HENRY STUART
CARDINAL OF YORK

THE KING OVER THE WATER

WATER

BY

A. SHIELD AND ANDREW LANG

With 4 Portraits and 3 other Illustrations

8vo.   15s. net

LONGMANS, GREEN AND CO.
LONDON, NEW YORK, BOMBAY, AND CALCUTTA

HENRY STUART
CARDINAL OF YORK

AND HIS TIMES

BY

ALICE SHIELD

JOINT-AUTHOR OF "THE KING OVER THE WATER"

WITH AN INTRODUCTION BY

ANDREW LANG

The old order changeth, giving place to new,
And God fulfils Himself in many ways,
Lest one good custom should corrupt the world.
TENNYSON.

WITH ILLUSTRATIONS

LONGMANS, GREEN AND CO.
39 PATERNOSTER ROW, LONDON
NEW YORK, BOMBAY, AND CALCUTTA
1908

PREFACE

THE life of the last grandson of James II., entwined as it was
with the more important life of his father and the more stirring
life of his brother, would be lamentably incomplete without
an account of the men and movements among which he was
born and bred, the influences which guided and controlled
his development. He, too, stood in the centre of the storm.
The vicissitudes of his near kindred were his ; the activities
that pressed so closely round them moved and shaped his
destiny too, in spite of the quiet resolution with which he
eventually took his career into his own hands. Torn from his
natural setting, the intrigues and struggles that surrounded
him, his life were a formless fragment. Apart from the high
lights and deep shadows of his brother's history, it must
be a colourless, unintelligible irrelevance. Hence it has been
necessary to include in this biography much of the political
and domestic history that fell within the term of Prince
Henry's life and so deeply concerned the fortunes of his
house, though he himself played little more than a passive part
therein.

The book was completed some time before the " King over
the Water," but it was judged better to keep it back until the
son's life should follow as a sequel to the father's. Both have
come from the same long and careful research. Until 1766,
the lives naturally overlap. Incidents common to both lives
that are given at length in King Jame's life, are noted here as
briefly as possible, that the biography should be complete in
itself ; while much that was taken from the former book, to
keep it within the limits of one volume, finds place here.

So the quiet shadowed story of the last Stuart prince is
the story of the passing of a dynasty ; a *Götterdämmerung*
through whose lightning-torn clouds echo clash of battle and
long-drawn notes of doom. We hear again the hero's trumpet-
call, the song of his sword, the wail of the spirits of Highland
flood and fell over the lost gold of a crown : the wild crash

v

and clangour of a funeral march to the forever flaming death-pyre of loyalty.

I must put on record my grateful thanks to those who have helped me by expert advice and most kind assistance ; before and above all, to Mr. Andrew Lang, who read and corrected the proofs, and gave me many valuable suggestions, with the benefit of his unequalled knowledge and understanding of the complicated history of the period, and who so greatly enhances the value of the book by contributing an introduction. Next, I must thank Monsignor Robert Fraser, for kind permission to reproduce the hitherto unpublished portraits of the Cardinal of York at the Scots College, Rome, and also the medals in his possession ; and Mr. Arthur Schomberg and Mr. James Mackay of Seend, Melksham, for the portrait of Queen Clementina.

For access to documents, I beg to thank the Reverend Father Ehrle, S.J., Prefect of the Vatican Library ; Professor Frati of the Bologna University Library ; and the Cavaliere Giovanni Livi, custodian of the Bologna Archives: for useful information, the Rev. Principal of the Seminary at Frascati ; the Very Reverend Father John Gerard, S.J.; the Right Honourable the Earl Nelson ; Dr. George A. Mason ; Mr. Henry Jenner, F.S.A. of the British Museum ; Mr. R. E. Francillon, who kindly allowed me to reprint from the *Royalist* the Appendix giving an account of the heirs of the Stuarts ; and the former editor of the *Gentleman's Magazine* (1898) who gave me permission to reprint the chapter, entitled "A call from America."

A. S.

MUNICH, 28*th September* 1908.

INTRODUCTION

A LONG chapter of history ended on July 13, 1807, when Henry Stuart, Cardinal York, "Duke of York," or "Henry IX." passed away. The origin of the Stuarts has been matter of eager debate. Scottish patriotism derived them, through Fleance, from the Scottish dynasty of Irish origin, whence Duncan and Malcolm Canmore came, but history regards them as of a younger branch of the Fitz Alans, who, long before the Norman Conquest, were Seneschals of Dol. They came into Scotland with other southern followers of David I.; they acquired large dominions in Renfrewshire and other parts of the south-west, and became hereditary Seneschals or Stewards of the Kingdom, their blazon, the *fesse chequy*, bearing reference to the exchequer-board. When the Steward married the daughter of Robert Bruce, the Kingdom was entailed by a Parliamentary title on his descendants, failing male issue of Robert and David Bruce, while the children of the Steward Robert (King Robert II.), born out of marriage, were legitimated when Robert and Elizabeth Muir of Rowallan "soudered sin wi' matrimony." It is a curious origin for a dynasty on whose behalf the doctrines of legitimism were pressed with unexampled ardour.

Misfortune constantly dogged the Stuarts, but, from the point of view of the singular ambition to wear the Scottish crown, they may be called lucky in the beginning. They were of no higher rank than the other members of the old Scottish noblesse, mainly of English or Anglo-Norman origin. Many great Houses were much more closely connected than they with the ancient Celtic dynasty, and the children of Robert II., born in later lawful marriage, were indisputably legitimate, while the House of Douglas held domains, and possessed a following much greater than those of the Steward. Yet, as the head of the House of Douglas, at the death of David II., was neither potent nor popular, while the Celtic *prétendants* were remote, and never possessed cavalry, Robert II.

and his heir succeeded without opposition to the throne—a heritage of sorrows.

The imbecility of Robert III., the intrigues of his brother Albany, the reckless character of his eldest son, the Duke of Rothesay—a prototype of Prince Charles—his captivity and death, and the seizure by the English of James I., threw Scotland into a state of anarchy, private war, and oppression by the nobles, which became chronic. The Stewards, except Robert III., had all been able men, vigorous warriors in the cause of national independence, even in the darkest hours of the reign of David II. James I., a poet, but a statesman, trained in English parliamentary ideas and methods, entered on the long conflict with the nobles, and was murdered in the moment of a success won by methods far from scrupulous. With him commenced the age of long Royal minorities and of misgovernment by factions. Each king, on coming to manhood, fought bravely the battle against feudal anarchy, and then perished, by accident, like James II.; or in conflict with the *noblesse*, like James III., in whom the family taste for art first appears. The minority of James IV. was brief, and his energy of character gave Scotland her first good days since the death of the last of the Kings of Peace, Alexander III. Scotland was richer, more civilised, more distinguished in literature than she had been, or, till 1760, was to be. But her very prosperity, her navy, her comparative strength brought her into the welter of European international politics. The energy of James IV. was fitful and untempered by discretion; he espoused the cause of France against Henry VIII., the brother of his wife, Margaret Tudor; he fell in the most crushing defeat ever inflicted on his country, and his death at Flodden opened another long Royal minority.

James V., more than any of his predecessors, was vexed by the intrigues of English ambition. To kidnap him, his advisers, and his infant daughter, Mary, was the unceasing policy of Henry VIII., who hoped to succeed, where Edward I. and Edward III. had failed, in mastering Scotland. James V. was thus forced into the French alliance, and to be the friend of France was necessarily to be the enemy of the new ideas in religion which were backed, intermittently, by England. A good Protestant, in Scotland, was bound to be "a good Englishman," while the cause of national independence was left in the hands of a Papist and a persecutor, Cardinal Beaton. The house of Douglas, driven into English exile by James V., became Protestant for political reasons ; for religious reasons the barons and the middle classes became allies of the English party. As the cause of the independent Crown of Scotland was bequeathed by Beaton to Mary of Loraine, a Guise and a Catholic, as in France and the Guises was her only hope, the web was woven of the net which, from her infancy, enveloped Mary Stuart. For her, from first to last, there was no hope, with her interests, her affection for her kindred, and her education. She never could turn Presbyterian, and though it seems not impossible that she might have "run the English course," and become Anglican, about 1562–1564, the intrigues of Elizabeth baffled and insulted her, and drove her into the fatal marriage with Darnley. His character, the insults of the bullying preachers, the violences of her perfidious nobles, and, finally, the passions of her own heart, love and revenge, consummated her tragedy.

Her son, James VI., was the most distasteful, the most astute, and the most fortunate of the family. He succeeded to his mother's struggle with the theocratic tyranny of the preachers. He had practically won his battle before he succeeded to the English throne ; by means quite unconstitutional he maintained his ground, but all was lost when his son, Charles I., not only maintained the rule of prelates, detested and despised both by nobles and commonalty, but attempted to alter the forms of worship, and introduced a Liturgy which was regarded as a Mass Book. Before Charles, as before Mary, there lay an inevitable war of Religion, and also a political war against the Tudor doctrine of Royal absolutism. No successor to the crown, after James V. and after James VI., would have been able, perhaps, to avoid these predestined sorrows, but neither Mary nor Charles I. had the kind of character which could cope with the situation.

The exile of the Royal family, during the Civil War, and the influence of a Catholic French mother and a French environment, made Charles II. a crypto-Catholic, and James II. an open Catholic. Demoralised by the perjuries forced on him by the Covenanters, and by his own insatiable love of ease and pleasure, Charles II. could not run a straight course. *Après moi le déluge* was his motto, and as his successor, James VII., was at least honestly a Catholic, the divorce between his propagandism and despotism, on one hand, and a people fiercely Protestant on the other, was complete.

In some mysterious way the ability of James VII. turned to folly, his strength to weakness, his courage to cowardice ; while his unfortunate son, "James VIII.," "The Old Pretender," with all the virtues, found that honour and Christian stoicism could not be allowed to atone for his unflinching attachment to his religion. Distasteful to the country as were his Hanoverian rivals, at least they were not Catholics. James VII. had convinced England and Scotland that the experiment of subjecting a Protestant country to the rule of a Catholic king was never again to be risked. Had James VIII. possessed the charm and the audacity of Prince Charles, he must have failed as the Prince failed, and he had neither charm nor reckless audacity. For Prince Charles all hope was over after his return to France ; his character, like that of James VII., had wholly broken down ; he was impossible.

In the subject of Miss Shield's book, Henry Stuart, there was never any hope. He was the last man to barter his Mass for three crowns ; and he was never the man to lead a forlorn hope. In childhood and early youth he had abundant charm, as the Earl Marischal, who disliked the rest of the family, attests. He had abundant spirit, too, and wept when he was not allowed, as a mere child, to make the campaign of Gaeta. The affection between the brothers, till Charles returned, "a wild man," from Culloden, was deep and tender—but there was something wrong. We do not know what it was. In a letter to Charles, James touches on some unpleasant set of circumstances, known to the Prince, and says, in effect, that Henry, for whom marriages had been planned, will never marry. He thus became a cypher, as far as the continuance of the dynasty went, while Charles, after various attempts to secure a bride of fitting rank, abandoned such ideas, and lived a wretched life with his unhappy Scottish mistress.

With all his accomplishments, and with all his private virtues, Henry was, and he knew it and acted on his knowledge, not the man to restore a fallen cause. It is difficult not to sympathise with the indignation of Prince Charles, when Henry fled secretly from Paris, and insured his own fortunes, and dealt a blow at his dying party by accepting a Cardinal's hat. James approved, but James, in his heart, had probably long despaired. He had a sad lucidity of spirit ; his deep affection for Charles did not blind him to the fact that Charles, save for some miracle of grace, had become a broken reed. Let Henry then provide for his own maintenance, and for that of the Prodigal Son, if ever he left his husks and his herding of the swine. Though James never ceased to aid Charles, when his help was asked, the Cardinalate of Henry was an abdication. In studying Miss Shield's book we attend, with all the invincibly loyal of Scotland, the long obsequies of a Dynasty ; but catch evasive glimpses of the dim working of heredity, the fading gleams of the talent of ancestral Stuarts ; of the virtues inherited from Mary of Modena ; sparkles of the energy of John Sobieski ; more of the wayward rebellious temper of the much-to-be-pitied Clementina Sobieska, mother of the two Princes. Human life, as we read, seems to be the sport of fate and of environment; it is a pageant of Royal shadows, growing fainter and yet more faint as the storm-cloud of Revolution and of the Napoleonic empire envelops them. The sun of the new century and of democracy falls on the Princes and they melt before it, "following darkness like a dream."

A fanciful picture of future history, written in the eighteenth century, represents the Stuarts as still lingering on at the end of the nineteenth. Fate was more merciful ; they were kings in exile for a century only, they were not bound longer on the rack of a world that was weary of the pageant of their miseries. Each of their names, save that of James VI., calls up the memory of some notable tragedy, something as of "Thebes and Atreus' line," till the long peaceful life of the Cardinal concludes with "a dying fall." Yet it is probable that the last of European kings will have in his veins a drop of the blood of the Stuarts.[1]

A. L.

---

[1] I may be permitted to say that, though I read through the proofs of this book, I had neither time nor opportunity to verify the references to authorities, and am not responsible for the accuracy of statements, often in matter which I have not studied.

CONTENTS

CHAP.   PAGE

     I. A Storm-Rocked Cradle 1

    II. Hopes Budding and Scattered 15

   III. The Boy Princes 29

   IV. The Shadow of the Forty-Five . . 47

    V. The Riding of the Prince 57

   VI. The Firing of the Heather 76

  VII. Forlorn Hope 87

 VIII. The Slings and Arrows of Outrageous Fortune 99

   IX. The Scarlet of the Seven Hills . . . 111

    X. The Priest-Prince 128

   XI. Music and Discord 141

  XII. The Cardinal Bishop 162

 XIII. The Close of a Long Reign 179

 XIV. King Charles III. 188

  XV. The Queen of Hearts 197

 XVI. A Call from America 210

 XVII. The Coming of the Poet 216

XVIII. A Royal Divorce 226

 XIX. The Bonnie Lass of Albany 234

  XX. Clear Shining after Rain 247

 XXI. To the Grave of the Cause 258

 XXII. King Henry the Ninth 267

XXIII. Sunset and Evening Star 295

       Appendix I 310

       Appendix II . . . . . *To face* 336

       Authorities Consulted 337

       Index 339

LIST OF ILLUSTRATIONS

HENRY, DUKE OF YORK (AFTERWARDS CARDINAL) . . . . . } *Photogravure Frontispiece*

From the painting in the Scots College, Rome

MARRIAGE BY PROXY OF THE PRINCESS CLEMENTINA SOBIESKA TO JAMES III. AT BOLOGNA . . . . . *To face page* 2

From a miniature on vellum in the Bologna Archives

HENRY, DUKE OF YORK . . . . ,, ,, 23

From a painting by NICOLAS LARGILLIÈRE *in the National Portrait Gallery*

THE DUKE OF YORK AND PRINCE CHARLES ,, ,, 29

PRINCESS CLEMENTINA SOBIESKA . . ,, ,, 32

From an oil painting by TREVISANI, *the property of Mr.* JAMES MACKAY *of Seend, Melksham, found in Falkland Palace*

PRINCE CHARLES EDWARD STUART . . ,, ,, 76

From a miniature by GILES HUSSEY, *Indian ink on card. The property of* LORD ARUNDELL OF WARDOUR

JAMES III. (CHEVALIER DE ST. GEORGE) . ,, ,, 124

From the portrait after ALEXIS SIMEON BELLE *in the National Portrait Gallery*

H.R.H. AND E., THE CARDINAL DUKE OF YORK . . . . . . ,, ,, 162

From the painting in the Scots College at Rome

PALACE OF THE CANCELLARIA, ROME . . ,, ,, 180

From a Photograph by POPPI, *Bologna*

MEDAL OF THE CARDINAL DUKE OF YORK,
  1766 . . . .

MEDAL OF HENRY IX., CARDINAL OF YORK,
  1788 . . . .

To face page 187

HENRY, CARDINAL OF YORK (HENRY IX.) .   ,,   ,,   267

    From the painting by POMPEO BATONI *in the
    National Portrait Gallery*

LOUISE OF STOLBERG . . . . .   ,,   ,,   284

    From the painting by F. S. FABRE *in the Uffizi
    Gallery, Florence*

H.R.H MARY THERESA OF AUSTRIA-ESTE .   ,,   ,,   310

    From a Photograph by B. DITTMAR, *Munich*

HENRY STUART

CARDINAL OF YORK

CHAPTER I

A STORM-ROCKED CRADLE

NOTHING is more trite than the incessantly repeated axiom that into the marriages of kings and queens, romance and sentiment do not enter : and this, like most parrot-phrases, is asserted in spite of well-known and cherished historical facts. In the matrimonial records of the House of Stuart alone, we have authentic love-stories as romantic as those of mediæval knights and simple peasants. The complicated marriages of Robert II. would furnish material for the most up-to-date novel. James I. fell in love with Joan Beaufort like any troubadour with his lady, as did James V. with Magdalen of France. Under circumstances of truly mediæval romance did the last James Stuart, eighth of his line, to his enemies the "old Pretender," James III. to the Jacobites, the Chevalier de St. George to all Europe, woo and win his Polish bride.

The story of that marriage has often been told ; of Wogan and his companions who, like Lancelot and Tristram of old with their companies, were sent to fetch the royal bride to her spouse. And this bride, though she and her knights remained prosaically faithful to the absent bridegroom, fulfilled in ante-matrimonial circumstances all that could be required by the canons of Arthurian legend, being a captive princess, the cynosure of hostile eyes—eyes of mighty sovereigns and statesmen, and of many loyal watchers over the sea ; whose prison was broken by romantic daring and faith and skill. From the fastness of Innsbruck, her deliverers carried her through storm and peril over the snowy passes of Tyrol to the friendly sunshine of Italy ; ultimately, to the arms of her king.

A

1725.   She was Clementina Sobieski, a pretty, fair girl, not quite seventeen, youngest of the three granddaughters of John III., King of Poland, who, last of a glorious trio of heroes—his forerunners, Charles Martel and Don John of Austria—checked the Moslem advance upon Christendom. She brought to her husband a great and welcome dowry in hard cash and famous jewels.

At the time of her rescue, May 1719, James was in Spain hoping vainly to win that crown which she expected him to set upon her head. He did not return at once upon hearing of her presence in Rome. His hopes of restoration to the throne of his fathers had been wrecked in Glenshiel. Perhaps it seemed no time for marrying and giving in marriage ; perhaps he had fallen in love with another woman. Not until September were they married at Montefiascone, and two months later he took her to the gloomy house in Rome given to him by the Pope, the Muti Palace, at the narrow end of the Piazza dei Sant' Apostoli.[1] Here on December 31, 1720, their elder son, Prince Charles, was born, and on March 6, 1725, their only other child, Henry, Duke of York.

The subject of this narrative came into the world at a moment of unusual perplexity even in his father's perpetually perplexed life. The Duke of Mar had been finally dismissed by James, whose seals he had held as Secretary of State since the dismissal of Bolingbroke after the hapless 'Fifteen. John Hay, brother of Lord Kinnoull, had been the king's chief agent in unveiling the treasons of Mar. It must be plain to all who have read the history of the Stuarts and their adherents since the revolution of 1688, what intrigues and heart-burnings, jealousies and scandals, such a change of ministry involved. Besides outside and inevitable political difficulties, ill-will, dissension, and distrust convulsed the peace of the exiled king within the walls of his home.

The girlish gaiety of Clementina had been chilled and crushed by five years of loneliness and ill-health. From shortly after Prince Charles's birth, things had gone wrong between her and her husband. He was fourteen years older than she, and the gaiety and energy of his youth had been quenched by continual and bitter disappointment, weighing

---

[1] Pope Clement XI. had recently rebuilt the church, said to have been founded by Pelagius I. who adapted the barracks of the ancient Vigiles, and took pillars and marbles from Trajan's Forum for its decoration.

MARRIAGE BY PROXY OF THE PRINCESS CLEMENTINA SOBIESKA TO JAMES III. AT BOLOGNA

From a miniature on vellum in the Bologna Archives

upon an extremely delicate physique. Clementina was natu- rally gay but of an hysterical temperament, as Polish women so often are ; bitterly jealous of her rights as a wife who was also a queen-consort. James, sweet-tempered and just all his life, was kind and considerate as a husband, but his cares and labours were great and incessant, and left little time for his wife's society. To every detail of his vast and complicated business he gave careful personal attention, keeping a very small secretarial staff, and refusing absolutely any share in his secrets and plans to his inexperienced young wife. This exclusion was bitterly resented by Clementina, and for whole months together she would refuse to speak to him.

Then came the matter of Mar's supersession. Mrs. Sheldon, Prince Charlie's nurse, was said to be a creature of Mar's. As she had boundless influence over her mistress, Clementina became the hot champion of Mar as against John Hay, then master of the household. James could not understand her hatred of Hay, but to please her, he took from him the direction of the household.

Lockhart, with the Scottish Jacobites, detested Hay; he describes him as "a cunning, false, avaricious creature, of very ordinary abilities . . . void of experience." He was married to Marjorie Murray, a daughter of Lord Stormont, sister of James Murray who had been James's Secretary for Scotland in Paris and a very devoted and intimate friend. Up to the spring of 1725, according to James, Clementina and Mrs. Hay were on affectionate terms, and Clementina wished much that Mrs. Hay should be with her at her coming confinement which was expected to take place in April. James's wish may have been father to this thought. Mrs. Hay never seems to have been a lovable person, but, according to common report among the Jacobites, "a vain, arrogant coquette."

In 1724, Hay's brother, Lord Kinnoull, made peace with the English government. Mrs. Hay went over to England to arrange her husband's affairs with the deserter ; to be detained for a while in Newgate as a Jacobite spy. During her absence, on March 5, James announced the promotion of Hay to Mar's place as Secretary of State and created him Earl of Inverness. On the following day, the second son of James and Clementina was born ; a month before he was due and "contrary to all expectation and the natural course of such matters," as James wrote later to Colonel O'Brien, his minister in Paris. Probably the appointment of the hated John Hay had caused a stormy scene, and hurried matters with the passionate young mother.

The news of the child's birth was immediately sent to the Pope, Benedict XIII. of the House of Orsini, who came at once to offer his congratulations at the Muti Palace. James received him at the entrance and led him to the queen's chamber, where he presented the " Duke of York," and prayed His Holiness to make him a Christian. The Pope baptized the babe in the chapel by twelve names, of which the four best remembered were, Henry Benedict Maria Clement ; the first a name dear to the English-hearted father as borne by eight English sovereigns ; the second conferred by Pope Benedict himself as godfather.

James at this period was deeply engaged with Spain, and his advisers, evidently the Hays, now in office, suggested that the child should be brought up at the Spanish Court, with the idea that the Stuart cause might be better advanced there by the presence of a Stuart prince who was, through his father, third cousin of King Philip V., and through his mother, first cousin once removed of Elizabeth Farnese, Queen of Spain. There was serious talk at the time of betrothing little Prince Charles to Philip's daughter, the rejected of Louis XV. The baby prince may have been suggested in the place of his elder. But Clementina angrily and absolutely refused to be parted from either of her sons, and the plan fell through. James, it was said, had been in favour of it, though he had had his own bitter experience of how little might come of personal contact with sympathising sovereigns. If the scheme originated with the Hays, it would not increase the little love Clementina had for the pair. Then a new element arose to quicken into fury her sullen hatred of her husband and his minister.

Prince Charles was four years old, and " very forward both in body and mind," said his father. He had been " getting among servants, where children never learn any good,"[1] and must be taken from his neglectful nurse, Mrs. Sheldon, and put into men's hands. In August, James sent for James Murray, brother of Lady Inverness, and appointed

---

[1] James's letter to Clementina, November 1725. Lockhart Papers, ii. 249, 276, &c. Printed also in many other collections.

him governor of the Prince of Wales, creating him Earl of 1725.
Dunbar to give him fitting rank. Walpole, historian of
George II.,[1] describes Murray, whom he saw in Rome, as "a
man of artful abilities, graceful in his person and manner, and
very attentive to please." James knew Murray to be "solely
and wholly devoted to himself." As Murray was a Protestant,
Sir Thomas Sheridan, a Catholic, was made sub-governor, and
the Chevalier Ramsay, a convert of Fénélon's, was appointed
tutor to the princes. Religious instruction would be imparted
by the Abbé Legouz of the University of Paris.

Mrs. Sheldon was furious at her deposition and stirred the
queen's indignation to hysterical frenzy ; stirred up also her
fierce Polish horror of heresy. Clementina declared passionately that her sons were to be brought up Protestants. James,
staunchest and sincerest of Catholics, who had practically renounced three kingdoms for his faith, assured her in vain that
there was not the slightest intention of Protestantising the
little princes. In November the quarrel reached its climax.
Clementina left her husband and children for the convent of
St. Cecilia ; then suddenly accused her indignant and undoubtedly innocent husband of having made Lady Inverness
his mistress.

The details of the miserable story have no place here.
James behaved all through with the greatest patience and
dignity and with the calm reasonableness of an innocent man.
But all Europe believed Clementina's story, and great injury
was done to his cause thereby.

Throughout these domestic troubles, James was immersed
in the business of a fresh attempt upon England. In the
chances of new conditions presented by the changing circumstances of continental powers had lain all Jacobite hope since
the death of Louis XIV., who alone for friendship's sake was
ready to sacrifice men and money, so long as he had them, in
the Stuart cause. No one knew better than the reasonable
Stuart prince, that kings cannot go to war to assist a brother
sovereign regardless of the advantage of their own countries.
Assistance must be at least likely to pay. Even the Pope, so
anxious to see a Catholic king on the British throne, was
bound as a temporal prince to act in the interest of his
temporal states ; and neither he nor the cousins of France

[1] " George II.," vol. i. p. 286.

1725. and Spain could afford to embroil their peoples in the horrors of war and risk their temporalities on such a very doubtful chance as the Stuart cause had become. France had, indeed, been bankrupt in 1715, and Law's schemes had ruined many adherents.

New opportunity, however, had come with the birth in 1716 of the Archduchess Maria Theresa, only child of the Emperor Charles VI. Charles settled his hereditary dominions upon her by his Pragmatic Sanction, but it was necessary to find friends among the powers to guarantee her succession. Spain was smarting from the insult offered to the Infanta at the hands of France and chafing at the retention of Gibraltar and Port Mahon by England and of her old Italian provinces by Austria. In Italy, the Medici family was dying out with the reigning Duke Gian Gastone, and the northern Italian powers had long been watching like vultures to snatch at the Tuscan succession. England had promised the heritage of the Medici to the Duke of Modena in 1717; hence coolness on the part of the Duke of Modena towards the kindred Stuart, anxious as he was to avoid offence by compromising himself with the cause sworn to destroy the English government. His unkindness did not give him success, for in the same year, by a secret treaty, England promised part of Modena to the Emperor as the price of his acquiescence in later arrangements. Later again, England proposed that all Modena should be ceded to Austria in exchange for Tuscany. All these arrangements about Tuscany were discussed and settled among the powers without so much as informing the Grand Duke Cosmo III., who reigned till 1723, or his feeble and childless son Gian Gastone, or the very masterful widow of his eldest son, Violante of Bavaria, or his daughter Anna Maria, widow of the Elector Palatine, who came to Florence in 1717 to look into affairs. The last of the Medici were treated as if mere Sultans of Morocco—of no account at all. Parma also mourned the extinction of the Farnese in the male line, the family of the Spanish Queen. Secret treaties were now drawn up. Spain promised to support the Pragmatic Sanction, receiving in return the Emperor's promise to support her in the recovery of Gibraltar and Port Mahon. Tuscany, Parma, and Piacenza were to be secured to the Emperor, who held also Naples and Sicily. There were also hopes privately held out of a marriage between the little Maria Theresa of Austria and 1725. the Infante, Don Carlos, Elizabeth Farnese's eldest son, who would rule over the northern Italian states under the Emperor. As all this would mean war between Spain and England, King James's cause was again to be used as a weapon by Spain, and his agents were busy.

No assistance could be expected until the winter was over, Lord Inverness wrote to Lockhart, the leader of the Scottish Jacobites (October 27, 1725) : but at the end of the year, the Spanish prime minister, Ripperda, openly took up the Stuart cause, and arranged an invasion ; with the ardent support of the Duke of Liria, eldest son of the Duke of Berwick, now married and settled in Spain. Unfortunely for James the Spanish sovereigns warmly championed Clementina and refused to receive him unless he came accompanied by his wife. Alberoni, though in disgrace and banished to Italy, also upheld Clementina. Ripperda had been good enough to side with James on the appointment of a Protestant governor for the Prince of Wales, and to declare that the king could not and should not part with Lord Inverness, but he acknowledged the impossibility of bringing his own sovereigns to reason on that subject. The Duke of Ormond, too, was on James's side in the quarrel ; indeed, declares in his memoirs that it was he who suggested the appointment of Murray. It was in hope of bribing Spanish ambition if not sympathy that the little Prince of Wales was offered as a bridegroom to the outraged Infanta, only four years older than himself, and James engaged himself to pay for Spanish assistance by the surrender of Gibraltar and Port Mahon : a promise shocking to English ears of to-day, until it is remembered that Gibraltar was then a recent acquisition of unknown value. Bishop Atterbury and his party fumed over the same idea, when the government was supposed to consider it. Into the counsels of the low-born Dutch adventurer, Ripperda, and the enthusiastic grandson of James II., the Duke of Liria, came a new actor, equally enthusiastic and of a certain importance.

The Marquis of Wharton, after devoting himself to James and then passing some years gaily abroad, had returned to England, been created a duke to compensate for loss of the strawberry leaves bestowed by James in 1716, and had taken his seat in the House of Lords. He was a clever young man,

1725. and his friends hoped he would now *ranger* himself and succeed in politics. In 1723 he was already shaking off his opportunism, unattractive as were Jacobite conditions at that date. Towards the end of August, after entertaining three-score country people at his house of Swaledale near Richmond, he and Sir Christopher Musgrave, half or more drunk, pulled off their coats and waistcoats, fell upon their knees to drink to King James, and compelled all their guests to do the same. Wives and daughters, ever more prudent, came crying to fetch their husbands away. This made a great noise, wrote Lord Lonsdale,[1] but the magistrate would not meddle with so great a man. Up to 1725 Wharton was corresponding with James, reporting parliamentary doings. For some time his loud Jacobitism was winked at. He was useful to the English government as "an everlasting talker and tippler" who let things out to them. In June 1725, his indiscretions could no longer be condoned and he was banished.[2] He ascribed his banishment to Ripperda, but gallantly declared to King James (June 8) that "he would rather carry a musket in an odd named Muscovite regiment than wallow in riches by favour of the usurper." He went to Rotterdam and, after some continental wandering, arrived in Vienna, to assist negotiations between James and the Emperor.

The Highlands were to be disarmed with the utmost cruelty, as he had reported to King James. It was therefore necessary to seize the hour before disarmament. Roads had been made that would be useful to insurgent movements. As the royal quarrel had done serious injury to the cause in Great Britain as in Spain, Lochiel's brother, Allan Cameron, was sent to Scotland (January 1726), to tell the king's side of the story to shocked Jacobites, to remove Scottish discontent with Mar's disgrace, and to plan the new rising. He went first to the Highlands; then to Edinburgh where he saw the Duke of Hamilton, another young ducal scapegrace, but by right of his rank the natural leader of Scotland. The cause suffered terribly all along by this insistence on mere rank as qualification for leadership, in default of the heaven-sent leader; who came indeed in 1745, only to be crushed

---

[1] Hist. MSS. Comm. Reports XIII., Appx. part vii. p. 123. Lonsdale MSS.
[2] He was outlawed two years later for joining in the Spanish attack upon Gibraltar, an act of high treason, though he declared he had attended the siege merely as a student of the art of war. During his exile he wrote his very clever memoirs.

by the old jealousies. Thus a cause that called for experienced statesmanship, experienced generalship, unflinching loyalty in a leader was handed over to drunken boys, too indolent to resist the winds of veering favour or the blandishments of unworthy women.

Lockhart of Carnwath, the real Scottish leader, welcomed Cameron coldly as a mere mouthpiece of Inverness. Nothing could or should be expected of Scotland, Cameron was told. She had suffered too much. The king must turn to England and land as near as possible to London. A foreign force would be necessary. Scotland could do little more than sympathise ; perhaps supply the natural leader in Hamilton, who might mend his ways if he had something to do. (To lead a nation to rise against its government was hardly the sort of thing to be chosen for his improvement !) He had sense and capacity, and was apparently devoted to the cause, which must make up for dissipation and addiction to low company. General Gordon might command the Highlanders. Lord Panmure, under the influence of his aggrieved heir, had been speaking contemptuously of James's right and saying that none but madmen would engage in his cause. The government of Scotland was in Campbell hands, and the officers in Edinburgh Castle were mostly English. The royal scandal came hard upon people suffering and striving for unanimity, mourned Lockhart. As for the Jacobites themselves, some minded nothing but diversions ; others were lazy. The Mackenzies had submitted *en masse* to the government ; also the Macdonalds of Glengarry, Keppoch, Skye, and Glencoe ; the Mackintoshes, Camerons, and Stuarts of Appin. Lockhart hoped to gain the Cameronians as they were a powerful body, but alas ! "a giddy-headed, humorous people ; 'tis no easy matter to manage them." What unexpected meanings words may bear !

It was doubtless at the same time and on the same errand that the Duke of Liria visited London, where he was the guest of Lord Strafford.[1]

In April the Duke of Wharton was sent by the Emperor to Spain to stir up cold hearts to at least Dutch courage. He and the Duke of Liria each drew up a plan of invasion which they submitted to Ripperda. Peter the Great had died in

---

[1] Liria to Strafford from Russia, 1728 : no date of his visit given.

1726. March 1725 and his widow and successor, the Empress
Catherine, was asserted to be heart and soul with King James.
She must be engaged to join in the invasion, providing 10,000
men with arms and transports for Scotland. The Earl
Marischal must raise the Highlanders and bring them to join
the Russian force. James must go at once incognito to Vienna
to see that the needful articles were included in the treaties
then being drawn up. He would then travel by St. Petersburg
to Archangel where he would embark, to avoid the Sound.
The King of Spain must send 8000 or 12,000 men from
Galicia under Ormond or another, and Liria offered himself to
serve in this expedition. Six thousand piastres were to be
advanced to one Morgan to provide six ships. The Emperor
would have 6000 men ready at Ostend and would obstruct the
sending of Dutch assistance to England. According to
Wharton, the Jacobites in England and France had ready two
million sterling and 20,000 stand of arms in France. It had
been proposed that the Spaniards should burn the English
ships at Chatham, but Liria was of opinion that even if that
could be done, it would be useless, as the alliance with Holland
ensured the easy procurement of a new fleet. King James
was to repeat his promise of the cession of Gibraltar and Port
Mahon and of important trading concessions to Spain and
Germany. The matter must be kept very secret.

Secrecy was to be found least of all with its advocates.
On King Philip's name-day, May 1, Wharton and Liria were
drinking enthusiastically to the saints of the day, Philip and
James. "What God had joined together, let not man separate." [1]
What the king wanted, said Wharton, was a Whig, a brisk
one, to put his affairs in the right train, and he (Wharton) was
the man. So he, with Ormond and Liria, went on drinking
to the cause and, in spite of royal discouragement,[2] shouting
that it would soon be a crime to speak of the Elector of
Hanover as King of England. Shortly after this, Ripperda
was disgraced, and a month later (June) Cardinal Fleury
replaced the Duke of Bourbon in France.

---

[1] Keen to Robinson. Paper Office. Miscellaneous State Papers 1501 to 1726
(Printed), vol. ii. p. 637.
[2] Ibid., p. 638, "Wharton, Liria, and the young Jacks are fond of a plan of an
expedition. Wharton says his master (James) does not love fox-hunting, but had promised
to go to Newmarket. He saw no immediate probability, but hoped the king would so
manage his affairs as to keep his word."

During the summer of 1726 the Catholic Church was adorned by the accession of the Duke of Wharton; to the profound sorrow and indignation of Bishop Atterbury, then resident at Paris. Ardently loyal to his own Church—had he not proclaimed as proof of James's freedom from bigotry the selection of himself, the stoutest Protestant in England, for his minister?—he could loyally accept a Catholic king, but conversions he could not away with. They seemed to him to play into the hands of the enemy by showing loyalty to James to be incompatible with Protestantism. James himself was both surprised and concerned to hear of young Wharton's conversion, so he wrote to Atterbury (August 14).[1]

There was now another and larger hope than in roystering young Jacobite dukes. George I. was old and in bad health. Walpole stood supreme in power, having lopped off the tallest poppyheads by dismissing all colleagues of competitive ability, Townshend, Carteret, Chesterfield, as well as smaller men. The heir-apparent was of the Opposition, after the fashion of Hanoverian heirs, and he and the prime minister were bitter enemies. Walpole hoped for no such supremacy in the next reign as he now enjoyed; unless, happily, England should separate from Hanover and the continental broils into which the German duchy dragged her. The Jacobites delicately but earnestly represented to Walpole the advantage of taking service under a grateful, English-born prince, and there is good reason to believe that Walpole inclined to the idea. After Atterbury's death in 1732, a paper was found among the bishop's possessions, written in the bishop's hand at the end of 1726 or beginning of 1727, in which he set forth a full and elaborate argument for the restoration of James by Walpole on the death of George I.[2] Twelve years later, Walpole was certainly debating the question of his allegiance.

Coxe suggests that the paper may have been written for a Jacobite tract; the plan of such a pamphlet had been mentioned by the Spanish minister at London to Ripperda. But Walpole was suspect at its date. In May 1726, Pulteney threatened to publish proofs not only of Walpole's financial dishonesty but of his readiness to sacrifice the House of Hanover and restore the " Pretender."

[1] Stuart Papers: Mahon, ii. Appx. p. xxii. James to Atterbury.
[2] Coxe's " Walpole," ii. 226 *sqq.*

1726.   James retired to Bologna from the difficulties of his position in Rome, still endeavouring to recover his wife by correspondence.[1] His letters were invariably affectionate but invariably dignified and reasonable.   Clementina remained obdurate.   It was a hopeless deadlock.

In August 1726, James was so ill as seriously to alarm his court ; the natural consequence of all the mental suffering caused by the quarrel combined with the anxious political business then going on.   He was even now trying to borrow money from the Pope on the queen's jewels for the projected expedition, if His Holiness should insist on security, a delicate matter in present conjugal circumstances though probably authorised by hope of the effect success might have on her majesty's mind towards reconciliation.   James recovered, and on September 10, perhaps to encourage the Pope by the promise of future triumphs for a generous Church in the brightness and piety of his heir, perhaps to allay papal suspicion of heresy in that quarter, he took little Prince Charles to see His Holiness in the Vatican gardens.   Unpleasant stories were rife in Rome and Paris as to the child's orthodoxy ; that Dunbar was seen to catch up his charge and put him in his carriage when the Angelus bell rang and the boy would have paused to pray, and had taught him to laugh at the pious custom of uncovering the head at the sound, as a "ridiculous superstition."[2]   In spite of Protestant influences, the prince said his catechism nicely to the Pope, who was much pleased.

In December, Inverness, in attendance on James at Pisa, again suggested the queen's jewels as security for a papal loan. (His letter is dated in his usual manner, "Vendredy au soir," and conjecturally dated in the margin "December 12 or 29, 1727," but by that date, Inverness had for some time ceased to be James's authorised minister, and the expedition had vanished into the limbo of many expeditions.   The year must be 1726.)   The Pope must not know that the king's friends were frankly looking to him for help, as that would frighten him as to secrecy.   He must be made to think that nobody should know the provenance of the money.

The Jacobites must also look to the Empress Catherine.

1 Letters dated February 20, June 27, and September 17, 1726. Hist. MSS. Comm. Reports X., vi. pp. 217, &c.
2 Letter from W. Connock at St. Germains to [Sir Timon ?] Connock at Madrid ; 1727. MSS. 21,896, ff. 11 and *verso*, British Museum.

She might not care so enthusiastically for King James as their 1727. fancy painted, but she hated England. In 1725 she had issued orders to her army and fleet, and laid out huge sums of money to be ready for attack. She was answered by the triple alliance of England, France, and Prussia, September 3, 1725. In December 1726, the Duke of Liria was sent on a special mission to Russia ;[1] partly, no doubt, to concert measures with the empress on behalf of King James. His journey was carefully arranged to divert suspicion, and a visit by the way to Gualterio in Rome was declined with polite regret. But he hinted that he would pass by Parma and probably by Bologna. James went to Pisa, Inverness in attendance, and Inverness, at least, met Liria, who then received the Garter or the promise thereof. He was certainly at King James's court early in January 1727, when he found Prince Charles "the most ideal prince he had ever seen, a marvel of beauty, dexterity, grace, and almost supernatural address."[2] If the gift of fascination is supernatural, Charles was certainly so endowed. As to address, at six and a half he could ride and shoot well, spoke English, French, and Italian perfectly, and danced at the carnival balls as if already a man. He had a stable of ponies, and Sir Nicholas Giraldin was his riding-master. According to Amedée Pichot, he had troops of Orcadian Amazons and dogs trained to fight. There is happily no evidence for the last statement.[3]

Atterbury in Paris discussed the conjugal quarrel with James's half-sister, the widowed Duchess of Buckingham, that pillar of the Anglican Church and one of the bishop's most beloved and affectionate friends. To the wrath of Atterbury, her half-brother, the Duke of Berwick, was urging her to give a Catholic tutor to her son, and under cover of asking and giving advice in the matter of the young duke's education, the bishop and the duchess met in the Bois de Boulogne and consulted how to end the wretched state of things between James and his wife. According to Coxe, the duchess, by Atterbury's advice, went to Rome and prevailed on James to

[1] He published an account of this journey to Muscovy in Spanish. His mission lasted until 1730. He also wrote his autobiography in English, of which there is a fragment in the British Museum, and an account in Spanish of his Gaeta campaign in 1734.
[2] "Prince Charles Edward." Lang, p. 27.
[3] Pichot is unreliable as to dates and other matters. The Orcadian dogs are a fable of 1745.

1727. remove Hay and Murray, and invest Atterbury with the principal management of his affairs in France.[1] Murray's removal was at most temporary, and as to Hay's, it is more probably the truth that the king, finding his kind letters to his wife of no avail and the situation impossible, yielded to Hay's own repeated advice and dismissed him (April 3, 1727). He replaced him by Sir John Graeme ;[2] at great cost of convenience, for Inverness "knew all his affairs by heart and Graeme had everything to learn." The retiring minister was created a duke (of Inverness) April 4.

At the meeting of parliament in January 1727, George I. announced that he had information that the restoration of the "Pretender" was one of the secret articles of the recent Vienna treaty, and that Gibraltar and Port Mahon were to be given up. England and Spain were not officially at war ; only "a sort of war" was in progress. On February 11, the Spaniards, assisted by the Duke of Wharton, began a siege of Gibraltar, which was raised in four months.

Storms matrimonial and high-political could little affect the baby Duke of York. The chief event of his present life was that in 1727 the heroic Lady Nithsdale, who helped her husband to escape from the Tower in 1716, was appointed his governess. But already he had received his character from his Polish mother, her hot temper, her haughty spirit. Charles, too, inherited much of his character from his mother. His father, always of delicate health and physique, had ever been too prone to yield to counsel, and the languor and melancholy that had possessed him since his twenty-fourth year increased with age. It almost seems as if the Stuarts in this late representative of their long royalty had grown weary of reigning, unavowedly and almost unconsciously, so placidly did he and his youngest son resign themselves to the inevitable : as if it were the newer Sobieski spirit that stirred so strongly in Prince Charles in his fight with fate.

---

[1] Coxe's "Walpole," vol. i. p. 173.
[2] A Protestant : afterwards Earl of Alford. Knighted now by James.

CHAPTER II

HOPES BUDDING AND SCATTERED

ON June 12 George I. died suddenly. What of statesmen's promises? James was aroused from the lethargy of hope deferred to take again a vigorous step. He set off for Lorraine, hoping to be able to go on to Paris—and England! Unfortunately this was just the moment chosen by Clementina for yielding to papal persuasion. Her enemy, Inverness, being out of the way, she announced her immediate departure from the convent to join the king at Bologna.

James had already vanished. He was at Nancy, burning to land at once in England, or if more feasible, in the Highlands. He was always ready for the moment; but at the moment, his friends always found themselves unready and drew back. Neither welcome nor encouragement met him at Nancy. As for the hoped-for English sympathy, the mob cheered the proclamation of George II. and the excitement of a new reign.[1] Then, to add to James's worries, Bishop Atterbury chose this inopportune moment to resign his leadership. He wrote to James from Paris, June 16,[2] that he had for some time had reason, now confirmed, to believe that his ceasing to deal in the king's affairs would not be unwelcome though his majesty had not yet seen fit to say anything of the sort to him. He had seen the royal countenance and encouragement gradually withdrawn, his methods disapproved, often crossed, and his prayers left ungranted, while certain persons "said things" of him and boasted that the most secret parts of his correspondence had been sent on to them. James refused to accept his resignation, and protested his perfect confidence in the bishop, who allowed himself to be persuaded into withdrawal of the resignation. It was probably here that the Duchess of Buckingham intervened : at Nancy, not in Rome.

[1] Strafford to James. Stuart Papers *ap*. Mahon, Appx. p. xxv.
[2] Mahon, ii. Appendix xxiii.

Then Allan Cameron arrived from Liège with Lockhart's discouraging response: there was no one prepared to join the king on landing but a few idle fellows, ready only for mischief, and James was strongly urged—as so often before—to keep away. Walpole, contrary to expectation, had been confirmed in his power by George II. Lord Orrery wrote to James that there was at present no hope of any opportunity from commotions in London ; only in the incapacity, haughtiness, and stubbornness of the new usurper. " Upon the whole, sir," he entreated, " let me beg of you never to think of making any rash attempt." [1] Atterbury, soothed and trusted, wrote to James, August 20, that a spirit of caution and fear possessed his subjects at home, so much that they dreaded a nearer approach of their king to the coast, fearful of its consequences to themselves ; that Orrery was wary to excess, yet that nothing could be hoped for without the ever-demanded and considerable foreign assistance which was so very far from obtainable. He too hoped in the unpopularity of the autocratic couple now on the British throne. He urged James to settle at Avignon, or somewhere at least on that side of the Alps. Fleury could not in his heart blame such a residence, and seemed to favour it somewhat. [2]

For alas! disappointment and humiliation had followed fast. Horatio Walpole, Sir Robert's brother, British minister at Paris *vice* Sir Luke Schaub, pushed out of his way, objected to the sojourn at Nancy, and on August 8, James had a holograph letter from the kind-hearted Duke of Lorraine, desiring him in the strongest terms to go out of his country in three days, with plain intimation that delay would only compel the use of force. The duke expressed the greatest concern ; the hard measure was much against his will, but he could not resist superior force. " Neither can I," says James in his letter to Atterbury, " so that I leave this place on Monday next." It was indeed " not right politics for me to expose myself manifestly to be drove out of different states, one after another." [3]

Switzerland had been suggested as an asylum, but he refused to enter any state against its will ; yet he was loth to recross the Alps. He took refuge once more at Avignon ;

---

[1] Stuart Papers : Mahon, ii. Appx. xxiii.   [2] Ibid. xxix.   [3] Ibid. xxvii.

so quietly, that ten days later rumour ran wild as to his whereabouts. Horatio Walpole was informed that he was to make a tour in Spain; that he was holding secret meetings with Atterbury and O'Brien at Mr. Ruth's house in Paris; that he had been at Cologne and at Liège; at O'Rourke's house at Comonges, and that O'Rourke had gone consequently to Vienna; that the Jacobites in Spain were preparing an armament for his service. Then it was rumoured in Havre among people of good credit and reported on oath to the British embassy, that James had been at Versailles with the German ambassador and had a two hours' private audience of Louis XV.: after which he immediately posted to Brussels with the German ambassador.[1] James, however, remained at Avignon.

And now a very forlorn hope sprung up, at least in the breast of Lockhart. The Duke of Berwick, suffering from gout in his right hand, came to Aix-les-Bains. Lockhart, who was with his king, caught at a new chance in this proximity.

He inquired eagerly of Sir John Graeme if he thought Berwick could be counted as a " thorow " friend, were his services to be required ? Graeme did not know. Lockhart was authorised to wait upon Berwick at Aix and get into private conversation. He did so and was civilly received, but he was too nervous to do more than keep to general topics and Berwick evaded all attempts at the desired private conversation. This was about October 6, and it was just then that the plot expired. Berwick's refusal had again " shown matters in their true light." [2]

Berwick's own recent dealings, though ambiguous, were certainly not such as to justify even such scantily hopeful approach. Since his great refusal to go with James to Scotland in 1715, a few letters of compliments only had passed between him and his royal brother.[3] In 1724 or in this same year 1727—the date in the MS. looks more like 1724, but Mahon reads it as 1727—Berwick took a step which Mahon construes as an attempt at reconciliation with the House of Hanover.[4] He wrote to Horatio Walpole, the English ambassador, for leave to visit his mother-in-law, Lady Sophia

---

[1] Hist. MSS. Comm. Reports XI., part iv. p. 200.
[2] Lockhart, ii. 372, &c.   [3] Ibid. p. 371.   [4] Mahon, ii. 261.

1727. Bulkeley, at Dover or elsewhere in England, whither she had retired on the death of Mary of Modena in 1718. By his attainder his life was forfeit should he set foot on British soil. George I. was willing to grant his request, promising his head should be safe ; but on finding that such a licence, even under the royal seal, would not ensure his liberty, he declined to risk being " clapped up according to the fancy or impertinence of any cross-grained magistrate," while thanking " his majesty " courteously for his generous intentions.[1]

James lingered at Avignon. His friends wished him to send for the queen, but his plans were so uncertain that he did not care to expose her to the risks of a dangerous journey, " though he wished more than any of his subjects that he might have her with him." [2] Rumours of her coming reached the French government, and notices combining official obligation with sympathy were sent to the commandants at Fort Barraux, Pont-de-Beaumoisin, Grenoble, Briançon, &c., dated 29th September 1727:

" The king [of France] is informed that the Princess Sobiesky, wife of the Chevalier de St. George, intends presently to leave Italy for Le Comtat to take up her residence with her husband, who has arrived there incognito. And as his majesty's engagements with his allies, and also the terms of the last treaties, require that his majesty should contribute as far as he can to keep that family at a distance from his dominions, he commands me to tell you that his intention is that you shall carefully observe all foreigners, male and female, who arrive in the place where you command : and that if Madame la Princesse de Sobiesky happens to turn up there, or any English, Scotch, or Irish of her suite, you will prevent them from passing further : explaining to them that his majesty, being unable for the above and for private reasons, to permit them to pass through his dominions, they must accept the alternative of retiring elsewhere. Independently of this order and its execution, his majesty wishes you to *retenir la main*. He will find it good that you shall use with respect to that princess all the attention and politeness that her birth demands, and that you shall procure for her all the assistance

[1] Berwick to Walpole, May 19, 1727 (or 1724). Add. MSS. 32,738, f. 415 (copy). Mahon, ii. 261. Coxe's " Horatio, Lord Walpole," i. 283.
[2] Lockhart Papers, ii. 369. Letter from Sir John Graeme, September 29.

1727.

she may require, should she find herself obliged to make any stay in the place." [1]

On October 24, James did send for Clementina to join him in Avignon as there seemed little prospect of moving. The children were to remain in Rome until the spring.[2] On November 15, he wrote that he could not prevail upon her to come, though he had given her every possible encouragement and full directions for her route. He believed Cardinal Alberoni and her other friends had dissuaded her, wishing to prolong the quarrel.[3] Clementina was Alberoni's "great heroine," according to Walton the spy. He believed in her wholly.

The queen wrote to Lady Southesk that she had declined the king's invitation to join him because "she did by no means think her children in such good hands as she in prudence and kindness could leave them: that she had been told the King of France would stop her on the way: that Lord Inverness was as much as ever in the king's favour and would soon be recalled."[4] Her majesty protested a little too much. Her hopeless obstinacy still stood in the way, while her tardy care for her children provokes a melancholy smile.

During James's absence, his little son wrote to him from Italy in careful roundhand the pretty letter first printed in Mr. Lang's "Prince Charles Edward": "I will be very dutiful to Mama and not jump too near her." She was neither a patient mother nor a patient wife and carried her nerves into the nursery. The little prince had for some time been signing his own complimentary letters to cardinals and princes, in handwriting which remained curiously unchanged through all his later years. What might not a child of such promise have grown to be, had his natural qualities been guarded and trained as his wise and gentle father desired? But no slave ever had less of his way with his children than this king of a free country, pressed upon by a mother's natural claims and a nation's angry demands; deceived by false friends and trusted traitors.

James returned to Italy after the New Year and joined his wife at Bologna on January 7. He found her "very much resigned to his will," says the Duke of Liria, again on a visit to the court. This must be the date of Liria's K.G. for he

[1] Add. MSS. British Museum 32,752, f. 80.   [2] Ibid.
[3] Lockhart Papers, ii. 379.   [4] Ibid. pp. 379, 380.

1728. states that it was given to him as a reward for making peace between the sovereigns which triumph of diplomacy had certainly not been achieved in 1727. He anticipated "a new falling-out," but for a month or so, all went well. The queen had sent Mrs. Sheldon to a convent the day before the king arrived : in recompense for which concession, he took back a servant whom the queen liked, whom he had dismissed. Liria hoped for the best but there was never more than a cool reconciliation. There was soon bitter quarrelling between them over who should pay Mrs. Sheldon's expenses home.[1] They lived on at Bologna in great seclusion. James was as much absorbed in business as before. Until September he had no Secretary of State : Graeme had been left behind in Avignon. In September, Lord Dunbar was appointed Secretary of State.

In March James lost one of his best and most generous friends in Cardinal Gualterio, who had suffered for some time from cancer or paralysis of the tongue. Their friendship dated from old Legatine days in Paris. Cardinal Davia was appointed Protector of England in his place.

In May James went to Venice ; perhaps to escape from his wife and the dulness of Bologna. He went incognito for the sake of the republic's susceptibilities. His visit was reported to the English government but there was no mystery in it. He went only to see the historic Ascension Day ceremonies,[2] and stayed at the White Lion. Here he met the Duke of Wharton who wrote to him from Parma, May 21, of the bewildering ecstasy of that interview.

New hope was now given to him in the promise of another child. On May 1, Clementina wrote to the Pope, begging his blessing upon her condition,[3] and James announced publicly and privately "the prospect of a near increase to his family." Clementina was sufficiently amiable to receive Lord and Lady Inverness graciously when in early July they came over from Padua to kiss her hand. She was seriously ill shortly after the Hays' visit, but the baby was expected towards the end of October. The Cardinal Legate of Bologna and other dignities were invited to be present on its arrival, but time went by and no baby appeared. Even in January 1729,

---

[1] State Papers : Italian States, 16.
[2] Hist. MSS. Commission Reports XI., part v. 119 : Townshend Papers. Also State Papers, Italian States (Rome), 16.
[3] Vatican Archives : Principi 226, f. 6.

Clementina went on hoping and the Duke of Liria, from Moscow, wrote: "God send us another prince"; but all Rome was laughing.[1] The baby had existed only in the queen's hysterical imagination. She never had another child.

In October, just while the phantom baby was being expected, James fell so suddenly, seriously, and mysteriously ill, that Walton, agent of the British government in Rome, supposed him to have been poisoned. A few months before, his cook had been murdered and the affair was so vigorously hushed up that to Italian minds, and even to Walton's, it seemed that the murder must have been done by James's orders! Perhaps the new cook had tried to carry out an attempt previously baulked by the angry energy of the royal servants. James was not out of danger until the middle of November.

All these matters were carefully noted and reported to the British government by their accredited agent in Rome, known to them and to certain historians as "John Walton," but known to the better informed as Baron Philipp Stosch, who combined the pursuits of an antiquary with a semi-official position as "servant of the King of England in Rome"; there being no avowed diplomatic relations between the Pope and St. James's. He was protected there by Cardinal Alexander Albani, now the one cardinal devoted to Hanoverian interests. The identity of Walton with Stosch is placed beyond question by letters in the State Papers (Tuscany) from the British envoys at Florence, and from his nephew on his death. George I. paid him £400 a year for his services, to which £120 was added in 1731, when he had been turned out of Rome and arrears were paid up.[2] He left at his death a large collection of antiquities besides his important papers, and such results as his highly valued espionage had on the fortunes of the exiled princes.

Rumour of probable increase in the number of "pretenders" quickened British apprehensions and vigilance. Jesse, in his "Pretenders and their Adherents," says that "Mr. S. who pretended to be an antiquary" was set to spy upon King James when he took the air in the wide gardens of the Palazzo Alla Lungara on the outskirts of Rome. He places, as if in 1756, circumstances that must be placed here. Accord-

---

[1] Hist. MSS. Comm. Reports X., part i. p. 166. State Papers: Italian States, 16.
[2] State Papers: Tuscany.

1729. ing to Jesse, Alberoni (who died in 1752 and whose inter-
ferences in James's affairs were chiefly during his earlier
married life) had proposed that James should remove altogether to the Palazza Lungara or Langhara, the Muti Palace
being too small, but that Mr. S. objected, as in that surburban
retreat James could have received friends and could have
absented himself, unknown to spies. A new wing was therefore
added to the Muti Palace to accommodate his household of
about forty persons. Mr. S. is, of course, Stosch, " John
Walton," whose authority in Rome lasted only between 1722
and January 1731. Jesse (p. 52) quotes from Keysler.

The disappointment of the baby further chilled the royal
re-union, and Clementina's temper grew still more trying.
They were a hopelessly ill-matched couple, whose natural discords were increased by circumstance. The fourteen years
between them were as forty. James had been a king from
childhood, supremely exalted and responsible. He had seen
much of life and understood human nature down to the
ground. His was the self-possessed dignity that came of a
long line of kingly ancestors. Clementina's royalty was new,
self-made, and assertive. James's temperament was calm, his
piety firm, quiet, and tolerant. Clementina's temperament was
hysterical, her piety hysterical and narrow.

The Pope had granted to James the ancient Savelli Palace
at Albano for *villeggiatura*, close to his own country palace of
Castelgandolfo, and until nearly the end of his life James
never failed to spend the spring and autumn months in that
beautiful spot, 1230 feet high ; upward vine-clad slopes, famed
for scenery and pure air since the days of Horace ; specially
interesting to an Englishman as the see of Nicholas Break-
speare, Pope Adrian IV. Clementina preferred Bologna and
Rome.

In March 1729 the Duke of Hamilton came to Rome, but
there was nothing at present to do for King James. English
Jacobites nevertheless kept coming and going and chattering of
the king's ever imminent departure. Nothing happened without or within the Muti Palace save that during the carnival
of 1730 there was an epidemic of smallpox, followed by an
epidemic of quite modern influenza ; " a sort of rheumatism
with fever," Walton called it. The Muti Palace was like a
hospital and the little Duke of York was one of the victims.

HENRY, DUKE OF YORK

From a painting by Nicolas Largillière in the National Portrait Gallery

James's chief policital care at present was to get the dangerous 1730. Walton turned out of Rome.

He was bringing his little boys forward. He went out with Prince Charles often ; "at extraordinary hours," Walton complained, whose spies thus missed opportunities. The boys were taken about wherever English tourists congregated. Prince Charles was made to dance and Prince Henry to sing little French songs for their delectation. Walton said these exhibitions were considered very affected. The priorship of Rome fell vacant and though the future cardinal was only five, the ecclesiastical life was already recommended as provision for his future and he was made a candidate for the priorship ; which was ultimately bestowed on Cardinal Cibo. In the summer James went to Albano with his sons but Clementina stayed in Rome to enjoy her devotions, occasionally driving over to Albano for the day, while James occasionally came to see her in Rome. Quarrels and reconciliations alone broke the monotony of their lives, but, " My children give me a great dale of comfort," James wrote to Inverness (1729), "I am really in love with the little duke, for he is the finest child can be seen." [1]

The children were indeed in more wholesome surroundings with their sad and much occupied father at Albano than had they remained in the care of their excitable mother, whose life was now wholly given to devotion and good works. James was melancholy, but not wilfully nor chronically so. His devotions were frequent and regular but not all-absorbing. He was fond of young people and Albano was gay enough with the boys and girls he liked to gather round him. Sir Toby Bourke, once his minister in Spain, brought his pretty daughter of whom Walton pretended Clementina was jealous. Lady Derwentwater, Countess of Newburgh, also brought a pretty daughter by her first marriage, and there was a pretty Mrs. Darcy who sometimes stayed there with her husband ; but there was no shadow of scandal, save in Walton's greedy imagination. He himself was presently turned out of Rome probably by the energy of the Duchess of Buckingham who arrived a month before his seizure (January 21, 1731). He took refuge at Florence under the immediate protection of Colman, the British minister, though he continued by means

[1] Stuart Papers : Windsor.

1731. of spies to find material for his constant and lengthy reports to the British government of the doings of the exiled court at Rome and Albano.

Honours and interest were still besought of the king who had so little to give. Some such appeals hurt his dignity as an English sovereign. Lady Nithsdale begged of the king to obtain from the Pope the title of a Roman countess for her sister, Lady Mary Herbert. The king refused: it would be improper for him to make any such request and he could not see what great advantage would ensue to Lady Mary thereby as "her own rank as an English duke's daughter was considered everywhere whilst the titles the Pope gives don't always meet with, even in Rome, the respect that is due to them."[1]

On February 21, 1730, the kind Benedict XIII. died; to be replaced by Cardinal Corsini as Clement XII.: a Pope less kindly disposed. James was said to be weary of Rome and longing for Avignon. In May he made a pilgrimage to Monte Cassino, near Naples. While he was absent, Clementina went with her sons to Albano. Charles had smallpox in July, but recovered without damage.

Their little boys at least were a great and increasing joy and pride. In the summer of 1731 William Hay arrived at the court from Naples to invest the princes, "the most lively and engaging two boys upon this earth," with rings as "protectors of the Order of Toboso"; an Order formed among the Jacobites of the court, from whose honours Lord Dunbar was excluded. Prince Charles had imbibed his mother's hatred of the governor. Two years later he even threatened him with personal violence. Dunbar, in spite of the king's trust, had certainly managed to counteract the Catholic element in his education: to make the prince a lax Catholic if not a good Protestant. In Dennistoun's life of Strange it is said that at eleven or twelve, this royal theologian was dissatisfied with his pedagogue's answers to religious questions! Dunbar was hated *ex officio* by the Jacobites as much as by the queen. A Mr. Stafford had been appointed the prince's tutor in 1728, James not having sufficient confidence in the Chevalier Ramsay to recall him. Ramsay was amusing his leisure by writing the life of Turenne. Presently he was appointed tutor to the

[1] Eliot Hodgkin MSS. p. 239; Hist. MSS. Comm. Reports.

prince's cousin, afterwards their fast friend, the son of the
Duke of Bouillon and Caroline Sobieska ; a fine young
prince, says Ramsay.

In July 1731, like a stormy petrel, the Earl Marischal with
a Moorish servant came from Spain to the court. James
received him with immense joy and distinction. The earl
was charmed by the little Duke of York, but he never liked
Prince Charles. "The little duke is much on his good
behaviour," he writes to his warrior brother. "He has ordered
a journal of his actions to be kept and given me, that you
may see how well he behaves. I never saw any child com-
parable to him. His brother has already got the better of his
governors, which makes him a little unruly ; but I fancy he
will be bold and no dissembler—two great and good qualities."

In the following October, 1732, Lord Marischal writes
again : "The Duke of York believes I send you a journal of
his actions : he stands in great awe of it, lest his faults should
be published in Europe and Asia, and is very fond to do any
good thing to be put in the journal."

Largillière's beautiful portraits of the princes in the National
Gallery [1] represent them at this time when they were about
seven and eleven years of age : in powdered wigs and scarlet
coats, lace ruffles and ribbons and stars of the Garter : the
Prince of Wales, a fair-complexioned boy, very handsome, with
fine regular features and erect soldierly bearing, all the dignity
and responsibility of the heir-apparent in his face ; the Duke
of York, sweetest and prettiest of little dark boys, a very
mother's darling. His father's darling he seems to have been
always, tenderly proud as James was of his first-born, his
"dearest Carluccio." Both children are painted with the
large, dark brown eyes of Mary of Modena and their father.
The Pope sent them a present of a gondola on which they
sailed on the Lake of Albano.

The Jacobites were naturally exhilarated by the glowing
accounts of the princes. Facts remained stubbornly discouraging but there was mystical promise in the Kalendar. It
had been discovered that in 1734 there would be an unusually
late Easter which would cause a rare series of coincidences in

---

[1] Largillière died in 1746 aged ninety, but it is more probable that he at the age of
seventy-five or thereabouts should have painted them—they are so completely in his
manner—than that the name should be lost or concealed of another artist of such skill.
In G. F. Watts we have had recent proof of art that time could not wither.

1731. feasts.   So Pollnitz in 1731 found all Rome repeating what was probably a very ancient saying adapted to the times: "When Mark sings Alleluia and Anthony sings Veni Creator and John censes the Blessed Sacrament,[1] King James will triumph and reign in England."

In the autumn of 1731, shortly after a miracle of telepathy was attributed to her, Clementina had a short dangerous illness, violent pain in her head.   James was in great distress.   She recovered and went to Albano to witness the launch of the splendid gondola the Pope had presented to her sons, but she was now in very bad health, profoundly melancholy, and the doctors looked grave.   On Prince Charles's eleventh birthday, new medals were distributed, bearing on the obverse his portrait surmounted by the star of his nativity with the motto, *Micat inter omnes;* on the reverse a bust of Prince Henry inscribed *Alter ab illo;* and all around the edge, *Extulit os sacrum cœlo Die* XXXI. *December :* MDCCXX.

1732. On February 22 O.S. (March 4 N.S.) Bishop Atterbury died.   He had been a very faithful servant, ever since he offered to go in his lawn sleeves to proclaim James at Charing Cross on Queen Anne's death, and mourned the good cause then lost for want of spirit.[2]   But he had officially attended the coronation of George I. in lawn sleeves and red robes too, in spite of his well-known politics.   He was a fair English bishop, a scholar and a gentleman, but the bench of bishops is no more limited to heroes and saints than was the cause of the Stuarts, and Atterbury was subject to the infirmities of gouty flesh.   Still, neither gout nor average infirmity can excuse perjury and blasphemy, and it is lamentable that Atterbury's conscience should have allowed him to call God to witness at his trial that he never had any sort of dealings with James.

He had served James loyally, at great cost, though he had also bowed the knee to Baal : a cost well counted.   He had a great and congenial position in the Church of England which would have been risked even by the success of the Catholic dynasty he supported.   Exiled, he lost not only place and possessions but a large affectionate circle of friends whom he

---

[1] That is, when Easter falls on April 25, Whitsuntide on June 13, and Corpus Christi on June 27.   If ecclesiastical feasts O.S. and N.S. coincided in 1688, which also is rare, the same omen prophesied at James's birth.

[2] Coxe's "Walpole," i. 167.

loved with his whole affectionate soul.[1] He was a man of 1732.
very handsome and stately presence, with a soft, graceful
address ; a high-churchman of Laud's beautiful, high-aimed
school, yet as stoutly Protestant as any traitor Whig. Lewis
Innes, a very narrow Catholic, disliked him, and feared that,
had King James been restored, the bishop had proved "uneasy to him in many respects, though he was otherwise a great
man—but he had many faults," adds Innes grudgingly.
Dicconson, who also knew him well in Paris, wrote of his rare
capacity in the king's service : of his rare wit, his knowledge
of his country, his elegance in speech and writing, the intrepidity of his temper, the steadfastness of his loyalty. James
well appreciated his fidelity and ability in which he "placed
the greatest trust and confidence" ; yet Atterbury was to suffer
the sharp pain of believing for a time that he had lost his
master's confidence, and the joy of reassurance must have been
sadly discounted by contemporary circumstances. The wound
never really healed. If Atterbury's temper was irritable, it
was sorely tried. Racked with the pain of deadly diseases,
heart-broken by the successive losses of wife and daughter,
deeply wounded by his master's seeming coldness, wandering,
poor and lonely, far from his beloved home, how could his
temper stand the sight and hearing of what was done in Paris
and England ostensibly for James and so ruinously against
him ? It was small consolation that his king's trust invariably
made his colleagues' distrust, that his own uprightness and
ability gained him only the jealous dislike of the less upright
and able. Being an ecclesiastic, he might not have made the
best of ministers to the throned king of a people jealous of
ecclesiastical rule, but he made an excellent minister for an
exiled sovereign, and he would have made a good Archbishop
of Canterbury. He sadly compared himself with Clarendon.
" I can indeed die in exile asserting the royal cause as he
did," he wrote to James, November 1731, " but I see not what
other way is now left me of contributing to the support of it."
He was no bigot but he hated the apparent disloyalty of conversions.

The last letter he wrote was probably the very long and
sorrowfully indignant reply to Lord Inverness's news of his

[1] The great demonstration of sorrowing friends who saw him off to exile as the
people of Miletus saw St. Paul, was very uneasily watched by the government.

1732. own conversion.[1] Inverness had left James at Pisa in 1727 and gone to Rome ; then to Avignon where he made his abjuration November 30, 1731. He had said that "since he saw nothing likely to be done for the king, he thought it high time to take care of his soul." The good bishop was very bitter on this reason for an act that public opinion must take only for a *coup de désespoir :* very reproachful that he, an experienced theologian, should not have been consulted by his old friend and colleague in such a presumably important spiritual difficulty. It was additional offence that Inverness should have chosen St. Andrew's Day for his abjuration—surely, to a Scot, a most propitious day—and the Cardinal's Inquisitor to receive the abjuration in public. He must have sought only to make a sensation ! Perhaps the emotions of writing this long letter exhausted the bishop's last remaining vital force, and it was Inverness's conversion that killed him. Two months after Atterbury's death, the Duke of Mar died at Aix-la-Chapelle.

Sister Rose Howard, a Dominican nun of the Spellekens convent at Brussels, had acted as intermediary between James and Atterbury. Her cousin, the Duchess of Gordon, was resident at Brussels, and even when there was nothing really doing in the king's affairs, they had managed to make a good deal of mischief in their fussy, restless correspondence, as the nuns of Chaillot probably did before them. When Sister Rose's priorship ended in 1731 the other nuns objected to their sister being used as a Jacobite agent. It brought danger to them all. A "remarkable sharp correspondence" then passed between the nuns and the Master-General of the Dominicans on the subject. The General took Sister Rose's part ; ordered that she should see her still busily intriguing cousin, the Duchess of Gordon, that "His Royal Majesty's" letters to her and hers to him were not to be opened by the prioress, and that the sisters were not to trouble "His Royal Majesty."[2]

---

[1] Endorsed 3 March ; the day before his death on the early morning of March 4. He wrote to King James the same day.

[2] Letters dated 1731 and 1732 : from the Registers of the Masters-General of the Order of St. Dominic.

THE DUKE OF YORK AND PRINCE CHARLES
Circa 1735

CHAPTER III

THE BOY PRINCES

DEARLY as James loved both his sons, Prince Henry was from 1733. the first his best beloved, his chief comfort. When in 1733 it was proposed to James by his father-in-law, Prince James Sobieski, that he should become a candidate for the crown of Poland, he declined it for himself, having another crown still in prospect, but suggested the Duke of York as a future candidate. "The blood of the Sobieskis runs in the veins," he wrote, " and by what may be judged of a child of such tender years, he will not be unworthy of it." [1]

When, a year later, Charles was sent to see war under the 1734. wing of the Duke of Liria, just become Duke of Berwick, at the siege of Gaeta, Prince Henry was wild to ride with his brother to the army, a warrior of nine years old, and passionately threw his little sword away when permission was refused. His father punished him by taking away his Garter, saying it did not become him to wear one without the other, but proudly wrote to O'Brien at Paris: "As far as one can judge of a child of his age, he promises yet more than the prince:" and to Lord Inverness, " I have all reason to hope that (he) will not be inferior to (his brother) when he makes his appearance in the world, for at present he promises at least as much, and I have also the satisfaction to see they love one another very well, though I believe the duke's affliction on his brother's journey proceeded as much from emulation as tenderness." [2]

On the prince's return from Naples in September he was received by his father at Albano. His mother was hopelessly ill and remained in Rome, but was able to nurse the dying Duchess of St. Aignan. She had the little Duke of York with her, and brought him to Albano to welcome his brother. The Marchesa Vitelleschi says that, after Gaeta, Prince Charles took part in the war in Lombardy, and that afterwards he and his

[1] Carte MSS. Bodleian 114, f. 272.
[2] Hist. MSS. Commission Reports XV., Appx. II. Eliot Hodgkin MSS., pp. 242, 243.

29

1734. brother spent some time together in Florence, returning to
Rome just in time for their mother's death in January 1735.
In Walton's detailed letters there is no room for this story.
Charles was conspicuously in evidence in Rome and Albano
until December.

According to Walton's informants, the English colony in
which the princes grew up was not calculated to impress them
with the excellence of English manners. As the rowdy exiles
at Avignon and Urbino had scandalised the decorous society
of the papal cities, so did the courtiers of the Muti Palace
shock the court of the Quirinal. The Derwentwater household seems to have been the most riotous of all, so that the
Pope compelled Lord Derwentwater to send his two pretty
step-daughters to the convent of St. Silvester to keep them
out of the disorderly assemblies of Jacobite youth.

Several legacies came at this time to rejoice King James.
Cardinal Falconieri left him 3000 scudi and 1000 to each of
his sons. Sir Mark Forester left them a collection of Indian
jewels and curiosities, and the King of Sardinia made James
a present of some splendid jewels. These windfalls were the
more welcome since the withdrawal of James's Spanish pension,
and other outstanding arrears of income caused an even
sharper pinch of poverty than usual at the Muti Palace. The
war naturally strained the finances of the belligerent powers, or
compelled thrift with a view to possible developments.

Relations were still strained between Spain and England,
and news was daily expected of England rushing into the war
on the Emperor's side. Spain's great poverty partly excused
her remissness as to King James's pension. He had heard that
the old queen-dowager had some months ago been starving,
and that the present queen's heavy dressmaker's bills were
unpaid. So poverty pinched terribly, and debts could not
readily be paid. Ezekiel Hamilton gave much trouble about a
hundred pounds owing to him, dunning even the queen and
the prince "in a manner little respectful to the king," until
the Duke of Ormond managed to get his claim settled. Ormond
wanted James to keep a minister incognito at Madrid and suggested Hamilton, Oxburgh, or Sir Charles Wogan, but James
could not afford to pay one, and saw little good that any
minister of his would do "in the present situation of that
court." The Prince of Asturias was in such bad health as to

make it probable that the new King of Naples would become 1734. King of Spain—as he did ; and there was hope in the friendship formed between Prince Charles and the Spanish princes.

The beautiful Strathtyrum miniatures were painted about this time. The St. Andrew worn by the king, who looks almost jovial and quite robust, is probably that preserved with the regalia in Edinburgh Castle. It contains at the back a portrait, officially described as that of Anne of Denmark. It could hardly be less like any other woman. It is undoubtedly Louisa, Countess of Albany, the wife of Prince Charles, and probably replaced an earlier portrait which may have been Anne of Denmark. The miniatures show us the king quite a happy *père-de-famille*, the queen, thin, fair, and sad ; the Prince of Wales, bright-eyed, erect, and soldierly. He, also, wears the Thistle, as does the Duke of York ; still the prettier boy of the two, extremely sweet and gentle. It is always a puzzle to reconcile the unvarying sweetness of his expression with the passionate temper which undoubtedly characterised him from childhood upwards. He was dangerously ill in October 1734, but recovered.

James was hopeful that Prince Charles's short campaign would do great good in England, whose government had been uneasy at hearing of it. He had hoped the prince might make a campaign in France the following year, but O'Brien discouraged the idea, and James agreed to give up the plan under present circumstances. He fully understood that France was more afraid of England than of Spain, or would be kinder to him. Meantime he was "sorry our friends in England should seem so inactive at this critical juncture, but I much fear they won't easily alter their ways."

Clementina died of asthma January 18,[1] to the great grief 1735. of her husband and of her sons, who made themselves nearly ill with weeping. She was buried in St. Peter's. James and the princes did not attend her state funeral, as some histories say, but watched the cortége from their windows, and spent the day together in prayer.[2]

James at least had the comfort of finding that his wife had

---

[1] This is the date given by contemporary accounts. A requiem mass was sung for her every year in St. Peter's on the 17th, another in the Sant' Apostoli on the 19th. This might be because the Feast of St. Peter's Chair in Rome falling on the 18th would preclude a "Black Mass" on that day.

[2] State Papers : Tuscany. Walton's Letters.

1735. died in the odour of sanctity. Rumour of miracle had even preceded her death, and as soon as she was buried Cardinal Gotti came to James for "material" for his forthcoming work on her life and miracles. Many such were reported from time to time ; all miraculous cures from her relics or on her invocation.[1] The Emperor sent for a relic at once, and James sent him the cup she had used while on her sick-bed. Up to 1771 miracles are recorded. The last was the case of a learned German noble named Sturm who pleaded her merits, praying for the recovery of his sick son. Instantaneous cure resulted, and was formally attested as miraculous by the father.[2]

Shortly after "his great heroine" Clementina's death, Cardinal Alberoni, still living exiled in Italy, tried to make up a match between James and the widowed Duchess of Parma. The duchess declined, though one of Clementina's ladies, Countess Legnani, was sent to the court of Parma, perhaps to disabuse the duchess's mind of belief in the stories current of the miseries of the late queen. The duchess, says Walton, had no mind to become a saint at the price paid by Clementina. At the same time there was a project of marrying the Duke of York to the child-widow, heiress of Massa, but she too declined the alliance, as she declined Prince Charles a few months later. Stuart prospects looked dark just then.

After Clementina's death James gave himself up more and more to practices of devotion, but he attended as unweariedly as ever to business and brought up his sons with great care, though rather after the Persian fashion—to ride and shoot and speak the truth—than after the showy fashion of his day, for they were found by critics to be behind other princes of their years in book-learning. They were taught to be good Englishmen, and spoke English habitually among themselves.

1736. In the spring of 1736 it was arranged that Prince Charles should make the campaign in Lombardy, again with the Duke of Berwick and Liria, who had taken charge of him at Gaeta. But Berwick was ill of consumption ; preparations were made, but departure was postponed from date to date, hoping for his recovery. Berwick lingered in Naples and

[1] State Papers : Tuscany.
[2] Add. MSS. British Museum 34,638, f. 247, Lat. 1781.

Sicily, trying to shake off his illness, but the campaign never 1735.
occurred. Charles was obliged to console himself with such
sport as might be found in the Borghese Gardens, tilting at
the ring on horseback with his brother and shooting blackbirds.
Sometimes they amused themselves with flying illuminated
kites, in the form of comets and dragons ; they rode constantly
with the sons of the Duc de St. Aignan. Charles, according
to report, was to be given the title of Admiral of Spain.
It was seriously suggested that one of the Stuart princes
should be made king of Corsica, just revolted from Genoa.

In the following February Berwick came to Albano and
brought with him his eldest son, aged eighteen, James Francis
Edward, to place him at the Clementine College. Though
heir of his father's Spanish titles, he was then intended for
the priesthood, and known at first in Rome as the Abbé de
Berwick, but he soon discovered his vocation to be a pious
illusion. James was fond of the boy, and had him a great deal
at Albano and the Muti Palace, and he was much with the
two princes, though his superior years made him a less
constant and congenial comrade for them in riding and
shooting than the two young sons of the French ambassador,
the Duc de St. Aignan. In June 1738 the Duke of Berwick
died. His son stayed on to finish his studies, and King James,
who had dearly loved the devotedly loyal father, did his best
to act a father's part to the young man, his grand-nephew.

The sad little family was bound together by the warmest
affection : in striking contrast with the incessant domestic
broils among their rivals at St. James's and Leicester House.
" Not for all the crowns in the world would he lose his boy,"
said King James, when his " dearest Carluccio " left him for
Scotland. " Few brothers love as we do," said Charles,
aching for the anxiety of " poor Harry " during his perilous
campaign. Hence it became the restless care of the enemy
to break a union in which there was so much formidable
strength. Henry had been early intended for the Church, but
that idea lay dormant while it seemed probable his aid in the
field might be needed by his father and brother. " Nature
seems to have designed to make him a figure in a military
way," says the anonymous writer of a pamphlet, "Æneas and
his Two Sons," but it was feared that his quick temper must
have stood in his way of succeeding as a commander. He

c

1737. certainly showed little signs of priestly vocation in his boy-hood, though he was from the first deeply and sincerely religious. "Of high spirit and activity, always preferable to myself," Prince Charles lovingly described him. But he was haughty, impatient of contradiction, obstinate in his opinions, prone to fits of passion which were succeeded by days of sullenness—his mother's temperament over again! To those who pleased him he was "sweet as summer," always ready to look over offences of inadvertence. His moral character was absolutely stainless, and he required regularity of conduct in others as strictly as he required it in himself.[1]

In the spring of 1737, James sent Prince Charles to make a tour about Italy, incognito, as Count of Albany; a title he was to resume in sad years long after. The prince set off on April 29. He was splendidly received in the fair cities he visited. A ball was given in his honour at Bologna. From Bologna he went to Parma, Reggio, Milan, Genoa. Though his beauty was a much cared-for point,[2] his warlike spirit was much admired during the festivals made in his honour. At Genoa he stood by the sea, watching for the British flag.[3] His father wished him to ask for a commission to serve in Hungary, and he declared that he longed for soldiers of his own, that instead of feasting he might serve his friends. At Milan, in spite of his incognito, he received visits from the governor of Lombardy and from the Spanish ambassador who addressed him as Prince of Wales, while the Stampa family exerted themselves zealously for his entertainment. "It is hoped the Emperor will openly discountenance such practices in his officers," wrote a Whitehall official, who complained that Prince Lobkowitz at Parma also had treated the prince with distinction and allowed his royal highness to inspect the Parmese troops. That he should have had a pass-port at all from Rome was a grievance.[4]

At Venice, where he missed the Ascension Day ceremonies (May 10), he was received with all royal honours. It was reported in England that "he was admitted into the Senate by a peculiar door and sat upon a peculiar seat"; the Bench

[1] "Æneas and his Two Sons."
[2] Charles wore curl-papers in the morning. Murray asked Captain Redmond not to mention it at Dublin. "Prince Charles Edward," Lang, p. 38.
[3] Amedée Pichot.   [4] Hist. MSS. Comm. Reports X., part i. 268.

of Princes in the Council Chamber. The Venetian resident ^{1737.} in London consequently received forty-eight hours' notice to quit.[1] At Florence the English minister, now Mr. Fane, forbade such honours.[2] The easily turned young head was turned once more. He behaved beautifully in public, having a very full sense of his dignity, but in private he was " as before," and gave Dunbar and the rest " rather more uneasiness when he travels." As before, he wrote little to his father, who expostulated tenderly ; " don't forget a father who loves you better than himself." [3] He arrived at the Duchess Salviati's, near Albano, June 22, but extended his visits to Pistoja, Lucca, Pisa, Leghorn, and Siena, which he left for Rome, July 8. After his return the indignity of curl-papers was removed : his long golden hair was cut and he was promoted to a wig. There is a beautiful portrait of the prince, still, as in " Waverley " " wearing his own fair hair " in a curly cascade. The curls there are sometimes taken for the periwig of an earlier day, causing the portrait to be labelled as that of his father ; but the face is not the round chubby face of the little James, and the long black eyes and slightly pouting lips have a merry alertness that was never characteristic of the father in his least wistful days. It belongs to Mr. Howard of Corby.

It seemed, indeed, as if fate must be kind, since she had given such a prince to England. Foolishly enough, it was advertised that the prince was handicapped by no obstructive religion as his father had been, to counteract his brilliant promise. He was, of course, ceremonially a Catholic, but utterly devoid of any religious conviction, thanks to the mistaken measures of his tutors. It is possible that even James himself may have come to look upon his heir's possible Protestantism as a condonable necessity. So now Jacobite hope went up and a plot emerged from the gloom which came to a head only in 1745.

The death of Prince James Sobieski, in December 1737, brought something more substantial than hope to the Stuart cause. He had already made over to his two Stuart grandsons. a great quantity of historic jewels, pledged at the Roman

---

[1] Hist. MSS. Comm. Reports X., part i. 268.

[2] Envoy extraordinary and minister plenipotentiary to the Grand Duke John Gaston de Medici, who died July 9 that year (1737). Re-accredited to his successor Francis of Lorraine. In this same year Horace Mann went to Florence as Fane's assistant.

[3] " Prince Charles Edward." Lang, p. 39.

1737. Monte de Pietà. These included the Polish crown jewels, pledged to himself by the republic of Poland. He had also made over to them all the sums due to him from the republic, inclusive of 400,000 Rhenish florins, advanced on the security of his duchy of Ohlau.[1] These florins the princes never recovered, and the legacy brought prolonged litigation with their aunt, the Duchess of Bouillon, and after her death in 1740, with her son and daughter ; but unlike most family disputes, the law-proceedings never made a family quarrel. The Duc de Bouillon was always the affectionate friend of both princes, and his sister, Madame de Montbazon, was afterwards one of the intimate circle of Prince Charles.

In 1737, Colonel Cecil became leader of the English Jacobites, a fussy and futile conspirator, much mixed up with Carte the historian, and with the Oglethorpe sisters, whose cousin he had married. The Jacobites roused themselves from the lethargy of late years. In 1738, a new plot was supposed to be discovered, and a Mr. Beaumont[2] was arrested with papers of Carte's and imprisoned in Newgate, though he earnestly denied being concerned in any plot. His arrest was said to have been a ministerial plot, got up to obtain possession of Carte's papers and to surprise the Jacobites into revelations. On January 21, 1738, a nameless correspondent wrote to Carte that he did not believe a certain Jacobite designated as " M. B." (Beaumont ?)[3] had had any interview with the Chev. W. (Charles Wogan), at St. Omer, and that even if such an interview had occurred it could have no authoritative significance.[4] Carte protested that his " History of England" alone occupied his attention and that, as the Lord Mayor had just promised him £300 towards its expenses, and the City was to promise £100 a year at the next meeting, he was not likely to risk such assistance.[5] The Lord Mayor and the City, however, were Jacobite and suspect. Carte did not lose the City subscription until his first volume was out, December 1747, when he offended with a note on the king's evil. Intrigues at this time are more than usually bewildering, charges of complicity more daring and more daringly denied, but it is the fact that at this time there was much under way, and that Carte was a

[1] Hist. MSS. Commission Reports X., part vi. p. 218. Lord Braye's MSS.
[2] Add. MSS. 34,522, f. 59. Carte MSS. 234, ff. 7, 8.
[3] Certainly not Bolingbroke, as is conjectured in the margin of the Carte MSS.
[4] MSS. Carte 230, ff. 16, and verso.   [5] Ibid., ff. 16 and verso.

chief agent therein. James himself was kept quite in the dark, had "no expectation of any enterprise in his favour: in the raising of which report he trusted the government had no hand in." So he wrote, March 4, 1738.[1]

In 1737 or 1738, John Murray of Broughton, name of sinister memory, arrived in Rome. The "Genuine Memoirs of John Murray," published 1747, give 1741 as the date of his visit, but the former is the date accepted by the Scottish History Society on the strength of the documents. Murray himself declared on his examination that he had not been in Rome or seen the prince since 1738 until he met him in Paris in 1744. He came to Rome after two years of study at Leyden, a Jacobite from family tradition, and a Protestant; not very truthful but not then a traitor, nor even a spy; but on the look-out for employment in the cause. The history purporting to be his "Genuine Memoirs" is more than "coloured." His really genuine "Memorials" were printed by the Scottish History Society in 1898.

He had no intention but to act in what seemed to him the best possible way for the advantage of the king and his sons if he reported to "a Lady" for publication that the princes were being brought up Protestants with the Pope's connivance, who hoped thus to get rid of them by their acceptance in England. Murray was not presented to James, but the princes, who vere very fond of talking to strangers, heard of Murray's presence in Rome and sent for him to come and kiss their hands. He was fascinated by the enchanting person and manner of Prince Charles and had a long conference with him. Henry he found "a very fine person, somewhat shorter than his brother, of a complexion not altogether so delicate, extraordinarily well made, with a certain agreeable robustness in his mien and a more than common sparkle in his eyes." Charles was an agreeable mixture of Stuart and Sobieski, Henry was actuated more entirely by the Sobieski spirit, "all the fire of his great ancestors on that side seems collected in him," and Murray believed that if ever Henry should get such a chance, as John Sobieski got at Vienna, "this warlike young prince would have the same success." Anxious that the unpopular religion of the princes should not outweigh their personal merits, he described the king's

[1] State Papers (Domestic), George II., Bundle 45. No. 54 Record Office.

1739. chapel in a way that would have considerably astonished him. There was nothing to distinguish it from an English (Anglican) chapel, he said ; neither confessional, crucifix, nor picture except an altarpiece. Perhaps he described only the room used as a Protestant chapel, where Dr. Cooper officiated for the Protestant members of the court: but in any case, the Archetto Chapel is much too small to hold a confessional, a very superfluous piece of furniture in a domestic chapel : and as the king was at Albano, the movable fittings were probably taken with him.[1]

During the carnival of 1739, Fanny Burney's correspondent, "Daddy" Crisp, came to Rome to be charmed by the princes, especially by the Duke of York. " I never saw anything so genteel," he wrote, "as this young one's paying his court to the electoral prince [of Saxony and Poland]. His looks, his gesture, all was the finest and most expressive that can be imagined. . . ."[2]

Whether or no the so-called "Ministerial Plot" had been a government trap or not, the most important of English politicians, Sir Robert Walpole, was in 1739 considering whether he might not save his tottering power by declaring war against Spain: or, should such a step be too late to serve him, declare himself for the king over the water. His carefully veiled overtures brought a visit from Carte in the autumn of 1739, which led to nothing, and in October England declared war against Spain and Walpole saved himself at the expense of his conscience.

War made opportunity for the Stuarts less hopeful and less agreeable than the treason of a prime minister, but beggars could not be choosers. But now the cause was represented not only by a king who, though persistent ill-luck had prejudiced his cause, was only fifty-one, but by his two sons full of promise and valour.

Prince Charles was to sail in the spring of 1740, probably accompanied by his brother, and from early in 1739 they had been endeavouring to obtain the sinews of war from their Ohlau property. The Duchess de Bouillon protested and caused delay. The princes won their case, but the Prussian invasion of Silesia in 1741 and seizure of the

---

[1] "Genuine Memoirs of Murray of Broughton," p. 5. London, 1747. (Dubious Tract.)

[2] "The Last of the Royal Stuarts," by H. M. Vaughan.

castle of Ohlau with its contents stopped payment of the money.

The death of Clement XII. in February 1740 suggested postponement of the expedition until the election of his successor should determine continuation of his policy or otherwise. A long and unusually stormy conclave followed. But Fleury was far from enthusiastic in his official friendship with England, though as yet peace between France and England was unbroken.

Hope in Walpole must be entirely abandoned. On March 22 James wrote to O'Brien that he did not believe Walpole had any serious intention of helping the cause unless he were forced to do it for his private interests, and the less the subject was worked on the better. It was not worth while to approach Fleury on the matter.[1] Walpole was indeed a broken reed that pierced Jacobite hands, for he betrayed to the government the secrets his pretence at Jacobitism had brought to him. He was now anxious as to his own reputation for Whiggism, and eagerly throwing suspicion of Jacobitism upon his rivals. He suspected Lord Granville of holding communication with James, and, through his influence, the Duke of Argyll, always more or less suspect of Jacobite sympathies at least, was again deprived of all his offices. Argyll (John of Argyll and Greenwich, " Red John of the Battles," who distinguished himself at Malplaquet and is so well known as the duke who assisted Jeanie Deans to obtain her sister's pardon) had been approached by James at the end of his attempt in 1715-16. Argyll, like his forebears, had been very wary in his dealings with the Jacobites, but that James had good reason for his hopes of the great Whig chieftain is proved by letters among the Stuart Papers at Windsor. In 1718, James had offered an English earldom to Argyll's brother, Lord Islay, Fanny Oglethorpe being the acting intermediary. This was not a very potent bait for a man who was heir-presumptive to his sonless brother, the lord of the lochs and of the mighty westland clan. After the ineffectual attempt in 1740 to dislodge Walpole, Lord Chesterfield was sent to Avignon by the Opposition to solicit, by means of Ormond, then resident there, an order from King James to the Jacobites to concur

<hr>

[1] " Prince Charles Edward." Lang, second edition, p. 46.

1740. roundly in any measure for Walpole's destruction.[1] But in the disgrace of Argyll there might be a glimmer of hope. James Keith was in London in June, sounding the duke, who was very nice indeed ; only would not discuss King James's affairs, though in a moment of irritation he exclaimed to Keith, "We must get rid of these people;" which might imply both George and Walpole.[2]

May was fixed for the prince's departure, in spite of discouragements which in the light of hope seemed of little account. A fleet of unknown destination was fitted out at Cadiz in the spring, and Prince Charles was summoned to Spain. Twenty-eight Spanish ships sailed out of Cadiz bay and passed Ferrol. Prince Charles was supposed to be on board, bound for Ireland. The armada found themselves far outnumbered by the English fleet in the channel and dared not attack.[3] But Charles was not absent from the view of Roman society and English spies for a sufficient length of time. A hint that his departure was to take place in May may be read in an application made by Madame de Mezières to the Duke of Newcastle for a passport to England that month. She applied through Lady Mary Herbert of Powis— a very *suspect* channel ! But the minister made such particular inquiries as to the servants she intended to bring with her that she changed her mind and did not go [4]—unless she smuggled herself over undiscovered. Her home at Godalming on the Portsmouth road was easily accessible to the Sussex smugglers. Some one evidently purposed to travel in her train whose identity dared not stand scrutiny. That the expedition to England was planned for both princes seems also to be suggested by a document among the Gualterio papers in the British Museum, a draft for the inscription on Charles's tomb, continued on the *verso* by texts "allusive to the expedition of the two royal princes to England in the wars of 1740."[5] The texts are given in Latin : "And they two being appointed were delivered out of the danger from

[1] Walpole's "George II.," i. 52.

[2] In a contemporary political tract on James III., King of Scots, the career of "Sir Robert" Cochrane is held up for warning to Sir Robert Walpole, as having "stumbled into power by dissimulated crimes and corruptions and supported himself thus in possession of it." Copy in the Foster Collection, Victoria and Albert Museum.

[3] "The Fallen Stuarts," F. W. Head. "Journal d'Argenson," ii. 413 ; iii. 59.

[4] Add. MSS. British Museum 32,840, f. 268.

[5] Ibid. 30,476, f. 189.

among the number of six hundred thousand men on foot, to 1740.
bring them into their inheritance " (Ecclus. xlvi. 10) ; "Who
redeemeth thy life from destruction : who crowneth thee with
mercy and compassion" (Psalm cii. 4) ; then, "alluding to
the return of 'S. A. R.'" to Rome : " Before the time of the
end of his life in the world, he protested before the Lord and
his anointed" (Ecclus. xlvi. 22) ; "He did that which pleased
God and walked valiantly in the way of his father, as he
commanded him" (Ecclus. xlviii. 25). Perhaps after the lapse
of forty-three years, Roman memory confused 1740 with
1745.

It was a very brilliant spring that year in Rome. The
Prince and Princess de Craon, regents for the new Grand
Duke of Tuscany, Francis of Lorraine, faithfully though
covertly a friend to James, came to Rome, and to the wrath
of the English embassy at Florence, chose to treat the English
royal family as old friends. Gray the poet came to Rome at
the same time (April). He was no less interested in the
princes than the other English visitors who swarmed in Rome
that Easter, though he affected extreme indifference. He was
present at the great ball given by Count Patrizzi to the Craons,
where *Il Serenissimo Pretendente* " displayed his rueful length of
person, with his two young ones and his ministry around
him." " They are good and fine boys," Gray said of the
"young ones," "especially the younger, who has the more
spirit of the two, and both danced incessantly all night long."
He found their father "a thin, ill-made man, extremely tall
and awkward, of a most unpromising countenance, a good
deal resembling James II., and has extremely the look and air
of an idiot, particularly when he laughs or prays : the first he
does not often, the latter continually." [1] Gray liked Dunbar,
whom he found " very sensible, very agreeable, and well-bred." [2]
De Brosses, who also came to Rome in 1740, was of the
same opinion as to the likeness to James II. ; also to the Duke
of Berwick, his half-brother. De Brosses greatly admired the
extraordinary majesty of the Chevalier's manners ; had never
seen any prince hold a *grand cercle* with so much grace and
dignity. He described James's life as very retired. He gave
entertainments only for the amusement of his sons, where he

---

[1] Gray's Letters. Ed. 1900, by D. C. Tovey, i. 74.
[2] "Gray and his Friends." D. C. Tovey, p. 52.

1740. made brief appearances, and passed much of every morning in the neighbouring church. His conduct was reasonable and his behaviour dignified. "He speaks seldom at [dinner] but always courteously and pleasantly. . . . When he sits down to dinner his two sons, before seating themselves, go to kneel before him for his blessing. He usually speaks to them in English, but to the others in Italian or French. The young princes have a small supper in the evening at which the king never appears. . . .

"Both have a family look," he goes on, "but the face of the Duke of York is still that of a handsome child. They are amiable and graceful in their manners, both showing a moderate understanding, and less cultivated than princes should have at their age. They are both passionately fond of music and understand it well; the eldest plays the violoncello with much skill; the youngest sings Italian airs in very good taste; once a week they give an excellent concert, which is the best music in Rome. The English who always swarm in this city, are most eager to have an opportunity of seeing the princes. The youngest especially is much liked on account of his handsome face and pretty manners; yet I hear from those who know them both thoroughly, that the eldest has far higher worth, and is much beloved by his friends; that he has a kind heart and a high courage, that he feels warmly for his family misfortunes; and that if some day he does not retrieve them, it will not be for want of intrepidity."[1]

De Brosses was much touched by the courteous kindness of Prince Charles. "Yesterday I entered while they were playing Corelli's Notte di Natale (the eighth concerto), and expressed my regret at not having arrived in time to hear the whole of it. When it was finished and they were about to pass on to another piece, Prince Charles said, 'No, wait. Let us begin over again, for I chanced to hear M. des Brosses say he would greatly like to hear the whole piece.'"[2]

Horace Walpole also came to Rome that spring on a flying visit from Florence. Though he saw the exiled court, he was not sufficiently interested to mention it in his "Letters"; only recalled his impression thereof in his "History of George II." His remembrance was harshly unflattering to persons, though

[1] As translated, very freely, by Mahon: "History," iii. 36, &c.
[2] L'Italie il y a cent ans. Charles de Brosses.

he praised the ordering of the Chevalier's household. The 1740.
intense interest taken in the princes by British tourists was
reported by the spies. These visitors dared not let themselves be presented to the father, but seized every opportunity
of meeting his attractive sons, who were easily accessible and
extremely charming. Murray of Broughton had found the
princes no such dunces as did De Brosses, fresh from the
polished French court ; he praised their industry in the pursuit
of knowledge. They were both fond of history, and spoke
English, French, and Italian, with a smattering of Latin.
Some said that Henry's capacity was superior to his brother's :
others, that he strove to make up by application for lack of
cleverness. His letters are well written, in a firm, clear hand,
and as a rule, correctly spelt. Prince Charles's spelling is
invariably the worst out of burlesque. The difference was
rather out of nature than capacity. Charles was born a
soldier, Henry a priest. Dundee and Marshal Saxe are well-
known examples of military inability to spell, and Charles with
fair chances might have been as great a soldier as either of
them. He proved so much in his one chance, his one hour
of glorious life. Sweet, sixteen-year-old Prince Henry, his
father's and society's darling, though "a little lively," had no
jealousy of his elder ; while Charles spoke enthusiastically of
Henry, of his high spirits and activity, "in all respects as one
preferable to himself." From all accounts, they were both
more Sobieski than Stuart, very much alike in feature, yet
very different in colour and form ; Charles, yellow-haired
like his mother, brown-eyed, tall like his father ; Henry, short,
strongly built like the sturdy crusader King of Poland, dark
to swarthiness like his father, but full of Sobieski fire, with
sparkling eyes. Charles had an iron constitution, Henry was
always delicate though so heavily and strongly built. Their
features were Polish, not Stuart, and their naturally fiery
temperaments, lack of staying power, inability to conquer fate,
were all Polish. But one gift Charles had inherited from his
Stuart forefathers, though his father and grandfather had
missed it ; that wonderful personal charm which, though he
lost it in later life in bitterness of soul and the self-indulgence
of despair, enhaloes his memory for ever. He lives on at his
best, not at his worst, ever young as Dionysus, brave and kind
and chivalrous ; for his bright youth was his real life, as God

1740. and he made it ; his age was made by the devils that beset him till despair let them in to possession.

By the middle of May all talk of Charles's expedition had died away. He had been with Henry shooting quail at Palo, then seeking sport with song-birds as usual in the Borghese gardens. Failing blackbirds, he shot bats at fall of evening. He was present at all the entertainments given for the Craons. At the end of May James and his sons went to Albano. On this occasion they had the society of an old friend to enliven the dulness of the prolonged conclave : Lady Inverness, who came from Avignon and stayed at the court till it returned to Rome.

At the beginning of June came the long awaited despatch from Ormond in Spain. The English fleet had captured Porto Bello and wrecked the Spanish fleet in the West Indies. Spain could do nothing at present for King James, but there was new hope in another quarter. Cardinal Tencin was now French ambassador at Rome, busily planning for the good estate of the royal patron to whom he owed his hat. On June 25 Walton wrote that Tencin was arranging that the young Duke of York should be made a cardinal by the coming Pope and provided by France and Spain with benefices amounting to 50,000 scudi a year. Tencin clung to this idea with ultimately successful tenacity. Its realisation would depend upon whether he should follow Fleury as French prime minister and whether the new Pope should prove as friendly as the old. On August 17, the protracted, very quarrelsome conclave ended in the election of Cardinal Lambertini as Pope Benedict XIV. ; a good friend to the Stuarts, though it was said that his exertions on their behalf were prompted less by friendship than desire to get them out of Rome.

Lady Inverness, after a pleasant sojourn in the Eternal City, returned with her royal friends to Albano in July, but in spite of her society, James was visibly bored, missing his cardinals. He expected Ormond, who failed to come and insisted that Charles must go to Spain, and there were many long nocturnal conferences with St. Aignan and Dunbar. The election and coronation of the Pope were followed by a sad and startling piece of news in October. Lord Inverness had died suddenly at Avignon. His wife hurried thither from Rome to look after his effects.

It was another sorrow for King James, whose old friends had been dropping off so fast ; the death of this old friend and long trusted minister : "one whom he had known so long, esteemed so justly, and who was so deeply attached to himself and his cause," he wrote to the Archbishop of Avignon who sent the sad news.[1] John Hay, desperately hated and angrily suspected as he was, had nevertheless been one of the few wholly faithful friends the king had ever had. No treason is ever laid to his charge—for one cannot count a silly report listened to at St. Germain's in the excitement of 1725–1727, that he had a pension of £2000 a year from the English government as a bribe to pervert the princes. Neither can any great mistake be laid to his charge though he was not a capable man. He left no children.

Three days before Inverness's death, Ormond, his great enemy, arrived at Avignon from Spain. Walton darkly notices the coincidence and hints at poison. Inverness had long been suffering from gout, but, according to Walton, there was a post-mortem examination.

Almost at the same time the great event happened that let loose all the dogs of war and gave the signal for the speeding of the Fiery Cross. In October, the Emperor Charles VI. died, and the continental powers whistled their promises down the wind. England alone stood for Maria Theresa and declared war on France, which, allied with Spain, abetted the new King Frederick II. of Prussia in his raid on Silesia. All Europe rushed into the fray, all hoping to snatch plunder out of it. France wanted to seize the Netherlands, Spain wanted the Milanese, Bavaria wanted Bohemia, and King James III. wanted the three kingdoms for his son.

Colonel Urquhart, chief correspondent in Scotland, had died in August, and John Murray of Broughton succeeded to the post. Macgregor of Balhaldy had come to France with glowing accounts of Scottish zeal. He was sent back to Scotland with promises from Louis XV. of arms and ammunition. Murray wanted a war-fund raised, but the Duke of Hamilton drew back on that point. Prince Charles appeared in a kilt at the carnival of 1741 : sure token in Walton's watchful eyes of a coming Highland expedition. Every precaution must be taken to prevent the prince's

---

[1] Archives of Avignon : October 12, 1741.

1741. escape from Rome, urged Walton. If possible, he must be seized.

The English government had almost forgotten the Stuart princes, except for those harmless reports brought by idle travellers of the " Pretender's" long hours of prayer in the Church of the Holy Apostles, the princes' singing and fiddling and their boar-hunts over the Campagna. Things were kept very quiet at Rome, and George II. was now too much absorbed by continental affairs, which were the affairs of Maria Theresa, Queen of Hungary, to remember that he was responsible for the security of British peace as well as for the security of the Protestant succession. The interests of his "despicable German electorate" were always paramount, and English money went to uphold the throne of Hungary, while the English throne was left to look after itself. Through the cloud of English and Prussian cannon-smoke, Rome appeared dim and far away. Nobody was greatly afraid of a king who, by all accounts, seemed to have renounced the world and to live like a monk ; who in his youth and best strength had never been personally a very formidable foe. Few gave serious thought to the boys who were happy and contented with their amusements and accomplishments and the deference paid them by their few and feeble folk. But the boys had not forgotten that they were strangers and sojourners in Rome.

Now court and parliament in England woke up to startled consciousness that the pretty engaging children had become young men : that the elder was ardent and resolute, burning to unsheath his sword for his father's right and his own : that he was indeed at the head of a new conspiracy : and report said that the invalid, exhausted old Chevalier had abdicated in favour of his more dangerously warlike son. But for the Duke of York Tencin was endeavouring to obtain a cardinal's hat.

CHAPTER IV

THE SHADOW OF THE FORTY-FIVE

EARLY in 1741, the Elector of Bavaria was elected Emperor 1741.
as Charles VII., to the indignation of Maria Theresa, Queen of
Hungary, who expected to see her husband on her father's
throne. The new Emperor was a cousin of the Stuart princes
through their mother, and it was a very gratifying circumstance
that the imperial ambassador to the court of Naples should
come in full state to notify his sovereign's accession to the
banished King of England.

There was not much else to cheer. Balhaldy returned to
Paris, April 1, 1741, with a renewed agreement from the
Scots, but the English as usual drew back, scared ; betrayed,
they said, by the unguarded behaviour and too lively zeal of
the Duchess of Buckingham on a visit she paid to Paris to
beg for help. She had always filled much such a place among
James's Protestant adherents as the Duchess of Gordon filled
among the Catholics, with the great advantage of her near
relationship to the king. " For the Duchess of Buckingham,
I cannot say enough to do her justice," wrote Lord Cornbury
to James (May 17, 1733).[1] Now she had constituted herself
ambassadress extraordinary and sent Colonel Brett as her
secretary to the French court, complained the angry Jacobites,
bitterly jealous of their king's sister ; " Princess Buckingham,"
as Horace Walpole called her, proud to midsummer madness
of her royal blood. This new withdrawal of the English
Jacobites gave Louis XV. an excellent pretext for new delay.[2]

On May 25 (1741) James issued a circular letter,[3] addressed to " a Scottish friend" (Argyll ?). He repeated his
so oft-repeated assurances, and his intention of profiting by

[1] Stuart Papers: Mahon, ii. xxxviii.
[2] Sempil's account of the transaction (copy) : Add. MSS. Brit. Museum 34,522,
ff. 59–61.
[3] Copy in Stowe MSS. 158, f. 188. Printed in Northern Notes and Queries, V. 12 :
" original is or was in the Charter Room of Cullen House." Also S. P. George II.
(Dom.) Bundle 60, No. 33.

47

1741. his predecessors' mistakes: of accepting the *fait accompli* of change made in the laws by the revolution. " I do not entertain the least thought of assuming the government on the footing my family left it." He regretted that his sentiments and those of his family should be so little known, and that some of his religion should have contributed to the false impression prevalent of its teaching. If any of his adherents declared for arbitrary power, they also acted against his sentiments. He declared himself utterly averse from all animosity on account of religion, from suspending the Habeas Corpus Act, from unnecessary or increased taxation, especially from the introduction of foreign excise. He ended: " I thank God I am without resentment against anybody: I shall never retain any memory of past mistakes. I have ever the greatest horror of dissimulation, and will certainly never promise anything during my exile but what I shall perform after my restoration."

A copy of this letter was put into Argyll's hands by Lord Barrymore. Argyll sent it on to George II. and professed himself " wounded to the very soul." Yet a year later, Argyll was claimed by Lord Perceval for the leader of the parliamentary Jacobites at an Opposition tavern meeting. Argyll died in 1743. His ultra-whig brother, Lord Islay, succeeded to the dukedom and there was no more room for hope that the Campbells were coming.

The Earl Marischal had no better fortune with the Spanish court than his brother and Lord Barrymore had with Argyll, but the prince's departure was declared imminent. Sir Horace Mann[1] was called up in the middle of the night of August 21 to receive an express with the news that he was gone.[2] Before the news was found out to be false, the British government had been informed and had taken such precautions as to make such a feat impossible for a long time to come. But Tencin at Rome with his nephew, Bailli de Tencin, ambassador of Malta, worked harder for James than any foreigner had worked before. The new Pope was economising in pensions but confirmed the king's, and began to erect the ugly but expensive monument to Clementina in St. Peter's. The Roman Jacobites were reported gay. This period of hope incessantly raised and overthrown was exceedingly dangerous

---

[1] Now envoy at Florence for the court of St. James's.
[2] State Papers: Tuscany.

for the two young princes, who between preparations for 1742. immediate campaigns had nothing better to distract their minds than games and dancing and inferior sport. "Another year of this will spoil them for ever," said Walton. Brought up in such softness, they would soon trouble no more about military exploits than any of the Roman nobility, and Walton reported with malevolent perverseness that Prince Charles was very fond of women's society. In an immoral sense this was quite untrue. He cared for nothing they could give him beyond, perhaps, a little flattery.

It was a tragically lamentable circumstance, just when the future looked so bright, especially with the promise of the young heir of the Stuarts, that cruel fate, which lay ever in wait for the princes of that house, should intervene to blight that radiant promise ; not in the form of his many open foes, but of false friends ; said indeed to have been subsidised by the British government for the corruption of the two princes. This noble work was now busily in hand, carried on by treachery the most despicable that even their father was to suffer. In 1742 James was cruelly shocked and pained on becoming aware that something was askew in his household. Mystery was in the air and it emanated from the *entourage* of his sons. He suspected secret intriguing, but was unable at the time to discover either its sources or its object. Shortly after the carnival, Walton knew he had been seriously angry with the prince, who "wanted to amuse himself in his own way." [1] Later, by putting two and two together, James found that a set of men, led by Francis Strickland and John Towneley,[2] were seeking popularity in England and the consequent "material advantages" by trying to gain his sons over to the irreligion they themselves professed, Catholic names though they bore.[3] With the Prince of Wales, they had a too easy success. He was excitable, fond of amusement, and even then too ready to indulge in wine. It was now impressed upon the princes that since religion alone stood between them and the crown, and though they might not as yet offend their father and their Catholic supporters by openly breaking with the

[1] State Papers (Tuscany) : Record Office.
[2] John Towneley was the second son of Charles Towneley of Towneley, Lancashire. His uncle Richard Towneley was out in '15. John, born 1697, and his younger brother Francis were at Philipsbourg under Berwick in 1734.
[3] See James's letters to Prince Charles ; 1745; Stuart Papers (Windsor) *ap.* Browne's "Highland Clans," ii. 470, 471 ; iii. 479-483.

1742. Church, they could prove to England a noble independence of her precepts by living an evil life.

Prince Henry was of a much more serious character than his brother. The cardinalate had already been spoken of as his destiny.[1] He was also too delicate in health to permit himself any excess. Since he was neither willing nor able to follow their lead, he incurred the bitter enmity of the clique: of Francis Strickland whom James called "the worst of men," and of Towneley whom he considered to be worthless but less wicked.[2] James's scorn of Towneley's capacity was somewhat misplaced. D'Eguilles told Argenson that he was the most intelligent and prudent of all who were at Blair Athol with the prince, February 1746. Later Towneley made a French translation of Hudibras, admired by Horace Walpole and Dean Milman.[3]

The prince's friends commenced an unceasing persecution of the Duke of York. They calumniated him to English travellers and Spanish officers, and even tried to embroil him with his father, and ascribed his incorruptibility to the bondage and foolishness of popery. Charles was urged to unfilial and disloyal independence. Walpole asserts that the seeds of faction were originally sown in that little court by "that masterhand of sedition, Bolingbroke," condemned by court disfavour to exile and literature at Battersea; who insinuated into their councils a project for the Chevalier's resigning his pretensions to his eldest son, as more likely to conciliate the affections of the English to his family: a plan which the boy and his adherents too eagerly embraced.[4]

While the manœuvres of the Strickland set were being carried on with careful secrecy so that the prince might be the more effectually drawn away from his duty to God and his father, Strickland was feigning all affectionate loyalty towards his master, who, though puzzled and anxious, was for the time half deceived.[5]

[1] State Papers: Tuscany, 46, 1742. The author of "Æneas and his Two Sons" says he was addicted to gallantry but kept it quiet. This is not likely to be true. He also says that Henry was ambitious.

[2] James to Colonel O'Brien. Browne's "History of the Highland Clans," iii. 446.

[3] "Dictionary of National Biography:" Towneley (John); the writer, however, is not aware of the evidence for Towneley's residence at the court in Rome.

[4] Walpole's "George II.," i. 288. "Gray and his Friends," Tovey, p. 280. Murray of Broughton was charged, falsely, he says, by Balhaldy in 1744 with advising the prince to make himself king and leave his father in Rome.

[5] James to Charles, 3rd February 1747. Stuart Papers ap. Browne, iii. 480.

A traitor of another sort was taken up by James that year, 1742. 1742 ; Alexander MacDonnell, young Glengarry, now so well known as *Pickle the Spy;* at this date studying under James's patronage at the Scots College at Paris.

Intrigues had been going on busily, ever in the teeth of unexpected French discouragement. In November 1741,[1] James had written to Balhaldy of some of the Opposition who might be brought into the true fold. The Scots, in despair at the new postponement, sent Lord Linton, now Earl of Traquair, to London early in 1742 to try to form some concert among the Jacobites that would satisfy Louis XV. Traquair made some progress, but political fermentation over the change of government in May, when Walpole fell, prevented hoped-for extension of the concert. Tracts in the form of letters poured into England and Scotland, praising the goodness and large-mindedness of "the rightful prince," the charm and promise of his sons. His subjects, chilled by recent rumours of the king's languor and piety, by memories of his dejection in Scotland, were reminded of his earlier vigour ; the resolution with which he exposed himself in 1715 to the dangers of wintry seas scoured by hostile ships. Another recalled his valour in Flanders ; how Marlborough had described him[2] as "of an excellent capacity, one of the best bred, best natured, and bravest persons upon the earth."[3] Suspicions, too, of the effect of soft Italian training upon the princes were to be dispelled. James himself wrote to Balhaldy (October 1, 1742) of his sons' fine qualities ; of Charles's longing to be with his "friends," wearied of Italy where he worked off his restlessness by almost incessant shooting, going out in all weathers before daybreak, out-tiring his hardiest servants ; yet playing after his return on the violoncello for an hour or two as if he had not been out at all.[4] He loved and understood music to a great degree, said his father, but his brother sang much better. "Were their friends to see them either at home or abroad, they could not but be infinitely charmed with them both ; though of different characters and tempers, they agree very well together and love one another

[1] Misprinted 1714 in Browne's "Highland Clans," ii. 430.
[2] To Dr. Cheyne of Bath.
[3] Letters signed respectively, "England," "Ireland," and "Scotland": Stowe MSS. 158, ff. 189, 190, 191, 1742.
[4] Vinciguerra, a huntsman, told the Pope how Charles endured rain and fatigue to harden himself. Archiv. Vat. Segret.

1742. very much." The intrigues of the Strickland clique to divide the brothers had failed so far, but James was evidently concerned to silence possible rumours of division. Prince Charles would sleep on a chair in his riding-coat that he might be off at two of a May morning to shoot. "What a pleasure it would be to see [them occupied with] better game than quails!" sighs a correspondent, probably Edgar, writing to the Earl Marischal.[1]

Though plots and plans went merrily on, they were thwarted incessantly by government vigilance. The Record Office is rich in intercepted letters from Edgar, Lochiel, and other Jacobites, while Walton and his fellow-spies were furnishing reports in plenty of machinations and "treasonable conversation." A Cameron was imprisoned for enlisting men for foreign service.

On December 12, 1742, Newcastle, Secretary of State, had Colonel Cecil arrested at his house in Masham Street, Westminster. His house and his very clothes were searched for treasonable papers. The colonel, a great invalid, protested that he had not left his room for three years past, and had for long been unable to read or write.[2]

Small wonder that James should be conspicuously melancholy that year, harassed by troubles within his home and without. He was worried also by the troubles about the Sobieski money. Hope of cash in hand having vanished before the conquering advance of Prussia, the princes in December 1742 divided their mother's jewels and those that were deposited in Rome. The Polish crown jewels were apportioned to Prince Charles, to be held by him until Poland should redeem them, the redemption money to be divided between the brothers. Of their mother's valuables, Henry chose for himself a gold watch and chain, a silver toilet service, and a walnut wardrobe, and gave up the rest to Charles.[3]

1743. In April 1743, the Duchess of Buckingham died; in the very thick of the plot that almost restored the Stuarts to the throne, and just when the sun of hope was rising once more on the French horizon.

Cardinal Fleury died January 29, 1743, and was suc-

---

[1] "Prince Charles Edward." A. Lang, p. 54.
[2] Murray of Broughton: Appendix, pp. 408–411 : Scottish Hist. Society.
[3] Hist. MSS. Comm Reports X., part ii. p. 219.

ceeded as French prime minister by Cardinal Tencin. As he owed his hat to King James's nomination, great things were expected of his gratitude. The plan so long projected had never been abandoned. It only awaited opportunity.[1] On May 28, "the Sieur W——," that is, Wogan, arrived in Paris as envoy of a large party of the Jacobite gentry of Yorkshire, Durham, and Lancashire. He was received by Amelot, the war minister at Versailles. The message was that the moment was propitious for a French descent with 10,000 or 12,000 men. Immediately on the arrival of this contingent, the northern gentlemen would declare for James III. and, if preferred, would at once ride to London to facilitate the rising of the city, confident that were James once proclaimed in the capital, the provincial towns would follow suit, and the revolution be accomplished in fifteen days. The best of the government troops were abroad; only 6000 could possibly be opposed. As for prejudice against French and Catholics, Turks would be welcome to put down the detested House of Hanover so long as the king or the prince were at their head, but without a royal leader the French would be mere invaders and the Jacobites would obtain no English recruits. Amelot demurred at the number of Frenchmen required, but agreed to send an accredited envoy to Colonel Cecil when he could find the right man. The Jacobites still insisted on absolute secrecy, to be kept even from King James, which Amelot must have thought strange. Madame de Mezières, of course, was in the secret, as Cecil's cousin and Carte's old friend. Indeed, De Luynes believed the whole scheme to be hers and "a Scotch lord's." At first, he says, the secret was to be known only to Louis XV., Amelot, and another minister. Then De Noailles was told, who protested vehemently against French support of a rising in England. Louis then kept his approval secret, but Cardinal Tencin was taken into confidence.

James wrote to Louis XV. (May 22, 1743) appealing to the memory of Louis XIV., under whose guardianship he had lived, in whose armies he had fought, and who had employed his arms for the restoration of the House of

---

[1] The Duke of York ordered a Highland dress to wear at the carnival of 1743 but the parcel went astray.

1743. Stuart. He appealed to the memory of the Dauphin who had been a father to him ; to the memory of the Duke of Burgundy, the king's father, who had been a brother to him. " I feel sure that you will be far from thinking it unworthy to imitate their sentiments towards me ; " all the more because during Louis's nonage James had been badly used. France had then found it good to ally herself with Hanover. Now it was otherwise. The real sentiments of Hanover for the House of Bourbon had been consistently proved. It was now the moment to restore a family as deeply attached to France as Hanover was hostile.

Nothing shows more forcibly the hoplessness of James's cause than the assurances he was obliged to make to the only sovereigns whom personal feeling could inspire to befriend him. Here he was, promising and leaning on the very friendship that had been dishonour to Charles II. and ruin to James II.: a friendship that England would have insisted upon his renouncing had she placed him on the throne. At the same time, the Roman clergy and nobles and the Roman monasteries were subscribing to the invasion fund as to a crusade in the firm conviction that Prince Charles was going to invade England with the purpose of overthrowing Protestantism and re-establishing the Catholic Church.[1] How was it possible that the English should believe in James's promises of toleration ?

In June Prince Charles was invited to Paris : to the surprise of his father who as usual knew rather less than anybody else concerned of the schemes for his restoration, and demurred. He wrote to Tencin, June 27, that a mere visit would only put the English government on its guard ; that if France really meditated a serious undertaking on his behalf, it would be better to defer the prince's journey until the great *coup* was at hand.[2] An envoy was thereupon despatched from Paris to Rome and secret conferences followed between James, the Pope, and the French envoy.[3] Prudence counselled a brief delay.

Now the Star of that Old Year's Night of 1720 rose to its meridian. James bestowed upon his son the regency of the

[1] State Papers (Tuscany) : Walton Letters. The court of Rome believed the same. Arch. Segr.
[2] Stuart Papers : Mahon, iii. viii.
[3] Bibl. Angelica. Cod. MS. 1613 ad. IV. Pontif. Bened. XIV. Vatican Library.

three kingdoms. A fleet was prepared at Dunkirk to transport 1743. forces to England under the command of Maurice de Saxe. The Duke of Ormond was to command in England, and James sent him a commission to act as regent until he himself or the prince should land, and ordered him to work in concert with the Duke of Beaufort, Lords Barrymore, Orrery[1], Cobham, and Westmorland, Sir John Hinde Cotton, Sir Robert Abdy, and Sir Watkin Wynn. At the proper time, Lord Derwent-water,[2] and any others in France whom Ormond might judge useful, would attend or follow him to England. Though the prince was naturally to head the expedition, Ormond must command in England and Ireland until his arrival. In case Ormond could not arrive in time or secretly, Barrymore was to command until the landing of king or prince. The Earl Marischal was to postpone classic study to command in Scotland, but must follow the directions of the King of France. James for once was so fully convinced of English fervour in his cause that he only feared lest Prince Charles, who was to leave Rome on January 11 or 12, might not arrive in time to take the tide at the flood.

Murray of Broughton had been travelling busily between Paris, London, and Scotland, but had found little to cheer his heart in Jacobite unanimity. He had hurried to Paris on Fleury's death, to the surprise and confusion of Balhaldy who, with the "smooth and insinuating" Sempil, had been filling the ears of Tencin and Amelot with exaggerated accounts of Jacobite enthusiasm. As the Earl Marischal, now at Boulogne, refused to accept and act upon their stories, they dismissed him from their councils as "an honourable Fool." Lord Marischal said that it was he who refused to have any further dealings with them, having proved their falsehoods. Murray had seen the Duke of Perth at York, who was "much shagreened" at the disappointing news from Cecil ; but the mayor and aldermen of York were professing devotion to the Stuarts, and would have sent to the duke of their city an address in a gold casket, but for fear of discovery by the workmen who were to prepare the gift.

Louis again drew back. His ministers found that the

---

[1] John Boyle ; succeeded his father Charles as Earl of Orrery in 1731.
[2] Charles Radclyffe, 5th earl ; succeeded to the title on the death of his nephew John, 4th earl, December 31, 1731.

1743. hopefulness of things in England had been grossly exaggerated by Balhaldy.   Balhaldy went to Rome, December 17, to fetch the prince, bearing the discouraging tidings, which Murray also had reported to the king.   James's first thought, in consequence of the report and of the French king's discouraging withdrawal, was to put off the prince's departure, but Charles would not hear of such a thing.   All had been arranged, and his departure must be kept absolutely secret.   He was to be accompanied only by Balhaldy and his valet.[1]   Cardinal Gonzaga had been requested by Sempil to provide a trusted courier for a friend going to France.   The prince was to travel by Switzerland, to enter French territory at Belfort,[2] in Franche Comté, and to stay hidden in Lord Sempil's house at Paris till he could embark for England.   James "could not restrain the ardour and vivacity of his son," he wrote to Louis XV., and spoke very touchingly of the comfort he felt at entrusting his son and the fate of his kingdom to so "respectable a prince."[3]

---

[1] Not with Murray, who did not reach Ostend, with Lord Elcho on his return from Britain, until hope had once more been wrecked by the staunchly Protestant wind.

[2] Called " Bedfort " in the correspondence.

[3] French Foreign Office Archives *ap.* Murray of Broughton, p. 493.   MSS. 34,222, British Museum, f. 49.   James issued a Declaration on December 23, MSS. 33,380: Stowe MSS. 158, f. 188.

CHAPTER V

THE RIDING OF THE PRINCE

ON the night of January 9, 1744, Prince Charles put fate to the touch to win or lose it all. " I go, sir, in search of three crowns," was his farewell to his father. " If I fail, your next sight of me shall be in my coffin." " Heaven forbid that all the crowns of the world should rob me of my son," the tender king responded. Not even coffined, with his hurts before, was James ever again to set eyes on his dear eldest-born.

His departure was kept so close a secret that his brother was not told. Only Cardinal Acquaviva, Spanish ambassador, Bailli de Tencin, ambassador of Malta, and the Duke Gaetani were in the secret. The Pope and his court, especially James's great friend Canillac, auditor of the Rota, were affronted at being excluded from confidence. All were sure that the King of France had nothing to do with the adventure. The King of Sardinia declared himself to be only the more closely drawn to Maria Theresa and George II. by Charles's flight.[1] The Pope said he would not have stopped him, had he known, for the Stuarts were not hostages in Rome.[2] So Charles galloped through the Gate of St. John, through the wintry dark to France—to England.

It had been arranged that the brothers were to set off the following morning for a boar-hunt at Cisterna, the place of the Duke Gaetani, but Prince Henry knew nothing of the midnight flight. Perhaps Charles had feared he could not or would not keep the secret. More probably the sad old father, who was always more than doubtful of the success of the expedition and who had nothing left to him but his boys, remembered his little son's eagerness to ride to Gaeta, and dreaded lest his Benjamin, now ten years older and as passionate and wilful as then, should insist upon accompanying

---

[1] Archivi IV. Vat. Segr. a.a O7 : 7 February 1744. Ministère des aff. etrangères a.a. O. fol. 92 : 29 February 1744.
[2] Ibid.

57

1744. his brother. Or it may have been that the pain of parting under conditions of such desperate uncertainty was dreaded for the duke, for he was young for his age, loving and sensitive.

So when he awoke on the morning of January 10, 1744, he was informed that the prince, impatient for sport, had gone on overnight, but would meet him at Albano. Only Dunbar turned up at Albano with the story that Charles had sprained his ankle and was detained.

It is an oft-told tale. Dunbar wrote and printed a full account [1] of how the prince drove through the Gate of St. John, south-east towards Albano, as if to hunt on the Campagna. Sheridan attended him some distance as a blind, and one servant who alone was to accompany him all the way. Safe out of Rome, he changed his clothes ; doubled ; found post-horses and passports provided by Cardinal Acquaviva, who had provided against detention by quarantine, so vexatious to travellers through Tuscany. Charles galloped for Massa and Genoa. After an awkward detention by bad weather, not quarantine,[2] at Savona, he slipped through the English fleet at Antibes ; landed at 2 P.M. on January 22, then was detained in quarantine eight days : [3] left Antibes January 29 ; was joined by Balhaldy, bearing the name of Mallock, and two servants ; and arrived in Paris January 30. On January 22 Sir Horace Mann knew of the flight and was describing the prince to the Duke of Newcastle ; on the 28th Walton was writing a full account of the great adventure. For the first five days of the journey the prince had neither slept or changed his clothes. Accounts are in conflict as to his companions' and his own incognito name.[4] One account says that on the northward way he had met a " Mr. Graeme " who looked after his comforts and business very kindly. This was, perhaps,

---

[1] State Papers (Tuscany) : Mann's Reports, vol. 48. Also French Foreign Office Papers *ap*. Murray of Broughton, Scottish Historical Society. Dunbar carried the news to the Pope, explaining that James had sent the prince to France only to keep him out of idleness, intending him to make a campaign with the French army. Bibl. Angel. Vatican.

[2] Archiv. Vat. Segreti. a.a. O.

[3] French Foreign Office Papers *ap*. Murray of Broughton. Scottish History Society, Appendix.

[4] The French official account says he travelled under the name of Graham, attended by Balhaldy under the name of Mallock. The account in the Archiv. Vat. Seg. says a priest accompanied him, who returned a fortnight later with the news for the Pope. The Pope's writings are startling evidence of the crusading light in which the prince's journey was viewed in Rome.

Balhaldy. " Both he and the two servants suffered by my impatience to arrive at the end of my journey," Charles wrote to his father. " If I had had to go much further I should have been obliged to get them ty'd behind the chase with my portmantle for they were quite *rendu*." [1] The prince's horses carried not only Cæsar and his fortunes, but the whole cause and its history, which passed out of Rome by St John's Gate that winter night.

As soon as the flight was made safe from pursuit, Henry was told the truth, and submitting with characteristic resignation to accomplished fact, he entered into the plot, and helped to keep up the fiction of the boar-hunt so long as it was required to cover his brother's tracks. The Duke Gaetani also keeping up the story, wrote to his duchess in Rome of his anxiety for the prince who went shooting woodcock two or three nights, regardless of the perils of night air.[2]

Here Henry showed the sunny sweetness that always lay behind his warm temper, the power of quick self-control, of ready adaptation to circumstance that made a happy life for him out of very unpromising materials. His great love for his brother must naturally have been wounded by the trick that had been played upon him, his pride hurt by the holding back of such great confidence. His father wrote to him to explain why he had not been told of the prince's great venture and to bid him keep the secret by deferring his return to Rome alone. Henry went therefore from Cisterna to Foligno, whence he replied to his father, January 15 :

" I am much obliged to your majesty for the honour of your two letters, your goodness has really been very great in giving me reasons for not revealing to me sooner this Affair. You may be very well assured, Sir, that I can never be anxious to know any things but what you think fit I should know, and that also but when you please ; certainly the thoughts of such a separation could not but at first have some impression on me, but that lasted very little, for those very reflections which your Majesty put under my Eyes in your letter, as also many other joifull prospects, immediately came into my mind, and not only put me at ease, but filled me with vast content and

---

[1] Charles to James, February 10, Paris. Stuart Papers (Windsor) *ap.* Prince Charles Edward, Lang, p. 63. The second servant may have been Balhaldy's.
[2] Bibl. Angelica. Vatican.

1744. satisfaction, so that the Road which of itself is very long and
tedious, passed away without my allmost perceiving it.   I have,
however, had a good deal of anxiety whilst I was at Cisterna,
for I really did not think it a good Air in the present conjuncture, but now that we are, thank God, at Foliagno, as I think
out of all harm's way, and that I perceive by your Majesty's
letter that all things continue quiet at Rome, I am very happy,
but I am at the same time very impatient to hear news of our
Dear Traveller which news I do not doubt will be but good,
for the hand of God seems to be remarquably upon him on
this occasion.   The pretence of staing on here longer is very
naturall and easy, so that I shall stay with a great deal of
Pleasure as long as your Majesty will think fit, were it to be of
any use in this occasion I would really be locked up very
willingly in the old Tower till Easter.   ("They also serve who
only stand and wait," he might have added.)   I am very much
ashamed of myself for not having writt sooner to your Majesty
as I have no good reason to give for my excuse I shall say
nothing but only aske your pardon for my negligence. . . ." [1]

On February 6 he wrote very affectionately to his brother.
He was then back in Rome.

"I really had not the heart to write to you before I heard
of your safe arrival at Antibes, but as soon as I got that comfortable news, I have saised on the first occasion, for to return
you many thanks for the great goodness you have showed me
on this occasion.   I can assure you, Dear Brother, that I am
here without you like a fish out of water, the only thing which
makes me bare our separation with patience and even with
Pleasure is the reflection of its being at present so necessary for
your honour, Reputation, and (I hope) Advantage, and besides
all that, I hope in God it shall not be for long.   I have allready
thanked the King and I also thank you particularly for not
having told me the secret of your journey beforehand, for
certainly the great love I have for you could not but have
show'd itself, may be imprudently on that occasion, the secret
has been kept here much longer I believe than you expected,
for it was the 11th day before any Courrier went of ; I
have already been upon thorns untill I heard you safely landed,
and particularly whilst I heard you was locked up at Savona,

[1] Stuart Papers (Windsor) *ap.* Lang's " Prince Charles Edward," p. 61.

for certainly you was there in a very ugly situation, but now I thank God that Providence has freed you from all these dangers. I am not sorry for them, for the manner in which you have made this journey will gain you a vast deal of honour all over the world, and I don't doubt but that you will daily increase it in all your future undertakings. I wish you cou'd see all the content and satisfaction my heart feels every time I hear anything that can redound to your honour and glory, and that I am sure proceeds from the Respectuous love and tenderness I have for you, which I can assure you, Dear Brother (were the king but to permit me) wou'd make me fly through fire and water to be with you. . . . I have nothing else to say to you, Dear Brother, at present, but waiting very impatiently for that happy day in which we shall meet again, wherever it be ; am with all respect your most loving Brother

" HENRY." [1]

Charles went to Lord Sempil's house, and remained there in hiding until February 25. Louis XV. alas! dared not see him, but Sempil received 10,000 livres from Amelot for his use,[2] and Charles wrote to cheer his father by saying that he had met with all that could be expected from the King of France, who talked much *of* him, expressed great tenderness for him, and would be careful of all his concerns. All looked roseate in the light of his own triumph ; that he should have done the deed that had been so long a-doing. James was not cheered so much as his hopeful son expected, and wrote to Sempil, February 13, "Your letter of January 27, gives small astonishment and concern. The promises of France are not to be reconciled with her negligent and indifferent behaviour to the prince." But Louis had done all and more that a king may do towards invasion of a country with which he was officially at peace. So James and Henry suffered cruelly from anxiety, aggravated by the tardiness of the posts.

The relations of the British government with the continental powers were peculiar. George II., as Elector of Hanover, was at war on behalf of Maria Theresa with Frederick of Prussia and his allies and abettors, and at the end of February had despatched English troops through Flanders into Germany

---

[1] Stuart Papers (Windsor) *ap*. Lang's " Prince Charles Edward," p. 63.
[2] French Foreign Office Papers *ap*. Murray of Broughton, 498. British Museum MSS. 34,522, ff. 65 and *verso ;* dated Versailles, 2nd February 1744.

1744. under Lord Stair. As Elector of Hanover, he had won the battle of Dettingen, June 27, 1743. As Elector of Hanover, he fed his German soldiers well, while the English in his army sometimes went entirely without food for two days, and the Earl Marischal showed him up in a pamphlet entitled "*Starve donc.*"[1] Diplomatic relations between France and the *de facto* King of England were as yet uninterrupted. In July, Horatio Walpole, ex-ambassador,[2] wrote to Horace Mann, "We have the name of war with Spain without the thing, and war with France without the name."

For now, at last, a French fleet lay off Brest and Dunkirk under Admiral Rocquefeuil, to transport troops under Count Maurice de Saxe for the invasion of England, to dethrone France's official ally, the Hanoverian occupant of the British thrones : all under the supreme command of Charles, Prince of Wales, Regent for His Majesty James III. and VIII., whom Louis XV. must not so much as speak to.

The prince chafed and champed in his Parisian hiding-place ; complained angrily to Tencin of delay (February 24), hinting at perfidy ; to which Tencin haughtily retorted (March 15) that he had never been suspected either by his own king or by H.R.H.'s father. Next day Charles set off for Gravelines to embark with Saxe, who carried a declaration from Louis XV., intended to reassure the English as to this seeming foreign invasion in time of peace. They were shown that France came as friend, not as foe ; had yielded only to the reiterated prayers of loyal Englishmen that she should aid them in breaking off a foreign yoke and in restoring the rightful dynasty, unjustly banished.[3] De Luynes says that the French ministers wished the prince had not departed so promptly, or at least so publicly.

On that same February 25, Newcastle was warned of the prince's presence in France by Mr. Edward Thompson, who was in charge of the English embassy at Paris during the absence of Lord Waldegrave. About the same time Captain Ridley of a packet brought tidings to England of the new armada making ready off Dunkirk. There were " excited debates " in both Houses of Parliament, and Mr Thompson

---

[1] Stuart Papers *ap.* Mahon, iii. Appx. viii.
[2] Succeeded by Lord Waldegrave at the Paris embassy in 1732.
[2] *Louis XV. et les Jacobites*, par J. Colin.

was requested to remind the Most Christian King of his 1744. engagements towards the court of St. James's. Amelot retorted that those engagements had already been broken by His Britannic Majesty and so made void. Parliament refused to believe that anything so audacious could be meditated as to dethrone by means of a foreign army the German House now reigning in England, but promised to stand by it in any difficulty.

A Bill was then brought into parliament to make it treason to correspond with "the Pretender's sons," as with himself.[1] Horace Walpole describes the debate in a letter to Sir Horace Mann, May 8, 1744. " We have had but one material day lately, last Thursday. The Opposition had brought in a Bill to make it treason to correspond with the young Pretenders ; the Lords added a clause after a long debate, to make it forfeiture of estates, as for dealing with the father. We sat till one in the morning, and then carried it by 286 to 106. It was the best debate I ever heard."

In Mr. Yorke's " MS. Parliamentary Journal," it is mentioned as " a warm and long debate, in which I think as much violence and dislike to the proposition was shown by the opposers, as any which had arisen during the whole winter. I thought neither Mr. Pelham's nor Pitt's performances equal on this occasion to what they are on most others. Many of the prince's (Frederick's) friends were absent, for what reason I cannot learn.[2] The king came and dismissed us on the 12th."

The hottest point of discussion in the Lords was upon the Lord Chancellor's amendment to the Correspondence Bill ; that the children of traitors should be attainted in blood. Lord Bathurst opened the debate upon the amendment. He maintained that no severity was superfluous which would help to secure the throne: that the laws of England had always ordained that children should suffer for their parents' treason. Best working argument of all, he set before his hearers the fact that a father would think more than twice about raising his hand against the powers in possession if he knew that failure must bring down ruin not only upon himself but upon his children and remote descendants, and reduce them from a great position to the lowest of the people. Lord Hervey spoke

[1] For verbatim account, see Parliamentary Debates, 1744.
[2] He was supposed to have Jacobite sympathies : probably only to spite his father.

1744. on the side of humanity and religion : the injustice of making an innocent heir suffer for his ancestor's sin, for no other reason than that his very blood was supposed to be corrupted by treason. He scorned the idea of the Jacobite party being so powerful as the proposed amendment implied, and recommended his peers to crush it rather with silent contempt. Lord Cholmondely complained that his predecessors in the discussion had drifted away from the question under consideration. He declared that no man pitied the innocent children of "forfeiting persons" more than he did, but the fact remained to be reckoned with that the innocent son generally wished to avenge his father. The debate fills nearly 190 pages of double-columned report. Lords and Commons repeated the same arguments day after day, and were dull, sarcastic, or blood-thirsty, according to the movement of sympathy or of party interest.

The English Jacobites apparently heard the tidings of the prince's coming with little less consternation than the government ; tidings of the long-prayed-for French help, whose absence alone had forbidden them to rise long ago in their thousands ! The battleships frightened them ; they had expected nothing more conspicuous than fishing-boats to transport their allies, said young Barry, Lord Barrymore's handsome son.[1] Many drew back ; winter was coming on ; they disliked the idea of leaving the fireside for the saddle.[2] Their Italian-bred prince had feared neither midwinter ride nor midwinter sea. Sir John Hinde Cotton was one of these comfortable gentlemen of England. Barrymore, like Gideon, said that they could do well enough without the lazy and effeminate. Parliament was sitting, too, and the Jacobite members dared not leave their places for the field.[3]

On March 4 (February 23 O.S.) Colonel Cecil was brought up for examination before Hardwicke, Newcastle, and Carteret. He denied all knowledge of anything and everybody connected with plots ; protested he did not understand the ciphers found in his breeches pockets and elsewhere ; knew nothing of Carte, though he admitted he knew Wogan. A letter was found from Madame de Mezières, dated December 10, no year, in which she stated that France meant

---

[1] *Louis XV. et les Jacobites*, par J. Colin, p. 49.
[2] Ibid.   [3] Ibid.

to make war on England "this summer," and that the Dutch would be neutral. Cecil declared his firm conviction that France never meant to help "the Pretender," but would have stirred up people in Wales and Scotland had they been fools enough to listen. Carte also was arrested and examined, with a Mr. Garth, but both were released. The subscription of the City of London towards his "History of England" was withdrawn, on pretext that he had declared his belief in the cure of one Christopher Lovel of Bristol of the king's evil by the touch of James III. at Avignon in 1716. His History nevertheless went on coming out.

James, as always, had had no confidence whatever in English support as represented by the Carte and Oglethorpe group; least of all in Madame de Mézières who, like so many women, helped to ruin the cause by her chatter and conceited folly. At the end of 1744 she wrote to the king, letters "in so extraordinary a style," he said, "that I could not in any decency so much as acknowledge them. As for the prince, he writes of them in a manner which I own raised my bile, but she is a madwoman and not to be minded."

Sempil warned Amelot to hold firm against whatever proposition Madame de Mezières should make. The most harmful would be to bring Carte from England. He admitted Carte's good intentions, but no one could trust him or Cecil with a secret. Sempil was as angry as Bolingbroke had been over self-constituted female ministers and ambassadresses.

Alas! while the prince waited at Gravelines, strictly concealed and all aglow with hope and daring, Saxe and the French government (March 2) received from England intelligence very unlike that which Sempil had provided. As always, there had been gross exaggeration and mis-statement. There were far more than 7000 troops in England; the navy was not in the least likely to declare for King James; the corporation of London had just renewed their oaths of fidelity to George II.; the Jacobites were only a feeble minority in the island.

The poor prince suspected nothing of this. The embarkation began. The landing was to be effected at Maldon, Essex, and pilots were to come over with a mysterious "Mr. Red." None turned up, nor "Mr. Red" (probably Rede), whom Saxe and the others supposed must be a mere Mrs.

E

1744. Harris. No one could find him or had seen him. The prince assured them there really was such a person, a gentleman of importance in Essex. There was—perhaps is still—an old Essex family of that name. It was said that Mr. Rede had reached Dunkirk, lost courage, and returned in the ship that brought him.

The prince had sent orders to the Highland chiefs to take up arms, promising twenty shillings per man. They had engaged to furnish 19,000 men. The Earl Marischal and the Prince of Monaco were with Charles and Saxe, and the Duke of Ormond was coming from Avignon to Paris. Then, once more, the wind rose and blew Jacobite hopes into the *Ewigkeit*. A terrific tempest on the night of March 6–7 shattered the ships at Dunkirk and Brest. The Marquise de Mezières' son, who was to sail in the expedition, at least distinguished himself by courage and good service, by riding into the raging sea and dragging out drowning sailors. Those of the only embarked battalion[1] who were not wrecked, suffered terribly from sea-sickness. The French government, as contemptuous of the English Jacobites as annoyed by the catastrophe, recalled Saxe.

How to tell the prince? Saxe's kind heart sank at the task before him.[2] He wrote a very sympathetic letter (March 13), assuring the prince that the expedition was only postponed.[3] Charles replied cheerfully, professing joy and gratitude.[4] Saxe had never been able to visit him, for such a visit would have betrayed the royal address so carefully concealed, and had spoken to no one but the Earl Marischal, who all along had thrown cold water on the expedition.[5] Charles understood well enough that the postponement was quite indefinite. He had written rather bitterly to Saxe, March 9; amazed to hear that Admiral Norris had been able to escape from Portsmouth, since Rocquefeuil's orders had been to blockade him there; puzzled as to why Rocquefeuil did not follow Norris if he were in the Downs, the wind being no less favourable to one than to the other.[6] Saxe went off to Flanders. Charles stayed to eat his heart out in sight of the white cliffs of his country, with Lord Caryll in attendance.

---

[1] The prince and Saxe had not embarked.
[2] *Louis XV. et les Jacobites*, Colin, p. 157.
[3] Ibid. p 177.   [4] Ibid.   [5] Ibid. p. 153.   [6] Ibid.

The prince wrote a long letter to Sempil for the French 1744. king's perusal, March 15 ;[1] eight full pages, a rare literary effort. He refused to leave the coast. He was safe enough, for no one knew of his exact whereabouts, only that he was near. He assured Sempil with pathetic earnestness that the havoc of the tempest had been exaggerated. True, eleven or twelve ships were lost, but enough were left. He was very sorry for the few men who were drowned, but he did not see that such a misfortune need change the French king's mind. If there were no other way, and if he knew that his presence " could deliver England," he would go alone in a boat without hesitation. It was his first big step in the world, he pleaded. If he were to draw back now after making such a fair show, posterity would receive a bad impression ; friends would be afflicted, and enemies encouraged. But it would be better to change the plan so far as to land in Scotland, not in England. Scotland was the country of his race. He knew the Irish regiment would follow him gladly, and if Louis would add two battalions and a regiment of dismounted dragoons, he would soon make himself master of the " ancient kingdom," whence, with an irresistible army, he could march into England. The long letter is very practical and clearly expressed though— perhaps because—written under great emotional stress ; and in the event, success proved the prince's plan to be the right one. Inexperienced, untutored as he was, there was the soul of a general in him, whether it were the soul of Sobieski or of the sometime Lord High Admiral, James, Duke of York. It had been suggested that he should join the French army in Flanders. He would have been charmed to fight in the army in which his father and grandfather had fought, but at present his mission was to " deliver " his kingdoms. " I know most of the Highlanders will join me when they see me come quite alone. Would it not be better to die, if die I must, at the head of these brave men, than drag out life in exile and dependence ? The length of this letter will show how I am touched by the accident which puts off our enterprise "—as indeed it does !—" I am not a bit cast down. I count on the kindness of your Majesty and the wisdom (*lumière*) of your ministers."

[1] Add. MSS. British Museum, 34,522, ff. 53 *verso*, and *sqq.* Copy. *Louis XV. et les Jacobites*, pp. 178-181.

1744.   His little stock of money ran out.   Saxe had been entrusted
with nothing but a letter of credit for the prince, drawn upon
an English bank, so now useless.   He appealed to his father
for help (March 7), "for arms, not for fine clothes," and asked
that his jewels might be pawned : "I should wear them with a
very sore heart on this side of the water."

D'Argenson wanted Charles to retire with the Earl Marischal
to Vie-sur-Aisne, a villa of his Fitz-James cousin, the Bishop
of Soissons ; he who in the following August was to send
"fair and haughty Châteauroux with wet cheeks and flaming
heart" flying from the supposed deathbed of Louis the Well-
beloved at Metz, and thereby to earn her undying enmity and
the displeasure of her restored lover.   Now Châteauroux ruled
the king and her sympathies were Jacobite ; hence the Most
Christian vacillations between mistress and ministry.   Charles
presently wearied of inaction in the lonely, wind-battered seaport, hidden within doors or bargaining for fish on the beach
for change and amusement.   Louis and Mme. de Châteauroux
had set off for Flanders, leaving a kind message with Sempil
that the prince must come to Paris, and the matter of his
household should be discussed with Maréchal de Noailles.
Louis had "always expressed remarkable tenderness for me,"
Charles wrote to his father from Paris, May 11, "but it is much
increased by my conduct at Gravelines."   But Charles yielded
to solicitation and arrived in Paris on the night of April 5–6.[1]
He went to a little house near Montmartre to live in strictest
seclusion.   He now looked forward to joining the French
army on the royal staff, though he feared the Earl Marischal
would stop that too, as he had helped to stop so much.   But
it is improbable that Charles had any serious intention of fighting under the French colours.   He was all the time making
plans for a campaign of his own.

Louis had been urged to "remove this nightmare (*fantôme*)
Pretender" since his adherents had been proved good-for-
nothing, but Charles refused to believe in perfidy though his
ride with the French colours failed to come off.   Murray of
Broughton extols his conduct under such trial ; the rare
moderation and temper with which he bore himself on finding
that he had been ill-used, imposed upon, and treated like a boy ;

---

[1] French Foreign Office Minute ; Murray of Broughton, p. 501, Scot. Hist.
Society.

marvels that at twenty-three years old, unaccustomed as he 1744. was to control, he should act with as much coolness, caution, and circumspection as the most experienced statesman.[1]

The prince treated Sempil and Balhaldy with cold neglect, and not until he had been a month in town did he give them audience. When Sheridan came, later on and invited them to dinner in the prince's name but in a very casual way, Sempil had a previous engagement, though Balhaldy went.

The Earl Marischal "pleaged" Charles with "letters that were rather books": would not hear of his disgusting the English by fighting with the French colours. The Earl Marischal had all along been much of his friend Voltaire's opinion—that the French expedition had had no defect except impossibility. So the prince had no occupation in the strict captivity of the little house at Montmartre but his weariful correspondence. He sent for Sir Thomas Sheridan, as he wanted "a man of sense" to be with him. James delayed sending Sheridan, so Charles, "in great ancteicty and pene" for Sheridan, sent to Avignon for the Reverend George Kelly:[2] to the relief of the Duke of Ormond, said Kelly, who found the non-juring parson a "great constrent on his Amoors."[3] The Duke of Berwick also was at Avignon and had responded joyously to the prince's summons in February, but the political ill-wind held him back.

Since his son's departure, James had become more and more depressed, but in March he was cheered by the promise of 4000 annual scudi from the Cathedral of Malaga, to which it was settled he should succeed upon the death of the present possessor, Cardinal Alberoni: "but Alberoni must die first," says the Vatican archivist, "and then we shall have to see how the bishop will be disposed to pay, for the Spanish bishops are rather queer about such payments."[4]

In July Murray of Broughton came to Paris to fan the flickering sparks. He told Charles there was no hope of further French help, but Charles assured him that the French expedition would be resumed in the autumn. Balhaldy had gone to Holland for arms and the prince was resolved to go, if with a single footman; as his father would and should have gone in 1708. France still tantalised with vague promises. Charles

[1] Murray of Broughton, p. 91 (note), Scot. Hist. Society.
[2] Then acting as secretary to Ormond.
[3] Charles to King James: Stuart Papers *ap.* Murray of Broughton, p. 369.
[4] Archiv. Vat. Segr.

1744. was living in a suburb called Francfort,[1] "in a few rooms which is but a hole," he wrote. Only Sheridan and George Kelly were with him. James wanted his son to come home. He was getting into debt, and seclusion that amounted to imprisonment might well have driven a more patient man to madness, but Charles would not hear of Rome and (September 18) thought of seeking the comparative liberty and comparative convenience of Avignon. However, he remained in Paris, which, until January, he could not leave because of debts.

In Rome there was no less a time of weary waiting, of mortification and hope deferred, while France played fast and loose with the royal adventurer. James was amazed and deeply wounded that his son should be compelled to remain incognito. The Pope, too, was greatly scandalised.[2] James, annoyed by the raids of German troops upon his hay at Albano, was further worried by the usual dissensions among his subjects. "For God's sake," he wrote to Lord John Drummond, the worst offender, 22 December 1744, "let us stifle as much as possible all little views and animosities. Let us have nothing in view but the common good."[3] He might as fruitfully have spoken to the winds at Dunkirk. He took the gloomiest view of the situation; believed in neither French nor English action, but he sent what supplies of money he could, and Charles sent to his brother a present of lace.

"All I have to say that is good," Charles wrote, November 30, "is as long as there is life there is hope." He was "pleaged out of his life" by the mischief-making among his people, who would rather sacrifice the whole cause than fail in any trivial object.

Letters from England, Sempil reported, December 1744, were excellent. James accepted the belief, but admitted fears and suspicions of the French, though so long as they did not patch up a peace with England all would be well. The prince must decide for all. James felt sadly disadvantaged by distance from the centre of action. He set his face against the prince going alone or even with a small following, but he did not see why the French should not transport as many troops as they

[1] There had been rumours that he was to go to Frankfort in Germany to see the Emperor Charles VII., but there is also a Parisian suburb of the name, and it is probable that Charles may have written the "Francfort" letters from there.

[2] Stuart Papers *ap.* Murray of Broughton, p. 371.

[3] Stuart Papers *ap.* Browne, ii. 447 (note).

liked to Scotland. In any case, it was better to risk too much 1744.
than too little. If they waited, seeing how things were in
England, they might possibly achieve the restoration without
foreign assistance at all.[1] This last hope looked more than
ever likely when in February three Jacobites, Lords Chesterfield
and Gower and Sir John Hinde Cotton, became members of
the government.

Balhaldy's accounts from England continued to be "very 1745.
comfortable" (February 2). The French court used the prince
scandalously, said the king, but anything must be submitted to
rather than abandon the scheme.[2] Sempil and the English
kept their secrets, such as they were, from Tencin, who, Sempil
made James believe, had little credit therefore with Louis XV.
Amelot, like the Bishop of Soissons, fell under Châteauroux'
displeasure, and the Marquis d'Argenson succeeded him as
French foreign minister. James reappointed O'Brien as his
representative at Paris.

Correspondence with England was suddenly interrupted
towards the end of February,[3] and the open passing of so
many people between France and England gave much cause
for uneasiness as to secrecy. James had no hope for the
present of anything better than that the prince should be
allowed to make a campaign with the French army.

In January 1745 the Emperor Charles VII. died ; to make
way for Maria Theresa's husband to the throne of the Cæsars.
England and France were now openly at war, and Prince
Charles might come out of his shell into social view, though
not into the full light of court recognition. As there was,
however, nothing doing for him as yet, in the "*triste état dans
lequel je languis*,"[4] he went on a visit to his cousins at Fitz-
James, in Picardy, near Clermont-sur-Oise, regretting only
that Fitz-James was out of the way of amusements into which
he must have entered with such zest after long seclusion. He
expected he would have the spleen there, though he would put
himself into a tub like Diogenes if necessary.

Confinement, only lately tempered by dancing, had somewhat relaxed his physical energies. "It is now two months

[1] Stuart Papers *ap.* Browne, ii. 452.
[2] Ibid. 453.
[3] Stuart Papers : Browne, ii. 454, 455.
[4] Charles to Argenson : 17th December 1744 ; Murray of Broughton, p. 504, Scottish
History Society.

1745. since I have handled a gun because of the bad weather and cold," he wrote home ; the duke would call him *cacciatore di pan bianco*. " As soon as I am arrived at Fitz-James, I intend to begin again to *shute* but not *whin* it *rens*." He was ill at the time of a severe cold, and being dull and depressed, he shortly after increased his father's worries by sending for Strickland and Towneley.

He found himself less cut off from carnival gaieties than he had feared, and wrote to his father (February 28) that between balls and diversions he had been too much hurried for regular correspondence, though he longed for "real business." Madame de Mezières' husband tried to have private talk with him, " but I always excused myself in a proper manner." De Luynes says that on Shrove Tuesday he sat very near Queen Marie Leczcinska at a masked ball, but she did not know him until after inquiry ; that he had been at another masked ball at the palace of Mesdames, the king's daughters. These at that date were Anne Henriette, second Daughter of France, born 1727, twin with Louise, who, in 1738, had married the Duke of Parma, brother of Charles III. of Naples, Prince Charles's brother-in-arms at Gaeta ; and the little princesses, Adelaide, Victoire, Sophie, and Louise. The last became a Carmelite nun : her three elders were the Mesdames who tormented Marie Antoinette. Anne was nearly eighteen, and was provisionally chosen by the prince for his future bride ; more of political than tender choice, perhaps, for his heart was too full of business to leave room for love, though it is not difficult to believe that the princess may have attracted him by her admiration. His companions supposed her to be the " Black Eye" he toasted in his Highland wanderings, though the bold black eyes of Miss Walkinshaw had perhaps extinguished the memory of those bright French eyes. He attended all these balls in strict incognito.

In April he went up to Paris for a week to see a " firework," and to attend a musical party at the Spanish embassy. He had been up in March on business. He also got a good deal into debt for clothes befitting the Prince of Wales moving in society, even incognito.[1]

---

[1] In 1745 his tailor's bills amounted to 3740 and 1348 livres for himself and 710 livres for servants' clothes. That he amused his time of suspense with science, like his merry royal namesake, is hinted by a bill for twenty-four livres for mending H.R.H.'s microscope. " History of the Highland Clans," Browne, iv. 35.

Sempil and the prince were becoming further and further 1745. estranged, though the prince made a show of trusting the man he had found out for the sake of apparent unity which was so very desirable. The Carte-Oglethorpe ministry harassed James as much as French duplicity and adherents' quarrels. Carte had sent for a certain Father Cruise to England to carry Jacobite reports back to France. James was much annoyed and disclaimed all knowledge of, much less authority for, Cruise, and feared "the Lady's" (Madame de Mézières or her sister Anne) "itch to meddle in politics without caution or prudence might be of ill consequence." Cruise and the Oglethorpes nevertheless busied themselves in England. "I wish no harm may come from their negotiations," James wrote to Charles, 23 March. "I have let the Father know that I can neither approve nor authorise negotiations into which I don't see quite clear." He hoped the French court would be cautious as to acting upon Cruise's representations, "for by what I know or can observe hitherto, I believe there are no people of a certain weight and consideration in England concerned in them but Colonel Cecil, with Carte and Mrs. Oglethorpe." Later, April 12, he wrote that Cecil and Carte had no weight among the best people.[1] On March 18 (N.S. 29) a hope that was rather a harassing perplexity was lost in the death of Sir Robert Walpole, Lord Orford.

While Charles danced and perhaps made love in Paris that carnival tide, the Duke of York also "made a shift to divert himself a good dale," his father writes to Charles. He attended a private comedy and a ball at Count Mariscolli's, a grand supper at Madame Bolognetti's, and gave three balls himself. After the carnival, his birthday, March 6, was the occasion of his giving a great conversazione which was well attended. The king was "extremely troubled with his usual ails," and unable to be present at these revels, for the *tramontana* was abroad and the weather extremely bad.

But he was too wise a father to be satisfied with dancing as an occupation for his younger son, nor was Henry, full of high spirit and military ambition despite the clerical career recommended for him, likely to be happy amid such gaieties while his brother was in daily expectation of embarking upon an enterprise of danger and glory, of life and death. Mann

[1] Stuart Papers: Browne's "Highland Clans," ii. p. 458.

1745. says he fainted on hearing of the failure of the intended
expedition with Saxe. But James had too little cause for
satisfaction with the result of Charles's sojourn in Paris to
send his other son there, and tried to get leave for Henry to
serve with the colours of the King of Spain in Italy. He was
anxious also that the boy should be parted from those who
were about him, and had refused permission to Towneley to
attend the duke on a campaign, should he make one. So
Towneley had joined Prince Charles in France, in defiance of
the king's orders. Strickland tried to obtain Henry's forgiveness, and then followed Towneley to Paris and the prince.
Old Sir Thomas Sheridan, the Falstaff of the party, for whom
the prince had the strongest affection, was already there, to
James's great vexation, who presently heard that Sheridan
had the prince quite in his hands.[1]

Between the jealousies of Sempil and Balhaldy, the evil
influence of Strickland and Towneley, and the meddling of
intriguers, anxiety was acute. James had written to Sempil
April 13, 1744, "Except what you may think proper to write
to me or Edgar on the subject of our unhappy tracasseries, the less these matters are stirred or talked of the
better, and yet I see with concern that everybody will be
criticising and meddling in matters which are not their
business . . . by which they certainly do a real and great
prejudice to the cause. . . . What occasions my saying
this at present is that I have had occasion to know lately of
a certain Lady Clifford . . . I suppose she is sincere in the
zeal she pretends to have for us, but . . . she is an intriguing
woman, capable of doing a great deal of hurt with a good
intention."

Sempil replied that Lady Clifford was a sister of the
Duchess of Gordon, who had taken up the prince's cause
only since he was in Paris: a good though very weak woman,
whose chief visitors were Mr. Stuart, of Lord John Drummond's
French regiment, and Sir Hector Maclean.

So the weary months dragged on, the end receding like
a mirage. The king and the duke waited in Rome, pursuing
the very monotonous round of their daily lives, expecting
nothing, but fearing much. Charles remained in Paris, keeping

---

[1] Stuart Papers: Browne's "Highland Clans," p. 459.

his own counsel. When on August 5,[1] 1745, they received 1745. the news of his sailing for Scotland, they were thunderstruck. Nothing had seemed more hopeless than waiting for French assistance, and without that assistance, surely such a step must be only a rush to prison or death. The Duke of York would have followed his brother at once, but this his father would not allow. When France should send the troops, without which it seemed that there could be no chance of success, the duke must be at their head with Ormond at his side, but until that happy day, James could not risk both his sons in so wild a venture.

[1] " August 11 ; a courier arrived on Thursday morning to the King of England with the news that the Prince of Wales had left France without saying for where, which has caused great agitation to the poor father who is really agonised, and endless gossip in Rome."—Archiv. Vat. Segr.

CHAPTER VI

THE FIRING OF THE HEATHER

1745. ON June 22 (O.S.—July 3 N.S.) the prince sailed from Nantes on board the *Doutelle*, incognito as Sheridan's son. The brave story has been told so often and so well that there needs little more than a summary here. All the world knows the names of the prince's seven companions : the Marquis of Tullibardine, rightful Duke of Athol, whose younger brother, being a Whig, held his lands and honours, Strickland, Sheridan, and Sullivan of the prince's household, the first distrusted and dreaded by the king, the second distrusted too, the third much trusted ; Sir John and Æneas Macdonald ; the Reverend George Kelly, the non-juror, once secretary to Atterbury, later, to Ormond ; a Buchanan ; and Antoine Vincent Walsh of Nantes, owner of the *Doutelle*. It was a brave venture and has been applauded by friend and foe, who, however, have quite forgotten to applaud the royal adventure of 1715, not on the summer seas but in bitter Christmas weather, and with two or three companions instead of seven. The *Elizabeth* joined the *Doutelle* at Belle Isle on July 4. They sailed for the west coast of Ireland, met the English *Lion* off the Lizard, fought her, disabled her, and drove her away, though she had disabled the *Elizabeth*, who must return to France. On July 23 the *Doutelle* reached Eriska by Long Island, and an eagle flew from the Highland cliffs to hail the prince come to the land of his fathers.

The chiefs did not so fly. Macdonald of Boisdale came to bid his prince go home. "I am come home," returned the Duke of Rothesay. Kinlochmoidart came and demurred. On July 25 the *Doutelle* landed the prince at Lochnanuagh, and he called Lochiel, Clanranald, Glenaladale, the Duke of Perth, and others. Lochiel who, by his paramount influence in the Highlands, held fate in his hand, hesitated, for there was no French help ; till his prince's taunt went home, struck the loyal heart to flame, and the heather was on fire.

PRINCE CHARLES EDWARD STUART

Circa 1745

From a miniature by Giles Hussey, Indian ink on card.
The property of Lord Arundell of Wardour

On August 19 (O.S.) the standard of King James was raised at Glenfinnan by Tullibardine. "The prince declared his commission and made a short but very pathetic speech," says Murray of Broughton, who had joined him the day before, and whom he had appointed secretary. Two days later, the prince set off on his march to London.

The Camerons, Macdonalds, and a few Macleods were nearly all his host. Lord Lovat sent a welcome message, and Stuart of Ardshiel brought in 200 Appin men, and though Glengarry stayed at home, 600 Macdonnells joined under Lochgarry and Angus of Glengarry, Pickle's brother. By August 27 the army was over 2000 strong. Sir John Cope advanced to meet the prince who out-generalled him at Corryarrick like an old campaigner and marched uninterruptedly towards Perth, joined as he swept along by the men from the glens. On August 31 he occupied Blair Athol. The usurping duke had fled, and the rightful duke, Tullibardine, became his prince's host. Lord George Murray joined Cope at Crieff, but left him for the prince a week or two later.

James had been greatly distressed by the rashness of the prince's step, but he was cheered to find that Rome and France applauded its daring and found much ground for hope. The Duke of York would wait no longer for the chance of a Spanish commission and was eager to join his brother at once. On August 11, the day he had news of the prince's sailing, James wrote to the King of France of Henry's strong desire, and that he would send him at once to Avignon to await Louis' orders. Henry had developed very much in his elder's absence, as James had written to Charles some months earlier. He had lost his pretty-boyishness in ardent admiration of his brother's daring and serious realisation of his perils. He pawned his own jewels to assist Charles, but for the present there was no more that he might do. The jewels had fallen very much in value. Many had already been sold for daily needs, and many had been set in the stars of the orders worn by the princes. On August 20 James had an audience of the Pope ; "the poor King of England," writes the Pope, "he is verily an object of compassion, unable to neglect his son's affairs, yet not knowing where to turn for help." [1]

By August 20 the Earl Marischal had fulfilled his mission

---

[1] Archiv. Vat. Segr.

1745. and obtained a promise from Louis to furnish the assistance required. There was no question left—except how to find the means for keeping the promise. Lord Clancarty had arrived as representative of the new Duke of Beaufort, whose brother and predecessor had died February 24 (1745) ; of Lords Lichfield, Orrery, and Barrymore, Sir Watkin Williams Wynn, and Sir John Hinde Cotton. These gentlemen, unaware of the fact that the prince had already arrived in Scotland, offered to raise the royal standard all over England on the moment of the French landing at Maldon. Clancarty was forbidden to take any one into his confidence except the King of France and his chosen minister, the Duke of Ormond, and the Earl Marischal. On October 13, De Maurepas, the war minister, reckoned up the force that could be furnished, and suggested that Walsh who had taken the prince to Scotland should superintend the fitting-out and embarkation thereof. Louis had sent an envoy to the prince, M. Boyer d'Eguilles, with assurances of affection and promises of assistance ; but for the present, with nothing more substantial.[1]

D'Argenson held back, on pretext that they had not the signatures of the party in England. They could not risk the French king's troops on the single word of Lord Clancarty, a very unprepossessing Irishman, dissolute, horribly slovenly, who had lost an eye in a drunken broil. The English Jacobites were ever careful to avoid setting pen to paper. Atterbury especially had been thus careful. They felt themselves pretty safe in their conditional promise. When they found the prince was actually in the island, they were shocked and did not even proclaim King James.

On August 29 (N.S.), by the advice of D'Argenson,[2] Henry left Rome as secretly as his brother had left. For some weeks before, he kept closely to the house. Walton reported him as ill of malaria. He really had a swelled face. It was presently given out that he had small-pox, that visitors might be held at bay. On the night of the 29th he stole out of the palace to Bailli de Tencin's house, who took him to the ever-helpful Cardinal Acquaviva, by whose means escape was achieved, and the duke crossed safely to Antibes, attended only by Sir

---

[1] Prince Charles to the King of France : Edinburgh, 15th October (O.S.) 1745. French Foreign Office Papers *ap.* Murray of Broughton, p. 513.
[2] Archivi Segreti ; Vatican.

John Graeme.   He went on to Avignon and stayed there with 1745.
the Duke of Ormond, with whom it was intended he should
sail.   But Ormond's wars and " amoors " were over.   He was
then very ill, and died on November 15 following.

Henry fell ill of fever, the fever that had really been hanging over him in Rome.   It helped to detain him two months
at Avignon.   He was detained also by disappointment at not
being called to England, or at least to Paris, to receive support
and encouragement.   But still the English Jacobites refused
to rise and so discouraged French sympathy.   D'Argenson
wrote to the Vatican, September 28, that the Chevalier de St.
George had risked much in giving up his two sons to the bold
adventure of the elder, but that it could not be believed that
the younger would be allowed to cross the sea until something
more substantial should come of the enterprise.[1]   There was
plenty of sympathy in England and Wales.   Lord Chesterfield,
who had visited Ormond at Avignon in 1740, was now Lord
Lieutenant of Ireland, though an avowed Jacobite.   " Being at
Dublin at the height of the rebellion," says Walpole in his
history of George II.,[2] "a zealous bishop came to him one
morning before he was out of bed and told him he had great
grounds to believe the Jacobites were going to rise.   The Lord
Lieutenant coolly looked at his watch and replied, ' I fancy
they are, my lord, for it is nine o'clock.' "   But the campaign
could not be nourished on sympathy, and James, watching the
situation through the clearing lens of distance, in the light of
his own profound experience, wrote to Henry as late as
November 8 (Prestonpans was won October 2 N.S.) that even
yet he had no great hopes in spite of the late successes.

Spain was faithful, and was fitting out a fleet at Ferrol for
a descent on England, and French troops for transport were
being leisurely drilled at the Channel ports.   It was expected
that Henry would go on to Madrid to fill the post of admiral,
but he was unanimously advised to wait for the French command.   Saxe was beating English troops in the Netherlands,
and England was sick of earning dishonour for the sake of
Hanover.

Towards the end of October, only half recovered from his
fever, the Duke showed courage and energy by taking a bold

---

[1] *Ministère des affaires étrangers ;* a.a. O., fol. 253 ; Versailles ; Vatican Archives.
[2] I. 53.

1745. step on his own account. Probably he had D'Argenson's advice and encouragement.[1] He was scarcely recovered from his fever, when he suddenly arrived in Paris, between October 20th and 28th, with the purpose of making a personal appeal to the French king on behalf of his brother. He went first to the friendly roof of his cousin, the Duc de Bouillon. On November 14, Lord Sempil and Balhaldy, "hastened to put themselves at his royal highness's feet ; extremely happy to find him so well recovered and in so much spirits." [2]

This loyal haste was really more than a fortnight's delay : an inexplicable breach of etiquette, unless it may be explained by the probability that the king's agents were not informed of the duke's arrival until due consultation had taken place with the Dukes of Bouillon and Fitz-James. James certainly never counselled, nor knew, nor would have approved of Henry's " forward policy." The Bouillons being of the prince's party, the forward party, may have persuaded the duke to flout his father's agents as Charles was used to flout them. The boy, though not by any means inexperienced in such cases, had walked into a perfect hornet's nest when he presented himself among the sworn supporters of his cause. As if he had not difficult cards enough to play with the French court and ministry, he had to cope with the numerous Jacobite leaders — numerous still, reduced though their numbers had been by the contingent that had followed the prince to Scotland.

Charles was going on from glory to glory, though there were already disappointments, even in the loyal Highlands. Cluny held back, as did Lovat. The chiefs, as is well known, tried to run with the hare and hunt with the hounds ; husband and wife divided the risks, fathers with children, brothers with brothers. James was very anxious ; grieved, too, that Strickland, and now Towneley, should be with the prince. He had forbidden the prince to take Strickland, and had been disobeyed ; " more than enough to have caused trouble between any father and son less attached than we are," James wrote to O'Brien, August 30.[3] Charles kept professing sorrow at his

---

[1] D'Argenson wrote October 12, 1745, to the French ambassador in Rome: "Le roi fera toujours par la maison Stuart qu'il regarde comme ancienne amie de la couronne." Arch. Seg. a.a. O.

[2] Balhaldy to James : Stuart Papers *ap.* Browne's " Highland Clans," iii. 454.

[3] Stuart Papers : Browne, iii. p. 145.

father's disapproval and promising to send Strickland away, but Strickland was never sent.

While at Perth the prince received, besides a large body of Macgregors and Robertsons, two important adherents. The loyal Duke of Perth joined: also Lord George Murray who had suddenly changed his mind and left the White Horse for the White Rose. The prince was quite undazzled by the prestige and reputation for military experience of this last recruit, and naturally never trusted such a sudden convert; even warned Lord Elcho, who joined a little later at Edinburgh, and whom he made his first aide-de-camp, never to confide in Lord George.[1] Tullibardine himself distrusted his brother; who on his side suspected all the suspicion afloat. Yet Lord George remained true, and doubtless did his best for the prince according to his lights. Those lights, alas! proved a less faithful guide than the star followed by the prince, and according to the statements published in Mr. Lang's "Life of Prince Charles Edward," the prince had, in Lord George's dealings with Cope, the gravest possible reason for his distrust. Yet King James always trusted Lord George. Space fails here to enter into the difficult matter.

Oliphant of Gask and his son also came in at Perth, brave in war, loyal and patient in defeat and exile; but the clan did not follow them. Passing through the happy autumn fields of Gask, ripe to harvest yet unreaped, the prince asked why the corn was not cut. Gask, he was told, had forbidden his disobedient men to reap. The prince with his sword slashed off some ears and declared the prohibition removed. Lords Strathallan and Ogilvie also came in and the Chevalier Johnstone. The army waited at Perth until September 11, and was drilled by Lord George, and the prince visited Scone where his forefathers had been crowned. On September 11 he marched from the Fair City: on Sunday the 16th he arrived before Edinburgh. Early next morning, Lochiel surprised the town, and before noon the heir of the Bruce had won his fathers' hall.

Then followed the march to meet Sir John Cope whom the young prince had already evaded so cleverly; who had hurried to the sea at Aberdeen, landed his army at Dunbar, and now marched upon the capital. At Preston-

[1] Lang: "Prince Charles Edward," pp. 124, 125.

F

1745. pans, September 21 O.S. (October 2 N.S.), Prince Charlie flung away his scabbard and with his merry men rushed upon "Johnnie Cope" in the mist of the early autumn morning and sent him flying to Berwick with the news of his own defeat.

But neither the prince's valour nor his victory nor his surprising success in the occupation of Edinburgh were potent to fetch the promised French help. On October 28 Charles sent a Jesuit, Alexander Gordon, to France to explain the position and waited at Edinburgh until November 1 O.S. (November 12). This delay gave the government the time it had lost by the celerity of the prince's previous movements. The Elector of Hanover, stricken in the person of his son and army at Fontenoy, had hurried back to the British Isles to look after his safety there. Parliament met, October 17, and the Habeas Corpus Act was suspended. Troops recalled from Flanders were sent to Newcastle under Marshal Wade, and on October 19 the lately defeated Duke of Cumberland arrived in England to wipe out the stain of Fontenoy. He certainly succeeded in obliterating it—by a ghastly smear of blood.

The prince kept up his heart bravely that his men might keep up theirs. Delay was hard to bear, now he had proved what dash could do, but how could he leave Edinburgh while the castle held for the Elector? Worse still, in spite of his successes there was no sign that the English Jacobites would rise: no sign of French help which was their excuse for throwing faith to the winds. News was slow to travel, as slow as French ministers to move, but the Scottish successes really had begun to take effect, and on October 24, D'Argenson and O'Brien drew up and signed a treaty at Fontainebleau on behalf of Louis XV. and James III., which, besides guaranteeing alliance between those monarchs with reasonable conditions, promised that a body of troops, drawn from the Irish French regiments, should be sent at once to Prince Charles under Lord John Drummond. These were sent to Scotland at once, but the prince had already marched south, hoping his numbers might be swelled by great accessions of English, so soon as he should be among them.

On October 31 (O.S.) the prince and his army marched out of Edinburgh. On November 6, they reached Jedburgh.

They kept along the border till they reached the Esk. On 1745.
November 8 (N.S. 19) the prince crossed the border into
Cumberland.   To mislead the enemy, a detachment marched
eastward, passing through the village of Haddon not far from
fatal Flodden.   An old man, hale and hearty in 1858, used
to tell how his wife's grandmother, a lassie named Telford,
was frightened with the other children at the sight of the
soldiers.   She herself in "a bit blue frockin'" fell down on
the road as she was running away and was pulled up by a
Scot who cried out laughing, "Weel dune, blue breeks!"
and asked "what she was frightened for?"[1]   On November
10 (O.S.) the prince opened the siege of Carlisle ; on the
16th Carlisle surrendered and delivered its keys to his royal
highness at Brampton, where he watched for Wade on the
Newcastle road.   He made a state entry into Carlisle, where
he stayed from the 17th to the 20th.

While he waited in Cumberland, the usual jealousies
sprang up to divert his mind, otherwise intent on Wade.
Lord George Murray's Protestantism protested against the
superior command of the papist Duke of Perth.   Perth was
perhaps less fit than Lord George for the command which
his rank had won for him, but he was brave and loyal through
and through ; the very Galahad of this quest.   His delicate
health had not held him back nor old Tullibardine from
working in the trenches before Carlisle, protected only by
their shirts from the snow and bitter cold which had welcomed
Charles to the frosty-hearted southern kingdom.   His soul
was too high, his loyalty too pure for selfish care.   He resigned rather than weaken force by division, and Lord George
was given the chief command.

On November 20 (O.S.) the prince marched on.   At
Manchester he was hailed with cheers and illumination and a
contingent of soldiers under Francis Towneley, brother of the
evil John.   At Chester he was greeted by an old lady who
had seen Charles II. land at Dover, and who had waited
till now to say her Nunc Dimittis.   On December 4 he
reached Derby, where he lodged at the Virgin's Inn.[2]   On
December 6, the hitherto undefeated army was in retreat.

Wise after the event, subsequent historical opinion is all

---

[1] " Northern Notes and Queries."
[2] See his bills for entertainment there.   Stowe MSS. 158, f. 201.

1745. for the march to London; confident that had the prince had his way, he would have triumphed. We know what the chiefs did not know; of the terror in London on hearing of the prince at Derby; of the run upon the bank; of even the plucky little Elector's preparation for flight: that Sir Watkin Williams Wynn was on the way to join with his Welsh contingent; and, cruellest ignorance of all, that a French fleet was waiting on the wind at Dunkirk to bring the longed-for French assistance and the Duke of York. If it seemed madness to go on, not knowing these things, had not the whole campaign been madness, and yet madness had won? With his one ship and seven men, the prince had escaped the English look-out and reached the desired Highland haven. With his little troop, scarcely armed save with enthusiasm and valour, he had baffled and beaten the experienced and well-equipped Cope; he had reigned in the palace of his ancestors; he had marched through a country, cold or hostile, unhurt by the mighty gathering hosts. Why should not unquenchable valour and the magic of his own personality carry him to the gates of London and into its streets, and up to the throne of St. Edward and the Stone of Scone? But pressure wrung assent to his own ruin, and he was dragged back from the prize almost in sight; dragged back to the north, as Fergus MacIvor said, like a dog on a string.

He knew the cause was lost, in spite of all the arguments of his officers, and he was right as he had always been right. His instinct had been true; the science of his experts false. He was the best officer in his army, Kinlochmoidart said, for all his inexperience. Charles blamed the ever-distrusted Lord George Murray for the fatal step back. When on January 6, Lord George in a memorial advised that the prince should call councils of war and vest discretionary power in those who had commands, the bitterness of the prince's soul came out in his reply. "Every one knew before he engaged in the cause, what he was to expect in case it miscarried, and should have stayed at home if he could not face death in any shape; but can I myself hope for better usage? At least I am the only person on whose head a price has been already set, and therefore I cannot indeed threaten at every other word to lay down my arms and make my peace with the government."[1]

---

[1] Athol MSS., Hist. MSS. Comm. Reports VII., pp. 703*b*–704*a* and *b*.

So Charles marched back with his sullen officers and angry men, he himself no longer the gay untiring leader who walked off his shoes, slept in the open, and ate where and how he could.   He now rose late, travelled much in his carriage, and sometimes strove to cheer his heart with mountain Malaga.[1] Cumberland was on his heels ; held back even at this dark hour by Lord George Murray at Clifton ; the moonlit skirmish in which Vich Ian Vohr was taken.   James Oglethorpe, Madame de Mézières' brother, commanding a body of volunteers detached from Wade's force, was ordered to follow the retreating army, but perhaps his heart was not in the work, and his " malingering " led to a court martial, though to acquittal.   In the early morning after that moonlight fight, December 19, the prince reached Carlisle out of which he had marched so merrily not a month before.   He left a tiny garrison to hold the town under Hamilton the governor and Colonel Francis Towneley of the Manchester regiment, and next evening[2] marched towards Glasgow.   Francis Strickland died at Carlisle, and Charles had at least one bad counsellor the less.   Cumberland reached Carlisle December 22, and forced the devoted garrison to surrender, December 30.   Hamilton and Towneley were taken prisoners in London.   Towneley was tried at Southwark, July 15, with James Dawson and six others, and suffered with them at Kennington.   His head and Dawson's were placed on Temple Bar.   Two Cumbrian heads were sent to adorn the English gate at Carlisle.   Hamilton suffered the same ghastly fate.

Charles has been blamed for sacrificing these brave men to the holding of an untenable post.   The fact was, he fully expected to return and relieve them in a few days.   The Frasers under Lovat, who had been caught by Lord Loudoun but had escaped, were marching south to join him, and Lords John Drummond and Strathallan were bringing reinforcements, the 800 French, from Perth.   But the three or four thousand Jacobites at Perth all quarrelled and refused to advance to the Border and Carlisle was lost.   They joined the prince at Glasgow, whence he went to besiege Stirling.

At Glasgow, the prince met fate in another form.   Sick at heart, feeling destiny and all the world against him, the world ill lost for men's selfish jealousies, he was thrown into the con-

---

[1] Lang: " Prince Charles Edward," p. 224.
[2] Terry, p. 75, " The Young Pretender."

1745. soling society of Clementina Walkinshaw, niece of the loyal Sir
Hugh Paterson of Bannockburn House, where the prince
stayed during the futile siege of Stirling : January 4 to 16 (O.S.)
The prince was ill of a chill and Miss Walkinshaw nursed him ;
with very usual consequences, at least as far as the lady was
concerned.   The prince had never before fallen in love unless
with Anne Henriette of France ; his mind had never been
sufficiently at leisure, sufficiently void, to admit soft thoughts.
Now he was sad, ill, and idle, and she was kind.   If she promised then, as Saint Simon says, to come to him whenever and
however he should call her, the promise was perhaps volunteered.   Charles seems to have forgotten the vow or cared
nothing for it, for, unless she were the Black Eye of his
Highland toasts, he thought no more of her for four years.

CHAPTER VII

FORLORN·HOPE

THE Duke of York, so anxiously expected, was still in Paris, 1745. doing what he could. He took a house at Bagneux, and sought through D'Argenson to obtain an audience of the King of France who was then at Fontainebleau. The duke's arrival was duly notified to Louis, who did not refuse the request : only forgot all about it until half-past six on the evening of the appointed day. Then he suddenly bethought himself of his engagement, and bewildered the Duc de Gesvres by sending for him in a violent hurry, to bid him summon " the prince." De Gesvres had no idea what prince nor where to find him, and it was against the laws of etiquette to ask the king for further information. While his Majesty impatiently awaited his visitor, De Gesvres discovered by dint of frantic inquiries that a foreign young gentleman, whose name must not be mentioned, but who possibly might be " the Prince of England," was waiting in a small closet below stairs. He was unearthed and brought into the Most Christian presence.

Tired and annoyed as he must have been, Henry's dignity and Stuart grace never failed him. He made a profound reverence and advanced to salute the king. Louis was helplessly embarrassed. Henry was incognito as Count of Albany, and it was contrary to etiquette, as it would be highly inconvenient, to recognise his rank by a royal embrace. He, however, came forward so confidently that the reluctant king yielded, and the duke was kissed. He conversed with his majesty for some time ; showing great good sense, according to the Duc de Luynes who was present and describes the interview.[1] That most fastidious of courts was impressed by his noble air and charming manners. He spoke gracefully of the obligations of his family to the House of France ; of his brother's brilliant prospects ; of the zeal and fidelity of the Scots towards their

---

[1] *Memoires du Duc de Luynes* (1861), vol. vii. pp. 104–108.

1745. lawful sovereign : then of the urgent need of his Majesty's support, so that those hopes and longings should be realised ; a need more pressing than ever, now Prince Charles was in England, lest he should be crushed by the numbers of his gathering enemies.

Louis, always shy and awkward with strangers, did not answer readily. He professed his conviction of the justice of the Stuart cause and kindly promised to continue his favours. Henry reminded him how Charles had vainly tried to procure an audience when he was in Paris. Louis was silent. De Luynes and De Gesvres promptly took up the conversational ball. Louis blundering, asked the duke if the Pope were not his godfather ? Henry knew well the grave disadvantage of papal sponsorship, even in the political eyes of the Most Christian king and eldest son of the Church, and suspected that it would be reckoned as against the success of any assistance sent to Protestant England. He replied that he had been given many names, but that he had chosen to be known by that round which English memories most proudly clung. Shirking politics—he was hardly attentive enough to wince at any hint of Agincourt—Louis went on with a weary catechism as to the prince's education, till he bethought himself of sending for the Dauphin to help him out of his difficulties. The Dauphin came in a hurry, not knowing whom he was to meet, for his father had forgotten to tell him of the duke's coming. He kissed the royal stranger on hearing that the king had done so, and everybody was worse at ease than ever.

The poor boy—he was twenty but little and young for his age [1]—his heart aching with suspense, his pride smarting, keenly aware of the embarrassment of his presence and of the unfriendliness and duplicity in the atmosphere, remained imperturbably graceful and self-possessed. He congratulated the Dauphin upon his recent campaign in Flanders, and prettily thanked the king for allowing him to see his son. After this, the conversation languished desperately. The audience had lasted half-an-hour when De Gesvres judged it to be full time to end it, and reminded the king that the young prince had evidently been ill and needed rest. Henry, who

---

[1] In the Vatican archives of this date, written by the Pope or his secretary, he is always styled *il Duchino di York*, as if he had been a child.

was shivering, admitted that he had recently had a fever. 1745.
He made his bow and retired without any more embracing.
He did not know the way out, and nobody seemed inclined to
trouble any more about him until De Gesvres presently
followed to see him off the premises. Henry asked his guide's
name and said he feared he had pressed too much the interests
he had so intensely at heart, but De Gesvres must see how
vitally necessary to the cause was the help and protection of
the King of France. He was then handed over to another
official and huddled down a dark staircase and out of the
palace to D'Argenson's lodgings.[1] From thence he went to
sup and stop the night with O'Brien, for whom he had a
strong affection.[2] There he met Tencin.

Henry was not particularly acute, but he now saw well
enough that France meant to do nothing that would sub-
stantially serve the Stuart cause, and Tencin and O'Brien
probably confirmed the conviction : for which assent they
would receive such small thanks as are the meed of unwelcome truthtellers. On November 29, Sempil wrote to King
James that the duke had prohibited him and Balhaldy in the
most peremptory manner from giving any information to the
French court until he, "with Kelly," had first considered
whether it might be proper to give such information.[3] This
Kelly, now the Duke of York's chosen counsellor, was the
Reverend George, the parson whom Prince Charles had taken
to Scotland, and sent back to Paris with news of his proceedings and authority to act for him. Kelly's genial Irish
optimism no doubt came in opportunely to cheer the duke's
spirits, and revive the hopes which the French king's conduct
and the discouraging counsels of Tencin and O'Brien had
cast down.

In spite, however, of shifts and evasions, the audience was
not without fruit ;[4] such apples of Sodom as might be gathered
in false France. De Maurepas, minister of marine, suggested
that 10,000 troops should be sent to England. Six thousand
were promised, to be commanded by the Duc de Richelieu,
Lord Clare, or the Duc de Fitz-James. Meantime ships were

[1] D'Argenson had been present at the audience.
[2] Memoires du Duc de Luynes, vii. 108.
[3] Stuart Papers : Browne, iii. 438.
[4] For " the Duke of York's energy, entreating help from France," see Campana, i. 54.
Letters to De Noailles.

1745. sent from time to time, at Henry's solicitation, to the assistance of Charles, but they were mostly captured by British privateers.

On December 15, the Queen Marie Leczcinska sent for the Duke of York to visit her privately, not having seen him at Fontainebleau. A Pole herself, she was always kindly disposed towards the sons of Clementina Sobieska. The Princesse de Conti, his cousin by marriage,[1] introduced him to her Majesty's presence, the Duchesse de Luynes and M. de la Mothe being of the company. The Dauphiness[2] was sent for, and on this occasion the duke received the unhesitating kisses of royalty, his incognito not being in force in private. But the audience was so short that no one so much as sat down.

The Pope, on receipt of the news of Charles's success, had secretly sent a large sum of money (amount unstated) to the Duke of York in Paris, while he was expecting to set off at once for Scotland to his brother's aid.[3] It was settled that he should sail at once from Dunkirk, with 11,000 men, according to D'Argenson, a train of artillery, and six or seven ships. His cousins, the Prince de Turenne and the Duc de Montbazon, son and son-in-law of the Duc de Bouillon, engaged to accompany him to Dunkirk as aides-de camp. The Prince de Montauban, son-in-law of the Marquise de Mezières and brother of the Duc de Montbazon, asked leave to attend his royal highness as another aide-de-camp. Henry consented, but refused to ask the necessary permission of the French king. After such treatment as he had received he would ask no further favours. De Montauban applied to Louis, who answered that the Duke of York must ask himself. Henry persisted in his refusal, and De Montauban was obliged to stay at home.

On Christmas Day the Duke of York left Paris for Dunkirk, to take command at once of the promised fleet. The Duc de Richelieu was to command under the young prince. No horses were embarked except a few for officers, but there was a supply of saddles and bridles.[4]

---

[1] The Prince de Conti of 1701 was first cousin of Mary of Modena, their mothers being sisters.
[2] She died shortly after.
[3] Bibl. Angelica. Cod. MSS. 1618 ad. an. VI. Pontif. Benedict XIV. Vatican.
[4] De Luynes, vii. 153.

The Duke of York waited about Dunkirk with the French
ships and soldiers, carefully watched by Admiral Vernon. He
was joined by Colonel John Macdonnell of Scottas, who, born
in 1728, had been three times wounded in the Spanish
service, which he relinquished when the service of his rightful
king demanded his sword. He had been presented to King
James shortly after Charles left Rome in January '44, and the
king and the Duke of York both helped him with money.
He served a while longer in Italy; then had leave to join
Prince Charles in Scotland, and hastened to meet the Duke of
York at Boulogne. He was kindly received and lived with
his royal highness until April 16, when he set off with a
letter and money to the prince from his brother. He did not
return to the Stuart Court and service, but remained in
Knoydart to look after his property.[1]

Even yet the situation might have been saved had France
been in loyal earnest; but alas! the tide had turned. Just
when success seemed almost assured, just when French
help was ready, the infatuated chiefs insisted upon retreat.
The fatal news reached France just in time to stop further
preparation. Louis XV. and Richelieu changed their minds
with the unfavourable wind. France had spent five million
francs over the business and would do no more.[2] Not
one ship was allowed to leave Dunkirk. The retreat had
ruined all.

The Duke of York with Lord Clare waited on at Dunkirk
and Boulogne all through the weary winter, as his brother had
waited before : the English cliffs on the horizon, the idle fleet
between, the idle army lying round. No effort was made to
put the forces under way. The Duc de Richelieu, weary of
inaction, returned to Paris, complaining impatiently of the
Duke of York's piety, which he had vainly tried to persuade
him to dissemble. " He never passed before a crucifix or an
altar without genuflecting like a sacristan," says D'Argenson

[1] Companions of Pickle; A. Lang, " A Gentleman of Knoydart."
[2] "Journal of the Marquis d'Argenson," vol. iii. p. 69. The King of France sent later
on to Prince Charles a million of francs, which D'Argenson supposed were lost, having
arrived after the catastrophe of Culloden. They were buried, as we know, beside or
beneath Loch Arkaig; a fairy hoard which brought much evil to its custodians, who
now and then saw fit to feed from it the dying cause—or their own pockets. This last
was, after all, hardly failing to fulfil the trust, for King James had commanded that
money sent over too late for the campaign should be applied to the necessities of his
impoverished adherents. Browne, iii. p. 462.

1745. scornfully. "Such customs may be in vogue in Rome but we never practise them in France;" where even to make the sign of the cross was out of courtly fashion. "Your royal highness may perhaps win the Kingdom of Heaven by your prayers but never the Kingdom of Great Britain," Richelieu told him when he kept a council of war waiting while he was at mass. D'Argenson tries to bring a charge of cowardice against the Duke of York. One foggy night, it was said, just before the New Year came in and a week before the project of embarkation was abandoned, there chanced an opportunity of getting out of Dunkirk harbour, watched as it was by English ships. In the thick darkness the watchful enemy being far enough off, the greater number of the French ships, with the Dukes of York and Richelieu at their head, might have slipped out unobserved. But though the danger was small, a certain amount of risk remained, and a council was held. The majority were for sailing, but two of the leaders declared the danger to be too great; that the prince's ship would be sunk at once. The prince decided against sailing and the opportunity, such as it was, passed.[1] The incident, even as reported, proves really nothing against Henry's courage, which all who knew him declared to be beyond doubt; but the story was repeated later to Prince Charles, with the object of embittering him against the brother to whom he was so warmly attached, and a painful quarrel was the result. D'Argenson disliked Henry and believed any story so long as it was against him.

There were frequent rumours of Henry having been captured and brought to London. A French ship, the *Soleil*, was taken by the *Sheerness*, and among the prisoners was one whom the fiercely exultant mob took for "the Youngest Pretender." They would hardly be held back from tearing him to pieces as he was marched along the streets to prison.[2] They had been thoroughly frightened, and were consequently savage from the memory of shame and the reaction of recent relief. The young man who so excited their fury was that son of the attainted Earl of Derwentwater, Charles Radclyffe, whom Walton had called the most impudent of all the Jacobites in Rome. Young Radclyffe was horrified at the

---

[1] *Journal et Mémoires du Marquis d'Argenson*, vi. p. 111, ed. 1863-4.
[2] Walpole's Letters, i. p. 410.

conduct of the London populace. He had been much in 1745. France and knew Parisian mobs, yet he said that though he had heard of London mobs, he had never imagined half of their terrors.

Later on, December 20, Horace Walpole writes : " We again think we have got the second son under the name of Macdonald."[1] No such peril ever came near the young Stuart 1746. prince ; nothing worse than the long months of torturing suspense, while Charles retreated back and back upon the desolate mountains, in the mists and snows of that terrible winter. In January, Henry, always energetic and eager to help his brother as he could, managed to send a letter to Sir Watkin Williams Wynn, who had made such magnificent promises, and who indeed professed himself to have been on the point of joining the prince with reinforcements when news reached him of his retreat ! The Duke of York urged him to rally with his Welsh friends to the assistance of Prince Charles and seize some seaport town. But Sir Watkin did not see his way to make good his boasts and promises. James, who had long ago given up what faint small hope he allowed himself, was greatly annoyed at this unauthorised and futile action of his younger son. *He* was fully aware of the state of things in England ; the gathering strength of the army round London, the real helplessness of the loyally-drinking loudly-talking Welsh squires, without arms and troops, and he declared with his invariable sense and patience that, though he had often blamed the indolence and timidity of the English, in the present moment he owned they would act imprudently and even rashly " not to lye quiet still."[2] But if Sir Watkin had taken his courage in both hands, supposing he had really been on the point of marching, he might have changed the fortune of the campaign.

Another rumour, that the Duke of York really did land in England, is accepted by Mr. T. F. Henderson in the " Dictionary of National Biography," in his article on that prince ; on the authority of " A genuine intercepted letter from Father Patrick Graham, Almoner and Confessor to the Pretender's son in Scotland, to Father Benedict Yorke, titular Bishop of St. David's at Bath ; published by authority," 1745 ; the authority

[1] Walpole's Letters, i. 413.
[2] James to Henry, 1 February 1746 : Stuart Papers *ap.* Browne, iii. 457.

1746· of some ignorant Whig pamphleteer.[1] The writer knows so little of his subject that he says "Father Benedict" (by whom he seems to mean Henry Benedict, Duke of York) "was soon translated from Bath to York, of which town he was duke, then cardinal: leaving England he died in Italy, &c." The letter is perhaps the very silliest of the many bogus "letters" published to fan the flame of Protestantism against the Stuarts. It even describes Prince Charles, that very doubtful Catholic, as "the most idolatrous, superstitious, and intolerant of Papists"; calling publicly upon the Blessed Virgin and St. Winifred; attributing the success of his arms to a medal he wore, and refusing to hear religious toleration so much as mentioned.

On January 17, Charles advanced to meet the government forces under Hawley at Falkirk where he won a complete victory; as much to his own surprise as to Hawley's, who wrote to Cumberland that his "heart was broke." Captain Lally was sent with the gladdening news to the Duke of York and the French court.[2] Lally was thereupon raised to the rank of Colonel by Louis XV., but nothing further came of the news; no more than came of the victory. James, who had been ill with melancholy, was made gay for a brief space,[3] only to fall again under the cloud when news came how, to the despair of the prince, further retreat had followed the victory.

On January 29, the prince had made ready for battle again, resolved to await Cumberland then advancing upon Edinburgh. On January 30, Cumberland slept in the prince's bed at Holyrood. That same January 30, ominous day! Lord George Murray sent the prince a memorial signed by the chiefs who insisted on the danger of giving battle since desertions had been so numerous. They proposed to take the northern forts, and wait in those fastnesses until the spring. Charles in despair struck his head against the wall and cried, "Good God, have I lived to see this day?" But he calmed himself and bore the unexpected proposal, says Warren of the French service, "with the greatness and constancy

---

[1] "Notes and Queries," 1st Series, xi. 477.

[2] "The duke was transported with joy at receiving news of his brother whom he loves passionately." De Luynes, vii. 220.

[3] On March 2, with the good news of Falkirk, James had returned from death to life. For some weeks he had heard nothing at all of Charles. Archiv. Vat.

of soul the prince is master of. However severe and un- 1746.
necessary it might appear to him, he generally waived his
own opinion."[1] He sent Sheridan to the chiefs to discuss the
memorial ; quietly stating the fact that if they were to retreat,
their men would be discouraged and the enemy elated. It
would be increasingly difficult to keep together deserting,
booty-laden Highlanders in their hills. Their Lowland friends
would be sacrificed, while France and Spain would refuse to
send succours to those who dared not wait to receive them.
But he was "too sensible of what [they had] already ventured
and done for [him], not to yield to [their] unanimous resolution if [they] persisted in it."

As before, the prince was right and the chiefs were wrong.
These desertions, inevitable with Highlanders, eager to rush
home with booty after a battle, were greatly exaggerated.
Lord George Murray, who counselled the retreat, admitted
that the army after Falkirk still made a fine appearance. In
the light of the review at Crieff a few days later, he called the
retreat "a disgraceful flight." Only a thousand men were
short. The chiefs took the desired forts and did nothing
with them. The government got time. The Highlanders,
disorganised, went on deserting, or starved. The arms of
courage and confidence had been victorious, and now they
were exchanged for arms of caution, dulled by discontent.
Charles could "see nothing but ruin and destruction to us
all in case we think of retreat." Had their defeat and disgrace and loss of officers and men at Falkirk made the
enemy more formidable? But he must yield, calling God to
witness that he did so with the greatest reluctance, and washed
his hands of the fatal consequences he foresaw but could
not help.

On February 1 (O.S.) the prince left Bannockburn House
with his army ; not as victors march forth, but hurried and
disorderly, as if flying from defeat. Stirling was evacuated
and St. Ninian's church was blown up with the powder
stored there. The prince marched by Crieff and Athol to
Moy (February 16), Lord George and Lord John Drummond
marching by Perth to Aberdeen. At Moy, Macleod attempted
to surprise the prince, but was driven off by a blacksmith

---

[1] Lang, "Prince Charles Edward," p. 254.

1746. and three or four men. On February 20, Inverness Castle surrendered to the prince's still undefeated arms.

Charles now had time to feel the strain of all he had so stoutly endured. He fell ill, and from March 11 to 20, was nursed at Elgin. He stayed as much as possible at Inverness ; his army was pursuing Lord Loudoun or besieging the forts. The rest abode by the sea-shore to find provisions. Cumberland reached Perth and garrisoned Blair Athol and other points by which Charles might escape to Aberdeen. Fort George and Fort Augustus surrendered to his arms, but Fort William held out till May. On April 14 (O.S.) the Duke of Perth marched out of Nairn and Cumberland marched in and kept his birthday there, April 15 (N.S. April 26).

That day the prince set his battle in array on Culloden Moor, but his men were starving, and after some weary waiting, scattered in search of food. A council met to discuss a night attack upon Cumberland's festively preoccupied and fuddled host. Had the prince's army been nearer, hunger might have driven them only the more fiercely to such a surprise rush as Prestonpans or Falkirk. The prince was all for the surprise. But the men had been drawn up all day, those who had not wearily roamed to seek food, and they were exhausted. At eight at night they marched towards Nairn, but in five hours only six miles had been covered, so long and so wasteful of weary men had been the halts. In the grey dawn they returned to Culloden. Charles afterwards (1759) declared that this return was carried out by Lord George in defiance of his orders. Much later, Charles said Lord George had convinced him for the moment of its necessity. It is impossible to find certainty from a very failing old man's memory.

Very early in the morning of Wednesday, April 16 (N.S. April 27), came the news of Cumberland's advance. The starving remnants of the prince's army were again drawn up ; to be further weakened, says legend, by the refusal of the Macdonalds to fight in the less dignified wing. The story of the battle is too well known. In a few hours, the murderous Hanoverians were slaughtering the dying and riding over the vanquished dead, and the prince, forcibly led from the field, was in flight to the west.

For the wonderful tale of his wanderings there is no space

here ; it has been too often told. But the memory of it will 1746.
never die. Hearts will never cease to thrill nor tears to flow
at the history of that marvellous courage and constancy.
James, so late as June, knew little of what had happened
beyond wild rumours of a great catastrophe, and urged Charles
to think of his safety, not to push matters to extremity. The
honour he had so far gained would remain with him,
wrote James, "and will, I think I may answer for it,
always engage the French to protect and assist you, and
to renew in time another project in your favour ; so that
you should really have no temptation to pursue rash or
desperate measures at this time, for should you do so, it
would be the ruin of all, and even a drawback from the
honour you have already gained. In fine, my dear child,
never separate prudence and courage. Providence has
wonderfully assisted you hitherto, and will not abandon you
for the time to come." [1]

Prince Henry had lingered on the coast until the end of
April when the news of Culloden was brought to him. Then
followed nearly six months of terrible suspense, while the
beloved prince was hunted like a partridge over the Highland
mountains, and James waited in Rome, suffering acutely,
lamenting that he had ever been persuaded to entrust his sons
to France. He entreated Henry to return home, but Henry
seems to have shrunk from the dulness and purposelessness of
the old Roman life. Suspense, too, could be better borne in
action. With practical common sense, he wasted no time
bemoaning fate and hoping for the impossible, and he asked
leave of the King of France to serve in the approaching
campaign in Flanders. He was permitted only to be present at
the siege of Antwerp as field adjutant under the Comte de
Clermont, where, as D'Argenson admits, "he behaved with a
valour which was at once natural and hereditary." [2] James,
who had lately been suffering much on his account, was greatly
comforted. [3]

Colonel Warren visited him at Arras in May to discuss
plans for fetching the fugitive prince from the Highlands :
again in June, when Henry was staying with the Duc de
Bouillon at the Château de Navarre, near Evreux. Warren

---

[1] Stuart Papers *ap*. Mahon, iii. Appx. xxviii.
[2] D'Argenson, vol. iii. p. 70. 1857.   [3] Archiv. Segret : Vatican.

G

1746. returned from Paris, whence he wrote to the king on August 1 :—

"The present orders were intimated to me just as I was about to part for Navarre, there to make my court to his royal highness the duke, and to receive from him due instructions relative to the present circumstances: it's wonderful how capable he is of giving good ones though so young."[1]

[1] Stuart Papers : Browne, iii. p. 460 : Warren to James.

CHAPTER VIII

THE SLINGS AND ARROWS OF OUTRAGEOUS FORTUNE

ON October 10, Prince Charles Edward landed at Roscoff, 1746. near Morlaix in Brittany; safe and sound, save for influenza and a slight deafness, the result of exposure during his wanderings. Warren also brought two prisoners, Barisdale and his son, who had wanted to betray the prince at Lochna-nuagh. The Duke of York was at Clichy when he received the anxiously awaited news; a letter to himself in the prince's own hand, enclosing "to lines" for his father who shook off his melancholy in relief at the news. Charles urged upon Henry the necessity of writing at once to the King of France to notify his own arrival. "The bearer will instruct you of the way I would wish you should meet me in Paris," says the Prince Regent, already putting his junior in his place. But Henry's affectionate heart was too full of joy to suspect any intention of domineering, despite the past, and he flew at once to the happy re-union which took place on October 15 (N.S.).

Crowds gathered along the road from Brest to Paris to greet the hero.[1] Hail to the vanquished who comes with such honours thick upon him! glory of chivalry, glamour of romance.

"It was roses, roses all the way."

He did not know Henry at first sight, though his brother thought him not in the least altered, except grown somewhat broader and fatter; surprising after all he had gone through. Those that were present at the meeting were profoundly touched at the affection of the princes. No brother could have shown himself more kind and loving than Charles. He refused himself to nearly everybody but Henry for a few days, that he might rest awhile, "before being plagued by all the world." The duke went every day to dine with

[1] D'Argenson, *Journal et Mémoires*, iv. 321, ed. 1862.

1746. him, took him privately to see the house he had taken for himself at Clichy, and was charmed to find him with as much *goût* for the chase as he ever had.[1]

Neither absence nor intrigue had as yet diminished the affection of the brothers, though at first they did not live under the same roof. Charles had expected a royal palace to be placed at his disposal. This was wholly out of the question. The hero-worshipping French court dared not irritate England by any official demonstration of sympathy and admiration. The ministry—or rather, D'Argenson who, as foreign minister, had the delicate care of keeping down Jacobite hopes and activity—said heartlessly that the less France did for the Stuarts the better, for the less would be their fall when, at the expected general peace, France must leave them to their fate. So Charles might be lodged only somewhere near the palace, and the Château of St. Antoine was lent to him.[2]

On October 21, he went to report himself at the court of Fontainebleau, accompanied by the Duke of York. Here expectation was again dashed to the ground. He must not on any account present himself as regent of Great Britain. There was even official demur whether or not the princes might wear their orders. Charles was permitted to come only on condition of coming incognito and very privately. He bowed perforce, poor sport of fortune, to the nervous necessities of French policy and allowed himself to be received as Baron Renfrew. His brother went as Earl of Albany. But, relying on royal sympathy, Charles went splendid and stately in rose-coloured velvet with silver lace and flashing stars. Again, crowds lined the road between Paris and Fontainebleau, turning his incognito into a triumph. The king left his council to receive him, embraced him most kindly, and assured him that a day would come when his high merit would meet with just reward. The Dauphin was friendly. Louis led him to the queen, who was most gracious. The court ladies smiled upon him. The Jacobites, says Sir Horace Mann, grew extremely insolent upon it all. All tried their best by flattery and petting to make him forget the disappointments of the past ; and to abandon hope for the future !

[1] Stuart Papers *ap*. Browne, iii. 466 : Henry to King James.
[2] Journal, D'Argenson, iv. 321.

He was not only keenly alive to what honour was due to his position, but boyishly full of his own personal importance. He was so irritably jealous even of a brother's share in his honours that he would not speak of his affairs to Louis XV. at this audience because Henry was present, but wrote next day to ask for another audience when he might see his Most Christian Majesty alone.

Great entertainments were given in honour of the princes by Parisian society, though officialdom held aloof. Music which they both so loved was a chief feature of these fêtes, though Charles was deaf from the bad cold remaining from Highland exposure. Henry was still delicate, unable to abstain from meat on *maigre* days, so that special dishes had to be provided for him. The extraordinary affection between the brothers was everywhere remarked upon. This did not last. D'Argenson, who liked and admired Charles though he firmly opposed anything like official countenance to his pretensions, blamed Henry for the rupture that presently took place. He was always hard on Henry ; called him " untrustworthy, thoroughly Italian, deceitful, superstitious, miserly, fond of his comforts."

Fond of his comforts he may have been, but in larger matters than these, the evidence is all against niggardliness. While he lived in Paris, he was obliged to practise the strictest economy, but the liberality with which he dispensed the wealth that came to him later—a liberality that was constant and, in the end, extreme, the kindness and honourableness with which he made up for his brother's many pecuniary shortcomings, emphatically disprove the charge.[1] He was too conscientious to be lavish while his means were small and his father so greatly embarrassed to find money for two Paris establishments.

Still, the princes continued for some weeks to live together on affectionate terms ; but the gulf of two and a half years which lay between their home life in the Muti Palace and

[1] " Æneas " also charges him with miserliness, attributing the fault to inheritance from John Sobieski. Cardinal Wiseman, on the other hand, in his "Four Last Popes," tells a story, related to him by one who knew the duke well, which proves his absolute ignorance of the value of money in his youth. " When he first came to Rome "—a curious inaccuracy—" having been shown some place or object of curiosity, he was asked what should be given to the attendant. As he was puzzled, his chamberlain suggested, ' Shall I give him a zecchino ? ' a gold piece worth about ten shillings. Thinking that the diminutive termination must indicate small coin, the duke replied, ' I think that is too little. Give him a grosso,' a silver five-pence."

1746. their re-union in Paris had widely stretched out the four years' difference in their ages. For Charles, the gulf was filled with experiences numerous and profound beyond the tale of most long lives. He had commanded an army and reigned as regent ; he had been the idol of a noble people's enthusiastic idolatry. Henry was a homebird, impatient though he had grown of the old dull, narrow Roman life ; very ignorant and inexperienced, and all the fonder of his own opinion and his own way. The licence of Parisian society under Louis XV. shocked him painfully, while society was impatient of what it considered his absurd prejudices. So Cardinal Alexander Albani wrote to Mann.

At this time of his life Henry had developed into a very handsome young man, very like his brother. There is an excellent portrait of him, in the scarlet coat of his pre-clerical days, in the Scots College at Rome, in which he looks older and manlier than his twenty odd Italian years might have made him. A miniature by an "artist unknown" in the Edinburgh National Portrait Gallery also represents him at this period : a slim figure in a coat of brownish red velvet, broadly laced with gold, crossed by the blue ribbon of the Garter ; a gentle-looking youth with a long pale face, straight nose, brown eyes, and a long upper lip which deprives the sweet bowed mouth of humour. Under the short powdered wig flows a cascade of dark curly hair, as he always wore it until the Church cut it short. The features, expression, and long hair are the same in the much earlier portrait where he wears armour with the Order of the Thistle, of which there are prints in the Edinburgh Gallery and elsewhere. De Luynes found Charles more serious than Henry, who " talks more, laughs freely, looks animated, and is passionately fond of music. He is much shorter than his brother, and his figure is not so good." [1]

Now came news of the ghastly punishment that fell upon the Highlands ; [2] such devastation of sword, scourge, and fire-brand as had not been known for two centuries. Let us who are so proud to be English, who have raged over Neapolitan

---

[1] De Luynes, vii. 462.

[2] The atrocities committed in the Highlands far exceeded those of Judge Jeffreys in the Bloody Assize, but the great majority of the Duke of Cumberland's victims were poor people, barely civilised, of no more account in the eyes of the victors than so much noxious vermin. Besides this, they suffered for the vanquished House of Stuart, while Jeffreys' victims suffered for the cause ultimately triumphant over that house. Hence the fiercer anger of history over the Bloody Assize.

prisons, Siberian mines, and Armenian atrocities ; who rose in 1746. righteous wrath to chastise the Austrian woman-flogger—let us, at least, remember to our small credit that the horrors of Culloden and Carlisle were authorised by no English prince, though he bore an English title. He won for himself a title to which his right has never been disputed, which will never fall into abeyance—the Butcher of Cumberland who made one hideous slaughter-house of the West Highlands of Scotland.

On July 30, seventeen English officers taken at Carlisle were hanged, drawn, and quartered at Kennington ; among them Francis Towneley and James Dawson. The pathetic story attending Dawson's death is well known. On July 28, Lords Kilmarnock, Cromarty, and Balmerino were arraigned in Westminster Hall. Cromarty was reprieved ; Kilmarnock and Balmerino were beheaded on Tower Hill, August 18.

In July, three hundred and eighty-five Scottish prisoners of all ranks were thrust into that Black Hole, the narrow prison chamber of Carlisle Castle, where many died from suffocation. On September 9, a hundred and thirty-three were arraigned. Eleven were recommended to mercy and thirty-six acquitted. On October 18, nine were hanged, drawn, and quartered at Harribee ; these included Kinlochmoidart, Cappock "the bishop," and Mr. Buchanan of Arnprior. On November 15, a batch of eleven more suffered at the same place. These included Sir Archibald Primrose of Dunipace, cousin and brother-in-law of the second Earl of Rosebery.[1] Six suffered at Brampton. At York twenty-two suffered. All died very bravely ; nearly all faithful to the last to their king. The others condemned were sent into exile ; many to slavery in the American plantations.

On December 8, Charles Radclyffe, Earl of Derwentwater, caught and imprisoned on his return to England to join Prince Charles, was executed on his old attainder of 1715. Of all the executions, this was the one which brought most sorrow to King James. He wrote in deep grief to condole with Lady Derwentwater. "My dear lord did but his duty," she replied.[2] It was the spirit of them all.

> "I ance had sons, that now hae nane :
> I bred them toiling sairly :
> And I wad bear them a' again,
> And lose them a' for Charlie."

---

[1] See Note at end of chapter.   [2] Stuart Papers : Browne, iii. p. 491.

1746.   Charles was only the more eager to return to avenge his slaughtered servants and save the rest. He sent up a memorial to Louis XV., showing him how much had been lost for want of more than half the money that had been promised. He had been unable to march on to London, though so near ; then, to pursue Hawley ; last of all, to meet Cumberland on equal terms at Culloden. If he had done so much with so little—as indeed he had—all could be repaired if France would even now give from 18,000 to 20,000 men. Was not the Stuarts' cause the cause of France ? The Duke of York shared the horror and sorrow, and it was he who appealed to his enemy D'Argenson to intercede with the murderous British government, Charles refusing to treat with faithless France. Perhaps this action took place when Charles was absent. D'Argenson's dates here are uncertain or wholly wanting.

Society exerted itself to find a royal bride for the prince, but he was in no humour for marriage, though he had a mysterious plan for marrying his brother,[1] who was not consulted. But there was much more pressing matter on hand than any vague scheme of marrying the Duke of York. France, faint and faltering, was repenting even her impulsive moment of cheap compliment. The prince, refused recognition as regent and Prince of Wales, was definitely refused all hope of assistance for another expedition. Practical people may decline to blame France for considering her own interests, seeing how futile such expenditure of life and money must be now that the clans and other adherents were too utterly crushed to be able effectively to meet foreign effort. But who could fail to sympathise with the prince, who, being an Englishman, wouldn't know when he was beaten ? Instead of troops and ships he was offered a French pension : 12,000 francs monthly and a residence ![2] He fiercely refused it. Acceptance would have implied acquiescence in the finality of his own defeat, and who that is worth anything would give up hope at twenty-six ; hope, not only of regaining a splendid and incontestable birthright, but of active service and independence ? He knew also what England thought of former acceptances of French pensions ; how little had been gained with them and how much had been lost.

So Fate drew her nets round the hapless prince. His

---

[1] Stuart Papers : Browne, iii. 472.   [2] Terry, "The Young Pretender," 128.

pride deeply wounded by the slights and broken faith of his 1746.
allies, he turned to his own immediate followers for companionship and counsel. Unfortunately he could have been driven
to no more dangerous associates. Here was a proud, self-
willed young prince, smarting under bitter disappointment and
the maddening strain of hope deferred but never to be
abandoned; the chafe of indignities and chilling change of
courtly countenance. There were the more respectable Jacobites
who were trusted by King James, with O'Brien and Tencin,
both bound to do their best for the king's sons. But the
prince would have little or nothing to do with them. He
called Tencin "a rogue and a rascal," and was persuaded that
they all worked against his interests; were even in the pay of
his enemies—as many doubtless were.

It was the fatal family tendency to lean upon unworthy
favourites, when those whose position should have placed them
in the first rank of friends and counsellors had turned opponents
or traitors. The tendency really came of the warm affection-
ateness of the Stuarts, and the easy familiarity in which they
liked to live with those who were near their persons; a tendency which too frequently failed to be guided by judgment.
Charles was here the true heritor of Edward II. and of
James V., rather than his father's son. Strickland had died at
Carlisle. Towneley was in Paris but as a reformed character;
little mixed up with the princes, but settling himself down to
literary life. The prince's familiars were George Kelly, the
non-juring parson, and Father Kelly, his Franciscan confessor.
Both, according to the Reverend Myles Macdonnell at St.
Germain's, were "false, perfidious, ambitious, and sordidly avaricious," which were "ever the inherent characteristics of their
respective families.[1] Friar Kelly, even among the notoriously
drunken Cordeliers, was conspicuous for his excesses: the very
wine at the prince's table was known as Friar Kelly's wine.
He was still the hapless prince's confessor, "and as he regulated
the diversions of his illustrious penitent as well as his conscience,
his royal highness's character on the point of sobriety had
been a little blemished on this friar's account."[2]

Sir Thomas Sheridan had left the prince in Scotland to
carry an appeal for help to France and Rome, but his son

---

[1] Stuart Papers : Browne, iv. 14.
[2] Mahon, iii. Appx. p. xlii : anonymous correspondent to Dunbar.

1746. was with the prince. In November 1746 Sir Thomas died of apoplexy [1] at Rome, so his evil influence was out of the way. James wrote at once to tell Prince Charles, who had been only too fond of his old tutor, and at the same time entreated him to dismiss Kelly with his other evil counsellors, who were now exercising as baleful an influence as Sheridan had once exercised.

The prince wrote back at great length (December 19), surprised to find his father had such a bad opinion of Kelly. It was the first time he had heard Kelly's honesty questioned: "it must be a mistake. . . . As Sir Thomas is dead and gone, it is useless to be troubling your majesty for to justify him. . . . I must own I am now entirely convinced F. S. [Frank Strickland] was an ill man by a circumstance your majesty mentions to me of him." He admitted also that Towneley was "not the discreetest man upon earth." He wrote of his grief for the poor Scots and of Louis XV.'s goodness to them, "so that I would go if necessary on my knees for them, but that I never would ask anything for myself." He commended O'Sullivan to the king, and asked that he might be rewarded by knighthood. James, knowing O'Sullivan to deserve it, granted the request. Charles had seen his Most Christian Majesty the other day, "who was extremely civil to us, as also all his family."

The prince was deceived, not deceiving. These men about him were bent on keeping him in tutelage in the name of his independence, acting as ministers or favourites, and the certain way to accomplish this was to widen and deepen the breach between the king's party and the prince's party, between the invalid James in distant Rome, who had officially though never really resigned the leadership of what was left of the cause, and the active young regent in Paris, whose was the only name with which any dream of a restoration could be associated. Henry expostulated. Charles was indignant. The Kellys and other boon companions worked upon his wounded pride and his jealousy of control, and irritated him into treating his young brother with a harshness that sorely tried Henry's affection and loyal admiration. This irritability was the natural effect of a most painful position

---

[1] He had had two strokes before he accompanied the prince to Scotland, where he did not fight but remained by the prince's side.—Vatican. Archiv. Segr.

upon a quick, impatient temperament, but it could hardly 1746.
be expected of a young man of two-and-twenty, also afflicted
with a haughty temper, to allow for such extenuating circumstances. The brothers quarrelled incessantly. The seeds of
jealousy were perhaps sown in the old days of the king's
fondness for his younger son. Charles sneered at Henry's
piety, and brought up the story of his supposed cowardice
at Boulogne. Henry was heartbroken. The bond between
the brothers was strained too severely. They could no longer
live under one roof, though they constantly exchanged visits,
and really loved each other at the bottom of their hearts.

No doubt it was hard to be advised by a younger brother
of the hopelessness of any further attempt at doing battle for
the cause on which his whole heart was set, to find faith and
sympathy lacking just when it should have been readiest and
warmest. France was all shifts and evasions; Spain implored
him to keep away from troubling her. It was hard that no
one, not even his brother, should believe in him, when he
believed so ardently in himself and his judgment, in his Right
and his Star, in the certainty that the crown of Britain was
only waiting to be won. How should Henry know, who had
never been in England or Scotland? These other men had
been with him there, had seen and known. Was not their
counsel infinitely better worth taking? So Henry's expostula-
tions, when not received with angry scorn, were dismissed with
affectionate contempt.

Henry reported the sad state of affairs to his father, who
rebuked the prince, but Charles declared, "I can assure
your majesty, I myself trust nobody more than I do him, as
with reason. I tell him everything I can, but I am afraid
some people have given him a bad opinion of me, for I
suppose I must own he does not open his heart to me. I
shall always love him and be united with him. Whatever
he does to me, I will always tell him face to face what I think
for his good, let him take it well or ill. I know him to be a
little lively, not much loving to be contradicted, but I also
know and am extremely sensible of his love and tenderness
for me in particular beyond expression, and of his good heart
in general." But he complained on his side that Henry did
not mind what he said to him, and contradicted him in the
least trifle.

1747. James blamed the influence of the prince's set. Charles protested, January 16, 1747 : "In reality, I do not doubt the honesty of those about me, though they may not have all the capacity in the world. I find it nowadays so rare to find an honest man, that any that has given me proofs of being so (unless your majesty orders me, or I find I am deceived by any of them on any the least trifle) I would part with them with a sore heart. Notwithstanding, I offered to my dear brother, that any one, or all about me that he had a disgust for, I would dismiss to make him easy : to which he assured me he had no dislike for anybody, and did not want any such thing. He does not open his heart to me, and yet I perceive he is grieved, which must proceed from malicious people putting things in his head, and preventing him against me. Notwithstanding, I am persuaded he loves me tenderly which is the occasion of my grief. God Almighty send us better days."

To end the miserable discords, and to provide occupation for his younger son, James decided to send Henry to Spain. Just at that time, the beginning of February 1747, Charles suddenly left Paris for Avignon, leaving his brother in charge of affairs. Henry wrote to tell him of their father's Spanish plan. Charles replied from Lyons that he little expected any transaction with the king would have been kept a secret from him. As it happened, he himself was going to Spain, and Henry must not go until he had returned. He would send O'Sullivan to Rome with a full account. It would never do if people should imagine the brothers did not act in concert. Henry must tell nobody but the King of France and Sir John Graeme. Young Sheridan, left behind in Paris, knew nothing of the Spanish journey.

The duke replied from Paris, February 15, that his province was blind obedience, and as the king could not have foreseen Prince Charles's journey, he would not act upon the permission given to himself.[1] He remained in Paris and attended the wedding of the Dauphin with his second wife, Marie Joséphe of Saxony, at Choissy. Charles's objective was kept a secret. The Spanish idea had probably come into his head only when he heard of his brother's intention ; less inspired by jealousy, perhaps, than by nervous insistence upon

[1] State Papers *ap*. Browne, iii. p. 486.

doing everything himself that was to be done for the cause. 1747. Of course he was missed, and there was much excited conjecture in diplomatic circles. La Roche, who spied in Paris for Horace Mann, reported that Charles had gone to avoid the royal wedding. He was of opinion that the Duke of York, in temporary charge of business, was much better fitted than his brother for the position.[1]

Charles returned, hustled out of Spain, about March 20 ; and in his disappointment and humiliation, all the devils lying in wait rushed to take possession of his soul.

He was a very bright little boy when he had those regrettable opportunities, during the disputes over his education, for keeping his ears open to controversy. We know how, at a very tender age, he was given to questioning Catholic dogmas propounded by his tutors,[2] and to making contemptuous remarks upon religious ceremonies. Cardinal Tencin, however, assured the Duc de Luynes that he was a good Catholic : that he had gone of his own accord to confession and communion before leaving Rome for France, and that he had had a chaplain with him in Scotland, disguised, and had heard mass regularly on Sundays and holidays.[3] Tencin probably did not know he had wanted to attend the Presbyterian service at Perth and was only restrained by the single-hearted Duke of Perth ; a bit of impulsive opportunism. Immediately upon landing in France on his return, he went to the sacraments, and again upon arriving in Paris, and continued to frequent them though such was by no means the fashion at the French court, for whom the ceremonial fulfilling of the Easter obligation sufficed.[4] Now he flung faith and morals alike to the winds.

With those who were about him, the austerely conducted and horrified Duke of York was unpopular.[5] The duke's equerry, Sir John Graeme, though he drank as hard as any of the prince's household, increased his own master's unpopularity by his hatred of English and Irish.[6] Charles was persuaded that his brother was jealous and a fool. His father

---

[1] State Papers (Tuscany) 56 : Tuscany. La Roche gives the prince's companions on this journey as Kelly, Sullivan, Sheridan, young Lochiel, and Mr. Vaughan. Young Sheridan may have joined him later. O'Sullivan was in Rome.
[2] Dennistoun's " Life of Sir Robert Strange."
[3] De Luynes, *Mémoires*, vol. ix. p. 264.   [4] Ibid.
[5] Letter of the Rev. Myles Macdonnell to James ; May 4, 1747. Browne, iii. 503.
[6] Ibid.

1747. expostulated tenderly but firmly. He was persuaded that his father was imbecile, and he heard his counsels held up to ridicule. He gave himself up to living as wild and rough a life as he had lived in his dear Highlands, defying not only French favour, but French canons of decency. He insulted and reviled his father's best friends, who were also his brother's friends; who, it was suspected then and afterwards, were secretly working in the interests of Hanover upon the Duke of York's tender conscience and fatalistic indolence. So the clouds rose between the brothers, which presently gathered so thick as to form an impenetrable barrier between them for nearly all the rest of their lives.

One friend the brothers seem to have had in common, Young Lochiel, who wrote to the king, January 16, 1747, of "the singular marks of favour and approbation" with which the Duke of York continued to honour him. James replied, he was glad the prince had so honest and worthy a man as Young Lochiel about him. Advice, he added, was the only authority he was inclined to employ with his children.

NOTE.—The dirge of these martyrs of loyalty is sung in "Carlisle Yetts," [1] one of the most plaintive of old Jacobite songs.

> "White was the rose in his gay bonnet
>   As he faulded me in his broached plaidie;
> His hand whilk clasped the truth o' luve,
>   O it was aye in battle ready!
> His lang, lang hair in yellow hanks,
>   Waved o'er his cheeks sae sweet an' ruddy,
> But now they wave o'er Carlisle Yetts,
>   In dripping ringlets, clotting bloodie.
>
> When I first cam' by merry Carlisle,
>   Was ne'er a town sae sweetly seeming;
> The White Rose flaunted owre the wall,
>   The thristled banners far were streaming.
> When next I cam' by merry Carlisle,
>   O sad, sad seemed the town and eerie.
> The auld, auld men cam' out an' wept,
>   'O maiden, come ye to seek your dearie.'"

[1] Probably by Allan Cunningham.

CHAPTER IX

THE SCARLET OF THE SEVEN HILLS

JAMES could not allow the state of things between his sons to continue. On April 17 he wrote to both of his sonsseparately. To Charles, after reference to his inevitable expul- sion from Paris at the coming peace, he wrote, " I cannot end this without expressing to you my concern to remark from your letters your uneasyness and jealousies in relation to your brother, by which means it is impossible he can be of any service to you. As he will even become a constant subject of uneasiness to you, so that I own I am tempted to send for him back hither, and tho' I don't order him to return to me, yet I now write to him that he may do so when he pleases, and the truth is, as matters now stand, I think it would be more for your service that he should be here, were it but for a few months, and were he to stay here, he would be of the less expence to me and I could be better able to supply you at a pinch. Enfin, my dear child, my whole thoughts are turned to provide, as much as is possible, for the real good and advantage of both of you."

James had already been obliged to reproach Charles with neglecting to read his letters with attention, and it seems as if this letter could hardly have been glanced at, so overwhelming was the surprise of his brother's subsequent action. As it would be useless to consult Charles on the matter, Henry consulted Tencin and O'Brien, who were fully of opinion that his duty and advantage lay in fulfilling his father's wish. But, though he was obliged for peace's sake to act secretly, he acted with apparent cruelty. He invited Charles to supper on the night of April 29. Three hours before the time appointed, he had slipped off to Rome. He had left a letter of apology to be delivered three days after his departure, during which period Charles believed he had been kidnapped, perhaps murdered, in mistake for himself. All the explanation that must satisfy him for the present was that Henry wanted to see

1747. his father, perhaps to stay with him only a fortnight. As to his return to France, he would abide by the king's advice.

James was as much surprised by Henry's sudden resolution as Charles was. He knew nothing of the journey until he had a letter from the duke, written on the way to announce his approach.[1] But very secret councils had been going on between the Pope, Cardinal Valenti, secretary of state, Cardinal Riviera, Protector of Scotland (both eminences being devoted and lifelong friends of King James), Rochefoucauld, the French ambassador, and the Bailli de Tencin as his uncle's mouthpiece, "for the great profit of the Duke of York and the great comfort of his most worthy father."[2] A cardinal's hat had just fallen vacant and was offered to the prince. James seems to have been excluded from the council until the matter should be ripe, but no doubt it was a sudden summons from this council that had broken up the duke's supper-party in most admired disorder. The chief urgency as to secrecy was to ensure that premature disclosure should not allow Prince Charles to oppose the project. James consented joyfully ; was indeed in a frenzy of nervousness lest delay should betray all to his elder son, and there was much galloping between Albano and Rome to hurry on the affair.

On June 9, James wrote to inform the King of France what had been settled. On June 13, he wrote as follows to Prince Charles :—

" I know not whether you will be surprised, my dearest Carluccio, when I tell you that your brother will be made a cardinal the first day of the next month. Naturally speaking, you should have been consulted about a resolution of that kind before it had been executed ; but as the duke and I were unalterably determined on the matter, and that we foresaw you might probably not approve of it, we thought it would be showing you more regard, and that it would even be more agreeable to you, that the thing should be done before your answer could come here, and so have it in your power to say it was done without your knowledge and approbation. It is very true I did not expect to see the duke here so soon, and that his tenderness and affection for me prompted him to

[1] James to Charles : Stuart Papers *ap.* Browne, iv. 2.
[2] Archivi Segreti : Vatican Library.

undertake the journey: but after I had seen him, I soon found 1747. that his chief motive for it was to discourse with me fully and freely on the vocation he had long had to embrace an ecclesiastical state, and which he had so long concealed from me and kept to himself, with a view, no doubt, of having it in his power of being of some use to you in the late conjunctures. But the case is now altered: and as I am fully convinced of the sincerity and solidity of his vocation, I should think it a resisting of the will of God, and acting directly against my conscience, if I should pretend to constrain him in a matter which so nearly concerns him. The maxim I have bred you up in and have always followed, of not constraining others in matters of religion, did not help a little to determine me in this particular : and that when I seriously consider all that has passed in relation to the duke for some years bygone, had he not had the vocation he has, I should have used my best endeavours, and all arguments, to have induced him to embrace that state. If Providence has made you the elder brother, he is as much my son as you, and my paternal care and affection are equally to be extended to you and him ; so that I should have thought I had greatly failed in both towards him, had I not endeavoured by all means to secure to him, as much as in me lay, that tranquillity and happiness which I was sensible it was impossible for him to enjoy in any other state. You will understand all that I mean without my enlarging further on this last so disagreeable article ; and you cannot, I am sure, complain that I deprive you of any service the duke might have been to you, since you must be sensible, that all things considered, he would have been useless to you remaining in the world.

"But let us look forward and not backward. The resolution is taken, and will be executed before your answer to this can come here. If you think proper to say you were ignorant of it and do not approve of it, I shall not take it amiss of you : but for God's sake, let not a step, which naturally should secure peace and union amongst us for the rest of our days, become a subject of scandal and *éclat*, which would fall heavier upon you than upon us in our present situation, and which a filial and brotherly conduct in you will easily prevent. Your silence towards your brother, and what you writ to me about him since he left Paris, would do you little honour if

1747. they were known, and are mortifications your brother did not deserve, but which cannot alter his sentiments towards you. . . . You must be sensible that on many occasions I have had reason to complain of you, and that I have acted for this long while towards you more like a son than a father. But I can assure you, my dear child, nothing of all that sticks with me, and I forgive you the more sincerely and cordially all the trouble you have given me, that I am persuaded it was not your intention to fail towards me, and that I shall have reason to be pleased with you for all time to come, since all I request of you hereafter is your personal love and affection for me and your brother. Those who may have had their own views in endeavouring to remove us from your affairs, have compassed their end. We are satisfied and you remain master ; so that I see no bone of contention remaining, nor any possible obstacle to a perfect peace and union amongst us for the future. God bless my dearest Carluccio, whom I tenderly embrace. I am all yours,

"JAMES R."[1]

The king enclosed with the above, a touching little letter from the cardinal-designate, the latter portion in his father's handwriting, assuring Charles of his own unchanging affection : of which communication his royal highness took not the slightest notice.[2]

He was beside himself with rage, and loudly blamed Tencin for his brother's action. He was very likely right. D'Argenson declared[3] on the authority of "a certain Madame * * * who was particularly well posted in the affairs of the Stuarts"—probably Madame de Mézières,[4]—that Tencin and the O'Briens had been bribed by a large sum of money from England to persuade the duke to become a cardinal, it being what England desired more than anything in the world. Henry himself would thus be excluded finally and for ever from the throne of his ancestors, while his purple would as fatally prejudice the prospects of his elder brother. Tencin was said to have received money over the transaction. That would be far from impossible. The English government were

---

[1] Printed by Mahon and Browne.
[2] Stuart Papers : Browne, iv. 9.
[3] Journal, v. 28 (November 1747).
[4] Or her sister, Anne Oglethorpe. Horace Walpole alludes to a " Mrs. A * * " who belonged to that family. Letters, vol. vi. p. 149.

pretty sure to offer it, and to consider such a transaction 1747.
cheaply done at a big price. O'Brien could not have been
bought. He was a faithful servant as James knew and proved
his confidence.

D'Argenson, who was all for this world, protested that
precisely the opposite mode of action should have been prescribed by the deeply indebted Tencin and followed by the
princes. They should have withdrawn from Rome altogether,
and avoided the very appearance of Catholicism. He says the
O'Briens played upon the king's conscience to persuade him to
act so violently against his interests: representing that if ever
Henry should, by default of his brother, come to the throne,
it must be by denying his faith and eating of meats sacrificed
to idols.[1]

The news of the cardinalate was a terrible shock not
only to the prince but to the whole party, who saw the last
fragment of hope shattered before them. The Scots College
at Paris hesitated to congratulate the young prince on his new
dignity, declaring that if it were known they had done so, they
would not be able to hold up their heads before their countrymen.[2] Mr. George Innes, now the Principal, wrote to James
Edgar on July 31, saying cannily that though he could not
compliment the duke, he enclosed a letter of congratulation to
be shown or not as Edgar thought best, in which he formally
begged for "his royal eminence's" protection.

Mr. Theodore Hay wrote to Edgar that the duke's change
of state was looked upon by everybody as of much worse
consequence than Culloden. The Reverend Myles Macdonnell
wrote to the king of the confusion his majesty's subjects were
in over the cardinalate. He believed the duke had been driven
to it by the perfidious attempts of some people to insult and
vex him.

Possibly it may have been James himself who prompted
Tencin and O'Brien to suggest the step to his son. Years
before he had destined Henry for the Church, and it was said
that he had been persuaded against the measure to his subsequent repentance.[3] No one had his sons' interest and happiness so deeply at heart as he, yet no one knew better what

---

[1] *Journal et Mémoires*, D'Argenson, v. 98 (ed. 1862).
[2] Stuart Papers (Windsor) *ap*. Browne, iv. 15.
[3] State Papers: Tuscany. Referred to in "Æneas and His Two Sons;" Pamphlet,
1746; that is, printed the year before this event.

1747. effect such a definite decision for Rome would have upon the Protestant mind of Britain. Had he not himself painfully learnt the lesson under Bolingbroke? Henry was deeply religious and pure of life, though in obedience to his father he had sought for military employment and had borne himself well in his one opportunity. Possibly his heart was never in a military career, though private inclination must be sacrificed so long as he might be useful to his brother. Perhaps he was shocked into flight from the temptations of royalty. Had not Charles's doings and the ways of the French court shown him how hardly should they who were born in earthly purple reach the kingdom of Heaven? He liked Rome and an easy life, too. A Roman cardinal's life need not be more saintly than his taste went. It was at least a provision : the secure position, with fixed precedence of a prince of the Church, which seemed to him more desirable than the position of a proscribed, disowned, rarely recognised English prince. The game was up. No further harm could be done to the ruined cause. Might he not hold himself free to act as seemed good towards himself?

There is no doubt that the acceptance of the cardinal's hat was virtual renunciation of the English crown. James and Henry were not clever men, but James was gifted with unfailing common sense, and had a true sense also of what was for the real good of his adherents. He had always felt so strongly that a king must be a father of his people ; to give them bread, not stones, for food ; above all, not cannon-balls! He knew, and Henry had learned and seen, that the cause was utterly beyond hope of even another struggle for life, much less of success : that all was done that man could do, and all was done in vain. If things had looked black enough two years ago, when the memory of the much less havoc made by the rising of '15 was thirty years old, how much blacker did they not look now the best and bravest of their followers were dead or ruined ; now the Highlands were disarmed, and the British government, once thoroughly frightened, was more vigilant than ever in the look-out for the least symptom of disaffection? Had not the reluctant chiefs, the wary English squires, been proved right? Had not the king himself been proved right, who never, even in the palmiest days of the campaign, had the least hope of its ultimate and permanent success ; who thankfully remembered that he at least was in ^{1747.} no degree to blame for the disastrous consequences ? With all the magnetic charm and prestige of rare daring and a success almost miraculous, they had failed, and the House of Hanover was settled more firmly than ever upon the throne. The Revolution, after a sixty years' struggle, was an accomplished fact. More useless than ever would it be to require sacrifice of life and lands in the lost cause. No action, politic or impolitic, admirable or obnoxious, on the part of the repudiated royal family could now serve or harm their interests : neither heroism, nor folly, nor sacrifice, nor crime. Nor " valour could avail, nor people's love." If the vocation of Heaven had come to the younger prince, he owed no duty to the country which had renounced him that he should disobey. If he sought occupation and a peaceful, honourable life where there was some certainty of finding it, there was no reason for blame on the part of those who had only a brilliant illusion with anxious and futile labours and the hard facts of poverty, humiliation, and bitter disappointment to offer as an alternative. And there were also the interests of their country for the Stuart princes to consider : no less their country because she had shut her gates upon them. The more remotely the native princes removed themselves from the throne, the more contentedly and prosperously England would submit to the rule of the foreign and younger branch of the family which her statesmen had chosen should sit upon that throne.

Prince Charles thought otherwise, and his proud spirit cried out with an exceeding bitter cry at the weakness with which the father and brother he had loved so dearly had yielded to force of circumstances and thrown up the battle. He believed it was still possible to make a fight for the right ; that the English people had but dissembled their love when they rejected him ; possible, at least, until that stout Protestant nation, who,

> " Pricked by the papal spur [had] rear'd
> And flung the burden of the second James,"

should hear how the son of that prince who had promised religious toleration so frequently and so earnestly, had put on the Roman scarlet ; the scarlet of the Abomination of the Seven Hills, of the fires of Smithfield, of the blood with which

1747. Jeffreys' assize had drenched the south-west of England. All the hope of all the faithful, that long-suffering remnant, was laid on those two pairs of young shoulders, and it beheld one pair clothed with the Church's purple as with a pall. Charles not only saw the Stuart race threatened with extinction ; he believed himself, with much good reason, in imminent danger of assassination, as the only Stuart to reckon with : for a rumour came that the duke was at once to enter the priesthood, not a necessary condition of the cardinalate.[1]

So Henry, as Mrs. Oliphant wrote, "set his red hat as a seal to the tomb of the Stuarts." Charles refused to hear his name mentioned, or to allow his health to be drunk in his house. He chose to do nothing himself to perpetuate the House of Stuart, but he could not forgive a like slackness on his brother's part, such treason of royalty against itself.

On June 30, 1747, Henry, Duke of York, received holy communion and the tonsure from the hands of the Pope in his private chapel, in the presence of the king and the Cardinal-Protectors of the three kingdoms. He put on the ecclesiastical habit which he wore till the following Monday,[2] July 3, 1747, when with specially splendid ceremonial, Pope Benedict XIV. created his royal highness a cardinal-deacon of the Holy Roman Church, of the title of Santa Maria in Portici[3] (or in Campitelli), near the theatre of Marcellus. The Pope presented the royal postulant for election, with a speech to the assembled cardinals, in which he recalled the services rendered to the Church by the prince's father and grandfather ; their sufferings in her cause ; the piety of King James III., the faith which had never flinched in severest temptations and darkest adversity ; the efforts he had made—unhappily in vain—for the restoration of the Church in his native land. He recalled the valour of King James in his youth, the graces and virtues of Queen Clementina ; assuring his hearers that the

---

[1] Even priestly vows have been dispensed with when the succession to the throne came in question, as in the case of Casimir the Monk, King of Poland. Cardinal Pole, too, was spoken of as a husband for Mary Tudor. Medici cardinals had reigned and married. The Princess Leonora, once spoken of as a bride for King James, was the widow of a Cardinal de' Medici.

[2] Archiv. Vat. Segr.

[3] To this church, near the English College, out of affection for his son's early connection with it, King James, in 1751, bequeathed money for a perpetual mass for the conversion of England. The mass is duly said, with Benediction, every Saturday at 9. The Duke of York never failed to be present while in Rome, frequently accompanied by his father. 1751 was the fiftieth year of James's reign.

son of such parents could not but increase the glory of the 1747. Sacred College if admitted within its pale. He was young, only just two-and-twenty ; but St. Charles Borromeo was no older when exalted to the same dignity, Peter of Luxemburg was only sixteen, Robert de Nobilibus only twelve when they received the hat, and these all had sustained the dignity to the love and admiration of the world.

The prince was unanimously elected. The Hat was given to him on July 6. The question of his precedence was complicated and caused much heart-burning, but precedence was granted to him as a prince of blood royal over all the other cardinals except the dean of the Sacred College,[1] the precedent of the Cardinal Infante of Spain being followed in all details. He wore ermine on his mantle and cardinals in their red robes of state, Roman princes and dukes paid him visits of ceremony not to be returned. This claim to high precedence rankled in the breasts of the cardinals and the Roman nobles, and bitter quarrels between them and the haughty young Cardinal of York tempered the satisfaction of James in his son's good fortune. Protest was unreasonable. It was not the precedence of ecclesiastic among ecclesiastics and secular princes nor the lawfulness of James III.'s sovereignty which was here in question, but the royal blood of James II.'s grandson. The royal cardinal's precedence was not a question of individual arrogance, but of the dignity of a royal race. After hot discussion it was decided that on his arms the cardinal's hat must surmount the ducal coronet, though in his titles Royal Highness preceded Eminence.[2]

Louis XV. was delighted at the reduction of his embarrassments by one, and promised the wealthy abbey of Anchin *in commendam* to the youthful ecclesiastic, who, however, had to live upon the promise for some years. The Bailli de Tencin, returning to Malta, left for the cardinal's use certain of his horses, carriages, and servants that he might not all at once be burdened by new expenses : to the great gratitude of James. The Catholic sovereigns of Europe had as good reason as the

---

[1] Vatican Archives : account by the Pope. Another authority, according to Mr. H. M. Vaughan, in the "Last of the Royal Stuarts," says that no precedence was given to him over cardinals in right of his royal blood ; that he ranked as the last of the cardinal-deacons.

[2] As he was Roman by birth, he placed above his door the arms also of the Roman Senate.

1747. Hanoverian government for rejoicing at the cardinalate, and might well bless it by substantial rewards. The Stuarts were a trouble and weakness to all Europe. Kings, who were relatives and who could not sympathise with the English revolution but were compelled in their own interests to condone it, were unhappy at being unable to help them to regain their crown. If England did not want them, it was nobody's prime concern to force them upon her, unless their claims happened to be useful as a pretext to harass her government. France and the rest had their own countries to consider, their own ambitions ; their trade and their peaceful home development. Dynastic sympathy must be laid aside, however regretfully. Peaces and treaties could not be signed between George II.—who, after all, was the only person who could legally sign in the name of Great Britain—and any government who befriended, or was even on speaking terms with, his most dangerous enemy. Henry Stuart was finally abolished as a possible pretender ; for the idea of making a Roman cardinal King of England, or even of accepting him as a peer of parliament or resident member of the royal family, never so much as occurred to anybody. It had been more practicable to restore the Heptarchy.

So there was only Charles left to disturb British relations, and he was alone, friendless, unlikely to find a wife, and almost as safely annulled in British eyes as a cardinal's brother as the cardinal was himself.

Charles, even under the shock of his brother's defection, went on railing against the French government, persisting in his demand of French assistance for an expedition to Britain. In vain his father represented to him that, anxious as Louis was for favourable conditions at the approaching peace, he was utterly unable to grant anything of the sort. Charles urged a new Declaration and asked for extension of his regency. James (June 20, 1747) saw no need for a new Declaration, and reminded Charles that his present powers as regent would subsist until recalled and provided him with full power and authority whenever he should be in the British dominions. Charles continued to ignore his brother, to his father's concern and surprise. "There was in such conduct," wrote James, July 4, "something so incomprehensible and so contrary to your natural temper and to that spirit of justice and mildness which gained you so much honour in Scotland, that I really know no more what to make or think of you. . . . One thing is indeed but too plain . . . that you are resolved to have no more to do with him, and I suppose you had a mind to drive him to take out of despair the party he is now taking (though unknown to you) by choice." Charles need hear nothing further of his brother except through the newspapers.

The prince had much just then to embitter his temper. The peace of Aix-la-Chapelle was being negotiated, one of the conditions of which was that Louis XV. should refuse him an asylum in France. Charles refused to remember his father's experience in 1713 and to believe such an outrage upon hospitality and the rights of an ally could be contemplated. He would not move ; even affected unconsciouness of what was going on. Puysieux was commanded to tell Sempil that he did not see how anything could be done to help Charles while his royal highness confided in persons disagreeable to his majesty : young Sheridan, Sir Thomas's son, and "that wretch Kelly," who engrossed his royal highness's whole confidence, and was in all respects unfit to be trusted. Sempil urged his master to take the promptest and best measures for saving the prince's reputation and preserving him from the dangers to which he was exposed.

James adjured the prince to submit to necessity, as he himself had had to submit in similar circumstances. How could he imagine he might stay in France without the king's leave ? But Charles persisted in defiance, encouraged by Madame de Talmond, a Pole, related to the French queen ; Madame de Mézières, whom he had flouted in earlier, better days, and his other female worshippers, mostly elderly and all more or less in love with him. He had cut himself off from sane counsellors. He had in vain called the Earl Marischal to his side. The earl, then at Treviso, had declined (September 13) on the score of broken health. Presently he went to join his brother, the marshal, in Berlin, where Frederick gave him a pension of 2000 crowns,[1] and he made himself very comfortable there, sunned by the royal philosopher's friendship. He still thought longingly of the sun of Spain but not of Charles or Scotland. Charles would never have taken counsel from Sempil, nor would he have

[1] The Earl Marischal to Edgar ; Stuart Papers *ap.* Browne, iv. p. 30.

1747. listened to sane counsel. Least of all would he have listened to O'Brien.

The Dunbar ministry had come to an end. Dunbar, long despotically powerful at the Muti Palace, according to Walton, had fallen under James's grave displeasure in the Strickland-Towneley affair. He was now dismissed on account of difference of opinion between him and his master upon the affairs of Prince Charles. He retired to Avignon to live with his sister, Lady Inverness.

In May 1747, just after the Duke of York's return and the fall of Lord Lovat's wicked old head on the scaffold, James summoned O'Brien to Rome. It would be a satisfaction to him, he wrote to Prince Charles, to have one near him whom he justly valued, and whom perhaps the prince would not be sorry to have at a distance.[1] The Prince Regent's relations with his father's ambassador had been the reverse of cordial and confidential, and it was Sir James Stewart of Coltness whom Charles had empowered to treat for him with the French ministers.

Some years previously James had created O'Brien Earl of Lismore, but the title was to remain latent, as were nearly all the patents in those days of fitful hope. Now the faithful envoy, become Secretary of State, the last to bear that title, was called up, as it were, to the House of Lords *in partibus*. D'Argenson erroneously supposed the earldom to have been now conferred as a reward for persuading the Duke of York to become a cardinal.

Prince Charles immediately demanded that Lochiel should be allowed to style himself baron according to his patent of 1717. James refused. He could not declare Lochiel's title unless he were to declare all the latent patents, which would be highly improper under present circumstances. Lord Lismore was not a precedent. His title would not have been declared, had he not gone to fill so high a post near the king's person. " Lochiel's interest and reputation in his own country, and being at the head of a regiment in France, will make him more considered there, than any empty title I could give him," wrote the ever-reasonable king to his ever-unreasonable son and heir. Even Warren's baronetcy, the reward for bringing Prince Charles from Scotland, was to remain a secret.

[1] Stuart Papers *ap.* Browne, iv. 2.

D'Argenson thought Lord Lismore was to have the Garter, 1747. but James gave no more Garters.

Lady Lismore, O'Brien by birth as well as by marriage, did not accompany her husband to Rome, but stayed in Paris with her handsome young son, now Lord Tallow, to plot. She was one of the shadiest of all the intriguing women who made themselves so busy in Jacobite plots. She was very pretty, and, rumour said, had attracted but repulsed the amorous fancy of Louis XV. In 1747–48, the Archbishop of Cambrai was said to have found her less obdurate. Owing to her scornful outspokenness over the treatment of Prince Charles by Louis XV., De Maurepas had her banished to Spain, but the fall of De Maurepas in 1749, restored her to the bosom of her family. Her husband went to meet her in Paris, but returned to Rome without her. James shortly after nominated Lismore for the Grand Cross of St. Louis, as a reward, says D'Argenson, for travelling back to Rome in December, regardless of gout and snow.

In 1747, Lord George Murray came to Rome ; very loyal and very penitent, and was warmly received by James.

On December 31, Prince Charles's birthday, his brother wrote to him again ; explaining that his months of silence had been in obedience to the king's command. The draft of this letter is in Edgar's hand, corrected and revised by the king. Henry declared himself heart-broken to see displeasure last so long, and sent repeated assurances of his affection. Charles vouchsafed no reply.

Henry was apparently much depressed at this time, Mann reported ; perhaps because he had now had time to realise all that he had renounced, his brother's affection being not the least thing ; but James was very happy.

On New Year's day, 1748, Charles wrote another bitter letter to his father ; "an unexpected New Year's gift."[1] On January 28, James wrote to Charles, reproaching him for continuing to make mysteries, keeping his life and plans a secret from his father and brother ; not out of temper and caprice, as James had hoped at first, but according to a fixed system. If he was deeply and hopefully engaged with a powerful party in England who were furnishing him with money, he did right to keep their secret, but the king failed to see why that should

---

[1] Stuart Papers *ap.* Browne, iv. 24.

1748. hinder him from behaving to his father and brother with kindness and, in other respects, with confidence. As to the grievance of the cardinalate, he reminded Charles that he had quite broken with his brother before that happened. Supposing Henry had failed ever so much towards his elder brother, were his letters and submissions always to be rejected? James disclaimed any wish to interfere with Charles's actions. He had no wish for a restoration, save to set a crown on his son's head, and he expected nothing from him but the love and tenderness that were naturally due.[1] "For God's sake, therefore, my dear child," he adds, "open your eyes at last and remain no longer in this enchantment I see you in. All we want is your love and affection, and as for business and politics, that as you please."[2]

Beyond the peace—or dulness—to which James and his younger son settled down, the great storm raged on; a storm that came of a peace and ended, not in clear shining, but in a great darkness. The warring powers were tired of fighting, but before England would make peace with France no such disturbing element as a Stuart prince must remain on French soil. Prince Charles still refused to believe that France would follow up coldness and neglect by deliberate breach of treaty obligations, and such a cruel insult as expulsion. He no doubt trusted to the real affection of Louis XV., who should have been as powerful as his predecessor to stand for hospitality against diplomacy. Even Sir Horace Mann did not believe that Charles would be turned out, and supposed the talk of expulsion to be merely a cover for his absence on some expedition. Charles took a little house in the Faubourg St. Honoré for the winter, where he supped and slept, but lived during the day at St. Ouen, two leagues from Paris.[3] Lord Lewis Gordon and young Lockhart were now of his household. He wanted to send them and Hepburn of Keith to his father, who regretfully declined, being unable to afford new salaries and pensions.

---

[1] In May, Lady Kenmure had been horrified on attending a dinner among Charles's adherents in Paris, to hear the prince's health drunk, without the king's. George Kelly had laughed at her anger, and called her old-fashioned. She declared that she was old-fashioned, and hoped God would permit her to remain in that sort of old fashion; then took a glass, saying, "God save and preserve our king, and grant him a long life and a happy reign over us." Balhaldy to Edgar: Stuart Papers *ap.* Browne, iv.

[2] Stuart Papers *ap.* Browne, iv. 24 and *sqq.*

[3] Towneley's Letters: State Papers (Tuscany).

JAMES III.

(CHEVALIER DE ST. GEORGE)

From the portrait after Alexis Simeon Belle in the National Portrait Gallery

James was very anxious to see Charles, that their differences 1748. might be healed.   There was some talk of the king's going to Avignon with a very small court as the prince would not come to Rome.   But Charles would not leave Paris, where he had interviews with the King and Dauphin,[1] who probably kept hope alight in his breast.   He wrote rarely and briefly to his father, though in September he sent him his portrait ; a good likeness, the king said, though smelling too much of musk.   He ignored his brother.

In February Sempil sent a memorial to James, signed also by Lochiel and Balhaldy, to lay before his majesty the prince's situation, whose dangers they attributed to young Sheridan and "his accomplice Kelly."   A few days later, February 23, 1748, Lochiel died.   His young son became chief under the guardianship of his uncle, Doctor Archibald Cameron.

In April Charles, still affecting ignorance of France's inhospitable intentions, was looking for a new house in the country near town where he might "brese a little fresh air." Wild women, his ministers, egged him on to his hopeless defiance of the French ministry.   He bought a new service of silver and entertained them royally at his house on the Quai des Théatins, and declared his intention of holding out like Charles XII. at Bender rather than submit to banishment.

Lord George Murray came to Paris, but Charles could not forgive the fatal counsel at Derby and refused him audience, to the great distress of King James, who found such conduct unchristian, unprincely, and impolitic.   Lord George, compunctious and anxious for reconciliation, had frankly owned himself wrong, and asked the king to offer his apologies to the prince for any failure in courtesy.   " I can scarce remember that ever any one made such an act of submission as he has done," James wrote.[2]   Lord Elcho, a person without any sense of humour, was making peace with the British government, and sent his duty by Lord George to their king, hoping he would excuse that step !   James returned that though he could hardly approve the step, he was very sensible of the zeal Elcho *had* shown.[3]

But peace was signed at Aix-la-Chapelle and the prince must go.   The Duke of Richmond was coming to Paris as

---

[1] Towneley's Letters : State Papers (Tuscany).
[2] Stuart Papers *ap.* Browne, iv.   [3] Ibid.

1748. English ambassador; "our hottest enemy," says Towneley,[1] trembling for inevitable collision between the ambassador and his royal cousin. King James from Albano, June 17, protested formally against the treaty, as was necessary for his son's interests. Charles sent up in July a protest in his father's name. James kindly approved the sentiments therein, but gently hoped the prince would publish no more papers in his name without his approbation. " My dear child," he sighed, " you really give me too many mortifications, and you must be sensible how little I deserve them from you."

Sir John Graeme asked permission of the prince to leave his service in October 1748, saying he could not afford to stay in Paris. He really wished to make his peace with the king and the Duke of York. Charles was furious and refused leave, and it was not for nearly a year that Sir John became reconciled to his old master. On August 20, 1749, he wrote to the king, thanking him for forgiveness and continuance again of his pension ; professing repentance for what was past, and grief for having incurred the displeasure of so good a master. On July 23, 1751, he went further still to concilliate James's favour by being received into the Catholic Church at Dijon.

There was extreme sympathy for the prince all over France, from the king to the mob. The faithless Louis XV. was stormed at by pasquinade, and D'Argenson wrote a play on the perfidy of the reigning ministry. The English Jacobites, says D'Argenson, lit feux-de-joie because Charles had quarrelled with France : stopped carriages and made their occupants drink to the brave prince who was now France's enemy. Jacobites were ready enough to see a silver lining to any cloud that did not come over their own heads, and it was certainly unfortunate that the Stuarts' friends should have been England's natural enemies.

The prince would not budge. Louis XV. was compelled to give notice that if he would not go otherwise, he must be turned out by force, and demanded of James that he should withdraw the commission of regency and command his son to obey the French court. James, perhaps sympathising with Charles, replied that he could not withdraw the act as the

---

[1] State Papers (Tuscany): Towneley to the court at Rome. Charles II.'s sons and grandsons were practically solid for the House of Hanover. The Duke of Northumberland was perhaps loyal to James II.

whole affair was more his son's than his own, and that as for giving him any orders, he was too much convinced that his son would not obey them, but he would urge him in the strongest manner possible to conform to the French king's pleasure. The Pope gave instructions for the reception of Charles at Avignon. It was proposed to send him to Fribourg but he indignantly refused to go. George II. also objected to Switzerland. Charles appeared at the opera in December, handsome and gay, the admired of all eyes. " Poor prince ! How hard it is for a king to be a friend," sighed the tender-hearted Louis XV. as he signed the warrant for his guest's arrest and forcible expulsion. On December 10, the prince was seized at the door of the opera-house, bound and searched like a common criminal, and carried to Vincennes where he was put in a cell seven feet by eight.[1] His gentlemen, Henry Goring and Sir James Harrington, were also arrested, to be imprisoned in the Bastille.

The surprising tranquillity of King James all through these troubles, as reported by Walton, puzzled Mann, who hardly believed that Charles was banished, and suspected Avignon to be a mere ruse to cover an expedition to England. The bitterness of death was past for James, who, finding Charles hopeless, was more interested in settling Henry for life. In 1748 the king and the cardinal duke made a pilgrimage to Loreto, in fulfilment of a vow made for Prince Charles's safe return from Scotland. James presented to the shrine a piece of armour with Prince Charles's picture engraved upon it and set with jewels.[2]

---

[1] Stuart Papers : Browne, iv. 50.   [2] State Papers : Tuscany.

CHAPTER X

THE PRIEST-PRINCE

1748. THE Duke of York had now decided upon entering the priesthood. There was no longer any possibility of his ever being required to continue the dynasty. He had as yet received only the easily dispensable minor orders.[1] "The Pope nearly wept on hearing of this heroic resolution of the holy youth."[2] On August 18, 1748, he was ordained sub-deacon; a week later he received the diaconate, the Pope ordaining. On September 1 he was ordained priest. September 8, the Nativity of the Blessed Virgin, had been chosen for his first mass, but he would not wait for it and said his first mass the day after his ordination in his father's private chapel.[3] Twelve days later he was made cardinal-priest, but retained his titular church of Santa Maria in Campitelli, to which he was much attached. France had promised benefices, but as yet she had not made good her promise. Spain bestowed three benefices, whose incomes amounted to 5000 or 6000 scudi a year.[4]

He continued to live with his father in the Muti Palace and at Albano. Silvagni records (as quoted by Hare in his "Walks in Rome") that the Cardinal of York used to drive from Albano to the Muti Palace with four horses at full gallop, attended by running footmen, who were so active and well-trained that they could tire out the fleetest horses. He was fond of walking, too, as his father and his grandfather James II. had been. It was in the course of one of his evening walks between the castle and the town that he met the Jesuit Cordara, afterwards the historian of the Stuart exile in Italy and Prince Charles's Scottish expedition. The prince accosted the father, a chance acquaintance that by

[1] "Should the English ever want him for a king, it would not be the first instance of dispensation given to a secular priest to marry, that he might fill a royal throne and continue his family."—Archiv. Vat. Segr., a.a. O.
[2] Archiv. Vat. Segr.
[3] State Papers: Tuscany.
[4] Ibid.

128

the discovery of mutual tastes ripened into a close and long 1749. friendship.

In November an incident occurred that must have looked like a good omen. News came from Macerata[1] of a new miracle performed upon a nun by a relic of Queen Clementina. James went to the Pope with the story, which was then passed on to the tribunal appointed to deal with such matters and to obtain more precise information with a view to beatification ;[2] information which obviously proved unsatisfactory.

Not till January 14 did news come to the Muti Palace of Charles's safe and surprising arrival at Avignon. He turned up there in the small hours of December 27, and stayed first with his mother's old enemy, Lady Inverness, and her brother, Dunbar. Nothing was further from Charles's mind than to live in the papal city ; it was as far from the mind of the British government. Wild horses would not take him to Rome whither his enemies were driving him. He would never see his brother in a cardinal's dress. But "the diplomacy of Europe had declared him *hostis humani generis*."[3] Where else should he go ?

He found Avignon pleasanter than his expectation. He was quite joyously received and entertained. The legate gave a ball on his birthday, which was attended by Don Philip of Spain who was staying there. When the Infante left, Charles removed from Lady Inverness's house and stayed with the vice-legate until a house should be ready for himself. He took one belonging to a merchant named Robert, the best in the town.[4] He diverted himself extremely, attended the carnival balls and tried to introduce boxing and bull-fighting, but these last diversions, to his wrath, were forbidden by the archbishop. To the extreme distress of his father, he was joined by one of his Parisian mistresses and lived with her "openly as his concubine," says Walton ; probably a star of the opera ; not Miss Walkinshaw who did not join him until 1752, nor a great lady like the Princesse de Talmond, whom Walton would have mentioned by name and not as "the Dulcinea who was the cause of his wild life in Paris."[5] James,

---

[1] State Papers: Tuscany. Charles was married at Macerata in 1772.
[2] Ibid.
[3] C. S. Terry: "The Young Pretender," p. 139.
[4] State Papers: Tuscany.
[5] Ibid.

I

1749. long depressed by accounts of his son's wild life, took this new scandal so terribly to heart that cardinals came to comfort him, though they excused themselves from interfering. They were not even sure that the Pope, a practical man of the world, would care to meddle. Even the Duke of York vainly tried to soothe ; then left Rome for Albano to avoid the carnival,[1] and wait till his father should hear reason as to Prince Charles's morals.

Charles went on defying fate and the unfriendly terrestrial powers, and sent a formal proposal of marriage to a Princess of Hesse Darmstadt on February 24. There was some talk of his election to the throne of Poland when it should fall vacant, and he proposed a visit to the reigning king, accompanied by his bride.

But not even at Avignon might the wanderer rest. The Duke de Nivernois went to Rome as French ambassador, and spent three evenings with James discussing the prince's future abode. Cardinal Alexander Albani,[2] representing the Emperor, threatened the Pope with French retaliation upon Avignon should it harbour the prince. The Pope held a council upon the difficulty. All possible remonstrance and persuasion were promised and a home in the States of the Church, but the Pope declared himself resolved to submit to the violence of France rather than, like France, use force to compel his guest. The French court admitted the Holy See had done what it could and promised to do its possessions no harm. On February 28, Charles rode out of Avignon with Henry Goring, released from the Bastille, and disappeared into the darkness of his long incognito.

From henceforth his movements were secret not only from the governments of Europe but nearly always from his father and brother. He lived as a wild man : a life in the dark where his star now shone so dimly ; the fitful Gleam he followed so faithfully through all the sins and miseries of his storm-tossed life. For thirteen years after Culloden the plots went on ; indeed, long after the Gleam had sunk under the waters of Quiberon Bay, it flashed, a false dawn, from the clouds that in 1749 closed over the shamed head.

---

[1] He left Rome every year to avoid the carnival orgies. State Papers : Tuscany.
[2] He was the only cardinal who was wholly for the House of Hanover, and corresponded in cipher with Walton.

He would not trust his father with his secrets, for every- 1746. thing known at Rome was known to the British government. Mann and Walton took care of that, and in their volumes of letters in the Record Office, the daily doings and hopes and fears of James are minutely chronicled. As there was no diplomatic representative of Great Britain in Rome, Horace Mann, resident at Florence, was the watch-dog who looked after the peace-breakers in Italy. He reported chiefly upon Walton's information ; who, in spite of the efforts of Francis of Lorraine, still lived and laboured in Florence. Since his kicking-out of Rome he had kept one spy after another in the Muti Palace ; Abbé Grant for one, it was suspected.

Walton is useful for facts that are open to the eyes, but not for facts that needed divination. Neither James nor his sons could have left Rome or Albano without his knowledge. He described every packet the king received, but he rarely found out what they contained and guessed from his spy's reports of the king's countenance. If James smiled, there was a promising expedition afoot under Prince Charles ; if he looked melancholy or was out of humour, there was bad news of the prince. His news of Charles was mostly founded on the guesses of the uninformed.

The Pope was not in the least anxious to receive such a turbulent and restless guest as Prince Charles, but offered him a home at any papal city in Italy. In the middle of March James heard from Charles that he had left Avignon but nothing further. In April he had news that Charles, after a sojourn in Lorraine, was in Paris, and he wanted to set off that very night to join him. He contented himself with sending Fitzmorris, one of his secretaries, with despatches. Walton could not find out what the letters had said, but counted for news on the Pope's inability to keep political secrets for long. James's melancholy deepened, and he would answer no questions as to Charles.

The Duke of York sang high mass on St. George's Day at the king's parish church of the Holy Apostles where the national feast was always kept with splendour. This year the festival was shadowed by the death of brave Lady Nithsdale, whose body lay in state in the church. It was reported that James had good news of Charles, who had announced himself as off to Poland to seek a bride of the princely but unroyal house of Radziwill. The Archbishop of Gnesen, primate of Poland,

1749. was much at the Muti Palace. James presently contradicted this marriage rumour emphatically at the house of his dear old friend, Duchess Salviati, whom he visited several times a week. He may have heard that Charles had transferred his hopes to a more desirable quarter, and he had business of his own in Poland connected with the Sobieski property, which probably accounted in part for the Polish primate's constant visits.

About May 17 the prince arrived suddenly in Venice, without luggage or money, attended by one servant in the Duke of Modena's livery. He put up at the Roman legation, and wrote to the Pope for money. The Pope sent the news at once to James who could not send any money, but the Pope sent 1000 sequins and ordered the nuncio to persuade the prince to remove to Bologna or Ferrara ; the latter for preference, as his presence at Bologna might frighten the many English visitors from bringing money to that city. Charles also wrote to Edgar at Rome, and to the Earl Marischal whom he again invited to join him, and who had been living in Venice until the preceding January, but had left for Berlin.

Though Charles stayed at Venice in strict seclusion, muffled in a Venetian cloak, it was not cheerless, hopeless seclusion, for his cousin, the hereditary Prince of Modena, was staying there and was very kind to him, as was the Modenese ambassador. This all suggests that the interval of time between Strasburg on April 26 and Venice, May 17, had been spent at Modena, wooing the duke's second daughter, Princess Fortunata Maria, whom he was certainly hoping to marry while at Venice. A year earlier he had amazed his father by proposing to the Czarina, in preference to the Modenese cousin, but the Czarina was too Hanoverphil to receive even the Earl Marischal in her territories, and was not likely to consider such an offer. The charms of Princess Fortunata d'Este may have diverted him on the very way to the plain little unroyal princess in Poland. He went to Padua several times ; perhaps with a view to the assistance of St. Anthony in his suit, as he had turned to his religion before in a difficult day. It was a measure certain to be recommended by Fortunata, if she were a consenting party.

There was still Jacobite fuel smouldering in England in high places. In this very month of May, Charles was invited by the University of Oxford to the opening of the Radcliffe

where Dr. King made a speech full of Jacobite *double-*
entendre.

Charles found Venice the best place for his interest next to France ; the only place in Italy, he told Edgar. The Pope, extremely annoyed by the obstinate refusal of Ferrara, compelled his nuncio to tell Charles, May 25, that his further stay in Venice was impossible. " What can a bird do that has not found a right nest ? He must flit from bough to bough, ainsi use les Irondel," Charles scribbled in a notebook. " As I have nothing further to do here," he wrote to his father (May 26), " and would not run the least risk of being found out, I depart this very morning." Rome was hopeful that he would end his *caravanes* at Bologna.

Homeless as he was, not only was he making love to Princess Fortunata, but marriage with the eleven-year-old Radziwill princess was being seriously negotiated by the Polish Princess de Talmond, the Archbishop of Gnesen, primate of Poland, and Monsignor Lascaris, who lived in the Radziwill family where he exerted much influence.[1] Lascaris was to have much future concern in James's affairs. The Radziwill marriage affair looked quite promising, and Lascaris was sent for to Rome. Sir Charles Hanbury Williams, British minister at Dresden whose elector was also King of Poland, offered to kidnap Lascaris on his way to Rome, ostensibly to keep the coming jubilee of 1750. He also offered to kidnap Charles himself, should he offer to go to Poland, and to carry him to some northern port. He had had several offers of agents to carry out the business. Lord Hyndford, British ambassador to Russia, also would have the " young vagabond " kidnapped.

When Charles left Venice is wrapped in mystery. Mann himself did not know for long that he had left, nor Lord Albemarle, British ambassador at Paris, nor the Pope. Charles did not reach Paris, his next abode, until the end of June. James had occasional short letters without date or address, that came by the Venice mail, but the little news was satisfactory. James was evidently easier in his mind, and appeared constantly at the Cardinal of York's musical parties. Not for many years had he looked so happy.[2]

The Prince of Wales being in hiding, Jacobites of all sorts

[1] State Papers: Tuscany.   [2] Ibid.

1749. turned to the poor king and the Duke of York for countenance and support. In June 1749, young Glengarry, " Pickle the Spy," wrote to Henry from Bagneux, reminding him of their acquaintance in Paris, and begging for interest and assistance on the ground of his royal highness's previous efforts to obtain relief from the French court for himself and Sir Hector Maclean and the other starving Jacobite prisoners in the Tower. It was little the cardinal could do. His new estate had brought new expenses and many promises but little money.

He took his ecclesiastical duties very seriously and devoted himself to his titular church. There he baptized a Jew who had abjured the Anglican Church, and married him to an Englishwoman, Elizabeth Whalley. He took extreme interest in the music of his choir, himself superintending rehearsals.[1]

Rumours of kidnapping were in the air. D'Argenson tells a story of the tranquillity of the exiled court being startlingly interrupted in the winter of 1749–50 by an attempt of Barbary pirates to kidnap the king and the Cardinal of York, with the object of handing them over to the British government to gain its clemency for themselves ; but that the royal servants were sufficient to put the pirates to flight.[2] There is no allusion whatever in the voluminous reports of Mann and Walton to this stirring event, though Walton frequently waxes scornful over James's nervousness as to brigands and demands for increased guard at Albano. The Barbary pirates were then " on the nerves" of every Mediterranean power. The Emperor having lately made peace with them, their activities had increased. On August 22, 1748, the court of the Quirinal had had notice that the pirates were fitting out vessels to cruise about the Sicilian coasts and all over Italy ; for several years ships were constantly prepared for protection and defence. The British government, had it possessed any jurisdiction over Barbary pirates, could hardly have cared to kidnap a helpless old man and a Roman cardinal, however pleased they might have been to catch the dangerous Prince Charles. There was an incident at the beginning of 1750 which may have been the origin of the legend. The Prince of Baden, come to Rome for the jubilee and exploring the lonely environs of

---

[1] State Papers : Tuscany.
[2] *Journal et Mémoires du Marquis d'Argenson*, vi. 119 (ed. 1864).

the city with one servant, was attacked by banditti. His 1749. other servants came up in time to drive off the assailants. The Duke of York occasionally visited Cardinal Corsini at Antium ; one such visit was paid in the early summer of 1749 ; but if there were any piratical attempt made upon him, it did not reach the Mann-and-Walton ear. James himself was never within easy reach of sea-rovers. Yet the politicians of England and France may have looked for such a solution of the Stuart problem. We have seen English ambassadors keen on kidnapping. Jacobitism was far from dead. Priestly vows may be dispensed with, as Mann found out to his surprise, to save a family of importance from extinction ; while James himself at sixty-one, might have married again. But for even a private piratical speculation in search of mere booty, there is no evidence.

In France the Jacobite party was strong, and at the New 1750. Year of 1750 there was a great deal of noise made over an almanack that appeared in Paris; with the imprimatur of authority, though its pages declared the English crown to belong of right to the House of Stuart, and that the kingdom would never be happy until the Stuarts were restored. The Duc de Richelieu was ready, said La Croix, to make terms for undertaking their cause.

The year 1750 was the jubilee year and James attended the opening of the Holy Door in full royal state, but he felt seriously ill and depressed. The Duke of York devoted himself to cheering his father, but he too was very anxious. Nothing ailed James except indigestion : the doctors pronounced him free from any internal malady, but like all dyspeptics he dwelt morbidly upon his health. Then his good friend, Monsignor de Canillac, came to see him ; said nothing of his illness, but gave him all the gossip of Rome, and James forgot his illness, and felt a little better. Cardinal Corsini also cheered him up, but conversation with the Duc de Nivernois, the French ambassador, would arouse his anger against the French government. Then he caught cold, visiting the basilicas to gain the jubilee indulgence, and even his moments of fitful cheerfulness passed away. More dateless notes from Charles rather increased the gloom. Neither he nor the Pope knew exactly where Charles was ; they sought news from one another, and " the Pope freely condemned that young man's

1750. conduct." Then there would be long silence on the subject at the Quirinal and at the Muti, as if Charles were no longer in the world. James was apparently in despair.

Yet all the time, sad and sick as he was, he busied himself incessantly with his immense correspondence. In April three more Scots came to Rome and were presented by Henry to the Pope: Sir Hector Maclean, young Glengarry, and Lochgarry. James said he loved to have his brave Highlanders about him, and the new Lochiel, the friend of his sons, had a place in his court.[1] The cardinal was as busy a man as his father. He took no interest in politics but, though absorbed chiefly in music, he often went to the Hospice of the Trinity to serve the table of the jubilee pilgrims, and was interested in the Academy of Roman History of which he was a member. He was present with the Pope when James's old friend Monsignor Bianchini, archæologist and astronomer, gave a lecture there on the Gladiators. The summer removal to fair Albano soothed James's troubled spirit, though he received no company there this year and was frequently suffering from gastric pains. News in May of Charles's house-rent at Avignon being paid seemed to promise his return thither, and his father appeared less melancholy for a while. In June he broke silence as to Charles, and talked of him incessantly and of good news he had from him. A great event was evidently imminent. Many believed Charles to be actually in Scotland. But when James returned to Rome as usual for the feast of St. Peter, he relapsed into melancholy, which was not dispelled even by vespers at St. Peter's, sung by two hundred voices to the accompaniment of twenty-eight hand organs! Fortunately without the expected effect, for the immense crowd absorbed the din. It was not a good period in Italy for the music with which the Duke of York alleviated the weariness of exile.

In August the king's spirits went up for a brief space. Repeated solicitation had succeeded, and the Duke of York was given a rich abbey in Naples. But James was ill or thought himself so nearly all the summer and autumn, and his son was closely occupied looking after him, trying to drive away his melancholy. Prince Charles, too, was busily occupied.

Young Glengarry returned to Rome in September, with

---

[1] Walton, State Papers: Tuscany.

news of the prince's plans in which he was so deep: begging 1750. this time of the Cardinal Duke only a relic of the true cross, and his protection and recommendation at the French court for *their* recommendation, as he was going to London. At this same date, "Pickle the Spy" began his traitorous correspondence with the British government.

In September, beguiled as usual by fair promises, even by news that much was doing, Charles went to England, met his supporters in London at Lord Westmoreland's house, turned a Protestant, and returned to his hiding-place on finding that there was nothing practical to be done. Even talking and promising were well-nigh over, for in that year the Welsh White Rose Cycle expired. It had been founded about 1727 to unite cavaliers and non-juring families in North Wales and Cheshire. Its headquarters were at Wynnstay, the lady of Wynnstay being always patroness. For many years it had been a real and definite political organisation ; then it became a mere dining-club, and in 1750 died a too natural death for lack of nourishment.[1]

James does not seem to have known of the prince's conversion. If he had heard rumours, he did not believe them. He wrote to Charles on New Year's Eve, his birthday, reproaching him for his secrecy and other things, *but not for apostasy*, urging him to marry and settle. Had he done as his father once wished, he had been by now himself the father of a family, "with a wife not beneath you to have married had you been in England." But he had put himself in a way of living which made marrying anybody absolutely impracticable. His father would rather see him married to a private gentlewoman than not at all. "I cannot think of any particular person to propose to you," James goes on, "who might be anyways proper, and at the same time willing to marry you. If this letter has the same fate with many others I have writ to you, I might have saved myself the trouble of writing it."[2]

Cardinal Alexander Albani, Austrian minister in Rome, told 1751. Sir Horace Mann, January 9, 1751, that James was in deep affliction ; something strange had happened about the elder son, and the cardinal was ill with grief. James had enough to

---

[1] Mr. G. W. E. Russell in "Seeing and Hearing," p. 15.
[2] Stuart Papers: Mahon, iv. Appendix, p. vi.

1751. afflict him in the late disappointment, and it turned out that the cardinal had smallpox, a new distress to increase his father's constant sorrows. He was very ill indeed, delirious, and there were prayers for him in all the churches. He was not out of danger till January 17.[1]

NOTE.

1750. Sir Walter Scott, in his preface to " Redgauntlet," declares that in 1750 there was a strong revival of Jacobitism in England. The riot of the Newcastle colliers in June of that year, when they proclaimed King Charles III., though a small and foolish thing, is interesting as a straw to show, if not quite distinctly whither, at least in what part of the island, the wind was blowing. That Northumberland was busy is revealed by a mysterious letter published by the late Dr. Charlton, of Hesleyside, one of the Jacobite holds of the Tyne. The letter was addressed to a certain " Dear Cambray," under cover to the government supervisor at Hexham, and refers to a Charlton known as Bowrie[2] from his residence, who was evidently the chief agent in Northumberland. The signature is " Pont. Max," dated " From the face of the Deep Waters July 17th, 1750." Bowrie had made certain proposals concerning one Carmichael, " of a piece with the general tenour of his benevolent sentiments towards the honest or indigent part of mankind . . . Carmichael is a good honest lad, but infected with that damned Scots disease never to spare his [life?] or his purse where friendship or necessity calls. Notwithstanding, he has three callants, will receive no arguments instead of a dinner . . . so that if the affair could be carried on, I would willingly contribute my mite, but I want courage to beg for a countryman. . . .

" *P.S.*—I almost dayly see men from North to South, intirely strangers to the habitation of the young Goodman of Bellnagih[3] [the prince]; only they tell me his father alone knows where he is, assures them he is well, and desires they may be content, and ask no more questions. Tom of Lubeck[4] is here from Lond., and greets you kindly in the covenant ; he intends to kiss your hands at Wylam, Sunday comes a week, where I must attend the conclave, but if he's diverted by his friends, I shall give you notice. Mention the honest Bp.[5] to Bowrie; he was once his guest upon the Bellingham tramp ! "

" It would be curious indeed if we could have obtained a report of what was discussed at the conclave at Wylam," says Dr. Charlton, " but no shorthand writer was present at these secret meetings to take down the dangerous words uttered or the treasonable toasts drunk by the Jacobite squires of Northumberland."

---

[1] State Papers : Tuscany.
[2] He was a well-known Jacobite, one of those as to whose complicity Murray of Broughton was examined when he turned traitor after the '45.
[3] Evidently a corruption of Ballangeich. Charles's ancestor, James V., called himself the Gudeman of Ballangeich.
[4] The prince had been recently at Lubeck. State Papers : Tuscany.
[5] Perhaps of Durham. The dean certainly was a Jacobite.

THE PRIEST-PRINCE

139

No doubt for a hundred years after the Revolution, several of the 1750. Northumbrian squires corresponded more or less with the exiled family and its adherents, says Dr. Charlton, but few mementos remain of those dealings. They were very cautious and did not keep incriminating evidence about them, not even medals and miniatures, still less letters. Wine-glasses exist for drinking "under the rose," one inscribed "take your advantage"; another had the prince's head engraved with motto, *Audentior Ibo;* a mull of 1745 inscribed, "O Charlie, ye've been laing a cummin'." (He came too soon for these loyal gentlemen.) A pair of silk garters exists bearing the inscription,

> " Come let us with one heart agree
> To pray that God may bless P.C."

One family possesses a pincushion bearing names of victims of 1746, white satin, blue tassels at corners. Inscriptions printed from copperplates and names run in circles round the centre, a double rose displayed and the inscription round it : MART : FOR : K : & CON : 1746.

OBVERSE.

Inner ring: Earl Kilmarnock. Earl Derwentwater. Lord Lovat. Lord Balmerino.
Second ring: T. Deacon. Syddall. T. Chadwicke. G. Fletcher. J. Berwick. J. A. Bradshaw. J. Dawson.
Third ring: P. Taylor. P. Lindsey. A. Kennedy. J. McGregor. A. Parker. P. Keir. L. Read. The Rev. T. Coppock. T. Park. A. Blyde.
Outer ring: J. McLewis. J. Thompson Murray. Mayrie. Stevenson. McDonald. Dempsey. Connolly. Endsworth. Sparks. Horn. D. Morgan, Esq. C. Gordon. McKenzie. J. McClain.

REVERSE.

Inner ring: Col. Townley. Sir L. Wedderburn. Sir A. Primrose. F. Buchanan, Esq. L. Hamilton, Esq.
Second ring: M. Deliard. C. Gordon. Cap. McDonald. Cap. Wood. Cap. Leith. Cap. Hamilton. Dan. M. Daniel.
Third ring: I. Wallis. Henderson. I. McNaughton. I. Roebottom. H. Cameron. I. Innies. I. Harvie. D. Fraizer. B. Mayson. Donald M'Donald.
Outer ring: The Rev. R. Lyon. Rol. Clavering. G. Read. Eaton. Heys. Brady. Ogilvie. Roper. Brand. Swan. Holt. Hunter. Mitchel-Nicholson. Matthews. Hint.

These pincushions were probably made at Lyons or somewhere else abroad. It is fitting that the last of our great poets, sprung of an old Northumbrian Jacobite house, should have sung the last great Jacobite hymn, the pæan of Northumbrian loyalty ; singing for once not as the bard of Revolution is wont to sing, but as Caiaphas prophesied, not of himself, but with the voice of a faithful Israel,

> " The faith our fathers fought for,
> The kings our fathers knew,
> We fight but as they fought for :
> We seek the goal they sought for,
> The chance they hailed and knew,
> The praise they strove and wrought for,
> To leave their blood as dew
> On fields that flower anew.

Our name the night may swallow,
Our lands the churl may take :
But night nor death may swallow,
Nor hell's nor heaven's dim hollow,
The star whose height we take,
The star whose light we follow
For faith's unfaltering sake
Till hope that sleeps awake."[1]

---

[1] A. C. Swinburne, " A Jacobite Song."

CHAPTER XI

MUSIC AND DISCORD

So the last Stuart prince settled down into the life that was 1751. given to him in exchange for the life that was his birthright, and the last page of the tragic Stuart history is the story of a happy life. That he made it so was not altogether due to temperament, for his hot temper and hot pride might have added yet more tragedy and misery to the lurid tale. But there was behind that hot Polish temper a great and enduring sweetness. The storms passed quickly like Italian storms, leaving softest sunshine behind. And stronger still for influence, there was the same high and steadfast principle as had ruled his father's life, the same consistency and common sense. His natural warmth was turned upon his work, his daily duty, and to that he brought the love and eagerness and unswerving conscientiousness that might have made the greatness of a king. No shadow of repining, no discord of vain ambition, disturbed the sunny peace of his life. He was never melancholy though he lived with a very melancholy father, and though his own health was extremely precarious. He had the happiness of warm and loyal friendships ; he had the happiness of love for a great art, always satisfying yet never to satiate ; and he had the happiness of worthy work, worthily done. The futile wars that made continued misery for his brother were no concern of his who had been fiercely thrust apart from them. He had found that the duties of royalty were not those to which he was called, so he turned to the duty laid upon him as a man, his share in the work of life.

All through his troubles the affectionate and careful companionship of the Duke of York had been his father's comfort. Even the spies admitted that Henry devoted himself to cheering the king's increasing melancholy. But the pleasant terms on which they lived began to be disturbed. They still shared one home and one table, Henry contributing to table expenses. Strong affection bound them together, but there was no bond of common interest or common taste. James was still immersed in business cares and harassed by continual anxiety as to Prince Charles. Henry had quite given up all interest in Jacobite politics. He had seen and realised their futility, and would not waste his life in crying for the moon. He had taken up his ecclesiastical state in great seriousness, as a profession to be worked in, as well as a divine vocation ; he was very far from looking upon it as a source of revenue and dignity, though he held so strongly by the temporal dignity which also was his as a royal prince. James, who had known so much of the stress of poverty and the worth of fixed income, seems rather to have looked upon the cardinalate as a handsome provision for life. Henry was a finished musician. Music had always been the chief delight of his life, and he spent much time in his titular church of Santa Maria in Campitelli, where he rehearsed masses and got up concerts with Buranello the Venetian, his choirmaster. Baldassare Galuppi, called Buranello from Burano, his birthplace, was born in 1706, and had attained success when only seventeen. Taught by his father, he was one of the most original comic composers of Italy. His lighter music was as charming as ever to the last, but his sacred music was poor, his masses feeble of invention and workmanship. All his music is as dead as the dear Venetian women with the golden hair of whom his gay Toccata sang to Browning. His few masses and cantatas and his many operas remained in manuscript. Their imperfections were chiefly owing to the insistent genius of production which governed him and refused him time for study ; not the genius that is the taking of pains.[1] He was also distinguished as a pianist—" stately at the clavichord."

Henry devoted himself also to the poor of his parish and to the fabric of his church, and erected therein a massive silver altar-piece. James cared nothing for music and had no sympathy with artists : objected to Henry's friendship with Buranello and to the musician's presence at their table, and accused his son of a fondness for low company. He was not musical enough to hear in Galuppi's music all that Browning heard in the Toccata,

---

[1] In 1762, he was appointed Maestro di Cappella at St. Mark's, Venice. Catherine II. invited him to Russia and honoured him greatly, but he returned to Venice in 1768, and took up his old work again. Dr. Burney saw him there in 1770, surrounded by his numerous family, full of honours and prosperity; full, too, of all the vivacity, fire, and gaiety of his youth. He composed operas till 1777, and church music till his death in 1785.

else there might have been more excuse for his strong disapproval, though Galuppi and his cardinal worked at masses and
cantatas, not at gay Toccatas. Bitter quarrels arose. James,
hitherto so invariably mild and kind, was used to absolute
obedience, and in his weak state of health, irritated perpetually
by great anxieties, he could not stand contradiction from his
younger son. He failed to realise that the little prince was
now a man of twenty-six, a personage in Rome, a priest and a
cardinal, with a right to independence. Henry, always gentle
and submissive with his father but perhaps inspired now by
outside influences, felt that since he asked no more than
freedom to use and enjoy his talent and to choose his friends
according to his taste, he should be conceded so much. He
was self-willed and quick-tempered, as we know, but that he
had a really bad temper, his portraits invariably deny. Like his
father, he was in very bad health. He had recovered from
smallpox with weakened lungs, and seemed to be falling into
consumption.

James's malady was indigestion, and indigestion makes a
man "gey ill to live with." Now that he had little of the real
work which had absorbed his mind for so many years, he gave
way to the depression caused by health and circumstances,
and his mind, like all dyspeptics' minds, concentrated upon his
malady and he was gloomy and irritable. Henry was good
and devoted but he was very much in earnest about his work,
and knowing that he did his duty, he found it hard that he
might not have a free hand, but be compelled to lay aside duty
as well as innocent pleasure, at his father's command. The
quarrels were no doubt exaggerated by the spies from whose
reports we learn of them. Like some journalists, they had their
living to get out of scandal. Henry had inherited his father's
thoroughness and business capacity, but he had in his larger
leisure acquired literary as well as musical tastes. James
never read, it was said, though an English bishop once found
him reading Voltaire's *Pucelle*. He also read much in the
Fathers.

James's objections were not limited to Buranello. In
August 1749, the cardinal dismissed his English chamberlain,
Monsignor Lee, a man of middle-class birth, and replaced him
by the Abbé John Lercari, a Genoese. Here at least Henry's
preference was for the better-born man, and Lercari had an

1751. uncle among the cardinals. James angrily attributed the change to Henry's confessor, Father Ildefonso, who, he declared, was setting his penitent against the English. Henry flew into a passion, and, according to Walton's informant, refused to go to bed until Ildefonso was called in to remonstrate. James accused Henry of extravagance. Since the cardinal had acquired that valuable Neapolitan abbey, he was rich, and his father, not unreasonably, insisted upon his increasing the sum he paid towards table expenses. Henry refused, and demanded a separate establishment that he might entertain his friends as he pleased. It was no doubt the king's refusal to welcome his son's guests, and so to keep to himself the absolute control of the table, that irritated Henry into refusing such a natural demand, as that he should pay according to his abundance for the maintenance of common hospitality. James said Henry's "favourites" were trying to get the management of his money into their hands, as may very probably have been true. Henry, who was really ill, rushed off to Foligno to take the waters of Nocera (there had been an earthquake at Nocera and the waters were carried to Foligno), and threatened to stay there until October ; or to return not at all unless to a separate establishment, for James had forbidden the obnoxious Ildefonso ever again to set foot in his house. The waters of Nocera, and a tour round by Perugia and Todi, cured the cardinal's health and his temper, and he relented so far as to join his father at Albano, though they did not speak until Ildefonso was banished from the papal states and replaced, as Henry's confessor, by a nominee of the Pope and King James.

As to the amount of money really in hand, not a penny had yet been paid to the Cardinal of York from the abbey of Anchin which Louis XV. had promised to him in 1748 as compensation for his enforced unkindness to Prince Charles. The abbey was useful only as an occasional refuge for the commendatory's fugitive brother. After much correspondence came news that the arrears should be paid up, and in December Henry was formally invested with the commendam, and the prefectorship of all Carthusians. The income promised amounted to 11,000 scudi, but would be enormously reduced not only by certain heavy charges upon the abbey funds but by renunciation of the 9000 scudi which the French government had paid to Henry since his cardinalate. James maintained that the income had been promised free of all charges, and there was more disheartening correspondence.[1] It was at last agreed that he should receive the full annual 11,000 scudi from Anchin, but that he must renounce the French pension.

At the same time the Pope not only confirmed his promise that the papal pension should be continued to Prince Charles on his father's death, but immensely increased the cardinal's income by appointing him archpriest of the Vatican, which very lucrative dignity carried with it the square house in the Piazza della Sagrestia, just outside the tribune wall of St. Peter's, now inhabited by the present archpriest, Cardinal Rampolla. Henry was installed November 14, 1751. He was required at his installation to make a long speech by rote. His memory failed him for a minute, which made his father ill with anger. But it was in the preceding July,[2] not in commemoration of this promotion[3] that the cardinal-duke presented to the treasury of St. Peter's the golden chalice studded with the Sobieski jewels, which is still preserved there. His first official appearance as archpriest was at the canonisation of St. Jane Frances de Chantal, November 21, 1751.

A portrait, of which there is a print in the National Portrait Gallery at Edinburgh, represents him at this period of his youthful cardinalship ; cardinal-priest, not yet bishop. It is the same sweet face but longer and thinner than the boy's face, the long upper lip pressed into the bow of the lower lip. The long curling hair no longer flows from beneath the stiff white wig. The print is inscribed : " Henricus Tit : S. Maria in Portici : S. R. E. : Presb : Card : Dux Eboracencis : Sacrosancta Basil : Vatic : Archpresb."

Henry remained at the Muti Palace, but he set about furnishing his own house and saw as little of his father as he could help. The new position had most likely been bestowed upon him for the very purpose of making him independent of his father in as pleasant and dignified a manner as possible. Unfortunately for peace, he carried into his new office the earnestness with which he had worked in his titular church. The dignified clergy of Rome had become mere high-placed

---

[1] State Papers : Tuscany.
[2] Probably to commemorate the jubilee year of his father's joyless reign.
[3] As other biographies say. The presentation is fully described in Walton's Letters.

1751. officials, with little of sacred calling about them outwardly, except when state ceremonial demanded prescribed robes. The cardinals were merely temporal princes. The Cardinal of York himself in his old age wore at home a dress secular in all but colour. The zealous young archpriest was determined on reform and earned the indignant animosity which is ever the meed of reformers, the chapter of St. Peter's being little accustomed to such despotism as he assumed. He had not been two months in office when he caused a canon to be reprimanded for coming into choir with his hair dressed and powdered. A few years later, a new Pope was to insist upon the same reform throughout the Church. But the chapter was furious and avenged itself by unanimously rejecting a Lenten preacher the Cardinal of York had recommended for the Vatican, to the extreme wrath of their royal Archpriest.

1752. Early in January 1752 James suffered a great sorrow in the sudden death of his dear friend, the Duchess Salviati, whom he used constantly to visit and to consult in all his difficulties. He was inconsolable for days and would see no company. Henry's patience was sorely tried. His father's mind was perhaps beginning to fail, and quarrels again broke out between them when James insisted on dismissing all Henry's servants and replacing them according to his own taste. Henry refused angrily to allow this to be done. James as usual went to complain to the Pope. Henry as usual followed with his story. The Pope scolded the young cardinal, who protested that his father's tyrannies had become quite insupportable; that it was impossible to comply with his humours or to live with him. The Pope stood by paternal authority, but reminded James that the cardinal was a dignified personage who had so far behaved well and besought him to use less rigour in the exercise of paternal authority. So quarrels and brief truces succeeded one another in the Muti Palace.

In 1751 Andrew Lumisden had come to Rome as James's secretary. He kept copies of every letter he wrote, fourteen or fifteen volumes stitched together into green paper, ranging from 1751 to 1773, now in the possession of Mr. Alexander Pelham Trotter, great-grandson of Lumisden's sister, Lady Strange. "The whole correspondence," writes Mrs. Mure, née Strange, "reveals a monotonous life

of devoted service (ill-requited too), that is very melancholy. 1752.
. . . For many years there is a weekly letter to Prince
Charles Edward, with a bulletin of his father's health
. . . enclosed to the prince's secretary [*sic :* he was, of course,
the prince's banker] Mr. Waters. . . . There are also weekly
letters throughout this period to Lord Alford and the titular
Lord Dunbar, reporting on health, and noticing any little
incident about the court or in Rome generally." Mrs.
Mure dates Lumisden's coming to Rome in 1749.[1]

In 1752 James took for private secretary that Monsignor
Lascaris who had, as Prince Radziwill's agent, tried to
arrange a marriage for Prince Charles. He was a Theatine
and mitred abbot of Olika in Poland. James never made
very much of Lumisden but Lascaris became his right hand,
and from the date of his arrival the king was again visibly
happy. The Cardinal of York appointed Lascaris his vicar
in the Vatican.

Lascaris from his arrival, says Walton, was supreme in
James's household, to the exceeding jealousy of the English
and of the Irish Fitzmorris. But poor Fitzmorris's work
was over. In the following February he had to retire in-
valided from James's service, who sent him to a convent,
paying his expenses until March 1753 when he died.
Royalty even *in partibus*, is expensive. James still kept
up something of sovereign state and went out with three
coaches, but the Italians were ceasing to regard him as a
sovereign and spoke of him now as " the king here " in
contradistinction to George II., " the king there." At the
opera, no Protestant stood up on his entrance, and when,
according to the custom of kings, he would cry " encore,"
nobody took any notice of the royal demand—except the
gleeful spies.[2]

In June the cardinal's income was again increased on the
death of Cardinal Alberoni ; which brought to him the reversion of 3000 scudi a year upon the bishopric of Malaga.
Henry was now persuaded by the Pope to dismiss his beloved
Lercari, who was exiled to Genoa, his native town, and James
assented to the recall of Father Ildefonso to Rome, but not to
the Muti Palace. Henry was resentful of Lercari's dismissal,

[1] Reminiscences by L. M. Mure. Privately printed.
[2] Jesse's " Pretenders and their Adherents," p. 52.

1752. and really ill, fainting and causing much alarm in his household. James believed Henry intended to remove to his house by the Vatican and recall Lercari. Henry flounced out of the Muti Palace and on pretext of making a retreat, went into a monastery—like his mother! He promised that much-tried intermediary, the Pope, that he would return to his father if he might be quite free and independent in the house, but he would not change his friends or his servants for anybody. James insisted upon complete cessation of communication with Ildefonso and Lercari. Highly incensed, Henry went off (July 20) to the baths of Nocera to stay till October. Ildefonso under obedience refused to return to him or to receive him. "The *tracasseries* of that family trouble the Pope more than all his states," said Walton.

James had much cause for irritation and anxiety in other and more serious matters. In 1751 his faithful friend Cardinal Tencin had fallen into disgrace at Paris and France opposed James's nomination of Tencin's nephew, the Bailli, for the cardinalate. A great scandal occurred in 1752 when Prince Charles took Miss Walkinshaw to live with him as his mistress, and in August the news of his apostasy had reached Rome and set all tongues wagging. At the same time a new plot was being organised by Charles and Murray of Elibank, and James was angry to see that the Duke of York took no interest in his brother's affairs, amatory or military. Henry at Nocera refused to return unless a separate table at least were promised to him. James was so angry that for several nights he went supperless to bed! Henry went from Nocera to Foligno; then to Bologna, where he had a state reception by the Cardinal-legate, Doria. He stayed with the Marquis Angelelli, brother of his own chamberlain, recently appointed by James *vice* Lercari. He went much into society and entertained profusely. This was much pleasanter than being shut up at Albano with an angry, silent father who treated him like a naughty child in disgrace. At Bologna he was described by one of that Riva family a member of which had belonged to James II.'s court of Whitehall, as exceedingly like James II., Mary of Modena, and Princess Louisa : which was absurd. As exaggerated is Riva's enthusiastic account of the duke's " great knowledge and exquisite gusto in science and in liberal arts wherein he exceeds in some measures professors," though

Henry was deeply interested in science and art and went "often to the institute in which he took much delight." He sent to Rome for his best vestments to wear on the Feast of the Nativity (September 8), but the Pope reminded him he might not pontificate in a papal diocese. James wanted the Pope to starve Henry into coming home by stopping his pension—a real prodigal son—but this the Pope refused to do.

There is no place except Rome and its neighbouring towns fuller of memories of the last Stuarts than the ancient papal city of Bologna. The palace of James for many years, Casa Belloni, now Casa Cantelli, stands practically unaltered ; now Via Gombruti 63, at its angle with Via Barberia (there is always bad luck with a corner house). A marble tablet on the staircase wall commemorates the residence of James III., King of England, &c. The Caprara Palace, scene of his last love affair, now belongs to the Duc de Montpensier. James also occupied the Villa Alamandini, beyond the gate of San Vitale. Clementina stayed a night in the Hotel Pellegrino, Via Ugo Bassi, at the time of her marriage by proxy, and lived after in the then Via Larga, near the old walls, behind Santa Maria Maggiore. The cardinal stayed frequently in the convent of St. Dominic. The Lambertini Palace, where the Duchess of Albany died, is now the Ranuzzi Palace in the Via San Stefano. In the archives may be seen miniature paintings on vellum of Clementina's wedding, of the baptisms of the two princes, and of fêtes at which James and Clementina were present.

The world abroad knew all about the quarrel. "Verily, it is a family of *têtes-de-fer*," said D'Argenson, and De Luynes knew that the Pope was at his wits' end trying to make peace.

"The Cardinal of York," writes Walpole, historian of George II.,[1] "whose devotion preserved him from disobedience to his father as little as his princely character preserved him from devotion, had entirely abandoned himself to the government of an abbé, who soon grew displeasing to the old Pretender. Commands, remonstrances, requests had no effect on the obstinacy of the young cardinal. The father . . . insisted on the dismission of the abbé. Instead of parting with his favourite, the young cardinal with his minion left Rome abruptly, and with little regard for the dignity of his purple. The Holy See, which was sunk to having few more important

[1] Vol. i. p. 284 and *sqq.*

1752. negotiations to manage, interested itself in the reconciliation, and the haughty young Eminence of York was induced to return to his father, but without being obliged to sacrifice his abbé." Some of these statements are incorrect. Lercari was not with the Duke. Walpole wrote to Mann, October 28 : "One hears of writings that have appeared in print on the quarrel of the Pretender and his second son. . . . Here is a bold epigram which the Jacobites give about :—

> 'In royal veins, how blood resembling runs!
> Like any George, James quarrels with his sons.
> Faith! I believe could he his crown resume,
> He'd hanker for his Herrenhausen, Rome!'

The second," comments Horace, "is a good line, but the thought of the last is too obscurely expressed ; and yet I don't believe it was designed for precaution."[1]

Lascaris wrote on the king's behalf. Henry refused to return without Lercari, bought horses and carriages at Milan, sent for his winter clothes and all his silver plate from Rome, and informed the Pope he meant to live at Bologna. The Pope reminded him that cardinals must not live out of Rome unless they were bishops or legates ; told him he owed his father entire obedience and submission, and that those who advised him otherwise were his worst enemies, and ordered him back to Rome. James was really ill, and it was rumoured that Prince Charles was in Scotland. Lascaris was again deputed to appeal to the rebel prince, who, now he found that the French king as well as the Pope took his father's part and thought less of him than before, submitted. He wrote to his father from Bologna, October 25 :[2]—

"The paternal and tender expressions made me by Monsignor Lascaris in your majesty's name, encourage me and oblige me to express myself to your majesty the extent of my gratitude, together with the assurance of the profound and dutiful respect I profess to your person. I beg your majesty to believe I have been truly sorry for whatever displeasure you may have had occasion, by my absence from Rome, which absence has never proceeded from the least want of that respect I owe to you ; but on the contrary, by a just and reasonable anxiety of

---

[1] Walpole's Letters to Mann, ii. 310.
[2] Printed by Browne, iv. 107. (Stuart Papers.)

not losing your good graces. Wholly, however, confiding at 1752. present on the tender expressions I find in Mr. Lascaris's letter, I shall dispose my return, after having complied with some necessary acts of attention with the cardinals of this neighbourhood, and particulary with Cardinal Crescenzi, having engaged myself with him in the time he was here to see me pass some days with him at Ferrara. I hope your majesty will not doubt of the comfort and satisfaction I shall have to find at your feet, and most humbly beg your blessing."

James replied, November 1 :[1]—

"It is very true, my dear son, that your leaving me has been a subject of grief and affliction to me, chiefly on your account, for these four months past, so that you may easily imagine with what satisfaction I perused your letter of the 25th October. I am sensible your absence was the effect of ill advice ; but I have the comfort to see that your return is your own work alone. Return, therefore, my dear child, without delay and with all confidence, into the arms of a tender father and true friend, who will forget what is past, and who will be as he has always been, wholly taken up with whatever may contribute to your real good and satisfaction. I beseech God to bless you and give you a good journey, and tenderly embrace you, my dear child."

What memories of the old correspondence with his rebellious wife re-awake in this letter ! How much of her temperament was inherited by her sons ! Now, the world was with James, and Mann says the French king threatened to cut off the cardinal's benefices.

Henry answered from Bologna, November 8, thanking his father for the kindness with which he had received his submission. He would return to Rome on the following Monday or Tuesday. Peace was made. Henry was allowed his separate table and to invite what guests he pleased. Lercari remained at Genoa. James was not to interfere with Henry's expenditure.

The cardinal returned to Rome on November 21, and the Pope, to avoid exciting the king, kindly met the cardinal at Santa Maria in Campitelli to discuss the situation. The Pope was satisfied with the cardinal's explanation and submission, and

Printed by Browne, iv. 107. (Stuart Papers.)

1752. bestowed upon him as reward the commendam of the Basilica of the Holy Apostles, with leave to keep at the same time the beloved Santa Maria in Campitelli. Henry on his side presented to the Pope's nephew two silver pots of artifical flowers.[1]

All this time, great events had been happening among Prince Charles's friends in England. Early in October, the Duke of Newcastle discovered that Madame de Mézières had come over secretly to England without a pass. Horace Walpole that same year had said that Jacobitism was silenced, but Newcastle knew better. The marquise declared she had come over only to see her sister Anne at Godalming who was ill, but admitted that she had stopped on the way to Godalming; first in Picardy where she had relations, and then to spend a pleasant week with Lady Westmoreland in Kent, according to an old promise. Lord Westmoreland was the leader of the Jacobites, and his palladian house at Mereworth in Kent was visited by Prince Charles certainly in the following year or 1755. Perhaps, in this autumn of 1752, he was hidden by Madame de Mézières at Westbrook Place, Godalming, where his ghost is said to wander and where there is a room said to have concealed him. The story of his hiding at Westbrook Place is quite alive in Godalming up to the present day. Carte, who did not die until April 1754, was busily carrying messages between his Oglethorpe friends and the other conspirators. The prince in September was expecting to be in London immediately, and he was not wont to hang back when business was doing. Pickle the Spy lost sight of him between September and the following March, but wrote to King James in March that in November the prince had been "on the coast, ready at a call to put himself at the head of his adherents, though mercifully he did not venture himself in London, where the plot was brewed." Godalming is not on the coast, but it is on the highroad to Portsmouth, easy of access, within convenient reach of London on the one hand and the prince's allies, the Sussex smugglers, on the other.

From Godalming, Madame de Mézières went to Bath; to take the waters for her rheumatism, she informed Newcastle, when he missed her. Bath was easy of access to the Welsh Jacobites. Tradition says that in 1753 the prince was hidden at Arlingham Court on the Severn, a house with a large park

[1] State Papers: Tuscany.

and surrounding estate. Perhaps he travelled there too in 1752. 1752 with Madame de Mézières when she went to Bath. The owner was a Mr. Yate, descendant of the Earls of Berkeley. He died in 1758, when the family became extinct. His mother succeeded him as proprietress.

But the Elibank plot blew up itself, not St. James's Palace and the House of Hanover as had been planned. November 10 had been fixed for action ; Murray of Elibank, with the assistance of Jacobite desperadoes, was to seize the reigning family and proclaim King James. From Menin, near Ghent, Charles had sent Lochgarry and Archy Cameron, Lochiel's uncle, to raise the Scottish clans, promising them the co-operation of Swedish troops under the Earl Marischal's brother, Marshal Keith, now of the Prussian service. The Prussian ambassador at Versailles knew all about it. Cameron of Fassifern and Cameron of Glen Nevis were in the plot ; also a brother of Lord Elcho, and Mr. Hepburn of Keith, still longing for dissolution of the Union. "When matters came to a pinch, some frivolous excuses retarded this great and glorious blow," Pickle told James. Archy Cameron was taken in the following March and hanged at Tyburn on the old charge of 1745 ; the last who died for the Stuart cause.

According to Miss Knight, lady-in-waiting to Princess Charlotte of Wales, Charles told Commander d'Olomien (?) that he visited England in 1752 at the invitation of "the minister" ; that would presumably be the French minister ; that he saw many people and was well received, though the person at whose house he lodged knew not who he was ; that at Dover he went to the house of a gentleman who belonged to the opposite party, but who treated him with great respect and civility. It was during this visit that he walked in suddenly upon his former hostess, Lady Primrose,[1] to the consternation of that loyal lady.

A Reverend Mr. Blacowe, who had discovered a "Jacobite gang" at Oxford, went to town "to complain of them and of the vice-chancellor for not doing justice against them." Mr. Blacowe was presently rewarded by recommendation for a vacant prebend at Durham.

In August 1752, James had summoned Lismore's son,

---

[1] Lord Elcho said the prince was at Lady Primrose's in London at the very time when Pickle said he was "on the coast."—Pickle the Spy.

1752. Lord Tallow, to Rome, and employed him in his household as a secretary. Probably James and Lismore wanted to keep the pretty bright boy out of the mischief of the Elibank plot. Walton took him to be Fitzmorris's son: then, anxious for his reputation for omniscience, pretended his mistake to have been due to Italian mis-pronunciation which had confused his title with a *tailor* to whom Fitzmorris's niece was married! Lord Tallow soon returned to Paris. Meantime, Prince Charles, as always, refused to look upon his plot as crushed. It was only postponed—or rather, the age-long plot was to be further drawn out. Had he not a mighty ally in Frederick of Prussia who, with his ambassador, the Earl Marischal, fanned the fainting embers of hope?

1753. In the spring of 1753, James Dawkins came to Paris, a wealthy West Indian proprietor and archæologist who had travelled much and written of Palmyra in collaboration with the Duke of Bridgewater. He was a hot Jacobite, and at once sought the Earl Marischal, and travelled between Paris and Berlin " on the king's business." The English Jacobites plotted as mysteriously and drank as heartily as ever ; and as they had never done more, why should there be less to hope for than in 1745—or 1715—or 1704? Jacobites were indicted in London for rioting and drinking to James III.[1] " Disaffected healths " were also drunk under the august roof of the Dean of Durham.[2] D'Argenson in 1753 declared that the English of the big towns, hating Hanoverian avarice, were for the prince; that Lords Chesterfield, Sandwich, Pulteney, and Bath were still for him, and that a revolution might break out at any moment. D'Argenson wanted his prophecy of 1752 to come true. France connived, inspired by D'Argenson and the sympathetic Prussian ambassador, and the British government complained that Scottish Jacobites were allowed to land constantly at La Rochelle. A council was called in London to protest against France giving asylum to these " malefactors," as John Hay once styled himself and his fellow-refugees.

Prince Charles, with whom hope died so hard, bestirred himself. Lengthy and elaborate accounts were given of his movements, but the spies who dogged and reported are ex-

---

[1] Eliot Hodgkin MSS., p. 250.
[2] Hist. MSS. Comm. Reports XI., part vii. p. 44. Also examination in council of the offenders ; Add. MSS. 33,050, ff. 201, &c.

ceedingly difficult to reconcile with one another.   He almost 1753.
certainly went again to England to look into proceedings
officered by Lord Westmoreland, Dr. King, and James Dawkins,
under Prussian patronage, but there is little more than tradition for that visit.   He not impossibly went to Scotland too.
He probably managed to evade the spies by keeping his own
secrets from his supposed friends.   Hume dates his surprise
visit to Lady Primrose in this year (1753), and also the story
of his presence in London being known to George II.   There
is also the story that he was hidden at Arlingham Court in
Gloucestershire, before mentioned.

Pickle was far from being the only active Jacobite at work
as a spy.   James Macgregor (or Drummond) "of Bohaldie,"
says the official report, better known as James Mohr, son of
Rob Roy, gave full information to the British government of
the Jacobite plot in France under the Earl Marischal, for the
simultaneous invasion of North Wales and Scotland from
Ireland by 14,000 Irish.[1]   Arlingham Court was therefore a
very likely point for the prince to make for.   By signed licence
of George II., dated 3rd November 1753, James Mohr returned to England for examination by Lord Holdernesse on
November 6 : when he "professed to give information of all
the agents in Scotland and elsewhere, he being one of the
most trusted himself."[2]   He was "wanted" by the British
government for the murder of Campbell of Glenure ; the
Leit Motif of Stevenson's "Catriona."   He had been living with
or near Allan Breck Stuart at Bièvre (he spells it "Baivre" in
his own notes), three leagues from Paris.   The Lord Justice
Clerk, in a letter of November 17, 1752, says positively that
James Mohr had committed the Appin murder and tried to
earn his pardon by betraying the Jacobite plot.[3]   There is also
a short, neatly written French "narrative," two and a half pages
of manuscript, which gives detailed accounts of the prince's
movements in 1753.[4]   The dates do not all perfectly fit in
with the dates given by Pickle and James Mohr, but are not

---

[1] Hist. MSS. Comm. Reports XI., part vii. p. 44.   (Leeds MSS.).
[2] Ibid.   From a series of papers among four parcels of letters to and from Lord
Albemarle, English ambassador at Paris.   Albemarle advised Holdernesse "not to
give much credit to M'Gregor for, upon reading his long declaration I find in it many
falsehoods and very few material circumstances, and upon the whole I believe him a
most notorious scoundrel."
[3] Ibid.
[4] Add MSS. 33,050, ff. 409, verso, and 410.

1753. irreconcilable when it is remembered that the spy of the
"narrative" spoke from memory, as he pleads, some time
after the events, and, that the prince was able occasionally
to baffle the spies.

According to this "narrative," Charles spent four early
months of 1753 at Lunéville. From other sources we
know that in March, Pickle met him in Paris,[1] at a *bal
masqué* and was surprised, having lost sight of him ;
that on May 6, Lochgarry came from Scotland with en-
couraging reports of Highland readiness. Dawkins went to
Berlin in May, says Pickle, and Charles to Coblentz, and,
in June, to Frankfort. The narrative says that during the
Lunéville period Charles went to Frankfort. From Lunéville
he went to Poland where he stayed a very short time ; from
thence to Prussia, where he stayed a fortnight to wait for the
envoy he had sent to Russia. As soon as the envoy (Dawkins ?)
arrived they went together back to Lunéville. On the way,
they spent two days at Strasbourg. The prince remained two
and a half months at Lunéville without leaving it. All these
journeys may be included in the interval of the four months'
headquarters at Lunéville. From Lunéville he went to Paris
where he stayed ten days and then departed for Liége where
he stayed nearly a month. He was certainly at Liége in July
when he wrote to Dormer for newspapers, describing himself
as a sedentary man seeking amusement in periodical literature.
Then comes the surprising, more than doubtful statement that
from Liége he went to Scotland, where he stayed *assez long tems*,
and on leaving, returned to Paris in the month of September,
where he stayed six days and received 2000 louis d'or. James
Mohr gives a very full account of this September visit to Paris,
but believed he came from south of Avignon. According to
Pickle, Charles had been called to meet him and Lochgarry
at Ternan in August to consult upon Scottish preparedness,
and they went from Ternan to Paris. Charles alluded to his
late wanderings, but it would not be surprising if he did
not describe them minutely. The former visit to Paris also
coincides with the "narrative," and the asserted visit to
Scotland might follow upon consultation with Lochgarry.
The traditional date of his visit to the Severn falls about
September. It would be strange if he never revisited Scotland.

[1] Pickle the Spy.

James Mohr said that in June 1753 Charles asked Balhaldy to take service with him. In June, according to the "narrative," Charles would be at Lunéville after the northern roaming, if it ever took place. Balhaldy refused to do anything whatever for the prince until he should be reconciled with his father and apologise to the King of France for his misconduct. On these conditions, Balhaldy would willingly enter upon his affairs in concert with the Earl Marischal, but with none other, for he could not trust any of the " fools " about the prince. In the middle of September Charles arrived in Paris attended by Trant and Fleetwood. James Mohr says that Trant was a son of Olive Trant. Olive had married the Prince of Auvergne and it was not likely that a son of her wild youth would bear her maiden name. He was perhaps a nephew. He had recently been much with James, according to Walton.

At Bièvre, where Balhaldy and Allan Breck Stuart lived, Charles met his supporters ; the Earl Marischal, Balhaldy, Mr. Gordon, Principal of the Scots College, who was to captain them for Scotland, Mr. Butler, master of the horse to Louis XV. with whom he was a great favourite, and some other English gentlemen. Balhaldy hoped the headstrong prince would now stick by the Earl Marischal and his advice, seeing " by what a parcel of fools he had been advised since 1745." The proposals from Ireland were accepted. James Mohr was to be sent to the people of Fingal ; Scottish affairs were entrusted to Stirling of Keir, Murray of Abercarnie, a Mr. Smith, and Sir Hugh Paterson. Abercarnie had waited on Charles in an abbé's house near Lille where he had been staying a month, perhaps the Duke of York's Abbey of Anchin ; but the visit is difficult to fit into the " narrative " dates.

Balhaldy said Charles had made a proposal to his father to resign the crown in his favour ; that the proposal was refused and the prince requested to make no more such proposals ; that Charles wanted Balhaldy to go to Rome to expostulate with the king, but that Balhaldy begged to be excused as he was strongly opposed to the idea and " would never desire the Old Gentleman to resign." This proposal was believed to proceed from the English, perhaps suggested during Charles's recent trip, since Charles had turned Protestant. Balhaldy says that Charles had certainly not written to his father for above two years and a half before this, nor would as yet, had not his friends

1753. made it a condition of acting with him. In the previous December, Edgar told Sir James Harrington that they were as much in the dark as he was. In July, King James told Lord George Murray that he did not know where Charles was or what had taken Archy Cameron, whose death he mourned, to Scotland. He recommended his family to the Spanish court : Edgar wrote to Charles for his interest in the matter on July 10. In September the king wrote to Sir John Graeme, " It is now more than two years since he (the prince) has writ at all here." James had been told some facts but they threw no light at all on the present situation.

Gordon was appointed the prince's manager in chief. As for money, Charles, says Balhaldy, had a good annual income from England. Mr. Trant told James Mohr that about 50,000 livres had been collected for him. Arms, too, were plentiful : 2000 stand concealed in Clanranald's country, all in good condition, though Archibald Cameron had taken away 250 stand without orders. George Kelly, Charles's secretary, who had returned to him now the Earl Marischal had retired, was told nothing, as he was suspected of having given information to the government. Young Sheridan was always with the prince. It was desired that the prince should wait hidden in Balhaldy's house till time for the invasion from Ireland. Nothing came of it all. Balhaldy said he was turned off by the Irish and that the Earl Marischal never would trust him.

The "narrative" says that from Paris the prince went to Prussia and from Prussia to Denmark ; that he spent two months on this journey, and on his return, spent three days in Paris : " as far as I can remember, this was in January 1754." But the narrator has forgotten, if he knew, that before the two months' journey ending in January, the prince was certainly at Liége, for his daughter was born there at the end of October and he himself carried her to her baptism.

"Since then " (January 1754), continues the "narrative," " he has lived nearly always in Liége or in Scotland, except for two visits to Paris : the last being at the end of August, when he stayed eight days, and returned to Liége. From Liége he went again to Prussia. You may have been told of his movements, but those who told you may easily have been deceived ; for I knew them *de bonne part*, seeing that the person of whom I told you has often been taken for him, and I myself have heard of him being in a certain place or that he has passed, even the *Gazette* has mentioned it, when I knew the contrary. His usual residence is in Scotland or in Liége, or in Lorraine. As for the project he had made for obtaining his ends, it was to send circular letters through all countries for deserters who might pass, to make of them a body of 6000 men, as well as a part of the 'reformed' French officers and soldiers. He wished to pay them in different ways. There must be magazines of arms and ammunition collected in many cellars of Scottish houses. When everything was ready, his plan was to take possession of a seaport, I cannot remember its name, and of some other place that would be given up to him, while at the same time his partisans should set fire to several places to cause diversion. I cannot repeat it to you exactly as it was planned, for in three years I have forgotten, but the plan was under way (approchant). I cannot make you [cipher] for the present but on his return, I will send you an account of what he aims at (butte) and what he was doing in Prussia, Russia, and Poland."

James Mohr was detained in prison but escaped. He died at the end of 1754, and there was one spy the less. Six leagues from Paris stood the Château de Montlin, crown property, granted to the Scottish Jacobites, as St. Germain's had once been granted to the English and Irish. Lady Lismore and Lady Kenmure lived there. James Mohr says this château was a *pied-à-terre* for the prince : that often when making a short tour in Germany he gave out that he was going to Poland and came to Montlin; "where he is at present," says James Mohr (November 1753), "sometimes dressed like an abbé, sometimes as a sportsman, and frequently hunts in the forest with other Scotsmen."

It was in that same month of November that Newcastle was confirmed in his suspicion as to Madame de Mézières' visit to England a year earlier : that he had "private and most secret" intelligence from a Mr. Roy Keith,[1] that the Earl Marischal was intriguing with Prussia on behalf of the Jacobites, and with "an English person of great importance at Paris," possessed of such great estates as to imply how

[1] This Mr. Keith may have been the "Baron de Mareschal," whom King James and the Cardinal of York received later with so much hospitable friendship in Rome : whom Walton took for a broken Prussian officer, ennobled by Frederick the Great. Spies were not necessarily working in partnership or even in rivalry, but kept their secrets from one another.

1753. "serious and safe" the venture must be. Newcastle was also informed that a young Mézières, probably a connection of Eleanor's, but said to be really one Charles Colin, was carrying messages between the Earl Marischal at Paris and King James in Rome. A mysterious "Lady," "whose name they have forgot," who was the *bonne amie* of the Bishop of Courtrai,—corrected later to Cambrai—must be watched to find where the prince were. It was she who employed young Mézières to carry the letters between Paris and Rome. This was beyond doubt Lady Lismore, wife of King James's secretary of state, O'Brien, once, scandal believed, the mistress of the Bishop of Cambrai, and now standing high in the self-appointed ministry of the prince regent. Lumisden calls her "a fair daughter of Eve." Whether Prince Charles, though furious against Lord Lismore as prime agent in his brother's flight, continued to employ her ladyship, or whether she acted on her own initiative like most of these plotters, she was deeply concerned in the conspiracy of 1752–54. Prince Charles's estimate of her is recorded in his memoranda : "O'Bryen is the greatest rogue there is . . . his wife is [little better than her] husband."[1]

"The most wicked conspiracy" of 1753 was discussed by the English Council. The Lord Chancellor believed there was no immediate danger, but that the case called for prudence, and one of the first things to be done was to arrest Madame de Mézières. No expense was to be spared to find "the pretender's son." Sir John Gooderich was to be sent after him, and Lord Anson must have frigates on the Scotch and Irish coasts. On December 3, Lord Albemarle was instructed to find out all about "the lady" unnamed and the person going under the name of Mézières.

In November 1753 Charles, in a fury of Protestantism, not only discharged his popish servants, but threatened to pack off his popish mistress, though it was only a month after their daughter's birth. On March 25 of the following year he wrote to Edgar that he was grieved his father should attribute his long silence either to neglect or want of duty, but in reality he had nothing to say but imprecations against the

---

[1] Browne, iv. 122, who transcribes the memorandum from the Stuart Papers, gives the words "is a little good other husband," out of which sense cannot be made. Browne does not always transcribe correctly (see "trial Kelly" for "Friar Kelly," iii. 503), and the Prince's English, as well as his handwriting, was now very confused.

fatality of having been born in such a detestable age. The 1754.
French ministry had made it impossible that he should
increase the amount of his misery by marrying and settling
down.[1]

At the end of 1754, a correspondent, anonymous at first,
later giving his name as Anderson, at Sens in Burgundy,
offered his services to Lord Chancellor Hardwick to spy
upon Charles. He boasted of intimacy with the Jacobite
party, and that his uncle had been twenty-seven years in the
immediate service and trust of the pretender. He specially
undertook to discover the prince's agent in Scotland. His
offer not being immediately accepted, he wrote again, March 8,
that the agent for seven years past had been Mr. Walkinshaw
of Scotstown. Again he received no reply, but his news was
acted upon and Walkinshaw was arrested. Presently this spy's
services were accepted by George II.[2]

[1] Stuart Papers : Browne, iv. 119.
[2] Hist. MSS. Comm. Reports XI., Appendix, part vii. p. 51.   (Leeds MSS.).

CHAPTER XII

THE CARDINAL BISHOP

1754. COMPARATIVE peace had reigned for four months between the Cardinal of York and his father since their reconciliation. Henry wanted the vice-chancellorship of St. Peter's and must propitiate the Pope by submissiveness; but that preferment was not yet for him. It went to Cardinal Colonna. Henry, however, failed to make himself popular with the chapter and increased their wrath by insisting that they, as well as all advocates at the Roman bar, should stand while giving him information, though all other cardinals had allowed them to sit.

In March 1753, a new quarrel broke out between James and Henry, and the Pope commanded the cardinal to dismiss his confessor, the *casus belli*, and replaced him by a secular priest. James was said to be treating his son with "insufferable haughtiness," and Henry complained of his father and his favourites and declared it to be impossible to manage the royal revenues. In July Henry fell seriously ill. The long dispute with his father had "spoilt his blood," says Walton. He was threatened with consumption, fainting and coughing and spitting blood, and was in great danger. He was kept to the house for two months; then ordered to Pisa, and it was supposed that he must go to a warmer climate for winter; but he mended somewhat, owing to the care of the Pope's doctor, Laurenti, and a milk diet. In September he went with his father to Albano; then to Monterassino in October for mountain air: attended, to his own considerable disgust, by Lascaris like a watch-dog, who had orders to bring him back to Albano without letting him go anywhere else. Monterassino and the good advice of Lascaris, says Walton, did him much good. He returned to Rome to interest himself in the magnificent furnishing of his house near the Vatican, and on November 18 he entertained the Pope and his father there, though he still lived at the Muti Palace. Besides costly furniture and good pictures, Henry had formed a collection

H.R.H. AND E., THE CARDINAL DUKE OF YORK

From the painting in the Scots College at Rome

of rare books and manuscripts, from which he presented to the Pope two cases, one of them containing holograph letters of Pope Pius II.

He was still in very bad health, unable to attend functions or entertainments. He was pronounced by the doctors to be doomed to a short life, and his father was in such distress that he withdrew altogether from society. James's grief was not, as Walton said, for the 30,000 crowns of ecclesiastical revenue imperilled by his son's dangerous state. But at Christmas Henry began to recover, and attended literary academical meetings.

Just before the New Year of 1754 Walton's informant at the court had been discovered and dismissed, and it was very difficult to glean information for the British government.

Louis XV. had recently offered to the Cardinal of York the great Flemish Abbey of St. Amand, free of charge, but it was found to be charged with a pension of 8000 crowns. Henry refused to receive it thus mutilated, and his father endeavoured through the Pope to obtain the entire income for his son, as it had been promised. Louis assured him that arrears up to 20,000 scudi should be paid. Differences arose again between James and Henry, but on the whole there was peace, and in February Henry gave a magnificent dinner to his father in his new house.

Fresh cause of dissension presented itself in the Cardinal Duke's friendship for Cardinal John Francis Albani. This Albani, five years older than the Cardinal of York, was one of the spoiled sons of the Church.[1] Nephew of Clement XI., who, however, died a year after his nephew's birth, he became Bishop of Ostia and Velletri at twenty-six. He was extremely handsome, witty, and charming, and had spent his youth in pleasure, neglectful of the duties of his station. His wisdom did not increase with years. He died Dean of the Sacred College, but he missed the tiara at two conclaves, it is said, owing to his infatuation for his chamberlain, Mariano, who, in Albani's old age, governed him despotically and was master of his see, till the Pope, Pius VII., amazed at hearing of the "principato di Marianino," called up the cardinal for rebuke. "Ah! Santissimo Padre!" replied the culprit humorously, "we all have our Marianinos, more or less:" a hit at the great confidence placed by the Pope in Cardinal Consalvi, his secretary

---

[1] Another cardinal of this name had been one of James's splendid hosts in 1717.

1754. of state. Such a man as John Francis Albani was doubtless not the best of friends and advisers for the Cardinal of York. James detested him, perhaps also distrusted his good faith, seeing that his kinsman, Cardinal Alexander, was entirely in the Hanoverian interest. He could not endure that Henry should so much as speak to Cardinal John Francis and refused to meet him at dinner at the archpriest's house.

In May, Henry went with Albani to Nettuno, to stay with his father's friend Cardinal Corsini, the chief correspondent of Tencin and the French Jacobites. There were great fêtes at Nettuno of which Henry sent his father newspaper accounts. The Pope had made Lercari Bishop of Brunato, to keep him away from Henry. All seemed more than usually cheerful; there was another hopeful scheme on hand for Prince Charles, and James was in high spirits; then all was overcast by the sudden and serious illness of the king.

Henry was called back from the gaieties of Nettuno. James had been suffering from what seemed to be rheumatic pains, and a letter, supposed to be from Prince Charles, had caused great agitation. He had probably had a slight stroke, for Henry on his return found his father so much altered that he fainted on leaving the sickroom. James recovered somewhat but was too weak to go to Albano. Henry, anxious about his father, remained in Rome and diverted his mind by enlarging his house in the Vatican precincts.

The Pope was very fond of James, and in the quarrels between the king and his son he always took the paternal side. He seems never to have liked the Duke of York. Benedict XIV. was one of the most delightful men who ever filled the Chair of St. Peter or any other throne. A saint in his private life, intolerant of every sort of laxity among his clergy, he was not only an unwearied worker in the duties of his office, a profound scholar and a skilled politician, but kind and wise and a witty companion. The Duke of York was not in the very least amusing. It is well known that after one occasion when he had talked inconsequently for an hour and a half, the bored Pope exclaimed that he did not wonder the English had got rid of the Stuarts if they were all as tiresome as this one. The Pope also laughed at Henry's stately airs, the elaborate ceremonial upon which he insisted as his and his father's due on every occasion.

The hauteur with which the young cardinal offended all 1754. the Roman notabilities, is curiously in contrast with the sweetness of his face in the portraits and with Lumisden's description of his bearing ; "extremely frank and free, far more like a companion than a superior, so that one would have taken him for the brother rather than the superior of " two travellers who at this time visited and dined frequently with the king. His position was extremely trying to a proud spirit, and consciousness of unwilling, perhaps sarcastic respect paid to his real rights embittered the tenacity with which he exacted his due. With those who accepted his claims and did him proper reverence, he could allow his real Stuart affability to have its way. Natural dignity made him shrink from being a mere " sight " for curious British trippers. Dennistoun says that his haughty temper made him as unpopular with English supporters as, combined with superior morality, it had made him with the Jacobites of Paris. Well-meaning English gentlemen made great complaints of the little notice he took of them when they put themselves in his way for the purpose of having the pleasure of seeing him as well as the honour to salute him, in churches and public places. They complained to Mr. Tyrrel,[1] who reported to James Edgar that he showed " slight and contempt of them, rather than any disposition to favour them with a kind and gracious look as the king does."

By the end of July James was well enough to be angered again by Henry's friendship with Cardinal Albani who was teaching him extravagance. Lercari was recalled to Rome, Henry's new friendship and splendid way of living having quite removed him from fear of the old favourite's influence. Henry had a natural and cultivated taste for splendour and also for learning, though far from learned himself. He felt that his money was his own, honestly worked for, and he asked nothing more unreasonable than that he should choose how to spend it. He was magnificently liberal, not only to the poor but to the Church. He was now having one of the Vatican altar-pictures copied in mosaic as the original was spoiling. But the king, God bless him, had no sympathy with any sort of art, and in October was quarrelling with Henry for frequenting conversazioni. However, in November he condescended to meet Cardinal Albani at dinner in Henry's house.

[1] A Tyrrel had been the king's agent in Florence. He died in 1752.

In 1754 Henry Pelham died, and his brother, the Duke of Newcastle [on-Tyne], succeeded him as Prime Minister. His dukedom was doubled by the addition of Newcastle-under-Lyme in 1756. In June 1754 Admiral Boscawen, with four warships, attacked and took two French ships on the banks of Newfoundland, a preliminary to the Seven Years' War. Lally advised the French to avenge the blow by sending Prince Charles to England. Charles, as usual eagerly seizing at hope in hostilities, insisted on secrecy and went on treating his father and brother as enemies to be baffled and opposed, always and in all things. Nothing must be told at Rome of his affairs, he says in a memorandum of 1st July 1754, "for everything there is known, and my brother who has got no confidence of my father, has always acted as far as in his power against my interests."[1]

Charles failed to keep his own secret inviolate, as he believed. He went to Navarre—("from Florence," says Amédée Pichot, a very uncertain guide); then to Lorraine to see King Stanislas and Lally; "but time was lost," says Pichot, "and a month later the project was abandoned, and Lally went to fight the English in India." Charles nevertheless went to England. Lord Albemarle reported as a fact to the British government that he was in London and at Nottingham.[2] It is said to have been during this visit that he was recognised in Hyde Park when a man tried to kneel to him. He lurked at Stoneleigh about this time, where tradition avers that he left a portrait of himself, painted in the Midlands, with the family of Mr. Dodson, rector of Leek Wootton. It is unlikely that a proscribed and concealed prince should sit for his portrait, but the picture may have been painted from memory, as were so many of his portraits, like those of his ancestress, Mary Queen of Scots.

The prince was now so poor that he had to dismiss five of his small establishment at Basle, with his valet. He sent them to Rome without waiting for any answer to his announcement that they were on their way. James was dismayed. All the refugees from Britain appealed to him and the cardinal for help, and he was not in a condition to give new pensions. In any case, he said, he could have kept them as well in France,

---

[1] Stuart Papers: Browne, iv. p. 122.
[2] Lansdowne MSS. Hist. MSS. Comm. Reports, vol. iii. p. 141.

while in Rome they would be in constant danger of being 1755. turned upon the streets at his death. He gave them forty crowns apiece out of Charles's own little revenue from the Licoghi di Monte, and the cardinal, always kind-hearted, gave them ten sequins apiece and sent them straight back to France. They passed through Florence on the way, where Mann set his spies upon them. Two men, pretending to be their friends, spent a jovial evening with them, but the Scots were loyal and wary. They drank "to the Boy that is lost and cannot be found," but Mann's spies found out nothing at all.[1]

Perhaps when Charles sent his servants to Rome he had heard of a new accession to his brother's income. The busy Lady Lismore had been exerting herself on the cardinal's behalf, and had asked for the vacant commendam of the Abbey of St. Médard for his royal eminence, as well as for the arrears of St. Amand. In December 1755 St. Amand was at last bestowed upon him in full, and he was formally invested with the commendam, but he did not get St. Médard.

James knew little of Charles's affairs, though he told De Stainville, now French ambassador at Rome, that he heard frequently from Charles, and was angry with France who, after promising assistance towards the new expedition, had put off as usual, with empty compliments, the fulfilling of her promise. Disappointment caused relapse into hypochondria. The doctors agreed that he had no other ailment and treated him as much of a *malade imaginaire*. He quarrelled anew with the Duke of York; again demanding that Henry should increase his contribution of 5000 scudi to their joint table; which Henry again refused to do. Henry had a mass composed by Galuppi (Buranello) at Venice at his own expense and angered his father by spending much time at Santa Maria in Campitelli over its rehearsals. James, though no critic, saw nothing in the masses, and offended Henry by his unskilled disparagement. For some days Henry ate in his own room and James kept away from Henry's musical evenings, staying dismally in his own apartments with Lismore and Lascaris. Then he was persuaded to go to hear the final rehearsal of the mass, which was brought out on July 20 (1755) at a *première* of much brilliance, eight cardinals assist-

[1] State Papers : Tuscany.

1755. ing privately. The wrangles were still going on between the archpriest and his over-governed chapter.

In the autumn James went to Albano, where, in a carefully contrived, accidental-seeming way he met the Elector of Cologne, who was paying a short visit in the neighbourhood and was very anxious to meet him. The Elector and the Cardinal of York met more than once. James looked happy once more, but early in November he caught a chill and was dangerously ill. The cardinal's musical receptions were stopped and he devoted himself to his father who recovered again.

How much money really came to the Cardinal of York from France is doubtful, but he had rich benefices in Spain and Naples, besides his Roman appointments. Walton supposed him to be the richest cardinal in the college, and was shocked to believe that he never sent a sou to Prince Charles. As Charles would hold no communication with his brother, it is difficult to see why Henry should have financed him, beyond giving up the reversion of the papal pension to his brother, as he did, finding himself sufficiently provided for. But there were heavy charges to pay in pensions, and even if he were one of the richest of the cardinals as far as his revenues went, none of them had the peculiar and necessary expenses of royalty to maintain. Though Charles for long had described himself as well provided for, and had taken the financing of the cause into his own hands, his father often sent him large sums of money. When he sent his dependents to Rome at a time of low exchequer, the cardinal cared for them. Henry also spent enormous sums over the decoration of Santa Maria in Campitelli.[1]

1756. Yet it seems as if James, at least on Henry's behalf, were insatiable in demands. In September, his old friend Cardinal Valenti, secretary of state, died. About the same time the great post of the vice-chancellorship of St. Peter's fell vacant by the death of Cardinal Ruffo. Much change of office, therefore, was going, and James asked for the vice-chancellorship for his son. The Pope gave it with the secretaryship to Cardinal Archinto. James, deeply offended, went off to Albano without either the usual *a rivederci* or the usual guard. Henry

[1] Storia dell' Immagine e la chiesa di Santa Maria in Portici di Campitelli; descritta da Carlo Antonio Erra: dedicata al Cardinale Duca di York, 1750.

seemed quite indifferent, which further exasperated his father. 1756.
The Pope kindly explained away the apparent slight, but James
was fated to be received by his old friend only once more.
Benedict fell seriously ill, and though he lingered more than
a year longer, and enjoyed occasional amelioration of health,
he avoided the many and varied embarrassments of James's
visits. The Pope, except as a very disobedient patient, was
a pattern to all his flock for the brave way in which he bore
his excruciating illness. He held Consistories in bed; he
showed himself whenever he could to his enthusiastic people;
he never lost his spirit for a moment, and carefully prepared
for vacating his throne; always cheerful, though as fully aware
as were those about him that he was a dying man. He dictated
a book that he was anxious to see finished before his death.
He was presently going about again, temporarily cured by
Tokay, sent by Maria Theresa; but he relapsed, and died on
May 2, 1758.

James, held aloof by the invalid Pope, was courted by 1757.
cardinals in view of an approaching conclave. Nothing else
broke the monotony of his life; alternations from gloom to
cheerfulness, and back to gloom; quarrels and reconciliations
with his son about his friends; now a Jesuit, Steffanucci, who
was said to have taken possession of Henry; later, the Guardian
of the Cordeliers. It was impossible that Henry should have
a friend of whom his father would approve. Henry busied
himself in the summer, getting up concerts at his church. He
and his father interested themselves in the wedding of the
Duke of Sermoneta with a Corsini, which took place in the
Cardinal of York's private chapel. Even Prince Charles emerged
from the shadows so far as to write a dateless letter of congratulation, and James gave a great entertainment in honour
of the marriage.

On November 6, 1757, Walton the spy, Baron Philip von
Stosch, died at Florence. His papers were immediately moved
to the English legation. He left his collection of antiquities
to his nephew, who had lived with him for two years, but
they had to be sold to pay debts.

In April 1758, just before his death, Pope Benedict XIV. 1758.
appointed the Cardinal of York to the office of Camerlengo.[1]

---

[1] The highest post at the Roman court: head of the treasury; empowered to coin
money, &c., during the Sede Vacante.

1758. He therefore presided at the conclave which met to elect Benedict's successor. Here his dignity was seriously affronted by the Austrian Cardinal Lanze, who abstained from giving him the royal title, calling him only Eminenza. Next, he came into new conflict with his father by supporting the Austrian candidate for the papacy, Cavalchini, against the will of the French court. James was exceedingly angry that his son should offend a court to which they were so deeply indebted. Henry returned that he would rather lose his head than act against his conscience. During the conclave, perhaps out of temper, James fell so ill at Albano that his death was momentarily expected by his frightened household and, according to Horace Mann, Henry was offered permission to leave the conclave for his father's deathbed and to return afterwards, contrary to all precedent ;[1] but he refused. He was too sadly accustomed to these attacks, and perhaps he knew that the illness had been magnified so that his father might try personal persuasion in the matter of his vote, the very danger against which the strict seclusion of conclaves is enforced. On July 6, Cardinal Rezzonico was elected Pope as Clement XIII. ; a very strict Pope in smaller matters of relaxed discipline, who forbade powder and ruffles to ecclesiastics. He bore no malice towards his opponent, the Cardinal of York, but re-instated him as Camerlengo, and presently offered him a bishopric. Clement XIII. was the last Pope to hold Avignon.

James was now almost always confined to bed, very weak, and suffering at times attacks of violent pain from indigestion. The doctors had pronounced his malady to be senile consumption. He was unable to be present at the magnificent ceremony in the Church of the Holy Apostles, when by the papal hands Henry was consecrated Archbishop of Corinth *in partibus infidelium*, November 19, 1758. In 1759. February 1759 he became a cardinal-priest and exchanged his commendam of the Sant' Apostoli for Santa Maria in Trastevere. This very ancient church, which still bears his arms, was founded by St. Calixtus in 222, where a spring of oil welled up on a Christmas night. Hence its style, Fons

---

[1] Great liberties were taken with ecclesiastical regulations in those days, or one would doubt Mann's report of such unwonted permission, but I am informed by a learned Jesuit that the permission might possibly have been given for once.

Olei, in early Christian documents. The beautiful mural 1759. tabernacle for the Holy Oil is by the most delicately noble of sculptors, Mino da Fiesole. Cardinal Campeggio, Shakespeare's Campeius, is buried here.[1] In this year was begun the voluminous official diary of the cardinal which is preserved in the British Museum.[2]

There was peace now in the Muti Palace, for James was too feeble and ill for jealousies and resentments. Beyond the quiet sickroom and the nearly as quiet routine of the Cardinal of York in his ecclesiastical duties, which he took so seriously, and his cultured recreations, the Seven Years' War thundered on. Prince Charles, longing to be in the fray and eagerly reckoning upon its chances, is said to have volunteered to serve in the attack on Minorca whose loss to France in 1755 demanded the sacrifice of Admiral Byng. In September 1759 Quebec fell to the arms of Wolfe. James revived sufficiently to be consulted in an avenging attempt upon England, but that hope sank under the waters of Quiberon Bay, October 1759.

In November, age and infirmities compelled Lord Lismore to resign the secretaryship of state to King James. He retired to Paris where he died the following year. On November 9 James summoned Sir John Graeme to take his place, but as chief secretary only ; there was no need now for a secretary of state. Graeme was created Earl of Alford. He was *persona gratissima* to the Cardinal of York, his old pupil, who had doubtless been the real fountain of his new honour. Lady Lismore, with her son, continued to act as James's diplomatic agent in Paris, and Graeme was commanded to inform her of his appointment and settle a correspondence with her. James wrote so kindly to Graeme, so much in his old gentle style, that it is evident his mind was not affected by his bodily weakness. He was no longer able to eat, save alone, he wrote. Yet Sir Horace Mann with stupid ill-will attributes not only this division of tables, but the cutttng down of the king's stable, to new quarrels with the Cardinal of York, though he knew James was now unable to go out.[3]

[1] The chapel to the right of the choir was restored in 1764 by the Cardinal of York, and the canopy of crimson damask used there at high functions bears his arms.
[2] Add. MSS. 30,463 and following volumes.
[3] State Papers : Tuscany, 66.

In March James again fell seriously ill. It seemed impossible that he could recover. Mann reports that the Duke of York was inconsolable, but adds sarcastically and self-contradictorily, that he found comfort in his ecclesiastical occupations. No doubt he did, and so much the better for him and the worse for nobody. James lingered, hanging between life and death but fully conscious. On April 16, his son gave him the last sacraments. Mann says that preparations were made for the instant departure of the cardinal with Cardinal John Francis Albani as soon as his father should be dead ; whither, Mann could not find out ; perhaps to seek —or to avoid—the new king. James recovered, but so slowly and so imperfectly that until well on in June the Church of the Holy Apostles was adorned by scaffolding in preparation for his funeral. From henceforth he could attend to no business beyond assenting to what was submitted to him for signature by the Cardinal of York and Lord Alford, who opened all his letters and troubled him as little as possible.[1]

While he lay so ill a great change was going on in Prince Charles's household. Miss Walkinshaw was trying to leave him ; had appealed for help to King James, who insisted that she and her child must retire to a convent where he engaged to maintain them decently (May 29, 1759). Charles was a consenting party to the arrangement, only dreading lest she should betray the many secrets she knew, were she free from him. But he changed his mind, or the lady did, for it was not until the following July, 1760, that Miss Walkinshaw fled with her daughter from Prince Charles and took refuge in a Parisian convent under the protection of Louis XV. James was unable to do more than authorise the Cardinal of York to give all possible assistance, and to rejoice in the ending of that unfortunate liaison. Miss Walkinshaw was liberally pensioned with £6000 a year, and the best of education was provided for her daughter, now seven years old. Charles stormed, threatened to burn down all the convents in Paris unless the fugitives were given up to him ; but Louis XV., armed with the authority of the King of England, refused to interfere between the prince and that monarch's obedient

---

[1] James's will was dated November 21, 1760 ; the codicil, May 26, 1762.

subjects.   They were hidden first in the Convent of the
Visitation, Rue du Bacq ; later they retired to the Saint Sacra-
ment.   Miss Walkinshaw from this period bore the title of
Countess Alberstroff.

In October of that year, 1760, George II. died.   Mann
heard that James had issued a protest against the new accession but failed to procure a copy.   Lord Lismore's death
happened a little later, and in the following January the
new Lord Lismore came to Rome, expecting to take up his
abode at the court and provided with splendour suitable
thereto.   He was kindly received but not invited to stay,
and suddenly returned to his mother in Paris.   The Cardinal
of York did not like Lady Lismore and her son.   Her ladyship had again been in deep disgrace with the French
government and in 1759 had been condemned to banishment
to Caen by *lettre de cachet.*   Through the intercession of Madame
de Pompadour, approached by De Stainville on behalf of King
James, her sentence was commuted, to her great content, to
banishment beyond fifteen leagues of Paris.   She established
herself at Montigny.

Weak and ill and living apart from politics as he was,
James was again much distressed by the independent action of
the Cardinal of York, who absented himself (January 1761)
from the congregation of cardinals who voted for the beatification of a Spanish missionary named Palafox, " whom the
Jesuits had persecuted," says Mann ; but it was rather Palafox
who had persecuted the Jesuits.   He was an American bishop
of high character, but a bitter enemy of the Society of Jesus
against which he had written an outrageous book.   At this
date of the approaching suppression of the Society, in which
France and Spain were particularly concerned, great efforts
were being made by the Society's enemies to secure his
beatification.   The Pope, endeavouring to escape from actual
suppression, used this contested beatification as an excuse for
delay, saying that he would combine the two acts ; but
the implacable court of Spain saw through the excuse, as the
process of beatification would necessarily be long, and insisted
on despatch.   James was distressed that Henry should oppose
and annoy Spain to whom they owed so much, and sent an
apologetic letter to the King of Spain which was unfavourably
received.   Mann attributed Henry's conscientious, most dis-

1761. interested action to Jesuit influence, thus seizing the opportunity further to injure the Stuarts in France as well as in England, as supporters of the unpopular Society against which animosity was so ominously gathering. But Mann is mistaken in saying that Henry atoned by his presence at the beatification of Palafox in March, having been threatened by Spain with forfeiture of his Spanish benefices and being anxious to assure Spain of his sympathy in the new war against England, for the simple reason that Palafox never was beatified. Prince Charles, according to Macallester, professed to go in fear of his life from the Jesuits ; this, no doubt to show the English that they had nothing to fear from his popularity with the Society.

On July 13, 1761, the Cardinal Duke of York was enthroned as Bishop of Frascati, one of the six Roman sees that are the titular churches of the six cardinal-bishops, and until his death,[1] nearly half a century later, Frascati was his best loved home. This transfer of course involved the resignation of his cardinal-priest's titular church in Rome.

His triumphal entry into Frascati is described in the local records ;[2] how in the blazing July weather he was received by the joyous cries of holiday crowds and escorted by them to the episcopal palace, La Rocca, which fronts the level sweep of the Campagna like a grey fortress from its steep height : grim and strong enough for a prince of Guelf and Ghibelline wars rather than for a peaceful prince of the Church. Its gardens were said to be the site of the gardens of Lucullus. Deputations, banquets, free flowing of wine and illumination of the lovely villages round about, acclaimed the new bishop. He was well known in the neighbourhood, his life-long home at Albano being within an easy drive of Frascati. Henry always loved barbaric splendour and here he lived a life as splendid in its bounty as in its royal state.

He was now a wealthy man and he spent his wealth with boundless generosity, He lived most religiously and was ever loyal to the royal rights of his house, but his life was un-shadowed either by asceticism or the melancholy of exile.

---

[1] On the anniversary of his enthronement. Frascati was not long ago the see of another English bishop, Cardinal Howard.
[2] Given at length in " A Court in Exile," by the Marchesa Vitelleschi.

Truly, his name lives on in the small city he loved so much. 1761.
The very stones cry out its affection and gratitude in the
numerous marble inscriptions all about Frascati, testifying to
this day on wells, walls, and other buildings to the munificence
of Henry, Duke of York and cardinal. The old twelfth-century
castle was in such bad repair that at a banquet in 1775 the
floor gave way, and cardinal and guests were precipitated into
the coach-house beneath. The prince was caught by the
roofs of the coaches and less hurt than the guests. He then
put the old castle into thorough repair without taking from it
its look of hoary antiquity, a mercy rare in that age. He
adorned the private chapel which remains as he left it, though
in other respects the palace looks sadly in need of another
generous resident bishop. He interested himself intensely in
the Seminary. The Jesuits had been masters there since 1701,
but though English spies, to please their paymasters, had
accused him of overmuch sympathy with Jesuits, he probably
disliked their quasi-independence of himself as bishop. He
therefore persuaded the Pope to separate the Seminary entirely
from the college, and thus he had complete control thereof.
The whole institution was placed under episcopal jurisdiction,
inclusive even of the Jesuit church. In 1774 he founded
the fine library of the Seminary which still exists exactly
as he left it, chairs standing round the table and his marble
bust presiding from the wall. He spared no expense to
obtain rare editions and works in all languages and on all
subjects.

His hospitality was royal in the fullest sense. He kept a
suite of forty persons about him, forty horses, and many costly
equipages. His tenderness, alas! did not extend to his horses,
but his charity to the poor was boundless. There was not a
poor person left in Frascati or for miles round, and his inexhaustible efforts to improve their condition was not mere
almsgiving and pauperisation.

He had the faults of his qualities and his pride offended
those who were above his charities. His conversation was less
admired in society than his brother's, who was a good talker
and always interested people. His love of literature and
culture did not save him from following the vandal fashion
of his day and of previous days, which stripped the Colosseum
to build modern Roman palaces. He destroyed the last frag-

1761. ments of the famous temple of Jupiter Latiaris on Monte Cavo (the ancient Mons Albanus), one of the best preserved remains of ancient Rome, and used the huge blocks of stone for building a wall round the garden of the Passionist convent on the top of the hill where there are now a meteorological observatory and an inn.

There is in the British Museum an interesting collection of papers relating to him in his episcopal capacity; edicts and other documents, and sonnets addressed to him in Latin and Italian. Even discounting the effusiveness then considered due from sonnetteers to one of doubly princely rank, those remains are valuable evidences of the affection and honour in which he was held.

The accession of George III. recalled English attention to the princes over the water. " Pray is there any print of the Cardinal of York ? " Horace Walpole had written to Sir Horace Mann, January 2, 1761. " If there is, do send me one." Again, March 3 : " Pray, is there a print of the Cardinal of York or medal of him ? If there is, do be so good as to send them to me."

King James never saw his dear son in his beautiful new home. His pleasant sojourns at Albano had come to an end a year or two ago. He dragged out his fragile life in his room, while Henry went from honour to honour. Charles made his own terrible progress from shame to shame. He now had his headquarters at Liége, and, says Mann, took frequent journeys in disguise to Paris and Switzerland. He had taken to drinking harder since the loss of his child and her mother : " was drunk as soon as he rose and was carried senseless to bed at night." Yet if a famous story of that year is true, he must have exerted himself on one great occasion.

On September 22, George III. was crowned. To that magnificent and popular ceremony, the triumph of the new over the old,[1] two stories of old romance are attached : one,

---

[1] Many Jacobites took part in the ceremony, though Horace Walpole says the attendance of peers and peeresses was small. The Earl, of Errol, who officiated as High Constable of Scotland, was the son of Lord Kilmarnock, condemned to death in that same hall in 1746. He was not insensible to the tragic association of the spot. Buried in thought, he forgot to take off his hat when King George appeared. The king received his respectful apology with his own invariable generosity and prayed him to be covered, "for he looked upon his presence at the solemnity as a very particular honour." Gray's Letters : ed. Tovey, ii. preface, vii.

that the vanquished and banished heir of the Stuarts was present to see his victorious rival's coronation ; the other, that on the champion's challenge, the gauntlet was picked up by an Unknown, who left upon that historic floor, the stage of a Stuart king's trial and of the trials of those who had fought for his heirs, his gage of defiant protest.[1] Alas ! for the latter story there is no shadow of evidence, though Sir Walter Scott liked to believe in it a little. Neither in the contemporary and circumstantial newspaper accounts, nor in the minute and picturesque account of Horace Walpole who was present, is there any allusion whatever to such a dramatic incident. For the other and even more thrilling story, we have only the word of the Earl Marischal, but he was a very honest man, and there is nothing to discredit the story in the contemporary movements of the prince. The Earl Marischal, we know, told his friend Hume, the historian, that he had the information from a friend who was present and not only recognised the prince but whispered his surprise in the royal ear ; that the heir of all the Plantagenets and all the Stuarts had replied, that curiosity alone had brought him, and that, in other words, the grapes were very sour. Since the defeat of Conflans, Charles, according to Macallester, had often been hanging about the English coasts, looking for convenient landing-places for his still purposed invasion, and Dumont told Macallester that the French were determined on the invasion of England in the winter of 1762. The magnetism of a great and rare state ceremony is very strong, and it would surely have been against nature had it not drawn a rover like Charles once more across the silver streak. Danger was never more than salt of life to him. Access to the abbey could be managed with comparative ease in those days of rudimentary police, and seeing how many sympathisers were among the illustrious crowd. Even in these well-policed days, we know how elaborate must be the precautions to guard such ceremonies from the bomb of the modern conspirator. In 1773, Hume wrote to Sir John Pringle, giving him this story of the Earl Marischal's, with others. That the others are inaccurate or untrue, as the date of Charles's visit to London,

[1] Early in 1761, Alexander Murray from London informed Charles that his adherents were about to publish a protest against the coronation. If Charles should remain obdurate, they would approach the King of Sardinia, the next heir after Charles, exclusive of the impossible Cardinal of York.

M

1761. known to George II., and the silly lie that he had had to be carried on deck bound hand and foot, shrinking from his Scottish adventure in 1745, does not necessarily discredit the coronation story told to Hume very shortly after the event. "You see this story is so near traced from the fountain head," says Hume, "as to wear a great face of probability. Query, what if the Pretender had taken up Dymoke's gauntlet?" The innocence of this last query entirely disposes of the legend that the gauntlet *was* picked up. Horace Walpole more than half believed the story of the prince's presence at the coronation.

CHAPTER XIII

THE CLOSE OF A LONG REIGN

JAMES lingered on, so feeble and so shadow-like in his extreme 1762.
tenuity that he looked scarcely a being of flesh and blood ; yet
in spite of Mann's gloomy reports of his bodily and mental
decay, his mind seems to have been fairly clear to the last.
Mann expected every day to hear of his death, economically
adding to his bulletins to Pitt, now in office, that he supposed
it would not be worth while to send the news by express. The
spies continued to find James able to quarrel with the Duke
of York, making much of the querulousness of a hypochondria-
cal invalid. In 1760 he was able at times to return thanks
in person for visits of inquiry during his severe attacks, when
great concern had been shown for him by Roman society.
Charles never now wrote to him and he never mentioned
Charles.

On September 24, 1762, his good old secretary, James
Edgar, died, a Protestant as he had lived, in spite of the efforts
of the Cardinal of York at his deathbed to bring him into
the fold of the Church. John Kerrich, the correspondent responsible for this news, adds that, in Rome Henry was considered
" proud and foolish, but withal charitable and humane." [1] A
fortnight after Edgar's death, James had a stroke of paralysis,
and his death was again looked for as certain. To the
astonishment of his doctors and friends he recovered, but his
memory was gone and his speech hardly intelligible. Mann
censures Henry because at this time he was living at Frascati
and frequent expresses had to be sent to him ; forgetting that
he had duties there and could have little served or pleasured
his father by his continuous presence. He was in very delicate
health himself and needed country air, and Frascati was within
very easy reach.

On February 10, 1763, peace was signed at Fontainebleau 1763.
and ended not only the Seven Years' War but the last hope of

---

[1] Hist. MSS. Comm. Reports X., part i. p. 345. (C. F. Weston Underwood's MSS.)

1763. invasion of England on behalf of the Stuarts. Only a spark was to twinkle from the ashes of the cause some years later, to flicker out into darkness at once and for ever.

Early in 1763, Henry fell dangerously ill of typhus fever and was slow to recover his health. In May he was appointed vice-chancellor of St. Peter's, which great dignity carried with it the magnificent palace of the Cancellaria, built by Bramante for Cardinal Riario, Pope Sixtus IV.'s nephew, with stones from the Colosseum and decorated with marbles torn from the church of San Lorenzo in Damaso. There was much deliberation, even hot dispute, as to the consequent order of his titles ; whether the dukedom of York must be inserted on his official documents, and in what order. The difficulty came of the vice-chancellor's necessary contact with foreign courts who could not recognise the English title. The ducal title was retained, placed second on the list, the episcopal title and cardinalate preceding, the vice-chancellorship ending the roll. That there should be such discussion is significant of contemporary Roman feeling, now that the king lay more dead than alive in his silent room. He no longer even signed his name. The Duke of York acted in his stead, staying with his father that he might the better attend to him.

Henry was still in very bad health ; suffering from scurvy, says Mann, a result of his fever. In July he went to Pisa, and Marshal Botha, the Austrian representative in Tuscany, was warned by Mann not to be too polite. Etiquette was carefully arranged before his arrival. Prince Liechtenstein called on him as last comer, addressed him neither as royal highness nor as royal Eminence but simply as Monseigneur. This was highly disapproved by James and the papal court, says Mann. James could hardly know of it. Henry kept open house, invited all Pisan society, performed public functions in the cathedral, and recovered his health, but etiquette forbade a much desired visit to Florence. He spent a few days at Bologna with his friend Angelelli, and then travelled by Loreto to Rome.[1] He returned, however, to Pisa the following year, 1764, after removing into his palace of the Cancellaria, and on this occasion, Botha being absent, he did stop and see Florence.

Illness and the care of administering what was left of his

---

[1] August 19, 1763. *Diario di Bologna :* Galeati.

PALACE OF THE CANCELLARIA, ROME

father's kingdom did not diminish his unresting care for his 1763.
diocese, nor did the unpopularity his zeal had earned for him
with the chapter of St. Peter's hold him back from his duty to
his clergy of Frascati.   Scandals abounded in those lax, post-
Renaissance days, and they should not be tolerated under the
rule of this earnest young bishop.   In 1763 he summoned a
synod of his diocese for clerical reform, with real fatherly
kindness entertaining them hospitably at the Villa Aldobrandini
while he castigated their conduct and insisted, in the teeth
of angry opposition, upon root and branch reform.

In 1763, at the end of the year, old Lord Alford in his
turn was compelled by years and gout to resign the chief
secretaryship, and Andrew Lumisden became sole secretary.
There was very little to do now.   An important piece of preferment fell to the Cardinal of York in that same year on the
death of Cardinal Spinelli, Protector of Scotland, and Henry
obtained the protectorship for his friend John Francis Albani.

It was no light task to fill his father's place in administering
the limited sums that could be spared from necessities to
relieve the wants of the quite unlimited number of beggars,
noble and otherwise, who applied to the Muti Palace for relief.
So it had been from the first, from the old St. Germain's days,
though the Stuart family were themselves living on charity.

The duke was very willing to continue the king's charities
to his distressed subjects, but Lumisden was afraid that his
kindness would be tired out by constant ûnreasonable demands ; such as those, for instance, of the hopeless Lord
Strathallan, a typical case.   His lordship had had very
large sums from the king and had recently got through
a gift of 14,000 livres with remarkable speed.   Now he applied
for more to pay heavy debts.   Lumisden refused to pass
his letter on to the duke, who could not justly waste the
king's money in such a way, especially as James had a strong
aversion from Lord Strathallan.   However, in April 1765,
Henry granted 3000 livres to be paid to him, on condition
that he should ask for no more and keep the gift a secret,
lest similar applications should rush in, and he trusted his
lordship would live frugally, as his circumstances and those
of the royal family rendered so necessary.   He was even
very sorry when Lord Strathallan died in the following July ;
promised to do all he could for his family, and interested

1764. himself at the French court on the widow's behalf. Then the rapacious family, like the daughters of the horse-leech, annoyed him by demanding that their pension should be guaranteed to continue after the king's approaching death. This the duke would not promise.

Another burden upon the finances he administered was Miss Walkinshaw, with her daughter. He could never forgive their existence and would not communicate with them, except through Lumisden and Mr. Waters, the king's banker at Paris, though Miss Walkinshaw wrote persistently to the cardinal, the source of her income, sometimes politely with seasonable compliments, sometimes angrily with demands for more money. Lumisden's correspondence with her began 1765. in January 1765, when directed to answer her Christmas greetings to his royal highness. A Monsieur Brunet was the duke's confidential adviser in Paris, where Lady Lismore, with her son, had been managing Jacobite affairs until the Duke of York informed her that his majesty had no further occasion for her services.

Most unexpected applications came in constantly, ghosts from a long-dead past. One of these was from the woman of the little house in Bologna where Clementina Sobieska spent the few days before her marriage by proxy; where the marriage took place. About the end of 1759 and again in 1766, this woman, very old and reduced to extreme misery, applied to King James for help.[2]

Henry had been devoted in attendance upon his father till James became too weak and lethargic to care who was about him. Now he devoted himself to the interests of his brother. He reopened communication between himself and that difficult personage and entreated him to come to Rome before their father's death, as his presence would make all the difference in his future position. He strained every nerve to fight against the hostile influences that dominated the papal court, and behaved in a singularly disinterested way with regard to his brother, to the admiration of Lumisden. There were signs not to be mistaken that with King James the last shred of Stuart royalty would pass away. In 1764 George III.'s scape-

---

[1] Dennistoun's "Life of Sir Robert Strange," vol. i. p. 215. Henry kindly interested himself for Strange (the engraver), to obtain access for him to the pictures of the churlish Count Zampieri, applying again and again though always in vain.

[2] University Library, Bologna: MS. 3893, No. 23.

grace brother, Edward, Duke of York, arrived in Rome, travel- 1764. ling incognito as Earl of Ulster, but nevertheless much fêted in the towns he had visited.   Roman official society welcomed him with honour, to the profound annoyance of the Stuart court, though the French ambassador stood loyally aloof ; "behaved very uncivilly," says Mann.   Such an insult would not have happened, Lumisden says of Roman opportunism, had the king been in his former vigour.   The *de jure* Duke of York went out of town to avoid awkward encounters.   The Jacobites consoled themselves by talking bitterly and contemptuously, yet not untruly, of the Hanoverian prince as a low-bred covetous youth.   He drank himself to death at Monaco three years later.[1]

Henry induced the Pope to invite Prince Charles to Rome. 1765. To remove the objection of expense to the Camera, he proposed to resign the reversion of his Roman pension to his brother. He would also hand over to Charles whatever money he should inherit from his father.   But Charles refused to come unless the Pope would promise to recognise him as king in succession to his father.   This the Pope was compelled to refuse, though he promised him every kindness and every honour short of the supreme honour.   Charles would have nothing of Rome with the title of Prince of Wales, which he truly said would be absurd.   Again and again Henry urged him to come. Charles sent assurances of profound veneration for the Pope and would come at once—conditionally, upon recognition. He fully empowered his brother to act for him and waited at Bouillon.   Nobody must be told of his intended journey except those who were indispensable.   "If I had the wings of a bird," he wrote with more poetry than sincerity, "we should soon be satisfied."   But he wanted something else than wings and little less difficult to come by.   Henry was in despair ; consoled only by knowing that he had done all that lay in his power.

James lingered, all but dead.   He had no ascertained disease, Dennistoun repeats, who knew from Lumisden. Nothing ailed him but the universal decline of nature.   The doctors had always said the same.   Even now, digestion and appetite continued almost unimpaired, but he was weakened by the many surgical bleedings of the period.

On New Year's Day, 1766, about nine o'clock of the

---

[1] Some accounts give Cagliari for Monaco.

1766. evening,[1] the weary pilgrimage of "poor old Mr. James Misfortunate" came to an end. The Duke of York was not present at the very last, having retired, exhausted by the pain and suspense of the closing hours, to his chamberlain's lodging.

That quiet death ended as pure and noble a life as ever man lived in this difficult world. James III. had not been called upon to lay down his life in blood for his faith, but he had with firm will and open eyes laid down three kingdoms for it, and chosen a life of poverty, suffering, and contempt. No man ever wore more fitly a white flower for his symbol. Through all his nearly seventy-eight years, in spite of all the fierce temptations that beset a prince in his position and of his age, he had remained stainless and true. A confessor if not martyr he truly was.

> " A sweeter and a lovelier gentleman
> . . . valiant, wise and, no doubt, right royal,
> The spacious world cannot again afford."

> " His life was gentle ; and the elements
> So mixed in him, that Nature might stand up,
> And say to all the world, This was a man."

The Duke of York was too much overcome with grief to write to Charles, and commissioned Lumisden to do so. He does not seem to have had much confidence in papal promises already made, though he did not doubt that, with prudence, he would be able to procure everything his brother could require from the Roman court. But as it was a dilatory court and wedded to ceremonial, he asked Charles to stop at Bologna or Urbino till all difficulties should be removed. Casa Angelelli at Bologna was prepared for him,[2] and Cardinal John Francis Albani sent directions to have the Albani palace at Urbino also made ready for him. It was considered better that, until the Pope should have fully recognised him, he should stay in a private palace, not in the papal castle in which his father had lived before marriage. He must write a letter from thence to the Pope, thanking him for his kindness, and reminding His Holiness that he had come on his holy and warm invitation.

All Roman society was heartily with the Cardinal Duke, who, sensible that any countenance or recommendation to the Pope from France and Spain would remove every difficulty,

---

[1] State Papers : Tuscany.   Sir Horace Mann.
[2] *Il Palazzo Vizani*, by A. Longhi, Bologna.

wrote to both courts to that effect. The French and Spanish 1766. ambassadors supported him, but privately, they said ; not as representing their courts.[1] The Maltese envoy also supported him "privately" for old friendship's sake. This was now the Abbé de Breteuil, son of Laura O'Brien of Clare. Henry was advised by "persons of great distinction, not Italians," that Charles should come directly to Rome. His presence would force the papal hand, but he was warned that he would have much need for patience before all was finally settled. Lumisden was convinced that had Charles taken his brother's advice and been in Rome long ago, all difficulty would have been prevented.

In spite of his invitation and his sympathy, the Pope could not see his way to giving Charles the titles he insisted upon. He called a congregation of cardinals to discuss the matter. Cardinal Negroni, once in the Duke of York's service, was excluded from the congregation as thereby disqualified, but Cardinal Alexander Albani, accredited minister of the Emperor, and firm upholder of the House of Hanover,[2] was admitted, so that the influence of the House of Austria preponderated. The Pope refused to receive the Cardinal Duke's memorial, even though the French ambassador had been for the recognition ; which is suggestive, as compared with the movings of French diplomacy since 1747 ; even since 1712.

Sir Horace Mann credited himself with the thwarting of the French ambassador's sympathies. "Very trifling circumstances might turn the French scale," he admitted, January 17, 1766. He describes the conflict in a letter to Horace Walpole, September 18, 1784 :—

"You may remember the struggle which I then had with the Marquis d'Aubeterre, the French ambassador at Rome, which he never forgave me, and some years afterwards expressed himself to the Marquis de Barbautane, who questioned him about it, in these words : 'Hé ! M. le Marquis, je croyais faire le plus beau coup possible, mais je ne fis qu'un pas de clerc. Ce diable, M. Mann, m'avait prévenu et gâta mon projet,' which was to take the Pope by surprise. But in my letters to old Cardinal Albani,[3] which were read in the consistory held on

---

[1] Sir Horace Mann. State Papers : Tuscany.

[2] "As staunch as a heretic in our favour," says Mann, who expected little from the other cardinals, for the Pope was in failing health and a conclave drawing near. Hence France and Spain must not be offended by ambitious cardinals.

[3] Alexander, born 1692.

1766. the subject, I asserted that the French ambassador could not have received orders from his court, whose engagements with that of England had made it inconsistent with its honour to insist upon it ; that the ambassador had laid a snare for the Pope, which he might avoid by only waiting for an answer from Paris, which I was very sure would bring a disavowal of the ambassador's conduct. That encouraged the Pope to tell him that if his master would be the first, he would be the second to acknowledge him under the title he contended for. The answer from France was such as I foretold ; and General Conway, who was then Secretary of State, conveyed to me the king's approbation of what I had done."

This action of French diplomacy proves what were the contemporary views of the French government with regard to Charles. It is out of the question to suppose that the ambassador acted without the direction of his government, though, France and England being officially at peace, that government must deny all complicity. But there was rankling in the soul of France the recent memory of the Seven Years' War which had resulted in the complete overthrow by England of French power in America and India. The British flag waved over Canada, and the peace of Paris had bereft France of Louisiana, several West Indian islands, and her African possessions. Such a peace was little less galling to a proud nation than the Peace of Versailles in 1871, and France was not likely to wait for retaliation longer than necessity compelled. Meantime she largely availed herself of any opportunity which lay at hand of embarrassing the British government. One safe card she always held in reserve. She must once more play "the Pretender." As yet, it must be done with great caution and secrecy.

"It is impossible to express the duke's zeal and activity at this critical conjuncture," Lumisden wrote to Lord Alford. In spite of his grief, and "the indecency of going abroad before his father's obsequies were performed," Henry sought and obtained an audience of the Pope on Friday night, January 3rd. The Pope repeated what he had said to Cardinal John Francis Albani. He intended no injustice, but in present circumstances he could not take any definite step ; though he allowed the duke's memorial to be shown to the Sacred

College. The indefatigable duke went immediately, that same night, to Cardinal Rezzonico and to Cardinal Torrigiani. He repeated what he had said to the Pope, but received the same answer. He then worked on the ambassadors of Spain and Naples. The French ambassador was still for the recognition and hoped with Henry that the Pope would even yet grant so reasonable a demand.

Next, the duke wrote to the kings themselves. The ambassadors forwarded his letters. To the King of France he also transmitted a letter left by King James to be forwarded after his death, praying His Most Christian Majesty to continue to Charles at least the proofs of generosity he himself had so long enjoyed.

For himself, the cardinal had a medal struck: it is given here and by Lord Mahon, dated 1766. It bears on the obverse his portrait, episcopally attired: a handsome profile with fine, prominent nose ; the parted lips giving something of vacancy to the sweetly innocent expression ; a remarkably youthful face for his forty-one years. The hair curls prettily under the zucchetta : his hair had once been a distinguishing feature in his portraits. The inscription runs : " Henricus M. D. Ep. Tusc : Card : Dux Ebor : S.R.E.V. Canc." On the reverse, a female figure leans against a cross ; a sorrowing lion crouches at her feet. St. Peter's basilica stands in the background. Around runs the famous legend : " Non desideriis hominum sed voluntate Dei." The inscriptions differ in several particulars with those of his "accession" in 1788.

King James was buried in St. Peter's on January 7, with all the splendour due to a king. It was the last "recognition." Lumisden as secretary, set his seal on the coffin. His services were transferred to King Charles III., whom he was at once sent to meet and inform of the papal will.

Sir Horace Mann heard that the Cardinal of York, from benefices in France, Spain, and Rome, had now an income of nearly 60,000 crowns : about £15,000 sterling. By his will, it was said James left all his French investments and other possessions to Prince Charles, his Roman monies, including 27,000 crowns in the public funds, to the Duke of York, charged with many legacies and pensions to his household. Accounts vary very much as to these moneys, as the actual sums varied and the dates of payment.

CHAPTER XIV

KING CHARLES III

1766. LUMISDEN and the new king met on January 20th between Florence and Bologna. Charles was now forty-nine years old, his birthday having fallen on New Year's Eve. Lumisden was agreeably surprised by his handsome, healthy appearance. Distressing rumours of sad disfigurement had reached the sorrowful court at Rome ; of pimples and other insignia of debauched living. But Lumisden found his new master no stouter than was " jolly," and the face that had fired the topmost peaks of Albyn was rosy, yet unpimpled.

He was in high good humour in spite of the unexpected check ; very affectionate ; pleased to hear that his mother's rooms had been prepared for him. He counted upon arriving in Rome on Thursday the 23rd, between ten and eleven at night. The roads were covered with snow and ice, and the travellers risked breaking their necks every moment. Charles had already, two days before the meeting, been upset over a precipice, but had taken no harm, though his legs were painfully swollen from the confinement and fatigue of the journey. As he could not be received at Rome *en roi*, he stayed at Albano. He had with him Mackintosh, master of the horse, Sir John Hay, groom of the bedchamber, and Eyre, an equerry. Stafford, who had been living at Avignon, joined him later.

He behaved like a true Christian hero, says his enthusiastic friend, Oliphant of Gask. As far as he could, he behaved like a king too, for he at once created Sir John Hay (of Restalrig) a baron and made him master of his household. Sir John is probably "the Giovannino" who, with the violoncello, was Charles's chief solace.

It really seemed as if Charles, now he had returned from his angry self-banishment and found himself head of the royal house, were doing his best to turn over a new leaf. To gain the support of the Pope and of his father's old allies, he must

188

of course be on good behaviour, and his old affection for his 1766. brother revived and influenced him strongly on seeing how much that brother was doing for him. Henry had renounced the world—in a measure—for himself, but he went on doing his utmost for the lofty claim of his forgiven brother and sovereign. He who had once been granted mortifying precedence as a prince of the church over his elder brother, the Prince of Wales, now rode publicly through the streets of Rome with that brother seated on his right hand ; a place due from a cardinal in Rome to nothing less than a crowned head. Roman society did not like it, says Mann. But St. Peter's had shaken hands with St. James's and refused to acknowledge another Stuart king.

There is a published letter from an English gentleman on his travels to a friend in London, dated March 21, 1766, which describes Charles as he was just after his accession. " His person is tall and rather lusty. His complexion has a redness in it, not unlike the effects of drinking. . . . He has ever since [Miss Walkinshaw left him] appeared calm and composed : talked very rationally, and read much and been fond of music. As to his religion, there is not a greater bigot upon earth. He has his bottle for Holy Water at his bed's head ; he never mounts a horse or goes out on a shooting party, but he crosses himself many times, and is strongly attached to the grossest fooleries of the Romish religion. The Romans had conceived him to be a debauchee ; but his behaviour at Rome has been perfectly sober and affable." [1]

But the ill seeds he had sown were still a-reaping. Miss Walkinshaw was giving trouble. One of the first consequences of King James's death was that as Charles would have nothing to do with her, the cardinal took her maintenance and her child's upon himself and was obliged to cut down her pension from 6000 to 5000 livres so that she was compelled to remove to the cheaper convent of Notre Dame at Meaux. She was highly indignant and protested loudly. The reduction was not owing so much to the cardinal's detestation of her existence, as to the very much reduced income of the royal family, so many of the late king's pensions having been discontinued. It could only be an incalculable satisfaction to the cardinal that Charles should take no notice of his late mistress, and Waters,

[1] *Gentleman's Magazine*, vol. xxxvi. p. 228.

1766. the banker, was recommended to mention her only when necessary and by a letter apart addressed to himself, marked on the top thus—X, "for she must never be named to his majesty." He refused absolutely to bring her name before his brother and advised her to refrain from any application in that quarter. She was furious. Lord Elcho visited her at Meaux and very ugly stories were poured by the discarded mistress into the greedy ears of that disappointed and disloyal adherent. Her next move was to set about a report that she had been married to the prince. Even then it was the cardinal who acted : Charles again took no notice. Furiously indignant, in reasonable dread of ultimate complications, Henry compelled her to sign a paper at Paris, 9th March 1767, denying that any sort of marriage had ever taken place between her and Charles. As soon as the deed passed out of her hands, she repented ; wrote the same day to the cardinal complaining of such treatment, and recalled her signature.[1]

Then, in spite of warnings, conditions, and experience, she applied to Charles.[2] He ignored all her letters. "She may write till the day of judgment without having any answer," the cardinal writes, July 7.[3] She wrote again to Charles, July 25, 1767 ; again December 16, 1768, enclosing a letter from Charlotte dated from her convent at Meaux.[4] Charles never replied.

In June 1766, the cardinal made over to his brother the *rentes* payable at the Hotel de Ville in Paris, which had been left to Henry by his father : 16,575 livres which James had inherited from Prince James Sobieski. Charles himself was entitled to 4000 livres of *rentes*, besides 4000 included in the above. All outstanding French loans were consolidated at Paris on March 31, 1767 ; after which he was entitled to the capital sum of 80,000 livres, and to 150,000 livres capital sum from moneys of his father, invested by Cardinal Tencin in 1725–6.[5]

The Pope still offered to call Charles Prince of Wales. The Romans were not allowed to give him the regal title. As

---

[1] *Histoire des Hommes Illustres*, by the Duc de Saint Simon, vol. iv. p. 204.
[2] Hist. MSS. Comm. Reports XV., part ii. p. 251. (Eliot Hodgkin MSS.)
[3] Hist. MSS. Comm. Reports III., p. 421. (MSS. of John Webster, Esq.)
[4] Hist. MSS. Comm. Reports XV., Appendix, part ii. p. 251. (Eliot Hodgkin MSS.)
[5] Hist. MSS. Comm. Reports X., part vi. p. 221. (Braye MSS.)

MEDAL OF HENRY IX., CARDINAL OF YORK, 1788

MEDAL OF THE CARDINAL DUKE OF YORK, 1766

he would receive nobody who refused it to him, his society
was thus limited to his brother and his household. The
English and the Scots Colleges, and the Irish Dominicans and
Franciscans in Rome, sang Te Deums for his accession and
prayed for him by name: wherefore the Pope banished their
Heads from Rome, though they considered themselves Charles's
subjects and not his. Abbé Grant, who received him at the
Scots College, was banished from the Pope's palace, and the
pension he had from the Datory was cut off.[1] In March,
the royal arms of England were removed from over the portals
of the Muti Palace.[2]

The patience Charles showed at first surprised every one,
and greatly increased the number of his friends.

The papal court, seeking about for an excuse for its in-
constancy, found one by raking up the very temporary apostasy
of 1750, when Charles renounced his Catholic faith in the
New Church in the Strand.   There was now set about a report
of the prince's heretical tendencies.   Charles indignantly denied
the charge.   " Thus," laments Lumisden, on the other side,
" in order to conciliate this court and the Roman Catholics in
Great Britain, he was driven to professions ill adapted to
forward his pretensions at home."   Charles naturally complained that while in Rome he was abhorred for a firm
Protestant, in England he was abhorred for a rank papist.
His conversion to Protestantism had been purely for reasons
of temporal interest ; his re-conversion to Catholicism was no
doubt little more sincere.   He was most likely without any
religious belief at all, though his brother's affectionate remonstrances, working upon the remains of his early training, may
have had some genuine effect.

For five of the nine months after his arrival in the Papal
States, he lived in the country, almost in solitude, with no
amusements beyond shooting and playing his beloved violoncello.   In April he went to Palidoro for a month's shooting.
" It is surprising how he resists fatigue," writes Lumisden to
Dunbar : but at Palidoro he over-exerted himself, and was
fatigued for once in his life.[3]   The Duke of York visited him
there.   The property was not then out of the lawyers' hands,

[1] Dennistoun's " Life of Sir Robert Strange," i. 94.   Lumisden to Lord Dunbar.
[2] Mann to Walpole, March 14, 1766.
[3] " Life of Sir Robert Strange," Dennistoun, i. 97.

1766. and Charles had not been granted the continuance of his father's pensions. He was therefore so poor that he had to give up taking in English newspapers and was unable to offer any hospitality to Lord Caryll beyond board and lodging.[1]

What wonder that the moral improvement did not stand the strain of mortification, disappointment, and want of occupation! He went to Albano in August, intending to stay until November ; "his only relief a little music and shooting, but game was scarce," says Lumisden. "Few people go to see him," writes Sir Horace Mann, November 5. Then on the 29th we hear, more in sorrow than in surprise, "he has committed great outrages against some of his people in a drunken fit, pursuing them with a drawn sword."

1767. This story is corroborated by friendly witnesses, but it must have been a temporary aberration and kept secret from gossips, followed by partial improvement. On April 7, 1767, Henry writes: "I have had no very bad account as to the bottle of late, but *ce qui me désole* is the singularity and incomprehensibility of his temper.[2] On May 1 following, Sir William Hamilton, British ambassador at Naples, who married Nelson's Lady Hamilton, writes to Lord Shelbourne that though Charles was "hardly thought of, even at Rome," the life he was then leading was "very regular and sober. His chief occupation is shooting in the environs of Rome, and the only people he can see and converse with are his few attendants, Messrs. Lumisden, Montgomery, &c." He goes on to say that their father's pension was now granted to the cardinal who gave it to Charles, "and, it is said, allowed him 1800 [scudi] more out of his own income." The cardinal's ecclesiastical benefices in Rome were said to amount to 18,000 [scudi] a year, "with which he does much good, being extremely generous. Besides the 3000 he allows the pretender, he is supposed to give at least 2000 more in private donations to support poor families in Rome." He kept open house. Lalande, who visited Rome in 1766, was much struck by the princely liberality of the Cardinal Duke's establishment, where it seemed that any one who had been presented to him might go to dine at will; unlike the use of the other cardinals

---

[1] " Life of Sir Robert Strange," Dennistoun, i. p. 105.
[2] Hist MSS. Comm. Reports IX., part ii. p. 479.

who sent out few invitations to dinner and always with long 1767. ceremonious notice.[1]

On May 12, the cardinal writes that "after much battleying about trifles," he had carried his brother privately, as a private nobleman, to see the Pope, who was "extremely well pleased" with the courtesy, while Charles seemed "well enough content" with his visit. The cardinal hoped all yet might be well, "if my brother does not obstruct all by his indocility and most singular way of thinking and arguing, which indeed passes anybody's comprehension."[2] The Pope presented to Charles a rosary of gold and precious stones. Charles, Henry writes to another correspondent, was "very well pleased of his visit . . . particularly so of having had . . . a present of a pair of beads, of such kind as are only given to Sovrains ; and cou'd wee but gett the better of the nasty bottle, which every now and then comes on by spurts, I would hope a great deal of even gaining a good deal as to other things, but I see that to gett the better of that nasty habit there must be the hand of God."[3]

But a terrible time followed, to the deep distress of the Duke of York. Charles's temper broke down and he flung all restraints to the winds. On June 10, the duke writes: "My brother was here (at Frascati) last Sunday, and is to come again on Saturday to see the ordination. I am persuaded we should gain ground as to everything, were it not for the nasty bottle, that goes on but too much, and certainly must at last kill him. Stafford is in desolation about it, but has no sway."[4]

On July 7th he deplores "the continuance of the bottle ; that, I own to you, makes me despair of everything, and I am of opinion that it is impossible for my brother to live if he continues in this strain."[5] Charles was all that was kind and affectionate, but behaved with "singular inflexibility and disregard for his own good," and the duke was in despair.

An applicant from the past more graciously received than Miss Walkinshaw, was that Routledge who procured the lost man-of-war *Elizabeth* for the expedition of '45, and who now

---

[1] Article upon the *Diario del Cardinale di York*, by A. Ademollo : Nuovo Antologia, 1880. Bologna.
[2] Hist. MSS. Comm. Reports III., p. 421. (MSS. of J. Webster, Esq.)
[3] Ibid. IX., part ii. p. 480.
[4] Ibid. III., p. 267. (Hopkinson MSS.)
[5] Ibid. III., p. 421. (Webster MSS.)

N

1768. wanted compensation for his losses. Charles was obliged to refer him to France, but expressed anxiety to give him and his family substantial marks of his gratitude, and applied to the Cardinal of York to find a benefice for "a very young friend," Routledge's son. This the cardinal gladly did.[1]

In 1768, Pope Clement XIII. died. Charles waited in Rome till the long conclave came to an end, and he should see what the new Pope would do for him. Unhappily he was drinking hard, though he attended public amusements, and had taken boxes at the opera for the last carnival. On December 8th, a great scandal happened. He insisted upon going drunk to an oratorio. His gentlemen-in-waiting, Andrew Lumisden, Hay of Restalrig, and Mr. Urquhart, refused to attend him in such a condition. He flew into a fury of passion, and dismissed them from his service.

The day before he left Rome, Lumisden went to take leave of the cardinal, "caged up like a bird in the conclave." His royal highness had been pleased publicly to approve of the conduct of the gentlemen and secretary, and to thank them for their behaviour in the most gracious manner. He was pleased with Lumisden's visit and gave him a snuff-box which had belonged to the late king, as a small token of grateful remembrance for faithful service. A day or two later Charles commanded his servants' return, but the cardinal advised them not to go back and replaced them by four Italians, one of whom had been at the court of Modena, as better fitted for the undesirable service than Scottish gentlemen. He wished John Stuart, an Athol man, had been dismissed too, but master and servant were unwilling to part, and Stuart stayed with his king until the last. He and Wagstaffe, the Protestant chaplain, were the only Britons Charles had left with him.

This incident of his gentlemen's departure shocked Charles into good behaviour for a while, for Lumisden said a few weeks later that he had never been seen in the least drunk since.

1769. In 1769, Clement XIV. (Ganganelli) was elected to the papal chair, and though the Cardinal of York had voted for him, his new holiness followed the policy of his predecessor and namesake with regard to the Stuarts. Sullen protest and

---

[1] Lumisden in Dennistoun's "Life of Sir Robert Strange," ii. 99. Also Stuart Papers *ap.* Browne's "Highland Clans," iv.: the last of Browne's transcripts.

furious resistance having availed nothing, Charles wearied of 1769. mortification and left Rome for Pisa, Siena, and other Italian towns. He assumed the incognito title of Count of Albany.

The Duke of York settled down to the life of splendid tranquillity that is the lot of a cardinal in Rome. " He sought consolation for the misfortunes of his predecessors," says Bohn, " in scrupulous observances of the duties of religion : apparently secured in his retirement from the storms and vicissitudes too often dependent upon political life." He was still a rich man, though he had denuded himself of so much for the benefit of his brother. He had the magnificent incomes of his Roman appointments, his abbeys of Anchin and St. Amand, and pensions from Spain charged on the bishoprics of Jaen, Malaga, Segovia and Cordova, and the prebends of Chinchilla, Moron, Heurta de Olmos, Gaca, Hermedes, Puerta de Santa Maria, Seville, Utrera, and Menco. The yield of these Spanish pensions and prebends together for one year—1787—was 19,840 scudi.[1] About 1769 he took for his secretary Canon Angelo Cesarini who remained for the whole remaining thirty-eight years of his life his most valued and faithful friend.[2]

Security from the storm and stress of politics for the cardinal was, indeed, only apparent. All the waves and winds that beat upon Charles set his brother's tender soul shaking with anxiety and aching with distress, and called him from the peace he naturally loved to the incessant and thankless labour of trying to guide that wayward and sadly disabled vessel through the surge of restless intrigue, the gloom of despair. His life for the next nineteen years, which would otherwise have been a period of eventless, monotonous peace, is the more interesting and important, if the sadder, through his concern in Charles's troubles.

The cardinal had failed to procure for his brother official recognition as king, but he went on serving him affectionately and loyally. Officious and self-interested favourites had for long years done their best to persuade Charles that Henry had always acted against his interests as far as lay in his power ; that the littleness of a mind never capable of arduous effort, had envied his superiority and thwarted his projects. They

---

[1] Sir William Hamilton.

[2] When later Cesarini was given the dignity of Bishop of Milevi i.p.i., the Cardinal of York settled upon him 600 scudi annually that he might be able to keep up his exalted position.

1771. had fanned the flame of jealousy, stirred by the duke's rising ascendancy at Rome and rank there above his brother and future sovereign ; but now at least there could be no doubt left of Henry's sincere affection as a brother, and loyalty as his brother's first subject. Loyally he served him when he fought against "that nasty bottle": loyally, too, when he gave his consent to his ill-starred marriage.

CHAPTER XV

THE QUEEN OF HEARTS

THE marriage of Charles Edward was only an incident in the new stirring of Jacobite hope and French intrigue which unfortunately happened at the very time when Sir Horace Mann was describing "the Pretender" as "a pitiful object, always drunk or fast asleep." French hatred of victorious England had been smouldering since 1763. In 1771, some French statesmen made up their minds to use the *de jure* King of England as a means of embarrassing the British government. It was easy now to lay hands upon him. He was no longer in hiding, out of sight and out of mind, but living quite openly though in gloomy, unrecognised retirement at Siena. It was perfectly well known that he had abandoned himself to intemperance and was hardly capable of leading a desperate enterprise, but he had never given up hope of recovering his lost crown, though his last and most faithful adherents had given him up, and the Pope, with the rest of Europe, had turned his back upon him. He lived in constant anticipation of being called "to speak to his subjects in Westminster Hall." To his dying day he kept sufficient sequins in a box under his bed to pay his journey to England : determined, as Réné Taillandier touchingly says, to die standing, standard in hand, that he might efface the memory of his miserable life.[1]

On March 15, 1771, Lord Caryll wrote to Charles of a conversation he had had with the Duc de Noailles on the subject of an impending invasion of England, preparation for which was being made beyond the Channel. "I have just received a letter from my agent in England," he says, "who assures me that things are now so far advanced that he only waited my answer to put an end to this long pending affair." He regretted that the new regulations of the French posts

[1] *Revue des Deux Mondes*, 1861 : Essay upon Von Reumont's "Life of the Countess of Albany."

1771. would interfere with his procuring the public papers from England.[1]

But Charles was fifty and his brother was a priest. Their next heir was the King of Sardinia—no name to conjure with in England, still less in Scotland, where it was rather the "auld Stuarts" than the kings by divine right that were beloved. A prince of the ancient dynasty, even handicapped by intemperance, might become formidable to the well-established and prolific House of Hanover, if provided at once with a direct and promising heir, but could not count for very much, however sober, without one. His cousin and ever faithful friend, the Duc de Fitz-James, was authorised by the French government to offer to Charles a handsome pension and a settlement of 240,000 livres if he would marry to please them.

Charles rose at once to the bait. For over thirty years he had been waiting for French help and French money, and at last it was offered. England had always professed her readiness to rise if these were forthcoming, so now, surely, England would stand by her word. He was perfectly willing to marry any selected princess. On August 18, 1771, he left Siena, with great secrecy and elaborate ruses for covering his trail. The world was given to suppose that he had gone to seek a wife in Poland. Sir Horace Mann found out that he had disappeared, but failed to guess whither ; only heard how the Cardinal of York had replied to another *porporato* who inquired : "God prosper him ! but he should have taken this resolution last year !"

"I am sorry that so watchful a cat should have let its mouse slip at last without knowing into what hole it has run," Walpole condoled with Mann, September 26. "To the dissidents in Poland, think you ? why, they have not a cheese-paring left. I should think rather to Spain, to be wafted to Ireland. . . . If it should be so, it will be diverting to hear the loyal ejaculations of the Scotch. . . . I question if my Lord Dunbar himself is a Jacobite now—except in principle. Should I guess right, you must positively come home : you prevented his receiving the crown of England at Rome, and must now keep him from receiving it at Dublin. I know nothing in his favour but the rule of contraries—as his father missed the

---

[1] Hist. MSS. Comm. Reports X., Appendix, part vi. p. 222. (Lord Braye's MSS.)

crown when Queen Anne was on his side: and he himself 1771.
when all Scotland and half England were Jacobites, when
he had conquered his way to Derby, he may be more fortunate
when even the University of Oxford scarce drinks his health."[1]

Charles arrived in Paris on September 9th and put up at
the Hotel de Brunswick, Rue des Prouvaires, calling himself
Mr. Stonor.[2]

Among Lord Braye's Stuart Papers are three scraps endorsed by Caryll as notes " of no consequence, found among
the papers brought from Paris by the king." There is a
sketch of a note to the Duc de Fitz-James ; also a memorandum
as follows :—

" Monday morning at 10½. The two houses by se or
land. The D signing present L. d. de F (le Duc de Fitz-James)
and only Down to be consulted before making any attempt
far off. My sayin to Gros and his brother in trede the
affair enjoining the secret, as also the soverain of the place ;
a renewal of Carignian's[3] proposition. The economy, as one
dose not even know if Gros (the King of France ?) will give
funds, which would derange me very much. Ryan's writing
immediately on or off. Iff on, wait for all things, and what
is desiered to be done, in as little time as possible, and come
with it himself, to give it in Mr. Gordon's name for a necessary
security and remain near or at Paris for the answer."

There are also two notes in his hand, dated Monday,
September 9, to Mr. Gordon, principal of the Scots College
at Paris, and to the Marquis d'Azi, Rue Neuve.

The Duc de Fitz-James was absent, but his son, the Marquis
de Fitz-James, wrote to say that they would both wait upon
his majesty upon the morning of September 10, and hoped
he would excuse their appearance in morning dress.

Several brides were under consideration, the favourite being
the young Princess Marie Louise Ferdinande of Salm-Kryburg.
Unfortunately Charles himself placed the chief difficulties in
his own way. He insisted that now he was about to be
married, he should be recognised as King of England without
further delay, and treated as his father had been ; and that

---

[1] Walpole's Letters to Mann, v. 341.
[2] Hist. MSS. Comm. Reports X., part vi. p. 223.
[3] Perhaps acting as agent for the King of Sardinia.

1771. the subsidies granted to James III., and stopped at his death, should be continued to him. The money was provided, but not the recognition.

More fatal still than that angry insistence was the fact that even now, when so much was at stake, Charles could not show himself fit to be trusted with the conduct of important business. Summoned by the Duc de Choiseul, the French prime minister, to discuss the organisation of the expedition with himself and the Duc de Broglie, Charles presented himself drunk.[1] The Duc d'Aiguillon says he was drunk and besotted during the whole time of his stay in Paris ; capable of committing any folly and absurdity ; quite unfit to be trusted with secrets and schemes.

And the moment seemed so propitious ! He was well received by the Dauphin (afterwards Louis XVI.), the old king's grandson ; whose treatment he described as "everything that could have been desired, if I had been upon the throne."[2]

In spite of the bridegroom's lamentable incapacity, the marriage negotiations, if not the preparations for invasion, went on. All was settled upon except the bride. Charles returned to Italy to make arrangements with his brother and the Pope, leaving full power with Colonel Ryan of Berwick's regiment to arrange matters with the Princess of Salm ; or, failing her, with any princess of suitable rank, birth, age, and appearance. The Marquis de Fitz-James accompanied him, but returned to Paris in November.[3]

Secrecy had been well kept. On October 22, Walpole still wrote to Mann: "The clouds that concealed the pretender's elopement seem to disperse. It is affirmed that he is in the *Highlands* of Poland, with the Catholics and dissidents. I hear from Paris that his cousin, the Marquis de Fitz-James, is going to him with a commission from Louis the *well behated*. . . . I do not comprehend it, and pity the poor *true blue* Sobieskists, who are to be betrayed and drawn into their destruction like the Jacobites in Scotland."[4]

In October, stopping at Genoa on the way to Rome, Charles encountered his Hanoverian cousin, the Duke of Gloucester,

---

[1] Sir Nathaniel Wraxall's " Memoirs of my own Time " (ed. 1904), pp. 181–182.
[2] Hist. MSS. Comm. Reports X., part vi. p. 229. (Lord Braye's MSS.)
[3] Ibid. p. 225. (Lord Braye's MSS.)
[4] Walpole's Letters, v. 344.

then resident there with his bride, Lady Waldegrave, for whose 1771.
unroyal sake he was in disgrace with his brother George III.
Several versions were given of the incident. Sir Horace Mann
says the princes met "full butt" in the streets of Genoa and
bowed most graciously to each other. Certain English papers
asserted that Charles had refused to allow the Duke of Gloucester's carriage to pass him. Lumisden declares this to be
all false ; that they met three times in the narrow streets, and
that each time "the denominated duke" voluntarily ordered
"his carriage by, and with the glasses down, very respectfully
saluted His Majesty."[1]

This courtesy gave immense pleasure to the crownless king,
whose proud heart had suffered so much bitter mortification,
and he brackets it triumphantly with the Dauphin's treatment.

Sir Horace Mann reports that Charles misbehaved himself sadly on his return to Rome, and was drunk every day.
Cardinal Marefoschi warned Caryll that his majesty must
not disgust the Pope and the Cardinal of York. He was
clamouring again at Rome to be recognised as king like his
father ; posing as a sufferer for conscience' sake, though all
Rome knew that he had once formally renounced his religion,
and was now practically of no religion at all.

The Salm marriage fell through, as did others. There
remained the two fatherless, penniless, princesses of Stolberg-
Gueldern, pensioners of the Empress Maria Theresa. Louise,
the elder, was nineteen, and had been provisionally provided
for as a canoness in a Chapter of Noble Ladies at Mons. She
had many quarterings, though no money. She was pretty in
a small, piquant, commonplace way, with dark blue eyes
(Alfieri described them as "nerissimi occhi"), a retroussé nose,
very fair hair, and a dazzling complexion, which she supposed
herself to improve by plastering with rouge. In her portrait
in the National Portrait Gallery, by Batoni, her features seem
too small for her broad German face. In middle age, all trace
of beauty was gone.[2] She was highly intellectual, fond of
literature and the arts, though it was under a later influence
that her intellect was to develop. Her letters are remarkably
well and gracefully written. Charles wrote to the Marquis de

[1] "Life of Sir Robert Strange," vol. ii., Appendix, p. 317.
[2] In her portrait by Fabre in the Uffizi, she is a plain, rather coarse German
Hausfrau.

1772. Fitz-James that he selected her in preference to her sister, as being of more suitable age and healthier, and they were married by proxy on March 28. Her sister Catherine was presently married to another Fitz-James, the Marquis of Jamaica, son of the third Duke of Berwick and Liria.

This piece of news travelled more swiftly to England, and on April 9 Walpole wrote to Mann: "It is uncommon for *me* to send you news of the pretender. He has been married in Paris by proxy to a Princess of Stolberg. The new pretendress is said to be but sixteen and a Lutheran. I suppose they mean to carry on the breed in the way it began, by a spurious child. . . . This event seems to explain the pretender's disappearance last autumn."

Charles and Louise were married at Macerata on Good Friday, April 17, 1772, "the mourning day of all Christendom," as the poor bride was to remember in the day of fulfilled omen. She was immensely admired, and Charles was much pleased with her. At first she was rather pleased with her king, who turned over a new leaf in honour of his wedding and showed himself as one not void of attraction; "a large lean man," he is described at this time by an English visitor, "of kindly disposition, talkative, delighted to talk of his adventures, and to speak English, and of perfectly sober habits." He was devoted to his young wife.

But she must be received in Rome with all the honours that had been accorded to his mother on her entry after marriage. He had written repeatedly to his brother and the other cardinals, urging them to obtain this recognition for her from the Pope, with a fitting escort; as even he himself had had as Prince of Wales, though incognito, on his return from Naples and Gaeta, he writes to Cardinal Marefoschi, the Secretary of State; that was a guard of fifty men, an officer, and a flag.[1]

The Cardinal of York managed to get up for the bride and bridegroom something of a royal reception, though he had to furnish the pageant chiefly from his own well-stocked stables and coach-houses. The entry took place on April 22, Easter Wednesday. He hastened to call upon the bride, on her arrival at the Muti Palace, and presented her with a gold snuff-box set with diamonds, containing an order on his

---

[1] Hist. MSS. Comm. Reports X., part vi. p. 229.

bankers to pay her down 40,000 scudi—nearly £10,000. He 1772. also settled upon her 4000 scudi a year.[1]

The Stolberg family name was Horn and hopeful Jacobites toasted her with her husband, "the lad that's been so kind to Louisa Horn." She was great-grand-daughter of James II.'s faithful servant, Lord Ailesbury. In Rome she was called the Queen of Hearts, as Clementina had been called *Regina Apostolorum*. She was immensely admired there for her dazzling fairness and her cleverness.

In 1773, Miss Walkinshaw, with her daughter, arrived in 1773. Rome to blackmail Charles, who as a newly married man might be willing to pay her well to be rid of her: at least, to dun the Cardinal of York and the Pope ; like a sturdy beggar, refusing to leave the place until she was served. The cardinal secretary of state was obliged to write to Lascaris, now Patriarch of Jerusalem and treasurer to the Cardinal of York, that "if Madame Clementine Walkinshaw refuses to leave Rome, he must convince her of the uselessness of her resistance and of the worse position she will consequently be in." On June 14 Lascaris wrote to represent the greater opportunities for molestation the ladies would have in Rome. As the Lady Charlotte wished to be removed from the convent at Meaux to one in Paris, his royal highness and eminence was perfectly indifferent as to the unfortunate young lady's place of retirement, provided she remained always in a nunnery.[2]

They were compelled to yield and depart. Charlotte wrote a farewell letter to Lascaris, thanking him for all the trouble he had taken "to soften a little her unhappy lot," and hoping that her uncle would not refuse her prayer to exchange Meaux for Paris. They were on the point of leaving for Lyons *via* Genoa, Antibes, and Avignon. She sent on behalf of her mother *mille homage* [*sic*]. In another letter in the same hand but headed "Madame la Comtesse d'Alberstroff," Lascaris was requested to send her letters under cover to the Marquise d'Alberi in the Faubourg St. Germain.[3]

"They formerly went to Rome but were sent back," Horace Walpole writes to Lady Ossory in 1784. "The House of Fitz-James, fearing their becoming a burden to themselves, prevented the acknowledgment of the daughter."

---

[1] "Life of Sir Robert Strange," vol. ii., Appendix, p. 316–317.
[2] Hist. MSS. Comm. Reports X., part vi. p. 234. Report IV., p. 403.
[3] Ibid.

1773.   As the influence of the House of Fitz-James could be potent only in Paris, the last words may refer to the memorial presented by Charlotte to the King of France on her return from Rome. The memorial is conjecturally dated "vers 1766" in the Stuart Papers printed by Mr. F. C. Madan, but allusions therein, especially to Charles's recent marriage, would seem rather to place it here on their return discouraged from Rome ; while the hint of recent favour from Charles towards his daughter might imply that he had seen her in Paris in the preceding year. The Duc de Saint Simon says that at the time of his marriage, Charles's affection for his daughter seemed to be renewed, and that he arranged for her joining him, but at the last moment obstacles intervened.[1] The Fitz-Jameses and the ladies were on very friendly terms, and may have arranged a meeting between father and daughter, which would have been more probable than a meeting in Rome. Mann, too, says the Fitz-Jameses prevented her recognition. In 1766 she was only a child of thirteen.

The memorial runs :—

"The Lady Charlotte, daughter of Prince Charles Edward, retired to Rome since the death of his father James III. of England, was born in 1753 in the prince's house at Liége. She was carried into church by his hands, baptized under the name he was then bearing, brought up as his daughter in his household until she was seven years old, and presented in that quality to all the English gentlemen who visited him during his sojourns at Basle and at Bouillon.

"Her mother, of one of the first Scottish families, allied to the House of Stuart for which many of her relatives have shed their blood and lost their lives, at that time treated by the prince as his wife, and known on his different journeys by the same name as himself, received in 1760 the command of the late King of England to take her daughter to Paris, to procure for her an education suitable to her birth and to give her masters which could not have been possible had she remained with the prince, then wandering from town to town. From that time the King of England placed the child under the protection of France. He took all their expenses upon himself, and so long as he lived he fulfilled these engagements with a generosity worthy of his kind heart.

[1] *Hommes Illustres* (Stuart), vol. iv. p. 206.

"At his death the prince, his son, was deprived of the subsidies which France and Spain had granted to his father. The Cardinal of York reduced the pension which the mother and daughter had enjoyed to 5000 livres, and for a crowning misfortune, they have not been able to find out what dispositions the late king may have made in their favour. In this state of distress they waited to see what might transpire. The new marriage of the prince has altered the condition of both. Exasperated by a separation which he felt very keenly, though it was commanded by the king his father, he has not continued to take the same interest in them. The Lady Charlotte, his daughter, is fully persuaded of his tenderness for her ; she has received recent proofs of his attachment ; she hopes everything from his kindness, but she is convinced that he cannot carry out the plans he has made for her without the help of France.[1] She ventures to implore the kindness and protection of the king. She reminds his majesty that she is the last scion of a sovereign House, allied to the House of France, celebrated for its misfortunes, and which has sacrificed its dominions for the sake of religion ; the only child of an unfortunate prince who has for long shared the fortunes of his majesty's arms, and who has made generous efforts to oblige France. The services rendered to his father by the Scottish gentlemen have gained for them annual subsistence. She dares to hope that the same assistance will not be refused to the daughter of him who fought at their head and who inspired them with that courage and zeal which rendered them worthy of his majesty's kindness and liberality."[2]

Whether or no this appeal touched the really kind heart of Louis XV., Charles and his brother remained adamant.

Sir Horace Mann says that before the end of 1773 Charles had relapsed into his old habits and drank harder than ever ; but Sir Horace was always over-eager to send evil reports to England. Rumour was always busy and rarely veracious as to the Stuarts, as when Horace Walpole wrote to Mann, August 29, 1772 : "It has been said in our newspapers that the Cardinal of York is dead ; but your silence makes me conclude it is not true ; which is probable, too, by its being in our papers, for

[1] This may very probably refer to an interview with promises in Paris, whether the "new marriage" means new project of marriage or recent marriage.

[2] Stuart Papers, relating chiefly to Mary of Modena, edited by F. C. Madan. (Roxburghe Club.)

1773. they are absolutely nothing but magazines of lies, blunders, scandal, virulence, and absurdity."

The papal court and Roman society in general had little attention free at this time for the affairs of Miss Walkinshaw or even of the Stuarts. The fiercely burning question of the Jesuits was being settled. After long reluctance Clement XIV. signed the brief for their suppression on July 27, 1773. The Cardinal of York was little concerned in the matter, officially. Probably, as a royal prince, he was obliged to remain neutral, for his interest and sympathy in ecclesiastical matters were always keen. His name appears among the "neutrals" in the lists of voting cardinals as for and against the suppression.[1] Though Father Stefanucci had been one of his great friends, and though he had incurred much blame from his father and the King of Spain by abstaining from voting for the beatification of Pala-fox, he had never identified himself with either side in the great controversy, and, partly as an act of submission to the Pope, had early taken the Seminary at Frascati out of Jesuit hands.

Charles was much more concerned in the papal recognition of his own claims than in the claims of the Society that had saved and given new life to the Church : more interested in the travelling English who came to Rome, who, as in his father's time, but in fewer numbers and with fainter interest, were pleased to find themselves in his company. His young consort was a new magnet to attract curiosity if not sympathy to the Muti Palace. One of these wandering islanders was young Coke of Norfolk, a very handsome young Whig of twenty, afterwards first Earl of Leicester. In 1773 he danced with Louise at a great fancy ball, and accepted from her a white cockade.[2] "Young Mr. Coke," writes Horace Walpole to Conway, August 18, 1774, "has returned from his travels in love with the Pretender's Queen, who has permitted him to have her picture."[3] The picture, which now hangs at Longford, Derbyshire, a seat of the Cokes, is really a portrait of the beautiful youth himself in the cavalier's costume of grey and rose in which he danced with her at the fancy ball. It was painted by Batoni at her majesty's command. But in the background

[1] See the articles on the Suppression of the Jesuits by Father Sydney F. Smith S.J., in the *Month*, 1905.
[2] "Coke of Norfolk and his Friends," by A. M. W. Stirling, pp. 107, 108.
[3] "Letters of Horace Walpole," vi. 109.

there is a statue of Ariadne, considered by Louise to bear a 1773. striking resemblance to herself, and whose presence in the picture was probably as near as she dared go to presenting him with her own portrait in such conjunction with his. If she converted him to Jacobitism, it was but an ephemeral conversion. Her situation naturally appealed to his sympathy ; perhaps, with some straining of allegory, he looked upon himself as a young Dionysos to save her from desolation worse than forsakenness. Indignant memory of such a princess tied to such a husband most likely re-established his aversion for the cause of Charles III.[1]

Charles, finally convinced that his kingship would never be recognised by Rome, withdrew in wrath with his wife to Leghorn at the end of 1773. From Leghorn he removed to Siena, the scene of the supposed birth of his son, according to the Hay-Allan romance.

And here may be dismissed that strange and foolish story which, in spite of its utter improbability and the absence of all proof, is considered worthy of recurrent refutation, even up to the present time : the pretension of two gentlemen calling themselves John Sobieski and Charles Edward Stuart, Counts d'Albanie, who died a few years ago, to be grandsons of Prince Charles by legitimate descent. They themselves pretended to believe in their royal lineage. They published their story in the "Tales of the Century" : a wild romance of a mysterious summons, a blindfolded doctor, a young mother and her new-born son ; a royal-looking father standing by, strangely resembling the portraits of a famous prince : the smuggling away of baby and doctor in the darkness : never any name given nor any address revealed.

The strongest evidence against the legend—stronger far than any carefully presented proofs that the Sobieski-Stuarts or Stuarts-d'Albanie were no more than Hay-Allans—is the fact that there was no reason whatever for such concealment. The child would have been in no danger ; the House of Hanover would hardly have noticed the event, strong in a popular and prolific sovereign of English birth : a sovereign,

---

[1] Towards the end of 1774, the year of his return, he dined at the Cocoa Tree Club (Jacobite) ; a dinner given in his honour, Sir Robert Burdett, grandfather of Sir Francis Burdett, being chairman. Mrs. Stirling (pp. 141, 142) gives an account of the curious and dramatic means young Coke's father took to warn him away from such gatherings. He never entered the Cocoa Tree again.

1773. too, who would never have stooped to countenance kidnapping or murder, whatever his predecessors might have winked at by way of ambassadorial effort. It would have been everything to Charles to have been able to proclaim the birth of a son and heir. A warming-pan baby would have been more probable than a suppressed prince. Had promise of issue blessed his marriage, he would most certainly have summoned the English and Scottish nobility, with the utmost flourish and state and triumph, to attend "the queen's labour," as James II. had done when Princess Louisa was born. He would not have been satisfied with the more modest and limited summons sent out in the case of his own birth.

He himself has declared in writing that the Duchess of Albany was the only child he ever had, and his wife absolutely denied having had a child.[1] Had this fairy babe ever been born, he would not have legitimatised his natural daughter, almost a stranger to him, and made her his heir. The Cardinal Duke would have known of the birth, and, most honourable of men as he was, would certainly have forborne to assume the title of King of England, had a legitimate nephew or niece been living : in whose name, and not in his own, he would have protested against the Duchess of Albany's legitimation in 1784.[2]

From Siena Charles went to Florence. After staying some time in an outlying palace lent by his old friend, Prince Corsini, he bought the San Clemente Palace (sometime called the Palazzo-Velluti-Zuli) in the Via Gino Capponi, formerly Via San Sebastiano ; a large yellow house with fine gardens. Here he took up his abode. His initials "C.R. 1777," on a weathercock, the royal arms on the staircase, and some medallion portraits remain to commemorate his occupancy. Then, it is said, the seven (intermittently) banished devils of drink rushed back to take possession.

As the Grand Duke of Tuscany [3] followed the lead of the great courts and declined to receive the royal couple as King and Queen of England, Charles refused to enter society on any

---

[1] To Napoleon, *par exemple.* It is said that he told her that had she had a son, he would have made him King of England.

[2] See " Tales of the Century," by John Sobieski Stuart.

[3] Leopold of Lorraine, son of Francis, Grand Duke and Emperor and of the Empress Maria Theresa ; married Maria Luisa, daughter of Charles III., King of Naples, afterwards of Spain.

lower footing, and his young wife was thrown entirely upon 1775. him for companionship. It is quite beyond dispute that even were the worst stories of brutal tyranny disproved, she had a very bad time of it. Jealousy was one of the features of his degraded character, as Miss Walkinshaw had experienced, and he would never allow his wife to be out of his sight. That he had cause enough for jealousy in her character and in the prevailing fashion of Italian society was presently to be proved ; and even a tipsy old man may be fond of his wife, and he was sad, ailing, and very lonely.

She tried to find interest in severe study, chiefly in mathematics. He still busied himself with plots. From the papers of Lord Dartmouth, interesting hints may be gathered that in 1775 he took a secret trip to England.

CHAPTER XVI

A CALL FROM AMERICA

1775. DISCONTENT with British rule had been growing in the American colonies, assiduously fomented by France, and aggravated by the insensate obstinacy of George III. and his minister, Lord Chatham. In 1773 Boston had dramatically expressed the mind of herself and her sister malcontents by throwing the very moderately taxed tea into her harbour. In the spring of 1775, open rebellion broke out, and the first blood was drawn at Lexington.

France fanned the flame and Charles watched eagerly from Florence. " Broken man " as he was, sadly deteriorated in health and character, a gleam of the old spirit lived within him, the old hope, a spark of the old daring. For all the fatal slavery to which he had abandoned himself, there were intervals in his life when he managed, after a startling warning, to forswear sack and live cleanly, and he was quite sharp enough to understand what the follies of his last Parisian trip had cost him. It is therefore not impossible that he may have slipped away from Florence, unobserved by the watchful Sir Horace Mann. Absence from sight might easily have been accounted for by a story of illness. He was often ill. We have as yet no proof that he did slip away, but neither have we proof that at this period he was continually in evidence.

Certain letters in Lord Dartmouth's papers suggest the possibility of such an adventure. They certainly prove that the British government had reason to remember his existence and its possibilities with uneasiness and increased vigilance.

Lord Dartmouth, great-grandson of James II.'s High Admiral, was Secretary of State for the colonies in Lord North's administration, and President of the Board of Trade and Foreign Plantations ; consequently the minister responsible under the prime minister for the business of the revolting American colonies. In November 1775 he became Lord Privy Seal.

On July 5, 1775, a correspondent who signs himself " A. Z." writes to the Reverend John Vardil : [1]—

" Captain John Hansen, who lately discovered some of the secrets of the French cabinet, for which he received a pension of £500, has now, it is said, discovered that the English (?) ministry are in league with the Pretender who must this year assert his right to the throne or be for ever barred.   This is supposed to be the reason of the present measures against America, that by drawing the forces out of Great Britain and Ireland, those countries will be subject to the incursions of the Pretender."

This was, of course, all nonsense.   The important matter is that such a letter should have been considered worth handing over to the government to be preserved among the colonial secretary's papers.   There was profound uneasiness about the American troubles, and no one could say what France might not see fit to do for the harassing of her natural enemy.

Presently information, much more definite and alarming, reached the government from a Mr. Taitt, "an eminent upholsterer in New Street, Hanover Square." A minute of his information is among the Dartmouth Papers, but, as with the letters, dates are scarce and incidents require placing according to context.

Mr. Taitt informed Mr. Pownall, M.P. for Minehead 1774–1780, and a strong supporter of Lord North, that a friend of his knew one Alexander Dorrett, who knew a Mrs. Leslie who kept a coffee-house in Princes Street, Leicester Fields, who knew the " Pretender," and who had stated that he was then in England, and that she had had an interview with him.   Letters for him and his adherents were addressed to her house to be called for.   She was a regular Jacobite agent.   Dorrett and Mrs. Leslie were, accordingly, summoned to Lord Dartmouth's office and interviewed there.

Lord Dartmouth writes to Sir Stanier Porten, under-secretary to Lord Rochford, who was then Secretary of State for the Southern Department and keeper of the State Papers at Whitehall:—

" Having repeated information that a traitorous correspondence is suspected to be carried on with the rebels of North

[1] Historical MSS. Commission Reports XIV., Appendix X.: Dartmouth MSS., vol. ii. p. 326.

1775. America, in letters conveyed thither in American ships, clearing out in ballast from the different ports in this kingdom," he sends a list of ships and suspected persons on board, destined for America. These men were known to be disaffected to the government, and were suspected of dangerous designs. He also encloses copies of three letters which were brought to him on the preceding evening by Alexander Dorrett's brother, which, Dorrett said, had been left at the Princes Street coffee-house since the examination of Mrs. Leslie. The originals had been returned to Dorrett, with directions to watch the person who should call for them at the coffee-house.[1] Thus were the Jacobites and their king almost invariably served by their agents.

One of these copies of the intercepted letters is dated August 8, signed "T. W." and addressed to "C. W. J." at Princes Street Coffee-house, Princes Street, Leicester Fields. Its purport is that as yet they have had no foreign letters, but hope, by the conveyance of their friend in Milford Haven, they will receive proper instructions. The movements of his highness were known only to Mrs. Leslie.

"Simon Dalton" also writes to "C. W. J." that he would be glad to know his orders "as to what comes from Milford Haven." Hamilton had written that "Brown" would have all ready in five days. He hoped that things would be "as faithfully obeyed in the other quarter as they are here." He desired "C. W. J." to ask his highness the particulars of their orders.

The third letter is from "N. B." to Mr. Statuvell (queried in the report "Hatwell"), addressed to the care of Mrs. Leslie. "Dear Friend, I received yours and make no doubt of the widow's punctuality, it's only your fears that makes you apprehend, the Seal being cracked is only your anxiety." The writer is now at the D. of N.'s, who assures him "the money is at a moment's warning," and if his highness had once received the intelligence of the landing in Milford Haven, the day would be their own. He had received a letter from the D. of Q. and proposed her taking a house in the country. All was going on according to their wishes, and she stated that "George" looked very sour-mouthed, especially at his regiments.

The last letter on this business among the Dartmouth papers

[1] Hist. MSS. Comm. Reports: Dartmouth MSS., ii. p. 368.

is from Lord Dartmouth to Sir Stanier Porten, and is dated from _{1775.}
Whitehall, September 2, 1775. Since his separate letter of the
morning, he had again seen Dorrett, who reported that Mrs.
Leslie had told him that the person who called for the letters left
in her care had carried them to a coffee-house somewhere near
Bow Church.[1]

The D. of N. is doubtless the Duc de Noailles who four
years previously was the chief French agent to summon Charles
from Italy to lead the expedition then contemplated. If De
Noailles in 1775 renewed that offer, he must have had reason,
remembering that dismal failure, to believe that Charles was a
reformed character. Therefore it may be hoped, if not proved,
that Sir Horace Mann's reports of his incessant drunkenness in
those early years of his married life, are calumnies. They
certainly were exaggerations. The D. of Q. is Catherine Hyde,
Duchess of Queensberry, Prior's Kitty, then a very old lady in
years, but always young in spirit and energy. Milford Haven
was not only a convenient port of embarkation for America,
but it was a port in a friendly country. Wales was a hotbed
of latent Jacobitism—very latent! The Welsh squires had done
nothing more useful for the Stuarts than to drink to the king
over the water. Had not Sir Watkin Williams Wynne declared
himself ready to join the prince at Derby with a thousand men,
when the chiefs and Lord George Murray turned tail? Charles
believed in his loyalty and accepted—it must have been with
a bitter smile—his very poor excuse. Why he and the Welsh
Jacobites did not follow the not very distant Jacobite army
on its northward march by Lancashire has never been satis-
factorily explained. But Welsh Jacobitism seems to have
expended itself in convivial "cycles" and bacchanalian song.
Still, the Welsh were sympathetic, and would at least place no
impediments in the way of other people who might wish to
sail from "that same blessed Milford Haven," to fight for their
noisily toasted king in his American colonies.

But there is more than guesswork to explain the mysterious
letters in the Dartmouth Papers, and to prove that though the
colonists refused the rule of George III., some of them by no
means wished to sever themselves from Great Britain and the
monarchy, to become a republic apart. It is curious that it
should not have been the loyal Carolinas, descendants of the

[1] Hist. MSS. Comm. Reports: Dartmouth MSS., ii. p. 369.

1775. cavaliers, who turned to the ancient dynasty, but Boston of the tea-strewn harbour. The Abbé Fabroni, rector of the university of Pisa, told the Reverend Louis Dutens,[1] rector of Elsdon, Northumberland, librarian to George, prince regent, and later, historiographer to George IV., that he had seen " at the time when the American rebellion broke out "—that is in 1775, the very year in which Charles was said to be in London on his way to America *viâ* Milford Haven — letters from Americans at Boston to the " Pretender," assuring him of their allegiance, and inviting him to put himself at their head.

The scheme, having been discovered to the British government, naturally came to an end. May it not have been this new disappointment which sent Charles back to the anæstheticising bottle ? It is pretty certain that from this date affairs at the Florentine Palace grew more and more deplorable.

There is a remarkably fine pencil drawing by Ozias Humphrey of Charles in the Scottish National Gallery, simply inscribed in handwriting, " Prince Charles Stewart : drawn from nature at Florence, 1776." The face at the first glance seems familiar enough from a print or engraving, but such reproductions have grossly exaggerated the harsh lines, the downward droop of the mouth and the heavy pendulous cheeks, while they have missed the fire of the angry eyes, fire that even yet might have burned for fame, leaving them only sullen. It is a fine strong face, in which much beauty and nobility remain for all the disfiguring work of thirty years of mortification, proud defiance, fierce revolt against fate, and reckless dissipation. But it is not such a face as one would see at the head of a happy home.[2]

The American rebellion proceeded victoriously. In March 1776, Washington entered Boston in triumph. On July 4, the Declaration of Independence announced the final separation of the colonies from the crown. But the war continued with varying fortune, and England might have recovered her sovereignty, had not France in 1778 allied herself openly with the rebels, in the hope of recovering Canada. She had apparently given up Charles Edward as a useful ally, for when she sent a

---

[1] *Mémoires d'un voyageur*, Rev. Louis Dutens, 1806. There is a portrait of Mr. Dutens in the National Portrait Gallery, Edinburgh.

[2] Mr. Lang has called attention in " Pickle the Spy " to the interesting resemblance between Prince Charles's young profile and Queen Victoria's. There is a still stronger likeness in the lower part of the aged faces.

French force that year to help the rebels, it was the Marquis de 1778. Lafayette who went with it and not the Stuart prince.

Yet in 1778 (?),[1] a memorial was sent to him from his adherents in America proposing to set up his standard in the back settlements. The arrival of a real French force, that long yearned-for auxiliary, must have stirred them to appeal once more to their king. Sir Walter Scott mentioned to Washington Irving that he had seen this memorial, dated 1778, among the Stuart Papers at Windsor, which had been submitted by the government to his inspection in 1829.[2] "This memorial," says Lord Mahon, "has now disappeared from its place in the collection. . . ."[3] "Few things indeed," he comments, "are more remarkable than the lingering attachment to kingly government which may be traced in these insurgent colonies . . . even when every hope was relinquished of returning to the sway of King George."[4]

It seems strange that such an appeal should have been made in vain to Charles, who was almost to the last so keenly on the alert for such opportunities, in spite of the habit which drugged his energies and was breaking up his splendid constitution : that he should not at least have gone with the French force to try his luck, forgetting his fifty-six years and all they held. The portrait of 1776 shows us a man with his natural force unabated. There is a wide difference between this face and that of the weary old man by Batoni in the National Portrait Gallery. His majesty's energies, it happened, were just then otherwise and quite absorbingly occupied.

---

[1] It is of course possible that either the Abbé Fabroni or Scott may have given a wrong date, and that the letters of 1775 and the memorial of 1778 may be of the same affair.

[2] "A visit to Abbotsford," by Washington Irving, 1850. Lord Mahon's "History of England," vol. vi. 185.

[3] Lord Mahon's "History of England," vol. vi. 185.

[4] Ibid. 184 (footnote).

CHAPTER XVII

THE COMING OF THE POET[1]

1776. AT the end of the summer of 1776 there had arrived in Florence a red-haired Piedmontese poet of noble birth and republican principles, Vittorio Alfieri, as yet unknown to fame. He brought introductions to the Countess of Albany, as to a lady of literary and artistic tastes, but he says he was not pre-

1777. sented to her until the autumn of 1777. He found her, this pretty, clever, cultivated woman of four-and-twenty, tied to "a querulous, unreasonable, and constantly intoxicated old husband," jealous to monomania ; she, pathetic as a foreigner among foreigners, though, at the same time, the object of general attention. He fell in love with her at once ; saw in her his Beatrice, his Laura, his Leonora. She was the one person, he said, whose golden chain could subjugate his vagrant and unconquerable heart. He would have done nothing distinguished without her friendship. In spite of her husband's vigilance—he never allowed the pair to be a moment out of his sight, further than the adjoining room with an open door between—they managed to exchange many confidences and much red-hot sympathy under the screen of study.

Alfieri's was an ardent nature. He had once had to have himself tied into a chair by his servant to restrain him from the pursuit of beauty to the detriment of literature. His queen was his fourth flame. One of her predecessors had been Lady Ligonier, whose husband wounded the poet in the consequent duel.

So they philandered about Florence, cut off from society by the strange circumstances of their position, and thrown upon poetry and philosophy for the whiling away of the long sunny hours, sitting within sight of the garden where Boccaccio told his stories, or driving by hill and river where memories

---

[1] The particulars of the transactions relating to the Countess of Albany, the Duchess of Albany, and the Cardinal of York are nearly all drawn from the correspondence preserved in the cardinal's papers. Add. MSS. British Museum 30,475, 30,476.

of Beatrice were more vivid and potent than the presence of 1780. the dozing old man in the corner of the carriage, until the end of 1780 when Louise escaped from her husband, her clever wits assisted by her lover's romantic experiences. She fled first to a convent and thence to Rome and the sympathetic protection of the only partially instructed Cardinal of York. Alfieri accompanied her part of the way, riding disguised at the back of her carriage ; then leaving her, to wait within easy recall when convenience should permit.

Her story, which the simple cardinal accepted in all good faith—he had seen enough in Rome and at Albano to believe anything—was that her husband's conduct had been loathsome beyond all toleration ; that he had insulted her innocence with coarse and groundless accusations ; had even barricaded her chamber door so that no one could enter it without passing through his ; that upon the last St. Andrew's night, when he had been keeping the feast with customary orgies, his brutal treatment had culminated in such outrageous violence that she went in fear of her life. But while loudly enlarging upon her husband's cruelty, tyranny, and degrading habits, she preserved a discreet silence upon those peccadilloes of her own which Charles afterwards declared, after the manner of his father Adam, to have been answerable for his relapse into those degrading habits. He denied the cruelty and tyranny altogether. Possibly he may have considered the "tyranny" to be no more than the lawful suzerainty of a husband, and forgotten the cruelty when the drunken fit was over.

The assertion of the lovers that their friendship in Florence had been purely Platonic may very well be believed. They had had no opportunity for anything more.[1] Charles was not fuddled beyond taking care of his honour. He was not an easy-going Tuscan or Roman husband of the day, accepting the *cicisbeo* as a necessary appendage to a matron of fashion. His defence should not be entirely dismissed ; that his own behaviour had at least given no just excuse for his wife's appeal to a stranger's sympathies and her subsequent desertion ; that Alfieri, writer of plays, had found a subject made

---

[1] They named one another in correspondence later, Psipsio and Psipsia, names invented to sound like kisses ; but it is not recorded whether or not this onomatopæia originated in Florence.

1780. to his hand in the young queen, pretty, *précieuse*, and bored, which he chose to work up to a dramatic climax. Alfieri's character and Louise's conduct are strong witnesses, if not for the husband's defence, at least against their own innocence and justification.

The cardinal had no idea of the truth of the case. He received the fugitive queen with the warmest brotherly kindness, though she unreasonably blamed him for the making up of her wretched marriage, in which he assured her he had had no hand beyond giving his formal consent. He arranged for her reception in the same convent of St. Cecilia where his mother had taken up her abode in circumstances somewhat similar. But marriage is marriage and inviolable, and he would not hear of the present situation being accepted as permanent.

" Let your mind be at rest, my dearest sister," he wrote, "and allow yourself to be guided by those who are devoted to you ; and above all, never tell any one, no matter whom, that you will never listen to proposals for returning to your husband. Do not fear, unless a miracle happens, that I shall have the courage to counsel such a step, but as it is probable that God has permitted what has just occurred in order to move you to the practice of an edifying life . . . it may be also that the Lord wishes to effect by the same means the conversion of my brother. . . . My dearest sister, be anxious about nothing. Monsignor Lascaris, Cantini, and I will arrange all that is necessary. I feel deeply for you."

1781. Louise had no intention whatever either of returning to her husband or of living shut up in a convent. The cardinal therefore placed at her disposal his own palace of the Cancellaria, and she established herself there before Easter, he himself being resident at Frascati where he welcomed her whenever she chose to visit him. With his invariable openhandedness, he lavished gifts upon her. They corresponded continually and affectionately.[1] During the first months of her residence in the Cancellaria, she chose to pose as an

---

[1] Her original letters with most of the cardinal's, which are chiefly in drafts and copies, are preserved with the rest of his extensive correspondence and his diaries in the fifty volumes of MSS. (Additional MSS. 30,428 to 30,477) presented to the British Museum by the Hon. Maria Otway Cave, whose mother, the Baroness Braye, purchased them in Rome, 1842. The Braye MSS., now at Stamford Hall, were overlooked at the time, but have been calendared by the Historical MSS. Commission. Louise invariably writes in French, in a clear, graceful hand.

interesting invalid, crushed by her troubles.   Nevertheless she
kept late hours, for she speaks of retirement at 1 A.M. as early.
She was able to attend the long Holy Week services and to
witness the Easter illumination of St. Peter's.   She repeated
over and over to the cardinal how fortunate she was in
having found such a brother, and though he presently complained of her temper, he was loyal to his belief in her
innocence.

She now felt herself safely settled after her mind, and
Alfieri was to come in May.   Even this arrangement did not
shake the cardinal's faith, which is high testimony to his own
innocent inexperience if not to his acuteness and knowledge
of the world ; but Louise, over-confident of his indulgence,
overstepped the mark by her insatiability.   Alfieri would find
her queening it in a splendid palace ; why should he not
find her fair in a queen's jewels ?   The cardinal still possessed
his share of his mother's diamonds, and his sister-in-law required them.   Generously as he had treated her with regard
to money, this request annoyed him, disillusion began, and
he refused to make them over to her.   She assured him she
wished to wear the jewels only as evidence before the world
of how fully she enjoyed his confidence.   Henry, a simple
man, but beginning to understand her, did not see the necessity of such evidence.   She had therefore to receive Alfieri
unadorned by their splendour, when, after hanging about
various Italian towns for appearance' sake, he arrived in
Rome in May.

" As I travelled towards Rome," he writes in his autobiography, " the approach to her made my heart beat.   I
arrived ! I saw her—O God ! the thought of it still cleaves my
heart in twain—I saw her a prisoner behind a grating : "
which is poetical licence dealing with chronology, for she had
left the convent.

He dined with her upon his arrival, and went next day
to pay his respects to the cardinal at Frascati, where he was
received as he had been received at his lady's convents of
refuge, on the footing of an intimate friend of the family.
Louise sent by him to her brother-in-law a little propitiatory
gift in the form of a Virgil, one of the finest copies she had
ever seen, having noticed the want of a good Virgil in the
handsome library at Frascati.

1781.   Alfieri recalled her to her love of literature, and the cardinal was next requested to get her books sent to her from Florence.[1]

Charles had not time to reply by the first post to his brother's letter of May 23, but he wrote by the next, May 29, expressing his gratitude that the cardinal should take so much "at hart" that his wife should come to herself and return to her duty to "her Man." (His English had evidently caught a German tincture from his wife.) "I sende here enclosed," he continues, "an exact Inventory of ye Books you desier, hoping you will examine them all: they are made by Abbé Sipolitu Language Master and of Mathematiques to ye Queen, being a very honest man, Chancellen to ye grande Duke."

It cannot be denied that there is no ill temper here, nor resentment, nor even unreadiness. Yet Charles felt himself justly aggrieved that his brother should have lavished sympathy and protection upon his runaway wife. As the books did not follow instantly, Louise complained to Spada, of the royal household at Florence. He replied that the king would not send them because he had not heard from the cardinal since he sent the catalogue. "He certainly is a most extraordinary man, this dearest husband of mine," Louise wrote to the cardinal. "I don't know what affection he can have for the books."

Though she chose to make a grievance of this very short delay, nobody was to blame for it but the cardinal, who was troubled with his servants just then and had forgotten to answer Charles's letter. He wrote at once to Charles and to Louise, explaining, and Spada wrote that as soon as his majesty had received his royal highness's letter, he had ordered the books to be sent. Some, Charles said, had already been sent to "the convent Shee went to" in Florence. But he refused to hold any communication with his wife until she should repent. This is the whole story of the supposed detention of the Countess of Albany's clothes.

[1] There has been much misunderstanding as to this matter. "Vernon Lee" in her "Countess of Albany," and A. E. Ewald say that Charles refused to send his wife her clothes and other personal belongings, but that on receiving a message from the Pope, he obeyed implicitly. Sir Horace Mann says, "he sent them at once, for reasons best known to himself." Vernon Lee presumes the Pope must have threatened to stop his pension. He was not in the least likely to have obeyed the Pope, had his holiness interfered in his domestic affairs, or had he wished to keep the books. Even his father, always a devout son of the Church, had refused for a moment to allow such sort of papal aggression. The true story of the affair is revealed in these letters.

Alfieri stayed on in Rome, welcomed not only in Roman 1781.
society but at Frascati, to Charles's very just indignation.
His letters to his brother were consequently short and cold,
haughtily silent upon the painful subject.   He sent his chief
and most important Florentine friend, Prince Corsini, to the
Vatican to demand that Alfieri should be turned out of Rome.
The Pope, now the unfortunate Pius VI., returned that he was
proud to have so distinguished a person as Alfieri residing in
Rome, and that the countess's conduct was perfectly correct.
Charles then demanded that his Roman pension should be
paid to him without any deduction for his wife's benefit.

Love, Alfieri confesses, made him stoop to expedients he
professed to hold in horror.   " I did everything," he writes ;
" I resorted to everything, and I remained in Rome, tolerated
by those charlatans, and even aided by those petty priests, who
had, or assumed, any influence in the affairs of my lady."   He
lived at the Villa Strozzi, near the Baths of Diocletian, worked
and rode until evening, which he spent with Louise, drawing
inspiration for his labours of the morrow.[1]   Sometimes she
rode with him.   " The fifteenth [of my horses] was my beautiful
roan Fido, the same that in Rome had often carried the
delightful burden of my lady, and for that reason was dearer
to me than all the rest of my stud."

Yet Pope and cardinals were all at the feet of the pretty
piece of injured innocence.   Cardinal Conti offered her his villa
at Frascati for July, and she expressed herself charmed with
the prospect of staying so near to the Cardinal Duke in that
healthy rural seclusion where she could walk straight from her
bed into the sweet air of the garden.   But the heat upset her
and made her legs swell ; so—she did not go to Frascati !
She found the heat of a Roman July pleasanter than the coolness and verdure of Frascati under the cardinal's eye.   She
was enjoying the unlimited society of Alfieri, riding with him
and talking poetry.   One day early in July Canon Cesarini,
the cardinal's confidential secretary, called at the Cancellaria,
and to his surprise, could not gain admission.   The house was
all shut up.   Louise wrote next day to her brother-in-law in
evident trepidation, explaining that she had gone to bed at
3 P.M., overcome by the heat, not having had any sleep the

---

[1] He says she had suggested his *Maria Stuarda* which he wrote to please her in
1778.

1781 previous night. She did not explain why the household also was invisible ; nor did she remove to Cardinal Conti's villa.

In August she had to feel her way in another delicate matter. Her mother with her sister and brother-in-law, the Marquise and Marquis of Jamaica, were coming to see her in the winter. She cherished privately the hope that they would be offered the splendid hospitality of the Cancellaria, and she craved to let them see her wearing the Sobieski diamonds. "They will live by themselves," she informed the cardinal tentatively, and added that she had been thinking again of those diamonds. If he had the least scruple about opening the casket, she begged him not to do it. She knew he had no desire but to please her and that was enough for her. Of course, as his brother's wife, she ought to have the diamonds, but she quite understood that circumstances must forbid, and that he was not to blame.

She did not get the diamonds. The cardinal's liberality had been so far boundless, but he drew the limit at his mother's jewels. It was curious that he should do so, for he did not yet suspect Louise's unworthiness to wear the jewels of the saintly Clementina, and he had already given many to the Church. Perhaps he cared more for jewels than he did for money, being a collector of taste. Later, Charles told Gustavus of Sweden that his brother had tried to keep all their mother's jewels to himself, that he had been obliged to have the Pope's assistance before he could get his own share from him. Charles's memory had then sadly failed and he probably confused the story of Louise's application with squabbles at the period of the division, for Henry had behaved with more than generosity when the brothers divided the property four decades earlier.

But though Louise must go without the jewels, in October she got the desired invitation for her relatives to the Cancellaria, its acceptableness being tempered by a hint that the cardinal had seen through her manœuvre. She protested ; she was sorry he should have misunderstood her. She had expected her sister only (having presumably forgotten her previous letters). Her mother arrived too, as it happened, and she didn't know how to put six people into a little lodging where there was only one bed and no convenience.

But if the cardinal insisted—and so on, with much protestation of "her *true* sentiments."[1]

Her mother had been managing business for her with Queen Marie Antoinette. Sir Horace Mann writes at the beginning of the following year, 1782, that the French queen had written very kindly to Louise, and that Louis XVI. had settled 20,000 Roman crowns a year upon her for life, while the Cardinal of York already provided 4000, besides palace and equipage.

Charles heard of this lucky stroke in France and tried a counterstroke. He had been quite sober since she left him, as both she and Sir Horace Mann confess. "The king gives frequent dinner parties and drinks less, for he can no longer exceed beyond a certain point," Louise puts it uncharitably. Prince Corsini was still acting as his counsellor, to her alarm and annoyance, though she tried to comfort herself by repeating to her brother-in-law how wholly and confidently she relied upon him, in spite of that ominous conjunction. The Archbishop of Florence was assisting Charles to get up a *placet* "against you and me," she tells Henry. It was to be sent on to Victor Amadeus III., King of Sardinia, now next in the succession to the Duke of York. Its object being the *rapprochement* of the royal brothers, it would naturally work against "her majesty's" schemes.

It was at the beginning of 1782 that the cardinal had another trouble on hand, besides his brother's conjugal difficulties, when a man named Venture claimed his interest, professing to be a natural son of King James. He had probably proved that there was nothing to be got out of the head of the family, before he turned to its younger but its rich and influential member. He asserted, too, that he had served in the prince's army in Scotland. Henry, shocked and distressed, but always conscientious, directed Lord Caryll to inquire into the case. Caryll inquired "among all the party on both sides of the water," and wrote to the cardinal, May 9, that he had proved the story to be "a most ridiculous invention."[2]

---

[1] Miss Cornelia Knight says the Princess of Stolberg and her younger daughter, a canoness, came to Rome in 1783; that the cardinal offered them apartments at Frascati which they declined, but that Henry consented to dine with them one day when he came up to town. (Autobiography.)

[2] See "The King over the Water," p. 377.

1782.   In May the Countess of Albany went to Baden, where she was joined by Alfieri. Rome, of course, knew all about it, but if any scandal reached the cardinal, he shut his ears to it, in loyalty to his distressed sister-in-law. His eyes were soon to be opened, his indignant voice to be raised against Alfieri as the source and sole origin of the scandals and discords of the royal household. One may find some excuse for Louise's treatment of her husband, but her falsehood towards the kindly, trusting brother who had done everything in his power to help and console her cannot be excused, and of itself must throw a doubt upon parts of her defence.

A curious slip is made by Horace Walpole on June 6, 1782 :—

"The Archbishop of Canterbury (Cornwallis) being confined by the gout, the Cardinal of York made the speech on the Birthday (George III.'s birthday, June 4), at the head of the Sacred College. He gloried in being admitted to that honour : he spoke with that truth which was their profession, and prayed for the Head of the Church in their public and *secret* devotions. He condoled with his majesty on many disagreeable things that he had been forced to undergo and must have felt, but he could take upon himself to assure him that he would not be deserted." [1]

Horace Walpole, immensely interested at the time in Sir Horace Mann's gossip from Italy about the Cardinal of York and the family quarrel, had, of course, in a fit of mental aberration, written the title of the Stuart prince for that of the Protestant Archbishop of York, and the Sacred College for the Bench of Bishops. Not all the misdoings of Charles twenty times aggravated would have permitted such an act of high treason on the part of the Duke of York to his brother's royal rights of which he was always loyally tenacious, submissively as he might bow to the inevitable in the case of his own. Still more impossible would it be that "a cardinal at the head of the Sacred College"—and he did not hold that position, as dean, until some years later—should pray for George III. as Head of the Church—of any church ! It is odd that such a slip should have passed so long unobserved and uncorrected.

[1] Walpole's Letters, vol. viii. p. 229.

Except for a long letter from Louise to the cardinal 1782. dated from Baden, June 2, without any hint of Alfieri, there is a gap in their correspondence until March of the following year. Into this gap falls a very serious occurrence, in which it verily seemed as if even in his quiet harmless life, the tragic doom of his house must be striving to find out the last of the race.

The office of corporal of the *birri* or police of Frascati falling vacant, one Felice Giannuzzi was appointed to the post, to the exclusion of Giacomo Merolli, called Il Zoppo Struggiono, or the wasted cripple. Merolli was greatly incensed at his defeat. He first refused to obey orders: then incited the other *birri* to leave the service. Finding them loyal, he proceeded to threats and violence. Mediation was in vain. He was disarmed and banished from the diocese, but kept hanging about the neighbourhood, furiously vowing vengeance against the authorities, especially against the cardinal-bishop and his officers. In July or August he managed to enter Frascati hidden in a load of hay, with the design of setting the little city on fire, to burn the bishop and those whom he accused of having robbed him of his bread. The plan was timely discovered and Merolli was banished again. Then he informed a friend that he was about to return with three other *birri* to leave a memento in the city that would last as long as the walls stood. He appeared armed at Frascati August 29, to the consternation of all its inhabitants from the bishop downwards. He was advised to be gone, but he went aside only a few steps, muttering that he must make an end of the place if he should hang for it. He then went towards the Capuchin church whither the cardinal was accustomed to go daily; ostensibly to petition his royal highness to be allowed a few days' sojourn in Frascati that he might move his wife who was ill. He took up his position, gun on shoulder, behind a wall whence he commanded the entire route usually taken by the cardinal from the Villa Belvedere to the Capuchin church. Quite accidentally, it happened that the cardinal went that day by another road. Merolli's successful rival, Giannuzzi, caught him with his loaded gun, knocked him down, took him prisoner, and the cardinal was saved.[1]

---

[1] From a printed account in Italian in the British Museum : Ristretto del processo informativo concordato con i Signori Defensori. Roma, 1783 : folio.

CHAPTER XVIII

A ROYAL DIVORCE

1783. ABOUT February 1783, Charles fell dangerously ill. Only in the previous month Mann, who had come wholly round to the husband's side of the quarrel, had written to Walpole that the royal dipsomaniac had totally altered his way of living and behaved in every respect with proper decency. But the wages of his past sins were overdue. He was at death's door. Mortification set in, beginning in his legs, and his body was swollen. He recovered, but the doctors agreed that he must fall into chronic disease from a dropsy in his breast. While he believed himself dying he sent for his brother and made full confession to him. He did not extenuate his own conduct, but he told the duke the whole miserable Alfieri story. Perhaps he only confirmed suspicions already aroused, for this time the cardinal believed and returned to Rome, burning with indignation.

He did not at once make a public scandal. According to Louise's own letter, he went to her privately and bade her dismiss Alfieri, which she promised to do but did not. Indignant at seeing the promise was not kept and that Alfieri still visited at the Cancellaria, the impulsive cardinal went to the Pope, whose credulity he fully undeceived, and obtained an order for Alfieri to quit Rome. He left for Siena on March 4.

Louise was furious; all outraged virtue and wounded confidence. She had presumed too much on her brother-in-law's ready sympathy which had been quickened by his long horror of Charles's conduct. Louise had not reckoned on a horror still greater of immorality. Henry had never been able to condone Charles's sins of 1747 and he could not condone Louise's, which were doubled by the treachery that had gained his sympathy at the expense of all fairness towards his brother. He acted as his father had acted on finding out Bolingbroke. Confidence was at an end, and all outward

friendship with it. Louise wrote instantly to him, dropping all 1783.
her customary terms of affection.

"After the advice you gave me, brother, and for which I
thanked you at the time, believing it to be private, I made
M. le Comte d'Alfieri promise to leave Rome. He has left it
this morning. I would have tried to persuade him to do so
earlier, had it not been that after ripe reflection and taking the
advice of the most sensible people, I feared a sudden departure
would have looked like compulsion, and confirmed the injurious reports about my conduct which, though groundless,
were only too prevalent. However that may be, your wish is
fulfilled, and your advice followed. The only annoyance is
that there should have been any publicity. It hurts my
reputation and my delicacy. See what trouble you would
have saved me . . . if you had not run off without the
slightest necessity to the Pope . . . and thus in the first
excitement allowed yourself to hurry to a proceeding which
the kindness of your heart must let you see was not very
courteous to me."

All Roman society was with Louise and indignant with the
cardinal. It would have been highly unpopular had such
severe treatment of so fashionable a situation been made a
precedent! It was declared that the cardinal had told "every
postilion between Florence and Rome" what he thought of
his sister-in-law and Alfieri, and that he confided the same to
all the common people about Frascati! Miss Cornelia Knight
found the city ringing with these stories; that the Cardinal of
York on his return had spoken only a few cold words to his
sister-in-law, and had gone on at once to the Pope with his
brother's demand that his wife must either be made to dismiss
Alfieri and return to himself, or to retire to a convent. Henry
was an impetuous person, and may well have been beside
himself with anger at finding how he had been tricked, how
his kindness and generosity had been misplaced, but angry
Romans and scornful Englishmen naturally exaggerated his
conduct. Roman society believed the Grand Duchess of
Tuscany to be at the bottom of the whole scandal, out of
jealousy of her husband's admiration for Louise. Florentine
society, as immoral as Roman and as fully recognisant of the
cicisbeo system, suddenly veered round to the side of Charles.
Sir Horace Mann, referring, April 26, to "the fracas between

1783. him (Charles) and his wife whom everybody then pitied and applauded," writes, "the tables are now turned, the cat is out of the bag," though he blames the cardinal for publishing the Alfieri intrigue in Rome ; "a more silly mortal never existed." The cardinal probably "published" nothing, but the truth could not but be quickly known and little gossip would set Roman tongues wagging.

Louise from this moment hated the cardinal who had found her out even more fiercely than her husband who, according to her story, had behaved to her with such amazing brutality. Drinking apart, she now declared him to be a much less despicable character than the cardinal. Years after, she described her husband as having possessed all the vices of all conditions, vices even incompatible with one another, to which he added the vice of the lower orders by drinking.[1]

Charles had convinced his brother that the story of ill-usage was of Alfieri's dramatic invention, but the proofs accepted by the Hanoverian envoy and by Florentine society must have been much more substantial than an angry husband's self-exculpation and his brother's shocked sympathy.

Alfieri himself admits that though his attentions to the queen "did not exceed the bounds of honour"—a word more or less elastic in that age, and indeed in all ages of poets—husband and brother were both right to disapprove of the intimacy which was *only* "better than the fashion of Rome and Florence," and *only* "much more on the safe side than the other."

The lovers were separated, but they corresponded secretly, and managed to meet now and then. The five passionate letters from Louise to Francesco Gori, friend of her poet, published by "Vernon Lee," are undated but fit in here. Louise was seldom careful as to dates. "Monday afternoon" —"Tuesday evening" as a rule sufficed to her, though she was frequently particular as to the hour. These letters, printed by her warm champion, are of deadly evidence against her, raving as she does of her passionate love for Alfieri and of the

---

[1] She spoke of her husband in varying strains as time softened or sharpened memory. Cornelia Knight in her "Autobiography" says that she spoke of him with great calmness and compassion. She would acknowledge that he possessed one good quality : he never betrayed a secret and never disclosed who had belonged to his party until after their death, nor would he ever listen to ill-natured things said of people.

misery of parting; longing for the death of "the man at 1783. Florence, who must be made of iron to spite us by living. It is so long since he is ill, and still he lives—may live another couple of years; though he may be suffocated any moment by the humours which have risen to his chest. What a cruel thing to look for one's happiness to the death of another, yet one cannot help wishing it. I love him (Alfieri) more than myself. . . . Peace by his side would suffice for me, and yet I am condemned to languish far from him. . . . That man does not seem inclined to depart."

A new factor now came into the affair in the shape of Gustavus III., King of Sweden, a connection of Louise's by marriage. He visited Charles at Florence late in 1783, and greatly cheered the royal exile, so long debarred, as he lamented, from "the society of his equals." Gustavus found "the old man very interesting." He was not bored by the stories of Scottish adventures which had so bored Louise, but conceived a strong liking and sympathy for Charles, which is good unbiassed testimony for the fallen prince. "The King of Sweden," Walpole wrote to Lady Ossory, November 12, 1784, "when here last, found the Count of Albany in a wretched condition, destitute even of an exchequer to pay his household. He imparted his sympathy at the opera to [Mann, of all people], and proposed, on a hint from [Mann], to make a free gift to [Charles] of £1000, to be followed by a like benevolence in six months, and an annual donative of more than both." Gustavus asked Mann to advance the money, for which he would give him a draft on the mines of Dalecarlia, but Mann declined.[1] Gustavus, however, exerted himself to get Charles's pecuniary affairs placed upon a more comfortable footing, and to arrange a separation between him and his wife that would be justice and relief for both. Unfortunately the impressionable Gustavus, "the king with two faces," went on to Rome, where he met the other party and heard the other story. The equally interesting and more charming Louise persuaded him that Charles neither deserved his compassion nor required his assistance. The latter statement she presently found it convenient to contradict, though unhappily it jumped with the King of Sweden's recollection of Charles, at his remarkably

---

[1] Letters of Horace Walpole, viii. 496.

1784. well-furnished table, describing himself pathetically as "an old soldier who wanted for bread."

On January 24, 1784, Charles had an apopletic seizure and lay speechless and insensible for two days. When he recovered consciousness, his doctors pronounced his illness to be inflammation of the brain and hopeless. He received Extreme Unction and recovered a little more. The Duke of York was sent for, but found himself unable to come. It is difficult to account for his absence. Lord Caryll, writing from St. Germain's, March 5, to congratulate him on his brother's recovery, declares that it was "a real mortification" to learn from his letter of February 11 the "motive" which had obliged his royal highness to deny himself the consolation of visiting his majesty, as he did the last year on a similar alarming occasion. Henry may have been ill. The road to Rome was blocked by snow so that not even the post could bring his reply to the news. *Aimant ses aises* as of old, he may not have cared to take another wintry journey to see a brother whom he expected to find unconscious or dead.[1] He certainly did not doubt the gravity of his brother's condition, for on January 27, he prepared a "protest" to be sent round to all European courts, announcing his own accession to the claims of his family, and that for the future he would use the title of Duke of York as a title of incognito only.

John Stuart, of his majesty's bedchamber, kept the cardinal informed as to his master's health and carefully locked up his stray possessions, "as there is no depending on most of those his majesty has about him"; the Irish so distrusted, not only by Louise but by the cardinal. Stuart was growing uneasy on another matter, and wrote to the cardinal, February 14, of "a strange hitch" which had apparently occurred, to hinder "the generous promise of the King of Sweden" from being fulfilled.[2]

The cardinal, though almost head of the family, was, in fact, kept much in the dark, and Gustavus and Louise negotiated the conditions of her separation without consulting him.

Gustavus managed to get Charles's signature to the settle-

---

[1] " A courier was despatched to his brother at Rome, who probably will not remove from thence with so little hopes of finding him alive." Sir Horace Mann's Letters: " Mann and Manners at the Court of Florence," Dr. Doran, ii. 403, 404.

[2] " Mann and Manners," Doran, ii. 404.

ment he suggested.   Eager to be free at any price to enjoy 1784.
the unlimited society of her lover, Louise agreed to give up
to her husband not only the three thousand crowns which
the cardinal allowed her, but the three thousand due to
her for pin-money by her marriage contract.   She even agreed
that Charles should take his diamonds from Rome.   She
admitted his necessities since Stuart vouched for them, she
said, and was proud of being able to help him ; to give up
of her superfluity to procure for him what was necessary.
Might it ensure the peace and comfort of his old age !   So
she wrote to the cardinal on April 1.

But the cardinal was not to be so easily hoodwinked.
He guessed the reason of Louise's generosity and of Charles's
acquiescence.   He knew, from three and a half years of
intimate acquaintance, that she was not by any means ready
to give up the means of easy living, even of royal state.   To
renounce money which it would have been extremely difficult
to obtain would simplify and hasten the business in hand,
while her consequent poverty would appeal to the more
accessible munificence of friendly courts.

The cardinal was very busy with Passiontide ceremonies
and did not reply for a week.   On April 9, he writes to his
sister-in-law :—

" . . . I have hardly time to answer your letter, and I
confine myself to telling you that while no one in the world
can desire more than I do a settlement between you and your
husband, I can never approve of a separation which has no
object but interest.

" I neither can nor ought to meddle in agreements which
you make together, but I beg of you to reflect that all you
have had from Cantini since you have lived at my house of
the Cancellaria, is mine ; that while you are my guest, Cantini
by my order will certainly pay it to nobody but to you ; but
the slight which my brother puts upon me by pretending to
dispense with the merest civilities, and to write without my
knowing anything about it, even deliberately to exclude me,
obliges me to take my own part and to make him see it.
I beg of you urgently, my dearest sister, to annoy me no
further on this point.   It really affects my health to see myself
treated in such a way by my brother, who endeavours by

1784. means of calumny and misrepresentation to have from me whatever [it] comes into his head [to ask,] without acknowledging the least obligation to me."

Louise replied at once, suddenly and boldly changing her tune. She sent a copy of the separation agreement, " which is based upon our mutual certainty of the impossibility of living together, seeing how different our characters are, and following the example of other personages as exalted as my husband and myself. You see now that your unhappy brother yielded only to reason and not to interest, as you think ; and that he disposes of nothing that is yours, since it is on my own suggestion that, knowing his necessities, I give up to him what he gave me for pin-money and which you said would be paid to me here ; a sacrifice which I repeat I would have made for him from the first, if I had not believed I ought not to do it, considering my circumstances. Believe me, brother, the king is in want. . . . Stuart can tell you that during his last illness he had not even money to pay for the masses that were said for him, and when Stuart wrote to you, he had not six sequins in the house. Believe me, brother, he has not enough to live upon: the 60,000 livres he draws from France are not enough for existence since he has no pension from the Camera. I used to think he saved, but I have verified all this with the bankers and I have found that he told the truth.[1] Therefore, I believed myself obliged to assist him. You know, my dear brother, that I thought the same when you proposed to me to keep the diamonds, to which I have some right, except the large stones in which you share with your brother ; but I could not do a thing that would make everybody cry out. . . . How is it possible, my dear brother, that you do not see it is more decent that we should be separated by mutual consent, and that you should not be pleased at my giving to your brother, since it is a sign that I have forgiven him his unkindness, and that I want to try to make him happy, since you give me this money ? What matter can it make to you if I give it to him ? It is quite a superfluous attention on my part to have told you of it. You need never have known it. And is it not better that he should be happy for the few years

---

[1] She had just been declaring that Charles was equally covetous and extravagant : that though his own table was always sumptuously provided, he used to grudge her a little mutton broth in the morning ! Cornelia Knight's " Autobiography."

he has to live, and that you should be left in peace? Also, 1784. why tease him by writing to him that he is disposing of what is yours, since it is I who dispose of what is mine by giving it to him of my free will. Your sister, LOUISE."

This cold signature is the last word she wrote to her offended brother-in-law for eight months. The deed of separation was signed by Charles on April 3, 1784.[1] His wife, amicably divorced *a mensâ et thoro*, was permitted to live at Rome or wherever she pleased, apart from her husband. As she was supposed by her advocates to live apart also from Alfieri, then in England, she did not join her poet until August 17, at Colmar. They were obliged to separate again before long for appearance' sake, and she went to Siena: then to Turin, probably to state her case to her husband's friend and cousin, Victor Amadeus. She had new plans in view.

Sir Horace Mann says that Charles took to drinking again as soon as his affairs were settled: a statement made most likely as carelessly and untruly as the others, for there is no evidence to support the charge, and much reason for its discredit. He also had new plans in view, a grand new scheme on hand for his happiness, and he was full of new hope.

[1] Hist. MSS. Comm. Reports X., part vi. p. 235. (Lord Braye's MSS.)

CHAPTER XIX

THE BONNIE LASS OF ALBANY

1784. DESERTED by his wife, estranged again from his brother, the heart of the dying exile turned to the daughter he had loved so dearly when she was a little child ; whom he had possibly seen again in the bloom of her eighteen years; now living " in the convent of St. Marie at Paris." He had made her his heir by a will signed March 23, 1783, on recovering from his nearly fatal illness.[1] On March 30 he legitimatised her in the French Parliament,[2] created her Duchess of Albany and royal highness, and sent for her to come and live with him. The act of legitimation was signed in July 1784 by " Charles Edward Stuart, grandson of James II., King of Great Britain," his ordinary " Charles R." not being recognised by French law. The King of France, Louis XVI., consented that all the acts should be registered in parliament and they were so registered on September 2. Louis also granted letters patent to the new duchess, which enabled her to inherit all goods which the prince, her father, possessed in France, with the right to dispose of them.[3] She was received as a duchess at the French court and granted the *tabouret*.

There was some necessary delay, while she bought herself new clothes in which to appear at the court of Versailles and made herself ready to take up her position at the head of her royal father's household. She had had a dull time at the convent, and though she had been received in French society, her enjoyment of the privilege was limited by poverty. Her chief recreation was to visit the Archbishop of Bordeaux, a Prince de Rohan ; hence, a Bouillon connection. Sir Horace Mann had this from the archbishop's nephew. John Stuart, once of Athol, was sent from Florence to fetch her : in

[1] Hist. MSS. Comm. Reports X., part vi. p. 235.
[2] Ibid.
[3] Letter of the Baron de Castille of the French Guards to Mr. Wilkes, December 22, 1784. Hist. MSS. Comm. Reports IV., Appx. p. 403 (Colonel Macaulay's Papers). Walpole's Letters, viii. 518 (note).

234

acknowledgment of which service he was created a baronet 1784. by Charles, November 4, 1784. She came attended by a small suite, which included Lord Nairne and a lady whom Charles presently created Countess of Norton, a Frenchwoman, who had married an Irish officer named O'Donnell.

"Her mother was not allowed to accompany her, lest she should disgrace her," writes Sir Horace Mann to his intensely interested correspondent. "The count purposes to marry her here; not, indeed, to one of the archdukes, but to a Florentine nobleman, and to leave her 12,000 crowns a year."[1] Horace Walpole writes to the Countess of Ossory, August 19, 1784:—

"The dying Pretender has acknowledged his natural daughter, Lady Charlotte Stuart, and created her Duchess of Albany, and declared her to be his heiress. I heard a report some time ago in town that his queen, so soon as she is dowager, intends to come to England and marry Alfieri, who is or was here, being sent out of Rome at the instance of the Cardinal of York."[2]

To Sir Horace Mann he writes, August 25:—

"Pray, send me the sequel of the Count of Albany and the Lady Charlotte FitzCharles, his daughter, the new duchess. I shall like to know, too, whether the cardinal assumes the royal title when his brother dies. I recollect but two king-cardinals, Henry of Portugal and the Cardinal of Bourbon, whom the League called Charles X., but who attained the crown no more than the Cardinal of York will do. If the count himself has any feeling, he must rejoice to hear that the descendants of so many of his martyrs are to be restored to their forfeited estates in Scotland by an Act just passed."[3]

Sir Horace Mann replied from Florence, September 18: "The affair relating to the Count of Albany and his natural daughter is drawing to a conclusion. Lady Charlotte Stuart (not FitzCharles), to which her father has on this occasion added the title of Duchess of Albany, is supposed to be on the road hither, attended by two ladies and two gentlemen, and is expected at the beginning of next month. The count

---

[1] Walpole's Letters, viii. 494.
[2] Ibid. 496.   [3] Ibid. 498.

1784. is very busy furnishing his house with all the valuables that he has lately received from Rome that his father left, which are numerous and costly ; besides these, he has received a large quantity of plate and his share of his mother's jewels, except the great ruby and one lesser which were pawned by the republic of Poland for a very large sum to his grandfather Sobieski, with a power, it is said, of redeeming them in the space of a hundred years, which are nearly elapsed. These, therefore, the cardinal would not trust to his brother, being persuaded that if he could find a purchaser, he would sell them, or even part with them for a large *rente viagère* to an Empress of Russia or some other court ; but it is not probable that he will ever have the disposal of them, but that when they fall to the cardinal, he will rather give them to the Madonna di Loreto than to his niece, with whose adoption he is not pleased, nor was consulted about it. Nobody can foresee what the cardinal will do with his crown after his brother's death. The Pope cannot permit him to wear it, as he never acknowledged or permitted the elder brother to assume it. . . . From all this I conclude that no future Pope will permit the Cardinal of York to install himself King of England."[1]

This new action of his brother's took the Duke of York wholly by surprise and he was furious : which Charles had presumably expected, as he did not consult him. He never did consult him upon anything if he could help it. Relations were still strained between them. The deathbed reconciliation of 1782 had been very temporary, owing first to Charles's suspicion of Henry's continued patronage of the revolted Louise, then to Henry's resentment against his brother's reserves as to the King of Sweden's intervention in the business of the divorce. Henry, always intolerant of the Walkinshaw scandal, now fancied his own rights to be endangered by the legitimation, with the unprecedented addition of "royal highness." The dukedom, too, must have been an annoyance to him personally : the Albany title usually given to the second son of the King of Scots. Charles I. and James II. had borne it when Dukes of York, and the Hanoverian monarchs had also bestowed it upon their second sons. It does not seem to

---

[1] Walpole's Letters, viii. 498–99.

have been given to Henry by his father, for it never appears 1784. officially among his titles and Charles treated it as dormant ; but the Duke of York would naturally look upon it as his due. He had assumed it in France as a title of incognito, and the French king and ministers continued to give it to him until he became a cardinal; perhaps for distinction, perhaps by preference, as they called Charles " Prince Edward." [1]   When Henry was an infant, the Scottish dukedom had apparently been expected, for Lockhart referred to him, in a letter to James, as the Duke of Albany, but James himself never gave him that title, referred to the child always as " Prince Henry," later, as "the duke," more rarely as "the Duke of York." Charles was really more moderate in his ambition for his daughter than one might have expected, for he could as lawfully (assuming his kingship) have created her Princess of Wales. Henry VIII. so created his daughters in succession. Princess Anne, afterwards queen, wished William of Orange to create her son Prince of Wales. Illegitimacy of birth would not affect a creation.

Henry immediately published his formal protest. "The Cardinal Duke of York cannot do less than complain strongly of the proceeding of his Royal Brother concerning the irregular and improper action taken in summoning a natural daughter of his to live with him with so much publicity. It will be easily perceived on what grounds he may complain, if it is considered in the first place, what an indecent uproar was made some time ago about supposed poverty and destitution, when it was pretended his Royal Brother had not enough to live upon, and the burden was thrown on the shoulders of the Cardinal Duke, against all justice ; who is now informed in the most outrageously pompous manner, that he has taken upon himself an expense which will naturally exceed the maintenance of his own consort ; an action which is in manifest contradiction to the former exaggerated statement.

"In the second place, the Cardinal Duke represents the situation in which he finds himself, on seeing follow immediately after a feigned reconciliation by means of autograph letters from his Royal Brother, a public proceeding of this description, as to which he has no information, and to which his consent was not asked.

---

[1] Charles was also called Prince Edward by the papal court. (Vatican Archives.)

1784. "In the third place, he represents the irregularity of this pretended legitimation, which was not necessary to enable his brother to give to this person a fair subsistence, which he had already been bound in conscience to do for thirty years past. As he did not do it, the Cardinal Duke, touched by pure compassion, supplied the money privately. But it was not necessary to give her those titles, and to place her in a position for which there can be no explanation to the mind of any intelligent person, aware of the facts and of present circumstances, except the intention of putting a public slight upon the Cardinal Duke and his sister-in-law.

"And here is reached the fourth point raised by the Cardinal Duke : that the said legitimation, as it seems to be intended, goes very much farther than has been the invariable custom in similar cases, and as in the recent example of James II. in the person of the Duke of Berwick, since it reaches the very height of presumption to pretend to have the lady recognised as of the stem of the royal house, by granting her titles which would be most justly contested if he were in actual possession of his lawful right. Nor in that case would his royal brother, according to the law of the kingdom, have the faculty thus to habilitate a natural child and place her in the succession to the throne ; a case utterly without precedent. In this state of things, the Cardinal Duke flatters himself that all his friends will accept his statement, convinced of its justice with regard to this business, so disgusting to him ; which he protests for his part to regard as null and void : in short, to ignore it so long as God gives him life." [1]

The cardinal may have been in one particular a little out in his history. However the law of succession in England and Scotland may have stood in 1784, the present supposed case was not by any means without a very notable precedent indeed ; that of the first Stuart king, Robert II., who settled the crown of Scotland upon his eldest illegitimate son by his cousin and mistress, Elizabeth Mure, John Earl of Carrick, afterwards Robert III. ; entailing it next upon his other children by Elizabeth Mure "for the love he bore her," to the exclusion of his lawful children, Walter, Earl of Strath-

[1] Additional MSS. British Museum 30,475.

earn and others, by Euphemia Ross.[1] As for instances in
earlier days of the succession passing to illegitimate sons,
they are plentiful though confused: and most confusing.

Ignored by the prince who was in himself the whole
royal family beyond its head—for the foreign cousins did
not count—the Duchess of Albany was welcomed by her
father with most touching eagerness. He had looked forward
to her arrival in a great state of joyful excitement, and he
found in her all his fond hope and reminiscent fancy had
painted. Florence welcomed her too, and Sir Horace Mann,
greatly interested, described her to Walpole, October 8, 1784 :—

" The arrival of the Lady Charlotte Stuart has caused
some little bustle in the town. A French lady, who for thirty
years had been totally neglected, but on a sudden transformed
into a duchess, was an object that excited the curiosity of
both sexes—the men to see her figure ; the ladies scrupulously
to examine that and the new modes she has brought from
Paris : the result of all which is that she is allowed to be a
good figure, tall and well made, but that the features of her
face resemble too much those of her father to be handsome " ;
a sad reminder of what time, disappointment, and Chianti had
done for " Bonnie Prince Charlie." " She is gay, lively, and
very affable, and has the behaviour of a well-bred Frenchwoman, without assuming the least distinction among our
ladies on account of her new dignity. They flock to her
door, and leave their cards, which she is to return ; though
the countess, her step-mother, did not, and therefore, or
perhaps for another reason, lived alone with Count Alfieri,
who as a writer of tragedies, formed the plot of her elopement, on which the acknowledgment of the natural daughter,
all the honours she has received, and the future advantage
she will have by being heiress to all her father can leave her,
depend. Perhaps neither the countess nor her lover foresaw
all this, and it is very probable that she will repent of it, and
consequently detest her adviser. . . . The new duchess has
appeared at the theatres, which were crowded on her account,
with all her father's jewels, which are very fine. He asked
leave of the duke to put a baldacchino or dais over her boxes
in each theatre, and a velvet carpet to hang before it, which

[1] See Stuart's " Genealogical History of the Stuarts " ; Bœthius ; Lesley, Bishop
of Ross ; Burton's " History of Scotland," &c. &c., for the marriage of Robert II.

1784. was refused, but had permission to line the boxes as he pleased. That in the great theatre is hung with crimson damask ; the cushion is velvet with gold lace. In the other theatre it is yellow damask. The count is much pleased with this distinction." [1]

She was really a handsome young woman with her father's fine profile—straight nose and sweet mouth ; very curly hair of a rich chestnut. In a beautiful portrait by an unknown painter, that thickly curling hair clusters under the odd square turban in fashion at the time, and falls softly on her long full neck. Her graceful shoulders are veiled by the fichu so familiar in contemporary portraits of Marie Antoinette and later, of Charlotte Corday. [2]

She presided over her father's house with all the grace and dignity of a real Stuart princess. For her sake, Charles emerged from his proudly sullen retirement, and together they entered into the gaieties of the Tuscan capital.

" The father's whole business seems to make her happy and settled according to her rank," writes her friend the Baron de Castille. " Many Italian princes have offered to her and one of the brothers of the King of Sweden. Her father, who wishes to see her on a throne, presses hard for the latter. He is commissioned to write to England. The duchess has suffered so much in her youth that she would prefer not to marry, if the court of England would make her an allowance so long as she remained single, and thus every idea of the unfortunate House of Stuart would be extinguished. The pursuit of the King of Sweden on behalf of his brother is a speculation : he hopes to make some advantage by the alliance." [3] " As [she] will inherit jewels and effects to the amount of at least £100,000," confirms Sir Horace Mann, " it is said that one of the royal Dukes of Ostrogothia or Vandalmania is to marry her ; but this I do not warrant." [4]

Money, indeed, the duchess wanted badly, and abstention from matrimony might bring her in as good a provision as any Italian or Swedish marriage. The cardinal stopped her allowance when she joined her father and Charles had very little to

[1] Walpole's Letters, viii. 517–8. Mann to Walpole (note).
[2] Miniature belonging (in 1861) to the Countess of Seafield. Published in " Prince Charles Edward," by Andrew Lang, first edition ; Goupil & Co.
[3] Hist. MSS. Comm. Reports IV., Appx. p. 403. (Col. Macaulay's Papers.)
[4] Walpole's Letters, viii. 522.

leave her, for of course the jewels Mann supposed would 1784. become hers were entailed beyond Charles's testamentary powers. The English government might have found it worth their while to buy her celibacy, seeing how the peace of the future might be disturbed by ambitious children of hers, reviving the story of her mother's marriage ; and it was stated later that she did make a formal promise to the government to remain single.

On October 8, the duchess wrote to the cardinal. The letter was no doubt suggested by Charles and the terms employed of his choosing. Her letters, some of them still sparkling with the bright sand she used to dry them, are all in French and very well written indeed.[1]

She notified to the cardinal her legitimation and her arrival in Florence, and assured him of her devotion to her father's health and comfort. She thanked him for his kindness to her since the death of "her grandfather," King James, and entreated him to continue her pension to her mother, who had nothing else to live upon. She addressed him as her "dearest uncle" and signed herself "Charlotte Stuart, Duchess of Albany."

The cardinal vouchsafed no reply beyond sending to his brother a copy of his manifesto. Charles replied in a holograph letter, in French, November 2 :—

"I have the pleasure of telling you myself that my dearest daughter, being recognised by me, by France, and by the Pope, is a royal highness to you and every one. I do not dispute your rights. They are fixed, since you are my brother ; but I beg of you not to dispute those of my dearest daughter."

The Pope had written kindly to the duchess, congratulating her upon her arrival. Charles thanked the Pope for his letter (November 16), entreated his protection for his daughter, and begged of him to grant to her the reversion of his pension after his death ; reminding him how the Cardinal of York had cut down the allowance made by King James and now had stopped it altogether.[2] Indeed, every one but the cardinal felt kindly towards this gentle Cordelia and was glad the poor old, sorrow-frenzied prince should have such promise of peace and

---

[1] Add. MSS. British Museum (Papers of the Cardinal of York) 30,475, 30,476.
[2] Hist. MSS. Comm. Reports X., part vi. p. 235. (Braye Papers, f. 147.)

Q

1784. affectionate care to soothe and brighten the last years of his dreary life. On that same November 16, the Count de Vergennes, French foreign minister, wrote to the duchess—" My lady Stuart d'Albany "—that Louis XVI. had granted her father an annual pension of 60,000 livres, with reversion in her favour on his death as to 10,000 livres thereof, charged on the royal treasury.[1]

Common wrath over the honours and praise of the new duchess drew the cardinal and his sister-in-law together again. The cardinal was under the impression that Louise had given up Alfieri, and he wrote to her at Turin. She replied, from Genoa, December 1. Nothing would astonish her that her husband could do! She was fully aware of " the follies he was carrying on at Florence," and attributed them to the influences of the Irish by whom he was surrounded. She went to spend Christmas at Bologna with her old friend, Princess Lambertini, and wrote again to the cardinal, on Christmas Eve, with seasonable greetings, and further and unseasonable sneers at her husband. He could no longer walk, but had to be carried from one room to another because of the swelling of his legs. He had bestowed the St. Andrew upon his daughter and " a certain lord who is with him," and it was all very droll.

Sir Horace Mann also mentions this investiture which took place on St. Andrew's Day, but he does not mock, and is full of praise for the strong and beneficent influence of the duchess, who checked her father when he drank too much and talked too much. He says they spent their time in abusing the unfriendly cardinal.[2] This is wholly untrue as regards Charlotte, who was doing her best to make peace between the brothers. The resentment Charles still felt at the cardinal's championship of the faithless wife was now sharpened by his refusal to acknowledge the faithful daughter and by his wounding her by such cruel slights.

" The pantomime carrying on at Florence and Rome is entertaining," Walpole writes to Mann, January 4, 1785.

1785. " So the Pope, who would not grant the title of king to the pretender allows his no-majesty to have created a duchess ; and the Cardinal of York, who is but a rag of the papacy,

---

[1] Hist. MSS. Comm. Reports X., part vi. p. 235. (Braye Papers, f. 149.)
[2] " Mann and Manners," Doran, ii. 410.

and who must think his brother a king, will not allow her 1785.
title."[1]

On February 26, Charlotte took the opportunity of the
cardinal's approaching birthday, March 6, to make another
very respectful advance : this time without her father's knowledge, who had probably forbidden correspondence without
repetition and recognition of her titles and relationship. She
submissively dropped the offending title, and signed herself
simply "Charlotte Stuart." After repeating her gratitude for
favours past, she asked with gentle pathos, how it was that
she had deserved to lose his protection, solely because she
had come to take care of her father who was ill, suffering, and
alone ? She had taken for granted that his royal highness
had known and approved of her coming, but she had not
had time to notify it herself. She was dreadfully distressed
at finding such courtesy had been omitted and assured him of
her sincere regret at having displeased him.

The cardinal answered this letter. (Sir Horace Mann
says he never answered any of her letters.) Though he had
been softened by her gentle persistence, he would not yet
acknowledge any relationship, and evidently objected even to
her use of the Stuart name, for thenceforth she ceased to
use it in writing to him. He probably knew from other
sources how gracious was her influence, and he saw how
useful an ally she might be to keep him *au courant* as to the
real state of things at Florence. He was anxious to be on
friendly terms with his brother, that they might now combine
against the Countess of Albany, who, he found, had tricked him
again about Alfieri, and who was endeavouring to engage for
herself the further sympathy and substantial assistance of
France. He was anxious that Charles should enlighten the
French court as to the true reason of his displeasure against
"madame" : the only name by which Louise is ever mentioned in the family. De Vergennes must threaten her with
the loss of her French pension if she should persist in her
misconduct.

The Duchess of Albany was delighted with the confidences
reposed in her, and promised to do everything in her power
to bring the king to terms with his brother. The cardinal
wrote to her so kindly, she said, in appreciation of her

[1] Walpole's Letters, viii. 536.

1785. conduct, that she was moved to tears. On April 9, she seized a favourable moment to get Charles to write a letter to De Vergennes, which should be submitted to the cardinal. Charles was unable to write himself but dictated to his secretary. He was willing enough to be reconciled to his brother, but the duchess insisted on the necessity of keeping her own correspondence with the cardinal a secret from her father, for he would never have suffered a word to have been sent out of the palace that he had not seen or dictated, and the cardinal would gain nothing by the correspondence. Charles himself would have gained nothing by openness. He was like a sick child who must be deceived for its good.

In his memorial to De Vergennes he set forth how his wife had left him nearly five years ago, for no other reason than to indulge an " unbridled passion for Monsieur Alfieri": how she had fled to Rome for that purpose and afterwards to Baden, and that there was every reason to suppose she meant to settle with Alfieri in Alsace. She had not brought a penny of dower to the king, who had settled upon her 15,000 francs for pin-money, and, besides, had paid all her expenses while she lived in his house. In spite of this, she had persuaded the Queen of France that he had let her want for the necessaries of life, and so had obtained from her majesty's kindness 60,000 francs which she had enjoyed during the whole time of her residence in Florence, unknown to her husband.

It may well have been that Charles kept her short. There is little room for doubt in the reports of his selfishness, if not miserliness, and husbands do exist from whom pin-money and household expenses must be extracted as with a forceps. He had heavy expenses of his own and little money to meet them, and was probably inclined to believe, after his kind, that a woman's expenses are always extravagances and will always wait to be paid. Louise's excuse was that the French money was paid to her personally and exclusively, and that if her husband had got hold of it, it would have been partially absorbed by Irish pockets, partially locked up against the next phantom expedition, and the remainder drunk away.

A copy of his memorial was sent by Charles to his brother, who highly approved of it and added his signature. " I conjure you," the cardinal wrote to Charles, "to do what 1785. in you lies to prevent a *quidam* like Alfieri from gaining his ends by a union so offensive to our family. It makes me furious, and it is well that you should know they are in constant communication by letter, and that there is no doubt it is he who governs madame in all these proceedings. She has deliberately broken her word to me upon this matter, and I broke off all communication with her several months ago. I am greatly obliged to your daughter for interesting herself so with you on my behalf. It proves the kindness of her heart, to which every one bears witness. . . . Take care of yourself."

Louise, in despair at Henry's silence, had written to him with repeated assurances of her attachment, excusing her conduct on various points with regard to which it had never been impeached, but saying not a word of Alfieri. She was in a terrible fright at the prospect of losing her jointure, which would be forfeited by misconduct, and of losing her French pension in case of war.[1] She left Bologna that April for France.

The cardinal did not do things by halves. Always impulsive as he was scrupulously just, now eager to atone for past unkindness, he wrote a second memorial to the Pope, in which he acknowledged that, though some circumstances attending the legitimation of the Duchess of Albany had been offensive to him, he had been won over by the young lady's goodness ; and that it was through her mediation that his brother had written him a letter of reconciliation.[2] At her anxious solicitation, he softened the formality of his address to her, but only to "Ma Cousine," still refusing to treat her as a niece. She was hurt. She could not show his letters to useful friends at Versailles, she told him, unless he would prove his confidence in her by calling her his niece. He could in no other way so gratify his brother. Charles would then consent to save himself fatigue by making her his authorised secretary.

So, though it was she who had drawn the brothers together, it was she who stood in the way of their perfect union ; held it from being more than a paper compact. Charles still

---

[1] Peace with England had been signed in January 1783, closing the great War of Independence in America. The chance of civil war in France was more likely to imperil the pension in 1785.

[2] Hist. MSS. Comm. Reports X., part vi. p. 237. (Lord Braye's MSS.)

1785. bitterly resented the cardinal's refusal to recognise her relationship and her rank ; Henry still sternly resented her existence, her conspicuous position, her pseudo-royalty. This intolerance was not out of cold obstinacy but out of unbending moral principle. Those who knew him best describe him as the kindest, most accessible of men. But, sincerely religious as he was, he was proud, passionate, and impulsive as he had been from childhood ; always as much of a prince as of a priest : "not a liitle lively" and fond of his own way, as Charles said of him nearly forty years earlier. And he had just been tricked out of confidence and generous sympathy by a woman, who had served herself by his impulsive kind-heartedness and his horror of vice.

His correspondence with the duchess nevertheless went on with the closest frequency and regularity. They wrote in French, but Henry was always apologetic for his French and wrote it with difficulty. He had almost forgotten his English, too, and had become very much Italianised. The duchess set to work to study Italian, that he might write to her in the language in which he was most at home. But she still annoyed him by an apparently tactless harping on her "recognition" string : chiefly, of course, with the object of soothing her father, who was suffering much that spring. She succeeded only in receiving another distressing snub from the cardinal. But upon receiving a most pathetic letter to beseech his forgiveness and continued kindness, the warm-hearted prince was touched and hastened to reassure her ; though, to her extreme sorrow, the reasons against her request for recognition as his niece were still insurmountable.

Charles wrote affectionately to his brother, thanking him warmly for the kind things he said about his dear daughter, who was their agent in the delicate business with De Vergennes and Vulpian, his own lawyer in Paris. Charles had requested De Vergennes to arrange that "madame's" dowry should be paid out of her French pension. The 40,000 livres had been guaranteed by subsidies from foreign courts. He would thus be relieved from all engagements, and she would have 60,000 francs for life. It would be most unjust if she should get 100,000, simply as a reward for misconduct.

CHAPTER XX

CLEAR SHINING AFTER RAIN

UNDER his daughter's gentle influence, a happy change came 1785. over Charles, physically and spiritually. He took great care of himself, she reported to the cardinal, and he had reconciled himself with the Church by going to the sacraments at Easter. Then to her consternation, he insisted upon going to Pisa, to attend the fêtes that were to be given at the beginning of May in honour of the King and Queen of Naples. He was quite unfit for any such exertion and excitement though he felt so much better. There was also a painful drawback to Pisa in the presence there of Alfieri, of which the duchess was aware. She appealed in vain to the cardinal, who dreaded the effect of the projected trip, but admitted there was no help for it : nothing but patience.

On May 4 the invalid himself wrote to his brother from Pisa, delighted with his outing, with the fresh air and gaiety of Pisa—which is a much hotter, stuffier place than Florence— and with the splendour of the fêtes. The journey had made his leg swell, the duchess reported, and the sore had become greatly inflamed, but he insisted on being present at everything, even though Alfieri paraded in his sight wherever he went, to his constant irritation. There were happier associations to divert his mind from late distresses, old battles to fight over again, and Charles was at the age when memories of boyhood are peculiarly clear and sweet. The King of Naples, Ferdinand IV., was the son of his old friend Charles now III. of Spain, with whom he had ridden to Gaeta in 1734. After a successful reign in Naples, Charles III. had been called to succeed his elder brother on the Spanish throne and had made over Naples to his third son. The Grand Duchess of Tuscany, Marie Louise de Bourbon, was Ferdinand's sister, while the Queen of Naples, Marie Caroline, and the Grand Duke of Tuscany, Leopold of Lorraine, were also brother and sister, and, with Queen Marie Antoinette, were children of the

1785. Emperor Francis I. and Maria Theresa. These royal persons were all much younger than Charles, but they were just the age of his daughter, and it was pleasant to be surrounded by so much youth and gaiety ; by "his equals," too, whose absence he had so lamented to Gustavus of Sweden. His life had of late been so hideously lonely! Now it was brightened by his daughter's loving presence and full of interest in making her happy. He was proud of her popularity and grace and anxious to make friends for her, so that his death should not leave her unprotected, lonely, and obscure.

Best of all, on May 3, the day before Charles wrote to his brother, his daughter had been presented to the Grand Duchess of Tuscany by the Duchess of Attry-Salviati, a very old friend of his, and had been accorded a most gratifying reception.

The grand duchess had never consented to receive Charlotte at the Florentine court as Duchess of Albany, in spite of Charles's urgent request ; not absolutely refusing, but putting him off with one excuse or another ; for one, it was objected that she had not brought credentials from the Queen of France. The grand duchess was at last persuaded to friendliness by her sister-in-law, Caroline of Naples, who received the Duchess of Albany most cordially. The grand duchess was now so full of sympathy with Charles on the subject of "madame," who had so forgotten what was due to the illustrious name she bore, that she was the more disposed to look kindly upon the step-daughter and rival who filled "madame's" place with so much wisdom and sweetness. It was whispered that the grand duchess had been jealous of the grand duke's admiration for Louise. The grand duchess said she had been under the impression that the family was still divided and that the Cardinal of York was in league with "madame." Charlotte took the opportunity of her interview to assure her royal highness that the cardinal disapproved of "madame" as strongly as she did, and to inform her of the excellent terms upon which the king now stood with his brother ; which the grand duchess was much pleased to hear.

Ill and suffering as he was, Charles would abstain from no amusement, and his health gave way. His daughter vainly urged him to be careful. How could he gain benefit from the change while he persisted in fatiguing himself by continual late hours and scanty repose ? She lamented to the cardinal 1785. that she was not listened to as she would wish as to the observance of a regimen which was for the king's good, but which he was very far from following. This need not imply that the excitement of the Pisan revels and subsequent exhaustion had sent Charles back to the bottle ; no more than a very self-willed invalid's impatience of laws of diet and early hours laid down by medical authority.

Even the end of the Pisan fêtes did not bring relief to his anxious daughter. He wanted to go on to the succeeding fêtes at Leghorn and Lucca. Then he became so much worse that he promised to give up that idea and return at once to Florence. After a relapse which sent him to bed for four days, they returned to Florence on May 22. He was very tired on the journey and was daily growing weaker.

It was a comfort to his daughter in her distress that French opinion (Marie Antoinette being the sister of the Queen of Naples) was now coming round to their side. Madame was staying in Paris with the Prince of Salm-Krybourg—whose daughter had so nearly stood in her shoes—and she had gone to Versailles to see M. de Vergennes, who, however, was forewarned and forearmed against her. French gossip reported a new flirtation of Louise with a valet-de-chambre, on account of which faithlessness Alfieri had broken with her. The valet was dismissed, but a certain Count Proly, a German, had followed her to Paris, and Alfieri raged loudly. The duchess suspected Louise had spies in Florence who sent her accounts of what passed in the royal household.

Alfieri unhappily followed Charles from Pisa to Florence, where he took a house for four months, and Charles was again perpetually exposed to chances of meeting him, which distressed and disturbed him greatly ; while Alfieri bore himself with the most consummate arrogance and defiance in his very sight. The duchess thought he had possibly come to Florence posing as an injured person, the better to conceal his intrigue : though in that case, he would hardly, she supposed, have "said things," as he did, about his beloved. These speeches confirm the story of his jealousy. Or he might have come to watch for the king's death.

Her next news for the cardinal was that after all Alfieri had given up his house in Florence, and was going privately

1785. to Paris to make up his quarrel with madame. She had it on the best authority. She supposed he had been disconcerted on finding out upon what friendly terms she (Charlotte) now stood with the grand duchess.

There was another interesting negotiation under way for raising the wind, and Charles was anxious to have his brother's support in the matter. He was as usual wretchedly short of money. Though he had lived in retirement for so many years, there had always been the expense and waste of a royal household to keep up. Now there was his daughter's household as well, which must befit her rank ; and he wished to provide for her in the event of his death, which could not be far distant. He bethought himself, or perhaps was reminded by Lord Caryll,[1] of the money really due to himself and his brother from England ; the jointure of their grandmother, Queen Mary of Modena, of which not one farthing had ever been paid, in spite of promises from the Prince of Orange and succeeding governments. Charles had, alas ! quarrelled with the faithful Caryll on a certain lamentable occasion seven years ago, but the gentle duchess had set herself to make peace here also, and in the preceding March Caryll had written to her from Dunkirk, thanking her for his restoration to the royal favour. He had lately been trying to get the long overdue jointure for his majesty, and suggested that the good offices of the French court should be solicited, as France had a right to demand payment of arrears which had been guaranteed by treaties. "There are in this present (British) Cabinet," he writes, "persons suspected of being at heart attached to their legitimate prince ; and further, I know for certain that the elector himself has more than once declared that if the king were ever in distress, it would be a real pleasure to assist him."

George III. made good those words twelve years later.

The jointure settled upon the queen of James II., by an Act of Parliament still unrepealed, amounted to £50,000, without the accumulations and interest for the eighty-four years that had elapsed since her widowhood. Indeed, it was contended on her behalf by the court of France, shortly after the revolution, that King James being banished and dead in law, she was even then entitled to the dowry as if she had

---

[1] Hist. MSS. Comm. Reports X., part vi. p. 226. (Lord Braye's MSS.)

been really his widow. The Prince of Orange did not deny the claim, but gave verbal promise only for its payment. Marshal Boufflers requested that the concession might at least be confirmed by a secret article in the Treaty of Ryswick, but William professing great indignation that his word should be held less satisfactory than his bond, the Marshal departed with full confidence in the prince's good faith. At the first demand for payment, William backed out, on some pretence of unfulfilled condition, though Boufflers swore the concession had been unconditional. The promoter of the Darien Scheme,[1] who reserved for his own uses, domestic and military, moneys voted by Parliament for the household and education of his nephew and presumptive heir, the little Duke of Gloucester, was not likely to be scrupulous as to money claimed by a helpless woman, whose husband he had conquered and banished. Another attempt had been made at the Peace of Utrecht to recover the money, and many private attempts were made on behalf of James III.: all equally in vain.

Vergennes agreed to set on foot new negotiations, and application for payment was made to Mr. Pitt through Lord Pembroke, who had visited Charles and his daughter at Florence. But Pitt refused to allow the subject to be so much as mentioned to the kindly conscientious George III. It was then recommended that the matter should be brought before the King's Bench, but on such extortionate terms that neither Charles nor Henry would agree to the measure. Louis XVI. refused to interfere, saying, " *C'est une famille malheureuse, dont je ne veux plus entendre parler.*" Four years later his own family was in a still more desperate plight! After endless correspondence, this new attempt came to nothing like its predecessors.

The weary litigation over " madame's " money matters dragged and fretted on. Charles's cousin, the Princesse de Montbazon, privately supported his side of the business ; a clever woman, says the Duchess of Albany, with a good head. Family interest was represented on the other side by Louise's sister, the Marquise of Jamaica, of the Fitz-James cousinship and " *forte-intrigante.*" It was presently hoped that

---

[1] " There's Mary the dochter and Willie the cheater." (Jacobite Song, "Cakes o' Croudy," by Lord Newbattle.)

1785. "madame" and her friends would consent to compromise by accepting through De Vergennes and Vulpian an annuity of 60,000 francs for dowry. She was in a hurry to leave Paris and had many schemes on hand. She had not met with the success she anticipated at the French court. Marie Antoinette had refused to receive her, and it had been hinted to her that the sooner she could make it convenient to depart the better. Vulpian assured Charles that she was the worst enemy of the Stuart family. She not only kept "saying things," but she compromised their friends in France. It was of the utmost importance that in the negotiations over the dowry, France should not appear to act for Charles as King of England ; yet his wife had caused profound annoyance to De Vergennes on one occasion at the Foreign Office when an Irishwoman flung herself on her knees before Louise and implored her protection as Queen of England. In the convents, too, she allowed herself to be received as a queen, which exasperated her royal husband as much as it did the French foreign minister. So Louise turned her attention to getting money out of England and Spain.

She left Paris for Alsace to visit a friend, Mlle. de Malzam. Alfieri, appeased and recovered, rejoined her there from Pisa. She purposed going on from Alsace to England on her money quest next year. She still held out for an outrageously extravagant alimony, and Charles held out for granting none at all out of his own pocket or prospects. The Duchess of Albany hoped he might be persuaded to grant 10,000 livres, but madame now wanted 100,000 down. She was told that that could not be done, and that it was not customary to pay dowries in advance. Hers, in any case, could be due only upon the death of her husband.

Charles was most anxious to see his brother. He was feeling better, but his tenure of life was precarious in the extreme, and failing memory no doubt helped to complicate matters with his wife and the lawyers as to what he had and had not really promised and settled. It was all down in black and white, but he was naturally anxious to avail himself of any legal loophole by which to escape from his wife's exorbitant demands. He was extremely desirous, too, that his brother should make his daughter's personal acquaintance, in the hope that she might find a second father in her uncle after his own death. Would Henry not come to pay him a visit after the celebration of St. Peter's Day, June 29 ? He began at once in delighted anticipation to prepare for the cardinal's reception, and assured him that he would make him as comfortable as he could.

The cardinal had found in Charlotte a useful ally as well as a devoted and tactful guardian of his brother, and he was anxious to see her that they might more conveniently discuss affairs and more effectively join forces against Louise, but for some occult reason, he would not come into the Duchy of Tuscany, even to please his invalid, possibly dying, brother. He suggested to Charlotte that she should pay him a visit ; a great condescension on his part and a striking tribute to her sense and devotion. But the difficulty was, how to persuade Charles to consent to her leaving him for ever so short a time ?

Charles was distressed and immensely puzzled by his brother's alleged inability to enter Tuscany, but profoundly touched by the kindness with which Henry deplored the fact ; still more, by the wish he expressed to meet the duchess ; but it did not enter Charles's head that a meeting could be contemplated which would part him from his daughter. He wrote, trusting that circumstances might change and allow the visit. The duchess wrote by the same post, rejoicing that so far all looked well for the success of their hoped-for meeting. She stipulated that her father should not know to what place the cardinal would come to meet her, or even the distance, for he was quite capable of insisting upon going too, which would fatigue him far too much in the feeble state of his health.

The negotiations which went on now between the duchess and the cardinal to contrive their meeting were as secret and anxious as those which concerned the thwarting of the Countess of Albany in her mercenary designs. But the cardinal, besides being in indifferent health, was a very busy man. He worked in his diocese with a minute and fatherly care. He was a bishop after the ideal of St. Paul and Ruskin,[1] for though he by no means despised the " shearer's feast," he was no " blind mouth," but saw and fed and watered like an honest overseer. He looked strictly after the morals

---

[1] See " Sesame and Lilies," Lecture I.

1785. of every member of his flock. That he had over-governed his canons in St. Peter's was perhaps true : he would not suffer laxities to obtain prescriptive right to remain under his rule. He worked as hard in the newer duties of the vice-chancellorship. He found close correspondence with his niece and brother fatiguing, and suggested that Charlotte should open a correspondence with his man of business, Canon Cesarini. Then he sent the Abbé Barbieri to Florence to talk things over.

The great heat of July caused Charles much suffering and sent him to bed now and then, but a pleasant visitor came to Florence at this time, the young Count de Banville, travelling for health and information. He brought introductions to Charles and the Cardinal Duke, and frequently visited and cheered the royal invalid. He was as greatly charmed with the duchess as she was with him, and praised her enthusiastically to the cardinal when he went on to Rome.

Weeks went by, and still Charlotte dared not mention to her father the intended meeting with her uncle. She had hoped the Duchess of Attry-Salviati, who was very fond of her and had great influence with the king, would manage the delicate business ; but the duchess went off to the waters of Pisa, and Charlotte must wait to see what came of the letter the Abbé Barbieri would bring from Canon Cesarini. She was quite ill with anxiety, but hoped all would come right, as her father saw how her heart was set upon the meeting. And madame was now clamouring for 400,000 livres down and at once ! But Vulpian was resolved she should have no more than 10,000 francs or he would upset the marriage contract. Nothing was due to her, in any case, Charlotte repeated, until her husband's death, and then only an annual sum.

The cardinal's emissary, Barbieri, arrived at Florence about September 1. Charles would not hear of his daughter leaving him. He could not be left without her ! She would never come back if she left him in her turn, as others had left him ! A thousand fears possessed him. She hoped the cardinal would write again to press the matter, but the worst of it was, she deplored, that reasons which would convince other people would not convince the king.

But Charles thought better of it, though even during the

dictation of his letter his reluctant mind wavered. He told 1785. his brother that the sacrifice he asked of him was certainly very great: one that he would make for nobody. So ill as he was, his dear daughter was absolutely necessary to him. It was only by her means that he could receive company without being bored. The days wherein he should miss her society would be very long and dull. But he would allow her to go, if only that Henry might understand how precious she must be to him, and to show him how real was the sacrifice he was making to prove his love for his brother.

The cardinal was suffering from influenza. The duchess recommended inhalations from which she had experienced much benefit. On his recovery, the meeting took place at Monte Freddo, near Perugia. Some accounts say he came to the Baths of Lucca to recuperate, but this would hardly be consistent with his refusal to enter Tuscany. The first result of the interview was the complete conquest of the reluctant but warm-hearted cardinal by his charming niece, his final conviction of her goodness and force of character.[1] The second result was the determination they came to that she must bring her father to Rome that he might be with his brother until the end.

Perhaps a third result was the epileptic fit with which Charles was attacked after his daughter's return. Excitement always brought him to death's door, and there was high excitement over the projected departure, pleasurable and other. Charles was delighted with the prospect of leaving Florence and living near his brother, once the subject was broken and had become familiarised, but there was the old difficulty of the "recognition." How should he consent to live in his father's palace in less than his father's state ? It is easy to imagine the stormy scenes that must have taken place before his daughter brought him to a more reasonable mind. *She* had no illusions on that point ; would shrug her shoulders sadly, says Sir Horace Mann, when her father talked of the never-abandoned hope.

Mann reported to Walpole that the cardinal was sent for and administered the Viaticum.[2] The only allusion to this visit in the correspondence is the mention that at the end of

[1] Letter of the Cardinal of York to the Pope : Lord Braye's MSS. Hist. MSS. Comm. Reports X., part vi. p. 237.
[2] "Mann and Manners," Doran, ii. 416.

1785. October the cardinal had just returned to Rome. Charles recovered and wrote to his brother on October 29; his last letter from Florence. It is written in Italian by a new hand, and signed in sprawling, shaky, blotted, almost illegible initials: " V. F. A. C. R." (Vostro Fratello Affezzionato, Carlo R.). Herein he set forth his views of the matter to his brother, who was busily occupied, preparing the Muti Palace for its master's reception. Charles thanked the cardinal warmly for his care and trouble, and assured him how he longed with his whole heart for the day that should bring them together. Then he bowed to the inevitable, the impossibility of "recognition." His daughter had managed him better than his impatient brother ; or Henry had reasoned with him effectually at Florence. It was his strong desire, he said, to preserve a strict incognito during his journey and his residence in Rome, and to be known only as the Count of Albany : clinging by that pathetic pretence at preference to his dignity as a free sovereign. He sent polite messages to the Pope and mentioned that he had been for some days confined to bed, and referred to the cardinal's recent return from a journey.

But the way was not yet made smooth. Charles changed his mind as to the desirability of a move and made himself ill again, but the duchess wrote a few days later, November 1, to Cesarini, a letter evidently dictated from her repentant father's sick-bed. She began by explaining his majesty's wishes, and described what he meant to bring in the way of equipage and house furniture. "The king no longer proposes to live at Rome differently from here," she says : and the concession is tempered by a touching hint that their stay in Rome is to be looked upon as only temporary: merely for the pleasure of the cardinal's society and to pay their respects to the Pope. Charles would not even yet consent to laying his bones far from the ashes of his forefathers. She was distressed that his royal highness should have been troubled with the details of their housekeeping. They did not wish to trespass upon his kindness further than the mere furnishing of the palace, where the simplest necessaries would suffice for such a flying visit ! They would keep their establishment at Rome on the same footing as at Florence. They hoped to live much with his royal highness, but would not for the world inconvenience

him. The expense of their removal would, of course, be a 1785.
strain upon the king's resources, but it was a very welcome
expense, not to be seriously considered, and other expenses
would be cut down. She was most anxious to meet his royal
highness's wishes in everything. The king was better and she
was writing from his bedroom. He had suffered cruelly but
the worst was over, though he would be obliged to stay in
bed for a month or six weeks longer.

She explained this startling news to the cardinal next day
at his command. Whether by evil design or gross ignorance,
the doctor had applied so violent a remedy to her father—
blisters which were left for twenty-two hours upon the soles
of his feet—as to cause him acute suffering. The king, she
said, had the blindest confidence in his doctor, who was a
young man, quite inexperienced. She was in a terrible state of
anxiety until another doctor was called in, who, on the previous
evening, had assured them that the king was quite able to
bear the journey, and that his illness had been occasioned only
by the wintry change in the weather. Thank God, he was
now going on as well as possible. She was afraid to judge
anybody, so perplexed as she was, but she knew their departure to be unpopular in Florence, that the withdrawal of the
little court would cause considerable loss to the tradespeople,
and many persons were strongly of the duchess's opinion that
an attempt had been made to keep the king in Florence.
Meantime he could talk and think of nothing but his journey,
though prudence ordered its postponement for the present.

On the 12th she wrote that her father was ready to set off
that very day if only his legs did not refuse to serve him ever
so little. Therefore the move was postponed until the beginning of December. Charles, in fact, would not leave until St.
Andrew's Day was past, which naturally roused the cardinal's
suspicions. He remembered old revels in honour of the
patron saint, and though the duchess wrote again and again,
recording uninterrupted convalescence, the date remained fixed.

" St. Andrew's Day," she admitted to him, November 22,
" would have had its perils in times past," but though they
should keep the feast at Florence, there was no fear : the king
was still only convalescent and on a strict regimen. Things
were very much changed. Their departure was fixed for
December 1 ; not again to be postponed.

R

CHAPTER XXI

TO THE GRAVE OF THE CAUSE

"Weep ye not for the dead, neither bemoan him ; but weep sore for him that goeth away ; for he shall return no more, nor see his native country."—JEREMIAS, xxii. 10.

1785. ON December 1, 1785, the removal took place. The travellers journeyed in easy stages, arriving in Rome on the evening of December 8. They travelled with their own horses. The Abbé Barbieri accompanied them as chaplain and travelling companion. Unfortunately there was a storm upon their arrival: some clashing of the two royal wills. Charles was, no doubt, tired and cross after his journey, and found things not exactly as he liked them in spite of his brother's pains to please. Perhaps he had forgotten his promise to lay aside his kingship. The storm blew over. Peace and sincere repentance succeeded the storm, the duchess wrote to the cardinal ; assuring him that all had been arranged according to his wishes, and that her father wished for nothing but to see his brother again.

So in Rome the storm-tossed grief-worn soul found rest : the torch flickered out which once "shook itself over Britain with such terrific glare." Charles and his daughter lived for the remaining two years of his life in the Muti Palace, where, thanks chiefly to the cardinal's influence and kind exertions, they enjoyed great comfort and honour. There is not the least reason for accepting Sir Horace Mann's light and stereotyped assertion that "drink was now his only solace,"[1] which Ewald as lightly and more culpably repeats. Better authority states that he used to lie dozing or half-conscious the best part of the day. He had moments of painful awakening, as when Mr. Greathead persuaded him to recall his Highland adventures: as when he fainted at the sight of M. de Vaudreuil whose father

[1] Sir Horace Mann did not see out the sequel of the departure of "the Albany family" from Florence. He died November 6, 1786 at Florence, and was succeeded at the legation by Lord Hervey.

had arrested him at the Paris opera-house : as when he burst 1786.
into tears, poor soul, at hearing "Lochaber no more." And
all the time he held on to the hope that he might yet be called
to his kingdom and kept his box of 12,000 sequins under his
bed to be ready.

His house was well kept, all in perfect order, under his
daughter's care. She was granted at Rome the style and
precedence of a duchess. By a deed of gift dated January 23,
1786, Charles and Henry made over to her the family jewels.
A hostile correspondent of the *Gentleman's Magazine*,[1] who was
in Rome in 1786, describes her as doing the honours of her
father's house "with great *éclat.*" He refuses to her even the
beauty of noble features and peaceful expression, as in her
portrait at Montpellier, but describes her as "a tall robust
woman, of a very dark complexion and coarse-grained skin,
with more of masculine boldness than feminine modesty or
elegance, but easy and unassuming in her manners. . . . Her
equipage was that of the pretender, with servants in the royal
livery of Great Britain, and with our royal coronet and cipher
of C.R. upon the carriage. As the English were received by
the duchess with the most marked attention, there were few
who had any scruples about partaking in the gaieties of a
house whose master was become an object of compassion
rather than of jealousy, whose birth and misfortune entitled
him to a sort of melancholy respect."

In April 1787 Sir J. T. Stanley, afterwards first Lord 1778.
Stanley of Alderley, visited Rome. "I have been presented to
the Count of Albany," he writes to his wife, "styled still by his
servants King of England. He wore the Order of the Garter,
but permitted himself to be addressed as count, and as to such
I was presented to him. The old man receives a great deal
of company in his house since he had his daughter with him.
It is one of the gayest in Rome. . . . The pretender, for so we
English still call him, received me with civility, made me sit
aside of him, and spoke to me in English. Poor old man ! he
is interesting from what he was but he is now in a second
childhood."[2]

"If goodness of heart were sufficient for the conquest of a
throne," says Mercier Dupaty,[3] "his daughter would occupy

---

[1] December 21, 1797.
[2] "Early Married Life of Maria Josepha Holroyd," ed. by J. H. Adeane," p. 52.
[3] Quoted by A. Longhi in *Il Palazzo Vizani* ; Bologna.

1787. it immediately, for she is goodness personified; such goodness as comes not of duty but rises from the heart, which clothes itself with grace, conquers hearts and compels veneration."

She was in very bad health. For three years she had been suffering from what turned out to be cancer; the result, it was said, of a riding accident; perhaps it was inherited from her great-grandmother, Mary of Modena, whose self-sacrificing devotion she certainly inherited, and was the guardian angel of her father's last days.

The Countess of Albany, who had never ceased to trouble, was meanwhile living off and on with Alfieri at Colmar and other places. She writes to Madame Alfieri, her poet's mother, in 1787, of her husband being better, but " dragging out his miserable life abandoned by all the world, without relations or friends "—which was not strictly true.

1788. Not wholly in gloom, no longer darkened by the clouds of bitterness and despair which had made stormy night of more than forty years, but in quiet twilight, those last days faded out. Sheltered by his brother's faithful care, blessed by his daughter's grateful love, the last Stuart prince who ever trod on British soil passed away. Loyal hearts were round his deathbed. His daughter rose from a sickbed on which fever had laid her low, to soothe his last hours. On January 31, 1788, he died in the arms of the Master of Nairne. Caryll and Gask and John Stuart stood by. After his many aberrations of the past, he died fully reconciled to the church of his fathers, attended by the Franciscan brothers, James and Michael McCormick. He had always been fond of Irishmen and Franciscans. He received the last sacraments " with every testimony of faith." In fulfilment of his last wishes, the friars remained by his body, saying the office for the dead from the moment of his departure until his burial.

There has always been a doubt as to the real day of his death. It was said that he had died, not at half-past nine of the morning of January 31, but at half-past nine of the evening of January 30, and that the date being so ominous, it was given out that he had lingered until the following morning that his adherents should not be discouraged. Not that his adherents could have saved any spar of hope from the wreck of the cause, but they kept their faith. The ship had

HENRY, CARDINAL OF YORK

(HENRY IX.)

From the painting by Pompeo Batoni in the National Portrait Gallery

CHAPTER XXII

KING HENRY THE NINTH

BY his will Charles had made his daughter his sole heiress. 1788. He left little or no ready money. His income from funded property had amounted to about £1740, half of which was assigned to his wife. His life pension from the French court was £2400, says Dennistoun (in the *Quarterly Review*, 1846) ;[1] but according to the Count de Montemorin who assisted the Duchess of Albany in the settlement of her French affairs, her father's French pension amounted only to £400 (10,000 livres) a year. To the reversion of this she was entitled, and Louis XVI. increased it, in March 1788, to 20,000 livres,[2] exactly double. She was charged to pay 3000 scudi to her mother (*une personne à Paris*), 100 to Lord Nairne, and 400 to Marie, Countess of Norton,[3] these two last being of her household. She was also charged by her father to continue their respective apartments to his servants in recompense for their faithful service, and to pay them annuities for life to the value of their wages. To his faithful servant and confidential secretary, Sir John Stuart, he left 100,000 ducats and an annuity of £750 a year. Stuart had been his valet ever since he was in Scotland. They had lurked together in the Hebrides. He had stuck to his master for the more than forty years of exile and miserable decline. Even Louise had trusted Stuart for his honesty. But the money bequeathed to him was repudiated by the Cardinal of York. There had been a stormy scene between

---

[1] " The Stuarts in Italy."

[2] The Count de Montemorin to the Duchess of Albany : Lord Braye's MSS. Hist. MSS. Comm. Reports X., part vi. pp. 238, 239.

[3] The Cardinal of York confirmed this lady in the private chapel of his episcopal palace at Frascati on June 6, 1788 : " our beloved niece, Charlotte, Duchess of Albany, being godmother," says the little blotted draft of the confirmation certificate, all in his handwriting ; interesting by its many orthographical errors and corrections to show how sadly the King of England had forgotten his English ; " conferred " being tried three times over in a corner of the paper, " conferred—conferd—confered." Add. MSS. British Museum 30,476, f. 33.

1788. the brothers over this point so late as January 12, 1788.[1] It is more than probable that Charles had left more legacies than his assets would cover, and the cardinal held out for justice to the Duchess of Albany who must suffer by such favouritism. After obstinate litigation, the annuity was compromised for about £270 (1250 scudi) yearly.

To his brother Charles had bequeathed two thousand ounces of silver. The tenancy of the Muti Palace passed by favour of the Pope to the Cardinal of York ; the Camera Apostolica paying the rent, £435, as before. The duchess was also entitled, in the event of her surviving the cardinal, to £650 yearly from the Camera. "This provision never fell to her," says Dennistoun (in the *Quarterly Review* already quoted), "but her kind uncle, apprehensive that the charges and annuities upon her succession might straiten her circumstances, not only gave up a large portion of his palace at the Cancellaria for her residence, but assigned over to her the entire allowance of £2200 which he enjoyed from the Camera, retaining only his benefices." On September 30, 1788, he made over to her the French rentes Charles had had.[2] "She made over to Henry the crown jewels, which included a sceptre, a richly enamelled collar, George and star of the Garter, and a St. Andrew's cross, all brought from England by James II." : those now preserved in the Crown Room of Edinburgh Castle. The St. Andrew contains the portrait of Louise, Countess of Albany, previously referred to. "On her death he succeeded to all her fortune, burdened with a pension to her mother."[3]

The palace at Florence was sold to the Duke of San Clemente for 30,000 scudi (£6517) inclusive of 10,000 (£2172) for the furniture, which was superb, in the very best taste of the period. It had been made for Charles at Lyons, regardless of expense. The present possessor of the palace is the cardinal-archbishop Duke of San Clemente. The duchess settled the 30,000, received for the sale, upon the Countess of Albany, in addition to the 10,000 already settled according to the agreement made for jointure, thus relieving herself of the burden of paying over the funds mortgaged

[1] *Diario del Cardinale Duca di York* ap. A. Ademollo.
[2] Lord Braye's MSS. : Hist. MSS. Comm. Reports X., part vi. p. 239.
[3] "The Stuarts in Italy : " *Quarterly Review*, December 1846.

for this object; a great advantage, since no other re-in- 1788. vestment would have paid so much interest. The cardinal fully approved the wisdom of the arrangement.[1]

The jewels and other valuables found by Charlotte at Florence and in the Muti and Albano palaces, with plate, were inventoried at £26,740.[2] On July 21, more than fifty packing-cases arrived from Florence containing such moveables. The duchess stowed these away in an upper room of the Muti Palace. There were a number of portraits of princes "and other personages" of the royal house, many valuables that had belonged to John Sobieski, King of Poland, and an infinite number of precious things that Waters the banker classed as "hardware." The duchess gratified her uncle immensely by presenting him with a magnificent gold chased salt-cellar, decorated with miniatures, surmounted by a Cleopatra flashing in pearls and diamonds, holding an enamelled serpent.

The Countess of Albany, says Alfieri, was overwhelmed with grief when news came of her husband's death : which, if true, looks as if there were kindly memories, after all, to recall, now that passion and self-interest no longer stood in the way of honesty and remorse. Immediately after, with curious taste, she took upon herself full royal state. Sir Nathaniel Wraxall saw her in Paris probably that same year,[3] with a throne-room and servants who were commanded to address her as queen. All her spoons, &c., bore the crown. Nuns in the convents also addressed her as majesty ; in grotesque inconsistency with her lover's fierce hatred of kings. Madame de Staël addressed her as "chère souveraine." Yet in 1791 she visited London, bowing her knee to the Hanoverian Baal with the object of getting money. She had herself presented at court by her kinswoman, Lady Ailesbury, as Princess of Stolberg. "Well! I have had an exact account of the interview of the two queens," writes Horace Walpole to Miss Berry. Louise, he says, was very well dressed and not at all embarrassed. The king and the prince chatted kindly with her, especially the Duke of Gloucester, whom she had probably known in Italy. The queen was observed to watch her with

---

[1] *Diario.*
[2] Inventories and other papers, realisation of Charles's property : Add MSS. 30,475, 30,476 ; British Museum. Catalogue of Charles's library, 34,638, f. 393.
[3] He says, in 1787, *after her husband's death ;* an error.

1791. profound interest. She went to the House of Lords where she was accommodated with a seat on the steps of the throne. It was remarked that the day of her visit was the 10th of June. Hannah More was a little shocked, being under the mistake that it was her husband's birthday on which she went thus holiday-making in the traitorous parliament house. She returned to Italy with Alfieri, whom she never married, and settled down with him in the palace on the Lung' Arno Corsini, which now bears a tablet commemorating the poet's residence.

1789. The Duchess of Albany did not survive her father for very long. There is little mention of her in the cardinal's diary ; nothing beyond notes of her visits to him at Frascati and of her failing health. She lived quietly with her little court, Lady Norton, Monsignor Stonor, the young (fifth) Duke of Berwick,[1] who, though a Spaniard, and nephew of the hostile Countess of Albany, followed his grandfather and great-grandfather in loyal personal devotion ; and, most constant in attendance, the Abbé Ercole Consalvi, who owed his first step on the ladder of promotion to the Cardinal of York. Her days were numbered. She had lived just long enough to fulfil the filial duty to which she had been born. An angelic creature her friends truly called her : angel of peace between the brothers, guardian angel to her dying father. Tortured by her terrible malady, she went in the autumn of 1789 to the baths of Nocera. There it was found that operation was necessary, and she went by Ancona to Bologna whose surgeons had a great reputation. She arrived on October 9 at the palace of the Countess of Albany's old friend, Princess Lambertini, once Vizani, now Ranuzzi Palace in the Via San Stefano, where she was received "with all the splendour and dignity due to her sublime rank."[2] But her malady was cancer on the liver and incurable, and to the inexpressible grief of her hostess and her uncle, she died there, November 17.[3]

According to her will, made November 13, she was buried in the closely neighbouring church of San Biagio (St. Blaise), with great state ; probably in one of the two Lambertini chapels

---

[1] Born 1773.
[2] *Il Palazzo Vizani;* A. Longhi. Also *Cronaca Manoscritti;* Galeati : Bibl. Communale Bologna.
[3] Add. MSS. British Museum 30,466 ; containing a large collection of letters relating to her illness and death.

that were there. A marble slab was placed over her grave, 1789. bearing the following inscription :—

A   ℞   Ω

Haic . iacet . Carlotta . Dux . Albanyensis
ex . Regia . Stirpe . Stuarda
F . Caroli III . olim . Jacobi III
Rægis . Angliæ . Scotiæ . et . Hiberniæ
Vixit . An . XXXVI . obyt . Bononiæ . Virgo . Clariss :
XV . Kal . Decemb : MDCCLXXXIX.
In Pace.[1]

This memorial was unveiled in August 1790. The Cardinal of York visited Bologna that month for the purpose, but it was all done so quietly that he had been staying some days at the monastery of St. Dominic before the fact of his presence and that he had been saying mass in San Biagio beside his niece's grave, became known.

Where the daughter of Charles Edward lies now is uncertain. In 1797, the church of San Biagio was closed by the French ; then pulled down. In 1806, when order was somewhat restored, the old parish was transferred to the adjoining church of the Trinità, and the memorial tablet of the Duchess of Albany was set into the pavement of the Trinità. Whether she sleeps under it cannot be known. All the bodies from San Biagio were removed to the Certosa in 1801, but there is no mention among the records of such translation of the Duchess of Albany, which Galeati, the chronicler of Bologna, takes for evidence against the re-burial of a duchess. The usual supposition of biographers that she was buried in the Certosa is untrue. Most likely the slab in the Trinità covers the ashes of that "spes ultima et exigua " of the Stuarts.[2]

By her will she left an annuity of 15,000 lire to her mother, says Longhi, and 100 scudi to the poor of the parish of San Biagio. The bulk of her property went to the Cardinal of York : "a welcome refreshment," says Longhi, "to resources much exhausted by extreme munificence."

The cardinal formally announced the death of "his beloved niece" to foreign courts and personal friends, but seized

---

[1] *Il Palazzo Vizani ;* A. Longhi. Also *Cronaca Manoscritti ;* Galeati : Bibl. Communale, Bologna.

[2] The slab is no longer to be found in the church pavement.

1789. the opportunity of once more denying that there had ever been any question of her legitimacy or of her bearing the title of royal highness, or even that of Duchess of Albany, save as "a title of affection." As she never married, and as the cardinal could never marry, one might wonder at the persistent uneasiness which urged such protest on behalf of a right that could never now be questioned. Yet a rumour of her legitimacy had been lately and widely believed in Scotland and inspired Burns's verses on "The Bonnie Lass of Albany," wronged and dispossessed of kingdoms three. The wish was father to the thought : the longing for one of the old blood towards whom loyal hearts might still yearn and whom loyal lips might honour as they had yearned and honoured for a century, but for whom they would never be called upon to leave the pleasant safety of sentiment for the difficulties and dangers of action. A handsome young woman of Scottish blood on both sides was a much more attractive subject for toast and song and romantic aspiration, than an old cardinal or an unknown Italian prince

Countess Alberstroff seized the opportunity of her daughter's death to dun "His Majesty, the King of England" for more money.[1] She was then living in Paris, but she removed later to Fribourg where she died in November 1802. She left only £12 sterling, six silver spoons, a geographical dictionary, and three devotional books, but bequeathed a louis apiece to each of her relatives, should any remain, in the hope that their existence might be discovered ; so long had communication ceased between her and her kindred.[2]

Considering the accessibility of Rome and Florence and the prominent position of the royal Stuarts in both cities, contemporary prints report their proceedings with strange inaccuracies and fables. One account records that Charles left a daughter by his wife whom he created Countess of Albany and who appeared later at the court of Queen Charlotte. Here of course the widow and the natural daughter are confused. Then, the *Gentleman's Magazine*, which had already given such full and accurate accounts of her father's death and

---

[1] Hist. MSS. Comm. Reports (Lord Braye's MSS.), February 15, 1790, and July 18, 1791.

[2] A. C. Ewald, in the "Dictionary of National Biography": art. Walkinshaw, Clementina.

funeral, records in November 1797 the death of "Maria 1789. Matilda, Dowager Duchess of Albany, natural daughter of the last pretender to the English throne, in her seventy-first year." A correspondent in the same magazine points out on December 21, at great length, the absurdities of the statement and the dates, which had been repeated in all the newspapers of the day: especially "the absurdity of styling the supposed deceased Dowager Duchess of Albany and calculating her age at 71, which would be only seven years less than that of her supposed father, if he had lived to the present time."

A plausible explanation of this story may be that at this time some lady did die who pretended to be a daughter of James III. Her birth in 1726 would occur at the time of his matrimonial troubles. There were several such fables afloat all equally vague and foolish; notably the legend of Gainsborough's wife.[1] It seems to have been a fashionable ambition of mysteriously or dubiously born persons to attribute their origin to the exiled King of England: the most virtuous of men, but also one of the least known to his countrymen: almost as workable a myth as descent from Romulus or Odin. And he was a Stuart, therefore he must have scattered any number of batons about contemporary heraldry! Was it not his nature so to do?

A rumour still more serious and still more foolishly false was discussed in the appendix to the *Tales of the Century*: the assertion that the generous, kindly cardinal, whose conduct to his niece was so "full of affectionate attention," had poisoned her for the sake of inheriting her money. This is only worth mentioning to show how little "the last and most blameless of the Stuarts" was known to his age, and of what the malevolence of those who hated his race and his religion was capable.

In 1788, the year of his brother's death, he was appointed Protector of all the Capuchins of Rome; an occasion of public congratulation upon his "incomparable merit" and the humility in which he veiled the splendours of his royalty. Humility was never one of Henry's virtues.

Curiously coincidental with the deaths of Charles and his

---

[1] One constantly hears up and down Italy of this and that insignificant person claiming to be "the last of the Stuarts." Even a family named *Sindaci*, hint that they might translate their name to Stewart and claim royal kin!

1789. daughter was a new inquiry set on foot in 1788 : a new search among the Vatican archives for the four-and-a-half centuries missing dispensation for the marriage of Robert II. with Elizabeth Mure from which the whole royal House of Stuart descended.   Obviously this inquiry must have been made at the instance of the Cardinal of York.   No one else existed who could be so deeply interested.   The dispensation had been sought in vain when in 1692 the Orange party sought to prove that the House of Stuart had never had more than a parliamentary title to the throne, Robert II. having settled the succession upon his eldest son who was born out of wedlock, John Earl of Carrick who reigned as Robert III.   Lewis Innes had sought to confute the Whigs by a charter he found in the Glasgow Chartularies which referred to the dispensation but the Whigs declared this to be a forgery.   In 1702 Lord Cromarty, Clerk Registrar, published his " Vindication of Robert III. and his descendants from bastardy," but he had no dispensation to support him.   He published a second edition in 1713 when Queen Anne was drawing to her grave.

Now, in 1789, so late in the day as to be grim irony, the dispensation was found, dated in the sixth year of Pope Clement VI. ; that is, in 1347.   It could hardly, however, bring much comfort, since if Robert " made ane honest woman " at all of " his lemmen " Elizabeth, of which there is no proof, he certainly married Euphemia Ross in 1355 and it is impossible that all his ten children by Elizabeth Mure could have been born between 1347 and 1355.   Hence the eldest must have been illegitimate, though according to canon law, a dispensation and subsequent marriage would legitimate them. But that Robert II. considered his eldest children to be illegitimate is proved by his legitimation of them by Act of Parliament on his accession in 1371 and by the formal and otherwise superfluous recognition of the Earl of Carrick as his heir by the kings of England and France.

The king-undesired-of-men lived on at his beloved Frascati in dignified retirement, enjoying his cultivated tastes [1] and forming a splendid collection of art treasures and a valuable library.   Like his brother, who found much solace in his sad old age playing his violoncello and the Highland pipes, Henry,

---

[1] He dabbled in literature in a small pamphleteering way.   A tract of his on the " Sins of the Drunkard " still exists.

who had played and sung so sweetly in his youth and had 1789.
relieved the melancholy of his middle age with Buranello's
masses, still delighted in music and was a member of the
Academy of St. Cecilia.

Cardinal Wiseman writes of him in his " Recollections of
the Four Last Popes"; with one slight inaccuracy. He did
ultimately exchange his see, though he continued to live at
Frascati to the end of his life :—

" The last of the Stuarts, the amiable and beneficent
Cardinal of York, was Bishop of Frascati. He never would
exchange his see for those which officially belonged to the
dean and sub-dean of the Sacred College. Of that prettily
situated city, successor of Tusculum, which yet gives the
bishop his title, he is still considered the great benefactor.
Whatever else may have been wanting for his title, to a royal
heart he was no pretender. His charities were without bounds :
poverty and distress were unknown in his see. The episcopal
palace was almost if not entirely rebuilt by him, though he
generally resided in a neighbouring villa. The cathedral was
much improved and richly furnished. But the Seminary or
Diocesan Ecclesiastical College was the object of his peculiar
care. Most of it was built by him, and the library, a most
elegant apartment, and rich in many English works, was the
fruit of his munificence. Though he was not himself either
learned or endowed with great abilities, he knew the value of
both, engaged excellent professors for his seminary, and
brought men of genius round him. Hence his college was
frequented not only by aspirants to the clerical state but by
youths of the best families. The diocese of Frascati was full
[when Cardinal Wiseman first knew it] of recollections of the
Cardinal Duke, all demonstrative of his singular goodness and
simplicity of character."

" He was a studious and well-informed prince," says a
biographer in the *Gentleman's Magazine*, on his death in 1807,
" and a sincerely pious prelate. His purse was always open
to suffering humanity: and British travellers particularly,
whether ruined by misfortune or imprudence, found in him
on all occasions, a compassionate benefactor." [1]

Such communications as passed between him and the

---

[1] *Annual Register* and *Gentleman's Magazine*, 1807.

1789. Jacobites at home seem to have been sentimental rather than important, though secrets may still be hidden among the inexhaustible Stuart Papers at Windsor, many of which have not even yet become accessible ; in the libraries of private families who were unwilling to disclose old secrets ; in unexplored archives at the Quai d'Orsai, the Vatican, and the Scots Colleges. Though all hope of a Stuart restoration had long been abandoned, there were still many in the British Isles, many serving in foreign armies, many scattered over western plantations, who remained faithful at heart to the ancient dynasty and the principle of divine right. But the utter futility of allegiance to a popish cardinal on the part of Protestant Britons was a strong reason for accepting the *de facto* sovereign. Even in 1786, two years before the death of Charles, the episcopal clergy of Scotland had debated whether they would not be compelled to pray for George III. when the Stuart king should be a cardinal. Oliphant of Gask was horrified at the mention of such apostasy and stood up for the rights of Henry IX. and for those of the King of Sardinia after him and no other. Who knew what might not happen ? Henry IX., by his influence and for his interest, might get the law of priestly celibacy repealed and take a wife and have a family, said the sanguine and desperately loyal Oliphant ![1] But evil days were upon all the world. The loss of the American colonies had warned British subjects of the necessity of standing shoulder to shoulder if they would save the British crown and empire. A year and a half after the death of Charles Edward, the Bastille fell, and the immediate peril of the Bourbon throne, the effect of its vicissitudes upon all other European thrones, was of more urgent interest to all monarchists than the long-lost throne of the Stuarts. It is to the last degree improbable that Henry authorised or encouraged any Jacobite plotting. Indeed, his well-known subsequent relations with the House of Hanover prove the contrary. Yet to this day, finger-bowls are never provided at English court dinners, lest glasses should be passed " over the water."

Yet—or rather therefore—he was always treated with the greatest courtesy by English travellers who came to Rome ; no longer with wild, illusive schemes, but some with sympathy,

---

[1] " The Jacobite Lairds of Gask," by Kingdon Oliphant.

some with curiosity. In 1790 he was visited at Frascati by 1790. Mr. Coutts, the banker, and his three daughters, the second of whom married Sir Francis Burdett and was mother of the late Baroness Burdett-Coutts. The Burdett family "had been much attached to the House of Stuart as late as 1745 and since," says the correspondent who described the visit. When Sir Francis was sent to the Tower in 1809, it was not for the following of hereditary principles! The cardinal gave to the youngest Miss Coutts the ring worn by Charles I. at his coronation.[1]

In that same year, 1790, a very hostile witness visited the cardinal, Gorani, the economist, who had known him already in 1780. Gorani describes the considerable part Henry played in Rome in right of his birth and his family misfortunes (well-deserved, says Gorani) and his father's kingly title and state. Though he spent more than 40,000 scudi annually at Frascati, Gorani declares that he was hated by the inhabitants for his strictness, his aversion from the most innocent pleasures. He would have a woman arrested on the slightest suspicion of immorality, beaten and imprisoned on bread and water. The least evil report was sufficient for the arrest of a priest or a monk.[2] He would have had every one spend their whole life in church and Frascati was nothing but a vast monastery. Gorani was presented and invited to dinners, but bored. Eagerly anxious to find stories of scandal in the austere cardinal's own private life, he was regretfully compelled to admit that there was not the faintest hint of any such scandals as were supposed to be prevalent in his order. "Finally, he is a lunatic of the House of Stuart and well worthy of his origin," says Gorani.[3]

Early in 1792, the cardinal was visited by the Marquise 1792. d'Osmond, *née* Dillon, granddaughter of Dicconson who had been treasurer at St. Germain's. She was accompanied by her husband and her daughter, afterwards Comtesse de Boigne,[4] who gives an amusing description of the visit in her memoirs.

---

[1] Hist. MSS. Comm. Reports XVI., p. 243.

[2] "En 1784, il s'y attira du ridicule par la défense qu'il fit de laisser errer les poules et les coqs dans les rues et places publiques, *propter scandalum*." De Brosses; Italie il y a cent ans; vol. ii. p. 96 (note): the only fact the editor, Colomb, finds worth mentioning of his life.

[3] A. Ademollo; *Diario del Cardinale Duca di York:* Nuova Antologia.

[4] Madame de Boigne errs in describing her great-grandfather as having been King James's governor.

1792. The old association with his father's household ensured a warm welcome from the cardinal, but as to material warmth his guests found his hospitality sadly lacking. They were received in his huge, scantily furnished palace of the Cancellaria where there was not a fire in any room, despite the bitter weather. He himself was wrapped in two thick overcoats, a hood over his head, his hands in a muff and his feet on a scaldino. His frozen guests would fain have worn the same attire. Out of extraordinary consideration for Madame d'Osmond, he allowed two or three pieces of wood to be lighted four rooms off, but declared that even at that distance the fire affected his breathing. Madame de Boigne ascribes this eccentricity to the effort of limited royalty to be distinguished where it could, but it is evident that the cardinal must have suffered from a form of spasmodic asthma; a neurosis akin to feminine hysteria, almost amounting to insanity on this particular point. He probably inherited it, in a manner, from his mother. He had been much with her in the last period of her life and the distressing impression made by her constant attacks of asthma might have remained in his young impressionable mind, to be revived even after sixty years. So says a medical expert.

Though his household styled him king, guests found it easy to combine diplomatic obligation with courtesy in the Italian use of the third person. The cardinal spoke only Italian, except for a little English. His French visitors found his English hardly intelligible, though he was deeply offended when it was not understood. Monsignor Ercole Consalvi, then about five-and-thirty, was now his constant companion, treated by him as a dearly loved son; a highly accomplished and distinguished man of European reputation, afterwards secretary of state to Pius VII. The cardinal could not do without "Ercole" for a moment, says Madame de Boigne. He had much to pour into sympathetic ears of his wrath against his sister-in-law who had so deeply wounded his royal dignity by accepting a pension from the English government; little dreaming that the day was not far off when he himself should thankfully accept a like indignity.

The protection of Hercules (Ercole) Consalvi, one of the foremost statesmen of his time, is good testimony to the judgment of the Cardinal of York. Born in 1757, he became a

student in the cardinal's beloved college at Frascati which had 1792.
just been taken out of the Jesuits' hands. Consalvi left it in
1776 for the Ecclesiastical Academy in Rome. Henry took a
deep interest in his protégé's progress and had him continually
at Frascati; a hospitality that cost Consalvi many sleepless
nights of study to make up for the time spent with his patron,
and therefore undermined his health. Henry presented him to
Mesdames, aunts of Louis XVI., refugees in Rome, whose
favour he won by his horror of the revolution, and through
their influence he was appointed auditor of the Rota. He was
a useful intermediary between Henry and his sister-in-law in
their correspondence on business affairs which lasted till the
cardinal's death. Consalvi was a very handsome man, of
somewhat stern or serious countenance; skilled in music
and literature as in theology and politics, and spending much
time with Cimarosa, his favourite composer. Through the
influence of the Cardinal of York he became archpriest and
vicar of St. Peter's.

A few months after Madame d'Osmond (1792), a more
illustrious visitor came to the Cancellaria; the youthful
Prince Augustus, afterwards Duke of Sussex, son of George III.
He behaved more prettily than did his uncle Edward, Duke of
York, in 1762, for he not only called upon the Stuart prince,
but with courteous grace remained standing in his presence,
though he addressed him only as royal highness. This necessarily limited title is supposed to have flattered the cardinal
king, and is quoted as an instance of Hanoverian " generosity,"
though to the grandson of a crowned king of England surely
such title at least must be due of right, not bestowed in half-
pitying condescension. The Chevalier Livingstone, who went
to Rome in Prince Augustus's suite, told Sir Robert Strange
that " on the compliment being returned, the cardinal was
received in a room containing only the seat he was intended
to occupy ; a studied politeness which had been inculcated by
his (Prince Augustus's) father, George III." [1] The cardinal was
in low spirits that year, says Oliphant of Gask. Clouds had
gathered thickly over church and throne in France and he was
expecting to lose his French benefices. His forebodings were
more than realised. The storm of the revolution reached him

---

[1] Add. MSS. 30,476, f. 33. The prince married Lady Augusta Murray in Rome
April 1793.

1794. in his peaceful retirement and in the turmoil his entire French income was lost; not only his benefices but the money he had inherited from his father and brother, which was nearly all invested in France. On February 1, 1794, Father Lescaillier, grand prior of the Abbey of Anchin in the Netherlands, wrote piteously to the cardinal commendatore of the sufferings of himself and his monks through the French revolution, and deprecated the distraints which he had heard the cardinal intended to levy, by means of the Comte de Walsh Serrant, on the property of the abbey to enforce payment of his income: a measure already taken with the Abbey of St. Amand. The grand prior had sent two monks to the nuncio at Brussels to implore his mediation, but M. de Limon, agent of Comte Walsh Serrant, assured the cardinal that the monks were intriguing with the nuncio. The nuncio, for his part, disapproved of M. de Walsh, the cardinal's agent; declared that the monks were insubordinate and only trying to gain time, for in February the sequestration on the abbey would be removed. But the cardinal did not get his money.[1]

In the midst of these anxieties, old family friends, also suffering from the revolution, brought their troubles to the cardinal. Monseigneur Henry Béthisy de Mézières, Bishop of Uzes, on behalf of himself and his once lovely cousin, Madame de Brionne, grandchildren of Eleanor Oglethorpe, Marquise de Mézières and godchildren of the cardinal, appealed to "his royal highness and eminence," to help them in their distress. The bishop trusted he was not importunate. He knew what trouble the cardinal was having with his abbeys and what he owed to the necessities of his rank, and he admitted that his own dignity must be enhanced by poverty and glorified in common with that of the other French bishops by the cause of their sufferings. But he hoped the cardinal would remember old family friendships and the obligations of sponsorship. Madame de Brionne carried the message, and beauty in distress did not appeal to old memories in vain.[2]

In 1796 Napoleon invaded Italy; advanced southwards, defeated the papal troops and occupied Ancona and Loreto. To help the Pope to make up the indemnity required by the Corsican conqueror, the Cardinal of York disposed of all the

---

[1] Hist. MSS. Comm. Reports X., part vi. p. 240. (Lord Braye's MSS.)
[2] Add MSS. Brittish Museum 34,636, f. 47.

family jewels, among them the famous Sobieski ruby, the 1796.
largest and most perfect known, valued at £50,000. He thus
deprived himself of the last means of an independent existence
and was reduced to great distress, say his biographers. No
doubt the distress was great, but the sale of his jewels could
not have been quite complete, since he was still able occasionally to bestow gifts. After the peace, the English crown jewels,
if pledged, must have been recovered.

A peace was made at Tolentino, between Pius VI. and 1797.
Napoleon, in February 1797. On October 17, of the same
year, the peace of Campo Formio between France and Austria
acknowledged the Cisalpine Republic which included the papal
states. At Christmas, the peace of Tolentino was broken by
riots, and there was a new invasion of Italy. Berthier marched
upon Rome, and entered the city on February 10, 1798, pro- 1798.
claimed a republic in the teeth of an outraged people, and
took the Pope prisoner. Pius was then sent from one Italian
town to another; finally to Valence, where he died in August
1799.

The Cardinal of York fled—he believed, for his life—on
the eve of Berthier's entry into Rome, and the palace of the
Cancellaria and his house at Frascati were sacked by the
French. His freedom may have been imperilled but there
was probably greater danger to his life in the exertions and
exposure of his wintry flight, than from Berthier's soldiers; but
he had lost the last remnant of his possessions and all the
comforts that had been so dear to him. He took refuge at the
Austrian-protected court at Naples.

"He possessed before 1798," says his biographer in the
Gentleman's Magazine, 1807, "a very valuable collection of
curiosities at his villa, where many scarce tracts and interesting
manuscripts concerning the unfortunate House of Stuart were
among the ornaments of his library. In his will, made January
1789, he had left the latter to his relation, Count Stuarton (?);
but they were all in 1798 either plundered by the French and
Italian Jacobins at Rome, or confiscated by the French Commissaries for the libraries and museums at Paris."

And now comes an interesting question as to which the full
answer may be yet to find.

France, relieved from war with Austria, turned her attention
to ever-defiant England. On May 19, 1798, Napoleon sailed

1798. for Egypt with the ultimate purpose of striking at England through India. But there was a weaker spot nearer home. As in Scottish discontent, the Bourbon kings had found opportunity of weakening British force, now in Irish hatred of British rule France hoped to find a weapon to break the strength of the enemy so fiercely united to resist her ever increasing advance to world power.

Ireland was anti-English, but she was before all things, Catholic. Her Chief-Justice Rice had threatened the Act of Settlement before James II. landed at Kinsale in 1689. William of Orange in the name of the Protestant succession had crushed the country beyond all hope of rising in '15 and '45, though the rage over the threatened debasing of the coinage in 1722 had been lashed to such dangerous force by Swift in his " Drapier's Letters " that Walpole was compelled to cancel the obnoxious patent. But misery and anger and fierce cravings for independence had increased with time, and the most severe of the laws penalising the Catholic religion were repealed. Then the Gordon riots of 1778 frightened the English government from further concession, and religious questions gave way for a while to temporal questions, desperately urgent to the starving country. Catholics were gradually won to alliance with Protestants. In 1779, Grattan, a Protestant, wrung from Lord North bills that at least promised to Ireland commercial equality with Great Britain. Agitation continued, legislative independence was fiercely demanded, and the statute of George I., which asserted the supremacy of the English Parliament, was repealed in 1782. But the demagogue Flood succeeded Grattan in the leadership of the rebellious party, and Pitt recognised the necessity of a new legislative union. Grattan's parliament had secured only Protestant ascendancy and, until 1793, when the Catholic Relief Bill was passed, Catholics were still excluded from power and nearly altogether from social position. The peasantry, tithed and rack-rented by Protestant landlords, were starving to death or despair. Murder reigned king in Ireland. Irish Protestants, poor and desperate, united with atheists and republicans and turned to revolutionary France for help, while Irish Catholics put on one side their age-long horror of heresy to join with Protestants against the Protestant rule. Lord Edward Fitzgerald went to France in 1796 and arranged for a French invasion of Ireland

under Hoche. Hoche sailed for Bantry Bay where a hurricane 1798.
swept his armada back to Brest.

Misery, murder, and conspiracy never ceased, and on
May 23, 1798, four days after Napoleon sailed for Egypt,
rebellion broke out. The tragedy of 1798 is too well known.
Fitzgerald, the leader, was killed at the moment of outbreak.
The rebellion was soon put down but the spirit of it was only
forced below ground to burst forth when fear again wore out.

It has been said that the Cardinal of York was implicated
in the rebellion of '98. For this charge there is no evidence
as yet available. The story is probably founded on certain
interesting coincidences and it is very possible that he may
have been approached on the matter. First, there is the fact
that Napoleon, breathing fury and destruction against England,
threatened to set Henry, by force of arms, on the English
throne ; an unexpected revival of the old French policy of
seeking to harass England by means of her native line of
princes, now so long thrust from her. Certainly, Henry had
never yet been an active pretender, but now times were
greatly changed. He was in desperate plight, owing to the
French and their revolution. So long as he had his beautiful
and beloved homes in Rome and Frascati, the occupations
and interests in which he had been happy for so long, it
would have taken a nearly inconceivable amount of temptation,
nothing less than a unanimous offer of the crown, to lure him
from the life in which he had grown old. But now he was
homeless, as his father had been eighty-five years earlier.
His roots had been torn up. Napoleon's angry threat might
well have served as a star of hope amid such a gathering of
angry clouds ; such a promise as his father and brother had
entreated in vain. Napoleon was apparently invincible. So
far he had worked his will upon the world. How easy for
him to do what Bourbon kings had been powerless to do!
He was busily intriguing in Ireland. Why should not that
most distressful country achieve her heart's desire under a
Stuart prince, as Catholic king of an independent Ireland ?
Americans, we have shown, had some such plan of independence under his brother as a prince of the royal house.

There was another coincident event. Deeply concerned
with Fitzgerald in the rebellion of '98 was Valentine Lawless,
Lord Cloncurry, whose friendship with the Cardinal of York

1798. was the chief ground for the charge of Henry's concern in the rebellion. It is maintained that their friendship did not begin until Cloncurry's second visit to Italy in 1803 ; the year, it must be remembered, of Emmett's rebellion. Whether or not Cloncurry visited the Cardinal of York at Naples—he makes no mention of such a visit in his memoirs—he did visit the Countess of Albany and Alfieri at Florence shortly before the '98 rebellion broke out, and it is very probable that that visit may have been connected with Irish politics, if not with the restoration of the Cardinal of York. It is curious, even suggestive, that he does not mention having been in Italy while describing the events of those years ; not until he comes to 1803. Then he gives a long account of this visit of five or six years ago, and it would not be too imaginative to allow for prudent suppressions as to its incidents, as its occurrence had been suppressed in its chronological place. Perhaps he had seen the cardinal, and meeting with no encouragement there, had turned his hopes to the widow of Prince Charlie and the chance that she might have had a child, long hidden away. We know how Burns and the Scots tried to see a future queen in the Duchess of Albany. Was there not the later story of the secret birth at Siena, perhaps afloat even then ?

The Countess of Albany, he says in his memoirs, was then one of the leaders of society both in Rome and Florence ; society not squeamish as to her relations with Alfieri, though it pretended to ignorance as to whether they might not be privately married. Lord Cloncurry found Alfieri's manners savage and repulsive ; in strong contrast to those of " Madame d'Albany," who was highly informed and very agreeable. At her receptions she used to stand at the tea-table, with an apron over her dress, serving tea with her own hands to her guests. Liberty, equality, and fraternity were in fashion—and had not even Marie Antoinette enjoyed such simplicity in the days of her highest queenliness ? Alfieri sat apart on a sofa in a sort of state and moody grandeur ; not mingling with the company but conversing with those who came about him, always provided there were no Frenchmen among the number. For the whole French nation he entertained the most cordial hatred, and lost no opportunity of exhibiting his feelings without disguise or modification.[1] But Cloncurry had no luck.

[1] " Personal Recollections of Lord Cloncurry," p. 201.

LOUISE OF STOLBERG

" Countess of Albany "

From the painting by F. S. Fabre in the Uffizi Gallery, Florence

The fact that only a year or two later the Cardinal of
York received great and substantial kindness from George III.
and his government, even at the critical moment when threat
of Catholic emancipation was helping to drive the king to
madness, proves that no suspicion of the royal exile's complicity in the rebellion can have existed.

Napoleon conquered Egypt, but against the white cliffs of
England and her wooden walls his fury raged in vain. On
August 1, at the Battle of the Nile, Nelson beat the French
fleet and shut up Napoleon and his army in Egypt. The
Cardinal of York was living at Naples when the great news
came. Sir William Hamilton, English ambassador at Naples,
returning from carrying Nelson's despatch to the King of
Naples, met the carriage of the Cardinal of York, and with
impulsive kindness stopped it to impart the glorious news.
The cardinal was quite carried away by excitement, hardly
believing for joy. Then young Capel of the *Mutine* was presented, who had seen the fight, and was carrying Nelson's
despatches to England. "In that case, sir," said Henry,
"when you arrive in England, do me the favour to say that
no man rejoices more sincerely than I do in the success and
glory of the British Navy." [1]

His acquaintance with the British navy and its great hero
was to be improved. It is a tradition in Nelson's family [2] that
when the victorious admiral came to Naples from the Nile, the
Cardinal of York was entertained by him on his flag-ship the
Agamemnon, and that the cardinal presented to Nelson a silver-
mounted dirk and cane that had belonged to Prince Charles.
This the admiral gave to Lieutenant Suckling of the *Agamemnon*
and it is now in the possession of Captain Suckling, R.N., of
Romsey. It is well known that the Pope specially thanked
Nelson for his kindness and courtesy towards the cardinals
who had fled to Naples. [3]

His Neapolitan shelter too failed the unfortunate Stuart
prince. Pitt set on foot the second great coalition. Naples
raised an army and made an effort for freedom but failed.
On the night of December 21, 1798, the king, queen, and

---

[1] Cornelia Knight's Autobiography.

[2] In 1788 Nelson had declined to attend the festivities at Holkham upon the
centenary of the revolution. Those festivites were not enthusiastically attended in spite
of the enthusiastic efforts of the promoters. (Coke of Norfolk, vol. i.)

[3] Information from the present Earl Nelson.

1798. court fled to Messina, and the Cardinal of York accompanied them. Then followed weary wanderings from Sicily to Corfu, to Padua and through Northern Italy—wanderings less romantic than his brother's in 1746 only because he was an aged priest and not a young knight-errant, but as bravely borne and, at his age, far more painful. Before the close of the year he arrived at Venice, ill and quite destitute save for some silver plate he had managed to bring with him, on which he supported himself for some weeks, living in abject poverty in humble lodgings near the Rialto. When the supply of plate was exhausted, he was forced to seek assistance at a neighbouring monastery.[1]

He had the consolation of meeting his dear friend Monsignor Consalvi who arrived in Venice at the end of 1798, whose business it had been to watch suspicious French in Rome ; and as his ardent loyalism caused him to do this with great severity, the French invaders imprisoned him when they came to Rome, and then banished him. On the way to Venice he saw Pius VI. a captive in the Certosa at Parma, and received his blessing. The Pope dying in the following August, the consequent conclave was held at Venice where thirty-five of the forty-six cardinals were present. In March Cardinal Chiara-

1799. monte was elected as Pius VII., chiefly through the influence of Consalvi, then his secretary, whom he therefore made a cardinal.

Help arrived from an unexpected quarter. The triumphant heir of George I. came to the rescue of the unfortunate heir of King James. Cardinal Borgia had been acquainted with Sir John Coxe Hippesley who represented England at the Vatican (in the usual *sub rosâ* fashion) from 1792 to 1796. He set forth the sad case of the last prince of the Royal Stuart line.[2] Hippesley probably knew the Cardinal of York too.

" It is greatly affecting to me," writes Cardinal Borgia, September 14, 1799, " to see so great a personage, the last descendant of his royal house, reduced to such distressed circumstances . . . the miseries of which greatly injured his health at the advanced age of seventy-five, and produced a

---

[1] *Times*, 28th February 1800.

[2] "The last prince of Darnley's house," say the lines that a sentimental poet wrote upon the circumstances : exalting the despicable Lennox Stewart to a chieftainship he never knew because he possessed two melodious syllables of courtesy-title.

very grievous sore in one of his legs." He had lost by the French revolution 48,000 crowns of income: also his Roman income from the Camera and his Roman investments. Nothing remained to him but about 14,000 crowns from Spain, which being paid in paper, suffered much depreciation. "The cardinal is heavily burthened with the annual sum of 4000 crowns for the dowry of the Countess of Albany, his sister-in-law ; 3000 for the mother of his deceased niece ; and 1500 for divers annuities of his father and brother."[1]

Sir John Coxe Hippesley represented the case of the royal cardinal's destitution to George III. through Dundas. The good old king at once ordered Lord Minto, his minister at the Court of Vienna, to offer the Cardinal of York, with all possible delicacy, a pension of £4000 for his life.[2] (The correspondence that took place on the subject is published at length in the *Annual Register* for 1807.) The Hanoverian sovereign paid grateful tribute, through his diplomatic representative, to "the eminent qualities of the august personage who was the object of his generosity" ; declaring his wish to repair as far as he could, the disaster into which the scourge of their age seemed to drag by preference all that was worthy of reverence and respect. The cardinal accepted the timely assistance gratefully and graciously ; much touched by "the expressions of singular regard and consideration for himself and the delicacy with which the business had been managed." It is suggestive, however, that he never mentions "the King of England" in his letters. He writes from the conclave to Sir John Hippesley :—

"VENICE, *26th February* 1800.

"I cannot sufficiently express how sensible I am to your good heart, and write these few lines, in the first place, to contest to you these my most sincere and grateful sentiments, and then to inform you that by means of Mr. Oakley, an English gentleman who arrived here last week, I have received a letter from Lord Minto from Vienna, advising me that he had orders from his court to remit to me at present the sum of £2000, and that in the month of July next I may again draw, if I desire it, for another equal sum. The letter is

---

[1] Letters of Cardinal Borgia ; printed by A. C. Ewald and others.
[2] George III. sent him £2000 at once, to be renewed within six months "should he be disposed to accept it."

1800. written in so extremely genteel and obliging a manner and with singular regard and consideration for me, that I assure you excited in me most particular and lively sentiments, not only of satisfaction for the delicacy with which the affair has been managed, but also of gratitude for the generosity that has provided for my necessity. . . .

"I own to you that the succour granted to me could not be more timely, for without it, it would have been impossible for me to subsist, on account of the absolutely irreparable loss of all my income ; the very funds being also destroyed, so that I would otherwise have been reduced for the short remainder of my life, to languish in misery and indigence. I would not lose a moment's time to apprise you of all this, and am very certain that your experimented good heart will find proper means to make known in an energetical and proper manner, these sentiments of my grateful acknowledgment. The signal obligations I am under to Mr. Andrew Stewart for all that he has, with so much cordiality, on this occasion done to assist me, renders it for me indispensable to desire that you may return him my most sincere thanks. . . . I have with great pleasure received from General Heton the genealogical history of our family[1] . . . and hope that he will from that General have already received my thanks for so valuable a proof of his attention for me. In the last place, if you think proper, and an occasion should offer itself, I beg you to make known to the other gentlemen who also have co-operated my most grateful acknowledgments."[2]

The cardinal's English had suffered in the course of years and trouble but his dignity never failed him and his heart remained in the right place.

As to the dignity that had been so outraged by the Countess of Albany's acceptance of an English pension, there were reasons besides expediency and the hard law of necessity to alter the point of view. The money was looked upon by the cardinal and his friends as no more than was really due to him from England in the payment of the long demanded and long withheld jointure of his grandmother, Mary of Modena. So much at least a prince who claimed to be King of England

---

[1] Andrew Stewart's "Genealogical History of the House of Stewart."
[2] Printed in Jesse's "Pretenders and their Adherents."

might accept without scruple from the prince who filled the 1800.
Stuarts' throne and was in possession of the revenues that had
been torn from James II. by a rebellious people.

As welcome to the proud heir of England's long line of
kings must have been Sir John's assurance that, severe as were
his sufferings, they would find some alleviation in the generous
sympathy of the British nation : " With all distinction of
parties, with all differences of communion, among all conditions
of men, but one voice was heard : all breathed one applauding
sentiment : all blessed the gracious act of the sovereign in
favour of his illustrious but unfortunate relation."

" I did not expect to see in writing," Henry writes to Lord
Minto, " so many and so obliging expressions that well calculated for persons who receive them and understand their force,
impress in their minds a most lively sense of tenderness and
gratitude : which I own to you, oblige me more than the
generosity spontaneously imparted. I am in reality at a loss
to express in writing all the sentiments of my heart."

To Sir John Hippesley he writes :—

" I have not words to explain the deep impression your
very obliging favour of March 31 made on me. What return
can I make of so many and so signal proofs of disinterested
benevolence ? Dear Sir John ! I confess I am at a loss to
express my feelings."

So the clouds lifted. The last of the Stuarts was destined
at least to end his days in his beloved home. When the
Concordat between Rome and the French Republic was con-
cluded in 1801, mainly through the influence and exertions of
Consalvi, the Cardinal of York returned to Rome and Frascati.
He was then made dean of the Sacred College of Cardinals,
" after being one of its most virtuous and disinterested members
upwards of sixty years."[1] In September 1803, he was translated 1803.
to the bishopric of Ostia and Velletri, but he could not leave
his beloved Frascati and made his home in the Muti Villa there.
Consalvi was made a cardinal and secretary of state by the
new Pope, and Henry presented him with a state carriage.

War was stopped for a while by the Peace of Amiens
(March 27, 1802), but it broke out afresh, May 18, 1803.
Ireland had in 1801 been legislatively united with England but

---

[1] *Annual Register*, 1807.

T

1803. not appeased. Napoleon again interfered to aggravate discontent, but the Catholics and others of the better class of Irish now shrank from associating themselves with the atheistical oppressors of the papacy. Robert Emmett, the new Irish leader, an obscure young man, visited Paris in 1802, had interviews with Napoleon, and returned to Ireland to stir up and organise. The rising was fixed to take place on July 23, 1803. Its futility was piteous. All that came of it was the murder of the Chief Justice, the execution of Emmett, and further severity and bitterness.

It was in this very year, 1803, as has been said, that Lord Cloncurry, a stormy petrel, visited Italy for the second time. He had not long been liberated from imprisonment meted for his concern in 1798. On this occasion he certainly visited the Cardinal of York and he describes their meeting in his memoirs.

He found the cardinal in those days of his old age one of the prominent members of Roman society. He claimed the distinction of being somewhat of a favourite with his royal eminence; which honour he attributed to his custom of addressing him as "Your Majesty": thus, as he says, going a step further than the Duke of Sussex had done. Perhaps Lord Cloncurry went several steps further than he confided to memoirs.

"The cardinal," he continues, "was in receipt of an income of £8000 or £9000 a year, of which he received £4000 from his royal rival George III., and the remainder from his ecclesiastical benefices. This revenue was then, in Italy, equivalent at least to £20,000; and it enabled his eminence to assume somewhat of royal state. He was waited upon with all suitable ceremony, and his equipages were numerous and splendid, and freely placed at the disposal of his guests. He was in the habit of receiving visitors very hospitably at his villa at Frascati, where I was often a guest, and was frequently amused by a reproduction of the scenes between Sancho Panza and his physician during the reign of the squire in the island of Barataria. His eminence was an invalid and under a strict regimen; but as he still retained his taste for savoury meals, a contest usually took place between him and his servants for the possession of rich diet, which they formally set before him, and then endeavoured to snatch away, while he, with greater eagerness, strove to seize it in its transit. Among the cardinal's 1803. most favourite attendants was a miserable cur dog, which, probably having been cast off by its master, as being neither useful nor ornamental, one day attached itself to his eminence at the gate of St. Peter's; an occurrence to which he constantly referred, as a proof of his true royal blood—the cur being, as he supposed, a King Charles spaniel, and therefore endowed with an instinctive hereditary acquaintance with the House of Stuart. Upon the occasion of my visit to Frascati, I presented the cardinal with a telescope, which he seemed to fancy, and received from him in return, the large medal struck in honour of his accession to his unsubstantial throne. So trifling an article as a telescope will scarcely seem to be a present worthy of the acceptance of a prince of the church and king, even though his sovereignty was not *de facto;* but it is scarcely possible at the present time to bring home to the mind a conception of the value which then, under the operation of the continental system, was set upon articles of English manufacture in Italy. The cardinal was in the highest delight with my gift." [1]

If Lord Cloncurry's visit was paid with the object of interesting the cardinal in Emmett's rebellion, the object failed. That Henry was loyal to the hand that fed him is certainly proved, not only by his known high character and by the absence of any evidence to the contrary, but by immediately subsequent communications with the House of Hanover.

Owing in a measure to his sister-in-law's drain upon him, the cardinal found his English pension insufficient, and application was made to have it increased. That this was done, he gratefully attributed to the influence of the Duke of Sussex; to whom his secretary, Cesarini, now Bishop of Milevi, wrote by command of the Cardinal Duke, October 15, 1806: "The cardinal was as well as his eighty-two years permitted, and comfortable in his circumstances, thanks to the generosity of the royal family." [2]

On October 8, 1803, Alfieri died at Florence and was buried with " the starry Galileo," Michel Angelo, and Machiavelli, in Santa Croce, where the Countess of Albany raised a magnificent monument to his memory, sculptured by Canova.

[1] " Personal Recollections of Lord Cloncurry," pp. 199, 200.
[2] Hist. MSS. Comm. Reports X., part vi. p. 248. (Lord Braye's MSS.)

1803. She mourned, " I am now alone in the world. I have lost all —consolation, support, society—all—all." But very shortly after, she took a new lover, the artist Fabre, with whom she lived until his death. Florentine gossip said that Alfieri had had occasion to be jealous of Fabre, also that Alfieri had given Louise occasion for jealousy. A few months after Alfieri's death, Louise installed Fabre in the palace on the Lung' Arno. He was thirty-seven, she fifty-one. She continued to fill an important place in society, and to fill it not only brilliantly but so as to gain universal honour and admiration in spite of scandals—but those were days when nearly everything was condoned to brilliant sinners. Indeed, her brilliance threatened the sole-brilliance insisted upon by Napoleon's star, and in 1809 she received an imperial order to repair at once to Paris. She went, accompanied by Fabre. At her first audience with the Emperor, he said to her : " I know your influence over the society of Florence. I know also that you employ it in a sense adverse to my policy. You are an obstacle to my projects of fusion between the Tuscans and the French." It is said that he told her also that if she had had a son, he would have made him King of England. She was not allowed to return to Florence until November 1810.

In 1810 Lamartine describes her as " a little woman whose figure had lost all lightness and elegance. The features of her face, too rounded and obtuse, also preserved no pure lines of ideal beauty. But her eyes had a light, her fair hair a tint, her mouth an attraction, all her physiognomy an intelligence and a grace of expression that made you remember if they no longer made you admire. Her soft way of speaking, her easy manner, her re-assuring familiarity, raised at once those who approached her to her level. You did not know whether she descended to yours or elevated you to hers, there was so much nature in her bearing."

In 1812 began her warm friendship with Ugo Foscolo.[1]

When the cardinal was living again at Rome, he was visited by two nuns who had arrived with relics to be placed in his charge.[2] The younger, an Austrian, who had lived at the court of Marie Antoinette, had recently been presented to

---

[1] Hayward's " Biographical and Critical Essays : The Countess of Albany and Alfieri," 1858.
[2] " On the Banks of the Seine," by A. M. Falls.

George III. and Queen Charlotte, and was greatly surprised 1804. that the handsome, magnificent-looking cardinal should be quite excited by her accounts of that interview, rather than by her much more thrilling reminiscences of the fated French royal family. "Did she not know," he enquired, "that he was the rightful King of England?" She did not, but replied, politely evasive, that he looked every inch a king. "You have been received by Henry of England," he said on dismissing her. She knelt for his blessing, feeling even more awed than she had ever felt in the august and sainted presence of Louis XVI.

She saw the royal cardinal next, walking in a procession at St. Peter's, next to the Pope, with a far-away look in his eyes. He often returned to the convent to see the lady abbess and to talk about England and his brother's campaign, nearly weeping over the misfortunes of their Scottish friends. His private chaplain who attended him was an Englishman ; eager too to hear about his country ; longing to return thither but too affectionately devoted to his king to leave him ; very sad at the thought that the cardinal should be the last of his race, though he would say cheerfully, "He will be king some day." His master's dearest treasures, he said, were the bethrothal ring given by Henrietta Maria to Charles I. and the small clock which was in Charles II.'s bedroom when he died ; the clock the dying king remembered he ought to wind up that day.

"A very handsome, saintly-looking man," the nun describes the cardinal : "the most refined-looking of all the Stuarts, with the exception of Charles I., without his brother's splendid physique, being more delicately made." After watching faithfully by his king's deathbed, the chaplain returned to England and went to see the lady abbess. The nuns used to wonder who was the King of England for whom masses were constantly said in the chapel.

The Marchesa Vitelleschi in "A Court in Exile" gives an elaborate account of a visit the cardinal received at Frascati from Pope Pius VII. and King Charles Emmanuel of Sardinia, who arrived there simultaneously, without concert. Charles Emmanuel had abdicated the Sardinian throne in 1802 in favour of his brother, Victor Emmanuel I.

Consalvi, the Cardinal of York's dear friend, now a

1804. cardinal himself, had been appointed by the new Pope his secretary of state. Consalvi had suffered imprisonment and exile like Pius VI., but on his return to Rome was a great but tactful reformer under Pius VII. He was the chief representative of the Church when the Concordat with France was being drawn up, and it was chiefly through his skill that difficulties were smoothed away and the Concordat accomplished. It was he who urged the Pope to consent to crown Napoleon in 1804.

In the new woes of the Niobe of Nations, the Cardinal of York was left in peace. The Pope returned from the imperial coronation in May 1805, bearing golden promises from France, but in the following October the French again occupied Ancona on pretence of protecting the papal see. They remained practically masters of Rome until the Congress of Vienna, 1814.

The cardinal's official diary, begun in 1759 by Giovanni Lando, was continued after Lando's death by Angelo Cesarini.

CHAPTER XXIII

SUNSET AND EVENING STAR

" Sunset and evening star,
  And one clear call for me !
And may there be no moaning of the bar,
  When I put out to sea,

But such a tide as moving seems asleep,
  Too full for sound or foam,
When that which drew from out the boundless deep
  Turns again home."

TENNYSON.

THOUGH the cardinal all his life had had delicate health and 1807. had come through severe illnesses and latterly through severe bodily distresses, he passed his eighty-second birthday without having become a real invalid such as his father had become in his last years. In Cesârini's careful diary where his patron's daily life is monotonously recorded, we find him still attending to his episcopal duties, still and frequently touching for the king's evil as he had done ever since his brother's death, still receiving incessant guests at his hospitable table. English, Scottish, and Irish travellers came in numbers, some of great distinction and more splendidly entertained, though Cesarini rarely remembers their foreign names. Henry suffered much from the long-standing ailment in his legs, but though he could not stand long Holy Week functions, he went on saying his daily mass. He was especially pleased at Easter 1807 to receive a visit from a niece of Pitt, the British minister ; also by attentions from the Portuguese ambassador, as he represented a never-friendly court. Pitt's niece and the lady and two English "lords" who accompanied her all treated the cardinal with the same respect and reverence as they could have shown to their sovereign, says Cesarini. He enjoyed his harmless royalty, which never for an hour endangered the peace of Great Britain. He was on most intimate and affectionate terms with his cousins, the two kings of Sardinia, the abdicated Charles Emmanuel who lived in Rome, and the

1807. reigning Victor Emmanuel I. who with his queen frequently visited him at Frascati.

Up to the middle of July this quiet pleasant life with its gentle royalty continued. Then the end came almost suddenly. On July 10 he fell seriously ill. All knew that there was no hope. The one thing that troubled his peaceful passing was care for his " family " ; the servants who had served him for so many years, and would be left with no certain means of living. Rich as he had once been, he had lost much and he had spent profusely, and from his estate there must be drawn heavy payments to his sister-in-law and the legacies of his brother. His own income had been irregular. Spanish payments were always behind, and he had received nothing from Jaen since 1801.

He died peacefully on the fourth day of his illness, in the evening of July 13, the anniversary of his translation to the see of Frascati forty-six years before. Cesarini, writing during that day to Manuel Pasquale, agent at Madrid, does not seem to have expected death to be so near.

Closing the history of the Stuarts with its sorrows and tragedies, its high lights and deep shadows, it was a good and happy, if an unromantic, life that ended here in calm sunset. He had known suffering, sorrow, and anxiety, with his father ; heavy clouds had darkened his evening before it brightened to peaceful light ; but as much real happiness had fallen to his share as mortal may expect. Of the romance of the Stuarts he had inherited only the name. Under other circumstances he might have played a far more strenuous part. As it was, his ardent nature had been governed by common sense, his pride had been controlled by the stern discipline of necessity. He had never grandly longed nor striven for the crown that was his birthright, and he had never raged nor repined and sunk under its withholding. If such resignation was not romantic, not brilliantly heroic, it was by far more dignified than the squalid sequel to his brother's crowded hour of glorious life. He had taken contentedly, even gladly, what good things a grudging world had spared to him, and had found in earnest following of duty the joy and peace that rarely surround a throne. Never deeming himself exempt by his frustrated royalty from taking up the burden of life, he had worked for his living honestly and with real love for his business.

He had not enjoyed the state and splendour of sovereignty, but 1807. he enjoyed to the full the sense of his royalty, the inalienable inheritance of great tradition.   " A captive void of noble rage," such as was his brother's glory and tragedy ; a linnet who had never known the summer woods, but could sing sweetly in such sun as reached his cage.   Proud to excess of his English blood, but born a Roman, soft Lydian airs of Italy had breathed into his nature and he had found content in the music and beauty of " lands of summer across the sea."   Out of wisdom, not out of scorn, he reconciled himself to exile and made it home.   Yet he never for a moment forgot that he was an English prince ; [1] though, content to rest and stand in his pleasant southern lot,[2] he, to all intents and purposes,

> " —— forgot the clouded Forth,
> The gloom that saddens Heaven and Earth,
> The bitter east, the misty summer,
> The gray metropolis of the North."

On the night of July 14, his body was carried to Rome, the carriage surrounded by his weeping people.   He lay in state during the two following days in the hall of the Cancellaria.   Dirges and requiems were sung in the neighbouring church of St. Andrea della Valle ; so by happy coincidence of neighbourhood, the patron saint of Scotland was associated with the passing of the last Stuart.   Thence he was borne to the north subterranean aisle of the Vatican basilica, to be buried with his father and mother.

At the same time, Charles Edward's body was brought privately from its temporary sepulchre at Frascati ; and on the evening of July 16, the royal brothers were laid together ; [3] far from the northern land they—or one of them, at least— loved so well ; where they would so fain have lived and died. There is a pathetic simplicity in those plain stone sarcophagi in the crypt of St. Peter's, among all the pomp of marble and bronze of that street of the illustrious dead.   They bear no

---

[1] He interested himself so early in his ecclesiastical career as 1749 in obtaining from the Pope special honours to English saints.   At his request, certain feasts previously granted to the English College at Rome were extended to "all ecclesiastics of the English nation wherever living.   Those were St. George, St. Edward, St. Ursula and companions, St. Edmund King and Martyr, and St. Thomas of Canterbury.   See the *Month*, March 1908.

[2] " Thou shalt rest and stand in thy lot at the end of the days."—Daniel xii. 13.

[3] Note at the end of the funeral oration by Dom Marco Mastrofino.

1807. trace whatever of sculpture beyond the cutting of the simple names on the tablets above the tombs, "Jacobus III."— "Carolus III."—"Henricus IX." It was so evidently intended they should be but temporary. Poverty may hardly account for the bareness in which James and Charles were left, for the Cardinal of York could well have afforded more stately houses for kings to sleep in, while to himself as dean of the College of Cardinals and archpriest of the Vatican basilica was certainly due some honour of memorial marble. But the Stuarts sleep in unique simplicity, as if still waiting till the time shall come when Westminster may open her gates to let those Kings of Sorrow come in.

The funeral oration on the death of "Henry, Cardinal, called the Duke of York" was preached in the Cathedral of Frascati on July 20, by Dom Marco Mastrofino, Public Professor of Theology, at the solemn requiem ordered by the magistracy. The oration may be read in printed form in the British Museum.

The preacher preluded his theme after the florid fashion of his day, with apostrophes so conventionally sentimental as almost to discount the sincerity of the panegyric that followed, in which he recounted the real merits of and the sterling work done by the royal bishop in his sphere. Frascati might well hang her walls in black and chant her hymns of sorrow, he proceeded, for such a lost benefactor, such a high exemplar. Not always has a prince of the church been praised with such truth as "he who clothed us with joy, who increased our glory, who made us greater than ourselves, the generous, kind, and zealous Henry. . . . Art thou broken, precious branch of kings?" cries the preacher. "Art thou fallen, last and sublimest glory of the House of Stuart? And we are left in darkness as in the terrible silence and shadow of nature under the quaking and eclipse and the horrors of desolate night.[1] As the royal prophet wept in Ziglag over Saul and Jonathan, fallen on Gilboa, and then burst into the most pathetic of elegies, so let my tearful words over the cold ashes of our beloved dead be a tribute of reverent and mournful praise. I have flowers to strew upon his grave, balsams incorruptible that will at least preserve his memory. The

---

[1] Here the preacher doubtless refers to the renewed anxieties at Rome while the French were occupying the Adriatic ports and Cività Vecchia.

field from which I gather them is wide, and abundant is the 1807.
harvest, but sincerity is moderate and brief ; scant and broken
the voice of supreme grief.   May just praise echo up to you,
O sublime soul, and assure you of the gratitude of a people and
a clergy who adored you."

The preacher went on to describe the bishop's zealous
care for his flock : first for the tender lambs, watching unweariedly that they should be instructed in the kingdom of
God, himself expounding the catechism to them in church ;
earnestly commending to the care of his clergy the delicate
shoots that have most need of the gardener's care.   How
often and how earnestly from that throne had he spoken to
his people, exhorting them with tears in his eyes to live well,
as if he longed to transfuse into them his own ardent spirit.
Then, fearing that he had spoken in vain, that his words
would pass with the air on which they were borne, to what
subtle arguments did not this loving shepherd turn !   Twice
he called together diocesan synods and there revealed the
abuses that existed among the clergy and pointed the way of
purgation, the sure way to heaven.   What a gracious example
for his clergy !   What a pious spectacle for the people who
revered him !   The public prints had revealed and repeated
memories of his piety, but his most eternally eloquent and
glorious memory would be this zeal of his for the Lord's
House.   His cleansing extended beyond the material walls of
that house.   He found out that a group of vagrant families
were settled in a corner of his diocese ; evidently a sort of
gypsies, as they were strangers to the faith.   With the zeal
of Onias, the third who tore up from Jerusalem the customs
and rites planted there by the infidel Antiochus, Henry investi-
gated and uprooted this source of evil.   He destroyed and
then planted.   He reopened the springs of healing grace upon
that neglected spot, himself carrying on foot from Frascati the
Sacred Host, followed by his people in triumph.   It seemed
as if the surrounding mountains must thrill and leap like
rams, as when Eleazar brought the ark of the living God over
Jordan into Canaan once sanctified by Melchisedek and
Abraham, and since profaned by heathen worship.   And now
a chapel in that once forgotten spot testified for ever to the
goodness of the bishop as the two piles of stones in Jordan
commemorated the passage of the ark to the Promised

1807. Land. So evident was the undying zeal of Henry for his diocese.

Then the preacher turned to the high standard the cardinal had set up for his not very docile clergy ; " how he laboured to make them an elect clergy, even with a certain emphasis or vehemence of paternal rigour" (as he had striven with the chapter of St. Peter's !) "endeavouring to restore the perfection of ancient discipline ; as if impelled by remembering the doom of Eli whom indolence held back from the correction of his priestly sons. He was as John the Evangelist whose prophetic ardour relit the waning lamps of the Asiatic churches. Blessings upon his memory ! might his clergy preserve all the fair virtues he had transmitted to them ! He had insisted upon their lives being pure, having grave reason for such insistence. When once a great personage told him that he would have to answer before God for having added nothing to the sum of humanity, he had answered quickly and enthusiastically that his children were those whom he had regenerated in the Lord."

Then for his private life : by prayer he anticipated the rising of the sun, by prayer he accompanied its setting. He was accustomed in the depth of winter to rise from bed to perform his devotions before he turned to the day's work. With what fervour he said his mass ; how tenderly he communicated his clergy and his people ; how rapt his countenance, as if his soul were rather in heaven than on earth ! How the virtuous and enviable mother who brought him up must have watched him with sweet sympathy from the depths of heaven ! Then his mass over and other masses heard, he would go to the seminary and study in its library. So retentive and full was his memory that few knew more of the Fathers and liturgies than he, and none excelled him. " Oh ! Father, that I might see you again in that library where I spent so much time to my profit in my tender years ; where you stooped to make yourself as a child with me that I might rise to heights of spiritual intellect. I now shed my tributary tears on your lifeless bust in gratitude and love for the early care that was given to me there."

Henry's last will, dated July 15, 1802, was registered at Rome in 1810. Therein he renewed his protest of 1784, and formally transmitted his right to the crown of Great Britain to "the nearest lawful heir." That heir at the date of his death 1807. was Charles Emmanuel IV. of Savoy.

There has been much misunderstanding over the legacy he bequeathed to George III.; the crown jewels of England carried away by James II., among them the George worn on the scaffold by Charles I. and handed by him to Bishop Juxon with the word "Remember." It is supposed that with those jewels the cardinal-king bequeathed to George III. the crown of England. The formal protest attached to his will proves the fallacy of such a supposition; besides the fact that no sovereign has more than a life-interest in the British crown. There are certain precedents of the sovereign's will having been esteemed as above the law, as in the cases of Henry VIII. and Edward VI.; the breathless suspense in which Elizabeth and Anne were watched to "name" their successors; but the crown could not lawfully be bequeathed by will or word.

The fact was that, in consideration of the gracious kindness with which George III. had provided for the necessities of the cardinal's old age, his executor, the Bishop of Milevi, on August 30, 1807, sent "as remembrances" to George, Prince Regent (George III. being then insane), a cross of St. Andrew set with diamonds worn by Charles I., and the ruby ring worn by the Kings of Scots at their coronation.[1] The prince graciously replied, professing profound respect for the late Cardinal Duke, and promising in his father's name to allow the Countess of Albany £1600 a year for life.[2]

The cardinal had duly provided for Louise by will, at which she professed herself very grateful. She condoled with the Bishop of Milevi (Angelo Cesarini, so long his man of business) upon an end of a friendship that had existed for forty years, highly approved his appointment as executor, and was confident that her jointure would be punctually paid. In November, the bishop sent her a watch and other things as "remembrances."[3] The papers and art treasures collected by Prince Charles Edward found their way to the Musée Fabre at Montpellier, founded by Louise's lover, the sculptor. The cardinal bequeathed to Sir John Coxe Hippesley a Plutarch in two volumes, folio, a MS. with miniatures, a gold medal, and the veil of Mary Queen of Scots.[4]

---

[1] Hist. MSS. Comm. Reports X., part vi. p. 249. (Braye MSS.)
[2] Ibid. pp. 249, 250, November 14, 1807.
[3] Ibid. pp. 219, 236.   [4] Ibid. p. 251.

1807.   The Bishop of Milevi applied to his friend Augustus, Duke of Sussex, to get the cardinal's pension continued for a year to provide for his poor household of fifty-six persons, who had nothing to depend upon but what might be due from his Spanish benefices at the date of his death, his assets being swallowed up by charges upon them.[1]

Cordara says that a considerable portion of his real property had been in Mexico and was lost in South American revolutions. He thinks it probable that he survived most of the heirlooms of his house. His library went to endow his favourite seminary at Frascati; his remaining furniture, plate, and family relics, were gradually absorbed by English collectors at Rome during the first half of the last century.[2]

It was understood that the Act with respect to attainder of blood was to expire at his death; which event therefore was the cause of much anxious expectation in England and Scotland.

An interesting account is given in that same *Quarterly* article of the vicissitudes of the cardinal's notable papers before the bulk of them was acquired by George IV. The remainder gradually followed them to the Royal Library at Windsor and the British Museum.[3]

Besides the fine portrait of the Cardinal of York by Batoni in the National Portrait Gallery, there is an oval in crayons by Rosalba Carriera (No. 378), where he appears as a very old man. The Earl of Orford possesses a full length portrait, the Earl of Galloway a miniature. The Scots College at Rome possesses two fine portraits in oil, one as a young man in lay dress, the other in his cardinal's robes. Another portrait was sent by Blairs College, Aberdeen, to the Stuart Exhibition of 1889, and Mr. Drummond of Edinburgh possesses a portrait by Gavin Hamilton. Literary memorials of the cardinal remain, besides the before-mentioned tract on Drunkenness, in the *Constitutiones Synodales ecclesiæ Tusculanæ*, published

---

[1] Hist. MSS. Comm. Reports X., part vi. pp. 234, 246, 257, 265.

[2] "The Stuarts in Italy," *Quarterly Review*, December 1846.

[3] The papers, or a considerable portion of them, were bequeathed to Cesarini who left them to his niece, the wife of a Malatesta who, at her death, sold them to Lord Orford. A portion of the cardinal's diary, the entries for the year 1788, was published in England in 1880; as a specimen, says Ademollo in his article in the *Nuova Antologia* before quoted. Ademollo inquired if any of the cardinal's papers remained in the Malatesta archives, and was told that there still remained four packets; 1. letters from Charles to Henry; 2. letters from the Countess of Albany; 3. letters from the Duchess of Albany; 4. other letters addressed to the cardinal.

writes, " which has a character and interest peculiarly its 1819.
own ; through which all Europe passes . . . which is entered
with intense curiosity, and left (to speak from the conviction of
my own feelings) with infinite regret—I mean, the little palace
on the Lung' Arno, where, on Saturday evenings, a congress of
Europeans . . . assembles, to offer its homage to the only
legitimate queen, who unites the suffrages of all parties in her
favour—the widow of that *true legitimate*, James the Third of
England " (Lady Morgan's accuracy is less remarkable than
\er enthusiastic emphasis), " Louisa, Princess of Stolberg,
ountess of Albany. This lady has, however, another, and
┐haps a deeper claim to interest, than these titles give her,
┐ing the ' *Mia Donna* ' of Alfieri . . .
since t went to my first interview with this illustrious lady,
import⌐d with the sense of all the respect due to my legitimate
brotheⁱᵘt still more with the recollection of that sweet picture
D of her by Alfieri. . . . Time has spared so much of the
brotⁱᵉⁿts of this fair portrait in the original, that it would be
the er just nor civil to record the thefts which he may have
mitted ; but enough remains to judge of the fidelity of the
ᵥing. If the ' dolce foco ' [*sic*] of the dark eyes has lost
ething of its lustre, the ' candidissima pelle ' still remains,
the intellect which gave a charm to all, brightened by
retains all the force and freshness of youth ; while a
\er at once so energetic and simple possesses a peculiar
to those with whom she converses *à demi voix* in the
/ of her rather formal circle, a charm which is infinitely
itful in the unceremonious morning receptions in her
it library . . . Madame d'Albany is the *Queen of Florence*,
her notice or neglect can always influence the character
1e stranger's sojourn in that interesting capital." " It was
good fortune frequently to occupy the place next to
ⁿe d'Albany (who habitually sits at the head of a very
like circle) and to enjoy her most pleasant conversation
besides being replete with acute and humorous ob-
n, sometimes turned on Alfieri. She spoke of him
unaffected simplicity, the very opposite of the senti-
jargon ascribed to her by many English travellers . . .
Ove d'Albany still reads a great deal ; and that passion
is said, fine arts ascribed to her by Alfieri still exists, to judge
from Gexcellent pictures of her library. She has one talent

U

1821. that is worth twenty others. She knows *how to laugh* and *at whom*, right well!"[1]

Other names, echoes of the cause, did it honour in Florence. Lady Morgan met there also the sixth Duke and Duchess of Berwick, "a favourable specimen of the Grandees of Spain. The Duke," he was the Countess of Albany's great-nephew,[2] "appears to us as conversant with modern English literature as if he had been in the habit of haunting the best circles in London and Edinburgh."[3] In 1802 he had become first Fitz-James Duke of Alba by inheritance from his aunt.

When Lady Morgan's "Italy" came out in 1821, Louise ordered copies both in English and French from her Paris bookseller. "Je sera curieux de voir coment elle nous traitera," [*sic*] wrote her learned majesty.[4] The treatment must have been found satisfactory.

She died at Florence in January 1824. With her, the last of the actors in the last scene of the Stuart drama passed away ; that tablet in Santa Croce is the curtain rung down upon that tale of sorrow, of doom, of beauty and romance. Her name links the dynasty, vanished in echo-laden Götter-dämmerung, to the prosaically tangible present. As we have seen, the present Earl of Leicester's father, "Coke of Norfolk," knew her in Rome in her youth. As a child, the late Lady Stanley of Alderley, mother of many living children, knew her familiarly in her old age. No doubt there are still living some who remember her. Her portrait and Alfieri's, painted by her later lover, Fabre, hang in the Uffizi at Florence.

So the ancient dynasty passed away, slain, extinguished by—Fate, or the perversity of man ?

In these so-called tolerant days, it may seem an astonishing injustice that princes, worthy men, who inherited their royal right from long lines of ancestors, should have been bereft of their inheritance because their chosen religion was not the religion of their people. Must one marvel for ever that the might of men's selfish interests should triumph over natural right and worth and whole-hearted self-sacrifice ; or that mere cruelty of Fate should turn aside the result of honest and patient effort ?

---

[1] "Italy," by Lady Morgan ; ii. 44.
[2] Grandson of her sister Catherine Augusta who married the fourth Duke of Berwick and Liria (Marquis of Jamaica). Blason de España.
[3] "Italy," by Lady Morgan ; ii. 111.
[4] Hist. MSS. Comm. Reports XV., Appx. ii. p. 251. (Eliot Hodgkin MSS.)

u
mig
for ever

One may
would have fol
Leith in 1708, o
in 1745, or the
Suppose this to ha   sive victory on the prince's side, as it actually was on Cumberland's ; no small victory like Prestonpans, but a trial of full strength. Decimated as they were, starving as they were, the valour of the Highlanders was so great, their prince's influence was so dominating, that, had they had the strength of union, had he been allowed to lead them as he would, they might well have been able to shock the trained forces brought against them and to recover the steps lost by retreat. Edinburgh, after a new pause of fear and nervous self-examination, would have risen enthusiastically to welcome home the victorious heir of her ancient kings. London would start dismayed and arm herself with a scornful smile ; to find that the people, changefully minded but sound-hearted, were cheering the brave young prince who, by might of his own sword and his dauntless spirit, had won his father's crown against terrific odds. They would remember only that he was brave and victorious ; English by near descent, and sound English of heart. If he was a papist—well, he had a right to his own religion, and a papist may be no worse than a German infidel. Away with the Germans who cannot even

at
be
people
small when
malcontents at

after another, and
again there are debts to pay. st redeem promises
to France and Spain, to Sweden and Russia—above all, to
Rome. But the people, long vexed by internal division and
danger, are for peace; or it is not the king's friends who have
their sympathy. What will come of that?

And what of Rome? James was the sincerest of men and
had promised incessantly all safeguard and protection for the
Protestant churches, but would he always be able to reconcile
his conscience with concession to Protestant demands? What
would come of that? The old story over again; the wars of
Charles I.; the Revolution; banishment or the scaffold?

Yet if James could have weathered the storm, would he not
have been, as Lumisden called him, the best of kings: un-
swervingly conscientious, unwearyingly anxious for the good
of his people, largely tolerant, of unflinching fidelity to his
word; loyally amenable to the constitution as he found it
established, ruling with wisdom come by painful and profound
experience? And were there not all the makings of a
popular sovereign in Prince Charles; his good qualities
sunned by success to beneficent development, not thwarted

and warped by the bitterness of disappointment and the blight 1807. of aimlessness ?   And Henry, never a priest ?   As an absolute ruler, he would have governed well, as Charles I. governed, admittedly, during the years called " of tyranny." But unless transplantation to England had taught him otherwise, one may guess that he would have yielded with difficulty to constitutional demands had they run counter to his fixed sense of duty, and, disdaining opportunism, he might perhaps have followed his great-grandfather to the block or his grandfather to exile.   The hot temper that his friends feared would prevent his success as a military leader would have balked the usefulness of his best qualities ; his undying energy, his single-eyed unswerving pursuit of duty.

It is idle to conjecture.   Circumstances so greatly alter cases, and we are glad to believe that all is for the best in this best of all possible worlds.

APPENDIX I

THE HEIRS OF THE STUARTS

1807. WHEN in 1807 the Cardinal of York died at Frascati, he bequeathed to George III. the crown jewels carried away from England by his grandfather James II. To the King of Sardinia he bequeathed his position as heir of the elder line of the royal house, his claim upon the succession.

That claim had become so shadowy, was so nearly forgotten, the House of Hanover was so firmly established on the throne, that hardly any one then thought of looking for the next brood of Pretenders, sprung from the dragon's teeth of hereditary right crushed under the iron heels of William of Orange and William of Cumberland.

There is no question of treason to the powers that be involved in tracing the elder line of the royal house from the date of accession of the House of Savoy to that title, up to the present day, for the Princes and Princesses of Savoy and Modena have never raised the faintest protest against their exclusion from the throne of the island kingdoms—for even the formal protest at the bar of the House of Lords by Anne, Duchess of Savoy, granddaughter of Charles I., against the passing of the Act which settled the succession upon the Electress Sophia, was forced upon her by James II. and Louis XIV. Yet it cannot but be interesting to look for a while into the lives of those princes who but for the Act of the Protestant Succession might have reigned over us ; only *might*, for circumstances would all have been changed, and the last two Stuarts, early married, might not have died childless. How were those monarchs *de jure* living ? What manner of men and women were they with regard to their qualities as potential British sovereigns ? What was befalling them in their southern principalities, while one George wandered, blind and mad, over the palace of their fathers ; while another George squandered English gold in profligacy like any blackest sheep of Stuart strain, only without the saving grace of a heart to spend with it ; while the faith for which the Stuart kings lost their crown was being set free to blossom in a second spring ; while the governing power was dropping into the hands of those who know not the lessons of history and have not yet learnt to govern themselves ; while English cannon thundered over Spain, Italy, and Belgium : in India, Russia, and Egypt ; while our Empire, half

Photo. B. Dittmar, Munich

H.R.H. MARY THERESA OF AUSTRIA-ESTE

PRINCESS LOUIS OF BAVARIA

Heiress-in-line of the Royal Houses of Plantagenet and Stuart

(Mary III. and IV.)

fallen in the west, was rising in the east; while loyalty and 1807.
with it faith, chivalry, and self-devotion, were near to perishing out
of the land; while the nation was being taught from day to day
that each man's duty is to himself alone, and that in furtherance
of his all-important private interests, faith and honour and loyalty
and self-sacrifice are worthless hindrances?

The line of James II. being extinct, his younger brother
Henry, Duke of Gloucester, having died unmarried, the succession
passed to the lines of his sisters. The eldest, Mary, Princess of
Orange, left only her son William who deposed James II., and died
childless. The second, Elizabeth, had died unmarried in Carisbrooke
Castle. Only the third and youngest daughter of Charles I., the
Princess Henrietta Anne, was represented by living descendants
on the death of the Cardinal of York. Of these there were abun-
dance, but all, being Catholics, were excluded from the throne by
the Act of the Protestant Succession; as were all the descendants
of the elder children of Charles the First's only sister, Elizabeth,
Queen of Bohemia. The Princess Henrietta, married to Philip,
Duke of Orleans, brother of Louis XIV., had left two daughters.
Of these the elder, married to Charles II. of Spain, died childless.
The younger, Anne, married in 1684 Victor Amadeus II., Duke
of Savoy, afterwards first King of Sardinia, and through Anne
of Orleans, Duchess of Savoy, the succession was ultimately
carried on.

Victor Amadeus II. was a prince whose tortuous line of
policy somewhat detracts from the splendid record he has left
among the high-minded and valiant chiefs of his illustrious
house. He succeeded in 1675, when only in his tenth year, to
the sovereignty of a country torn among contending factions, with
which his regent-mother, Marie de Nemours, was hardly able to
cope. Nevertheless she was extremely unwilling, when the time
came, to deliver the reins of power into his hands. Though he
married the niece of Louis XIV., he was so angry at being treated as
a mere vassal by that imperious monarch, who demanded of him
the most humiliating concessions, and so affronted by the airs of
superiority of the boy Philip V., that he deserted the French side
in the war of the Spanish Succession; for which desertion, at the
Peace of Utrecht he was rewarded with the kingdom of Sicily. This
fertile dominion he was, however, compelled by the Quadruple 1720.
Alliance to exchange for rocky Sardinia in 1720. By cunning
and luck, rather than by wisdom and patriotism, he raised his
kingdom of Sardinia, with Piedmont and Savoy, to a place among
the kingdoms of Europe and a position which, except for the
period of almost universal upheaval of the revolution, it ever after
maintained: until his distant cousin and distant successor, Victor
Emmanuel II., made himself master of the whole Italian peninsula.

Victor Amadeus was not a devout son of the Church. He
opposed himself in particular to the Jesuits, who held the education

1730. of youth almost entirely in their hands. He founded several public schools of science and letters from which Jesuit influence was rigidly excluded; among them the splendid University of Turin. Trade and manufacture received their share of his attention. Through his care, the cultivation of the mulberry tree and the rearing of silk-worms obtained in Piedmont the perfection they still retain. He reformed the criminal and civil laws, showing himself throughout a prince as sagacious as successful.

In 1728 his queen, the Princess Anne of Orleans, died. In 1730, wearied of the burden of sovereignty which he had borne for fifty-five years, he abdicated (many of the Savoyard kings abdicated) in favour of his son Charles Emmanuel. He soon repented of this step; his shoulders were too long used to the burden to feel comfortable without it, and twice he vainly attempted to recover the reins of government. He was at last shut up as a rebel, though in "honourable captivity," at Moncalieri, where he died two years later. Browning has dramatised the history of "King Victor and King Charles."

Charles Emmanuel III. was one of the best and greatest of his brilliant line, brave, prudent, and patriotic; a prince who covered himself with glory in the wars that convulsed Europe for nearly the whole period of his reign, and who yet found time to encourage art and literature, to found the universities of Cagliari and Sassari, and to introduce professors and teachers of the highest merit into his kingdom. He was too anxious for the power and strengthening of his kingdom to live on always friendly terms with his Stuart cousins, and vehemently declared himself opposed to Prince Charles's great venture in 1744. He died in 1773, at the venerable age of seventy-three, mourned by 'Italy and his own states as an irreparable loss. During his reign his dominions were increased by the cession to him of Vigevano and Bobbio by the Empress Maria Theresa in acknowledgment of his gallant services in her cause. He was married three times; two of his wives were Polyxena of Hesse-Rheinfeld and Anne of Sulzbach.

1773. His son Victor Amadeus III. succeeded him. With him our personal interest draws closer, as the father of two princes who might have reigned successively as English kings. He was a monarch athirst for military glory and had fought under his father at the battles of Coni and Bassignano. Frederick the Great of Prussia was his ideal of hero and ruler, and as soon as the reins of government came into his hands, he set to work to remodel his army after the Prussian type, and completed the building of the fortresses of Alessandria and Tortona. He was not only a soldier; he was a wise and conscientious sovereign. He busied himself energetically and enthusiastically with reforms in the administration of his country. He founded academies of arts and sciences; he fostered painting and sculpture, and availed himself of the services of men so distinguished as Lagrange, Gialuzzo, and

From this date, the younger son's crescent for difference 1788. disappears from the royal shield of Great Britain and Ireland which surmounts his episcopal proclamations and other official documents, and the ducal coronet beneath the cardinal's hat is exchanged for the crown. He no longer styles himself " Henry, Duke of York and Cardinal," but " Henry, called the Duke of York:" *Dux Eboracensis nuncupatus*, or *Duca di Yorck denominato*. So far, for conscience sake at least, he set forth his ancient right. He continued to sign his name " Henry, Cardinal ;" not " Henry R." after the use of his father and brother. From this date his household gave him kingly honours, but with few exceptions, no one else did so. His intimate friends, such as Princess Lambertini, continued to address him as " Royal Highness and Eminence :" the Roman prelates, friendly princes, ambassadors, and statesmen were compelled of state necessity to do so. Only Miss Walkinshaw dunning for money,[1] and crazy Irishmen like one Denis O'Dea, addressed him as " His Majesty the King of England."

The only official response to his announcement seems to have been from the Vatican, and that was a cruelly, even absurdly, evasive reply, utterly ignoring the chief subject in hand ; indeed, ignoring the new protest altogether and referring to that of four years earlier ; unless it happened that his protest then prepared had been kept and sent out without rectification of dates. The papal answer is given in his diary.

" From the Vatican, February 1, 1788.

" Most obliging is the attention rendered to us by the Lord Cardinal Duke of York, in communicating to us before any one else the protest made by him on the 27th of January 1784, for which you will return him lively thanks in our name. Having read that protest, we have found it moderate and prudent, and we have therefore nothing to say against it. At the same time you will add our condolences on the loss of his elder brother, for whom we shall not cease to intercede. And, meanwhile, we very heartily give you our paternal benediction."

Portraits of Charles in his old age are rare, and few memorials remain in Italy to recall the years he lived in that land of many memories. In the ancient basilica of San Clemente, not far from the Colosseum, the Irish Dominicans,

---

[1] Hist. MSS. Comm. Reports X., part vi. p. 239. (Lord Braye's MSS.)

1788. who have possessed the church since Urban VIII. presented it to them, remember the visit he paid them before leaving Rome for Scotland when they entertained him in their garden. They show two portraits which have hitherto been described as of James III. and Queen Clementina. The former portrait is not of James but of Charles in about his sixtieth year, and a good likeness.

Cigna. He was adored throughout Savoy for the benefits he con- *1773.*
ferred upon that land, the cradle of his race. He married Maria
Antonetta of Spain. Two of his daughters married Kings of
France, though neither wore the crown. The elder, Marie
Josephine, Queen of Louis XVIII., died an exile in England and
is buried in Westminster Abbey with her British forefathers; the
younger, Marie Thérèse, married the Comte d'Artois, but died long
before he became Charles X. This king lived on very friendly
terms wirh his cousin Prince Charles at Florence, and with the
Cardinal of York.

Unfortunately, military glory and liberal patronage of arts and
sciences are expensive tastes. In a very few years Victor Amadeus
got through more than the twelve million lire left by his father, and
the public debt was enormously increased. In spite of raising
money by new imposts and by the secularisation of several abbeys,
the treasury became exhausted and the people impoverished. *1792.*
The king was accused of favouring the nobles as against the
people, quite irrespective of merit; a dangerous proclivity then,
when just over his mountain border the French Revolution was
raging and the sovereign people were carrying the lately sovereign
nobles to the guillotine in tumbril-loads. All employments and all
offices, whether ecclesiastical or civil, were conferred upon the
nobles, with the lucrative sale of commissions and pensions to
refresh the exhausted treasury. Industry was paralysed by the
heavy taxation, and the people, despairing of justice, were deprived
of energy and exertion. History repeats itself to-day with slight
modification, under the House of Savoy! From the outbreak of
the revolution, Victor Amadeus proclaimed himself its inveterate
enemy, and he welcomed to his territories the first *emigrés* who
fled from its horrors, one of whom was his son-in-law, the Comte
d'Artois. His refusal to receive the ambassador of the new French
republic was the final cause of open hostilities breaking out
between Sardinia and France. Piedmont being the nearest
neighbour of the republic, naturally had to bear the brunt of the
revolutionary storm when it overflowed the French borders. In
1795 the French army, under Scherer, defeated the Sardinians in
several engagements of which the most decisive was at Loano.
In vain the king sought help from the wealth of England and the
arms of Russia. On the 15th of May 1796, after four years of
brave but ineffectual struggle, Napoleon entered Turin and Victor
Amadeus was compelled to sign a humiliating peace, by which
Savoy, Nice, and Oneglia were ceded to France, while French troops
overran the whole of Piedmont and held the chief fortresses of Coni
and Tortona in their hands. Five months later, a fit of apoplexy, *1796.*
or a broken heart, ended the king's life.

His son Charles Emmanuel IV. succeeded him on the perilously
shaken Sardinian throne; he who might have been styled Charles
IV. of Great Britain and Ireland, since it was on his shoulders there

1796. fell the mantle of hereditary right when in 1807 the last prince of the eldest line passed away. He was a gentle, pious man, not cast in heroic mould; nervously anxious to conciliate rather than to defy the all-conquering Corsican Cæsar. He was devotedly attached to his saintly wife, Marie Clotilde of France, sister of Louis XVI. and of that other saintly princess whose heroism shone so brightly through adversity deep as ever martyr bore, Madame Elizabeth of the Temple. Marie Clotilde had lived with extreme simplicity as Princess of Piedmont and now as Queen of Sardinia she devoted herself entirely to works of devotion and piety.

Before they came to the throne they were described by Sir J. T. Stanley, who visited the dull court of Turin in 1785 and found King Victor Amadeus old and stupid, his Spanish wife solemn and gloomy, Charles Emmanuel "as bigoted as they." The three princes were brought up very strictly, treated as boys when married men. But Lady Stanley, *née* Maria Josepha Holroyd, found Victor Amadeus "a well-looking man and a very worthy, well-meaning one, a very good king and well beloved by his subjects." The Prince of Piedmont was "very plain, but nevertheless his countenance is very agreeable and his manner extremely pleasing. His princess is without exception one of the most pleasing women one ever saw . . . rather handsome, but it was not for beauty one admired her, but for her amiable countenance, goodness of heart, her natural, unassuming, unaffected piety. She is accordingly adored here by everybody."[1]

It was the French policy to wheedle Charles Emmanuel, for he commanded the passes between France and Italy. As long as Buonaparte remained in command in Italy, he observed some degree of respect towards the Sardinian king, but after his departure, the generals, commissaries, and other agents of the Directory heaped insult after insult upon the fallen monarch and exaction after exaction upon his unfortunate subjects. Charles Emmanuel tried by flattery and concessions to obtain the goodwill of his mighty and arrogant neighbour. His ambassador at Paris was, by dint of bribery and intrigue, enabled to conclude a treaty which gave brief security to his country, but the French, being compelled to restore Naples for a while to its king, avenged their check in the south upon the northern Italian states, and Charles Emmanuel was subjected to further humiliating concessions. The French ambassador addressed the unfortunate king in the haughtiest terms, reflected upon the conduct of his government, and commanded a still more cordial compliance with the supreme will of the Directory. French troops surrounded his territories and the French republic was proclaimed in his own capital of Turin. Verily on his shoulders had fallen at least "all a true Stuart's heritage of woe." Bitterly did he repent the confidence he had placed in the republican govern-

---

[1] "Early Married Life of Maria Josepha Holroyd." Edited by J. H. Adeane.

ment.   In return for having faithfully adhered to his treaties, he 1797.
was driven ignominiously from his throne and all his continental
dominions were torn from him.   With his queen he withdrew to
Leghorn, to Rome, to Florence, wandering over the peninsula from
town to town, holding little courts here and there which were
attended not only by political refugees, but by men distinguished in
literature and art.   Among his courtiers appeared Vittorio Alfieri,
now the fierce opponent of revolution.   Alfieri sent " a greeting of
respect and sympathy to the royal fugitives; those princes, he
declared, whom in his heart of hearts he had always honoured while
avoiding them in the plenitude of their power, but whom now
adversity and threats of other not less incapable but less honest
rulers had almost consecrated in his eyes."[1]

While at Leghorn Charles Emmanuel received deputies from the
Statamenti of the island of Sardinia, assuring him of the entire
devotion of the people to his person and government.   Satisfied
with these assurances, he embarked, and, escorted by an English
fleet, arrived on the 3rd of March 1799 at Cagliari, where he was
enthusiastically welcomed.   After a time, the successes of Napoleon's
great Russian adversary, Souvaroff, induced him to return to the
mainland : but hearing in Tuscany of the battle of Marengo (June
14, 1800), he deemed it advisable to return once more to his island
dominions out of reach of Napoleon's victorious arms.

In 1802 his devoted wife died at Naples.   They had had no 1802.
children.   Pius VII., who had been witness of her private virtues
and endless charities, declared her Venerable in 1808.   The church
honours her yearly on March 7th.

Broken-hearted at this last and supreme loss, the childless king
abdicated the Sardinian throne in favour of his brother Victor
Emmanuel : an action which considerably disconcerted Napoleon's
plans.   Having thus thrown off the cares of state, Charles Emmanuel
gave himself up wholly to religious observances, living in the Jesuit
noviciate at the Quirinal from July 1802 to his death in 1819;
twelve years after the death of Henry IX., Cardinal of York, had
made him heir of the elder branch of the Royal House of Britain.

His death occasioned the raising of an interesting question as
to court mourning in England.   Lord Liverpool wrote to Canning
on the subject, being doubtful as to mourning for an "abdicated
king."   Canning replied, "The Sardinians are all relations, and
there are those who think that the ex-king was the lawful King of
Great Britain to the day of his death.   Therefore, I think we must
mourn."[2]

Victor Emmanuel I. was born on July 24, 1759, and was
consequently in his forty-fourth year when he became King of
Sardinia.   As Duke of Aosta he had commanded the Piedmontese
troops against the French in the campaign of 1792-96.   The

---

[1] Antonio Gallenga ; Storia del Piemonte.   Turin, 1856.
[2] " Some Official Correspondence of Canning," vol. i. p. 143.

1802. irreconcilable foe of the revolution and a man of enterprise and capacity besides, he successfully aroused the patriotism of the peasantry against the republican army.   When the Directory dethroned the House of Savoy, orders were given for his arrest, but he escaped by signing a declaration to bear arms no longer against France and withdrew with his brother to the island of Sardinia. His wife was Maria Theresa of Austria-Este, daughter of the Duchess (in her own right) of Modena.   Their only child at the time of their banishment was the Princess Mary Beatrice Victoria. Later were born twin girls, Maria Theresa and Marianna, who became respectively Duchess of Lucca and Empress of Austria, and Christina who became the almost sainted Queen of Naples, as first wife of Bomba.[1]   They never had any sons; hence it was Mary Beatrice who was to follow her father in the English succession. Whether the succession passed from her to her son or to her next sister is a difficult question of English law.

The House of Este is the oldest House in Europe, except perhaps that of Savoy, which has retained sovereign power.   Ercole Rinaldo, last Duke of Modena of the elder line of Este from which sprang Tasso's Leonora and the Queen of James II. of England, was, like the other Italian princes, driven from his dominions by the revolution.   The duchy of Modena became a portion of the Cisalpine republic, which, when Buonaparte became First Consul, was placed under the viceroyalty of Eugène Beauharnais.   Duke Ercole died in Austria in 1803.   He had married a princess of Massa and Carrara.   Their only child and heiress was Maria Beatrice Ricciarda, who married the Archduke Ferdinand, son of the Empress Maria Theresa, and therefore brother of Marie Antoinette and of Caroline Queen of Naples.   She was proud to excess and boundlessly ambitious.   There were seven children of this marriage.   Their eldest daughter, Maria Theresa, born 1773, married Victor Emmanuel, King of Sardinia; their eldest son, Francis, born 1779, presently married the daughter of his sister, Maria Theresa, Mary Beatrice of Savoy, and succeeded his mother in the Duchy of Modena as Francis IV.   Francis and his brothers were educated with the greatest care under the superintendence of their mother, whose pride of birth, though tempered by sincere piety, demanded that Francis, her heir, should be trained to rule as an ideal sovereign of the Middle Ages.   His governors were Valenti Gonzago, Knight of Malta, a gentleman of the chivalrous old school, and Keller, a kindly, honest, and devoted Austrian official.   His religious education was placed in the hands of Father Andrea Draghetti, an ex-Jesuit.   Thus from the very beginning he imbibed the doctrine of absolutism with love of ancient ordinances and also of daring enterprise, and in spite of his Italian mother and the Knight of Malta and the Jesuit

[1] She died in 1836, after the birth of her only child Francis II., last King of the two Sicilies, who died childless.

tutor, he became as German as his father and was consequently 1810. unpopular in Piedmont.

It is very difficult to form a just estimate of those who ruled the destinies of nations during an epoch of extreme party feeling. To justify the deposition of the other Italian sovereigns by the revolutionists, headed by the House of Savoy, led by Mazzini, Garibaldi, and Cavour, it was necessary to paint them in colours as black as those in which the friends of Henry VIII. painted the dispossessed monks, and in which the Whigs painted the Stuarts and the Jacobites. Galvani, the historian of Francis IV., describes him as both in public and domestic life a saint and hero. Bosellini[1] ("a low-class lawyer" says Lord Normanby[2]) holds in horror his religious training, is merciless upon him as a ruler, but speaks well of him in his private capacity. His portraits and medals represent him as a good-looking man, intelligent, earnest, thoughtful, but melancholy. He had the prominent nose of the Este family, with the loose-falling cheeks characteristic of the House of Lorraine. Though he was short-sighted he would not avail himself of spectacles, which gave to his anxiously peering eyes the appearance of slyness and suspicion. Indefatigable alike in exercise and business, he took very little rest. His tastes were very simple. Sparing in diet, he shared without inconvenience the food of peasants and mountaineers, and dispensed as far as state ceremonies would allow him with the attendance of servants : often waiting upon himself, rather than disturb their sleep. "In a word," says Bosellini, "nature had made him to be a good prince ; education and mistaken aims in policy made him a despot. We can say of him neither evil nor good." Yet modern Italians call him traitor, assassin—on no evidence whatever.

When he arrived at man's estate, Napoleon offered him the hand of his beautiful sister, Pauline. This alliance was contemptuously declined for her son by his haughty mother. Francis had chosen for himself a lady more worthy by birth to share the dignities of the House of Este in the young Archduchess Marie Louise. Metternich, who hated and feared the Este, stepped in and forbade the banns, and by means of his diplomacy, the archduchess was married to the Emperor Napoleon. Francis set off on foreign travel to recover from his disappointment, and to seek another wife. Hence his violent and undying hatred of the Corsican adventurer.

In 1810, the year of Napoleon's marriage with Marie Louise, Francis, after travelling through Bosnia to Salonica and Smyrna, visited Sardinia where his sister and her husband, Victor Emmanuel, were reigning while the French occupied Piedmont. It was a very joyful meeting, the brother and sister having been parted for ten

---

[1] Bosellini, "I Contemporanei Italiani," 14–15.
[2] "Vindication of the Duke of Modena." by the Marquis of Normandy.

1810. years. Upon the palace staircase, there met him the young princess, Mary Beatrice, then in her eighteenth year. Galvani speaks rapturously of this angelic creature, grown up so fair and pure to become the reward of the prince's virtuous self-denying youth. Francis was lodged at the palace of Villamarina, opposite to the king's palace, but lived chiefly with the royal family. The twin princesses, who were much younger than Mary Beatrice, lived in a villa apart, surrounded by lovely gardens.

Feasts and great rejoicings celebrated the visit of the queen's brother. The captain of the English warship stationed at Cagliari for King Victor's protection, gave a banquet on board on King George's birthday, the 4th of June, attended by the archduke.[1] There followed a splendid ball in the illuminated citadel at which the king and queen, their daughter and the archduke were present.

Many months of pleasant family life went by, devoid of great events, all that passed being carefully recorded in the diary in which the Archduke Francis revealed his simple soul. He shared in the homely pleasures and occupations of his relatives and in their continual practices of piety. "Hitherto he had known no love," says Galvani, "but for God, mother, and kindred;" his fancy for Marie Louise having doubtless concerned his pride rather than his heart. Now he fell in love. "He heard constantly the praises of the Princess Beatrice," says Galvani, "and beheld her goodness and rare gifts. Everything relating to her and her royal parents augured happiness for a closer union." But serious obstacles were in the way of such a marriage. The near relationship of uncle and niece required a dispensation from the Pope himself which, as his Holiness happened to be Napoleon's prisoner at Fontainebleau, was extremely difficult to obtain. The lady, too, was said by common report to be most unwilling, though on this matter Galvani is absolutely silent, determined on painting the whole affair in roseate colours. Her uncle inspired her with awe and reverence rather than with love. He was fourteen years older than herself and his student tastes ill fitted him to be the husband of a gay Italian girl of eighteen. But the strong wish of his mother alone would have broken down all opposition, even had not the king and queen been anxious for the match. The only difficulty in their eyes was how to get the dispensation from the captive Pope. Partly in hope that his absence might make the princess's heart grow fonder, partly to kill the weary time of waiting; also out of conscientious scruple against temptation to love-making, that until it had received the sanction of the Church must be a sin, the archduke left Sardinia on a visit to Sicily. He remained there three months, where he

---

[1] As his father was an archduke, Francis and all his brothers, sisters, and descendants became archi-ducal; an unfortunate accession of honour, for it turned the Italian house into a branch of Austria. Consequently, the tablet on the outer wall of Modena Cathedral, commemorating the Revolution, triumphs in the expulsion of the foreign House of Hapsburg-Lorraine.

lived in intimate companionship with Louis Philippe, Duke of Orleans, afterwards King of the French. He returned to Sardinia at the end of November, but no dispensation had arrived. He waited on, as patiently as he might, enjoying once more the pleasant home life of the palace. His journal describes the affection of court and people for the Princess Beatrice, whose nineteenth birthday was celebrated on December 6, 1811; how on the last day of the year, the high officials of the island paid homage not only to the king and queen, but to the princess royal, who received them separately attended by her ladies. The archduke next describes the carnival of 1812: how he enjoyed the gaieties only when his princess joined in them. To shorten again the time of delay, he now went on a three weeks' riding tour over the island. The king, besides providing him with riding horses, furnished an escort of soldiers, and commanded that he should be received everywhere with sovereign honours. He minutely describes his journey through the wild interior and its ancient cities; the Roman acqueducts, the Roman town of Crucium, the Roman bridge of seven well-preserved arches over the St. George river; the ancient subterranean church of St. Savino; lead mines, olive groves and gardens, and the strange contrasts and curious customs of the island. The bishops received him with stately hospitality; the civil and military authorities made feasts for him, though, it being Lent, he allowed himself only one meal a day. He returned to Cagliari on March 12.

Time went on, and still the dispensation tarried. Then the prince took a resolution which proves of itself, says Galvani, how much more religion was to him than any other sentiment, however permissible and good. Fearing an indefinite delay, and that all attempts to treat with Pius VII. must be useless, and distrusting his own power to conquer his love, he decided that if the dispensation had not come by the middle of May, he would sail at once for England, renouncing all hope of the marriage.

The middle of May arrived. On the day before that fixed upon as the turning-point, there arrived the papal brief so long expected. The world might see in this coincidence mere fortuitous chance. The pious archduke accepted it as direct answer to prayer and the reward of honest effort to do what was right.

Two days later, at Pentecost, the marriage was publicly announced by the king. On the 20th of June 1812, at six o'clock in the evening, it was celebrated with much pomp, in the cathedral of Cagliari, to the great delight of every one concerned; not even excepting the bride, according to Galvani, who declares that the royal couple had mutually found themselves mated after God's mind and their own. All sorts and conditions of their subjects shared with the royal family in common rejoicing. The archduke gave a banquet to the army, supplemented by all manner of games and horse-races by gentlemen riders, at which the ladies were present in their carriages.

Marginal notes: 1811. 1812.

After the very lengthy festivities, the newly-married pair turned to enjoy the quiet of home. The archduke had always known his young wife to be pious, charming, and accomplished: now that he had an opportunity of enjoying her intimate society, he found with admiration (Galvani) that the strength and energy of her character equalled her other gifts, and he knew that should circumstances ever call forth such qualities, the retiring girl whose innocence so greatly charmed him, would prove by courage in misfortune or danger that the heroic blood of Savoy ran in her veins. All the pride of Este and Savoy was there too, latent in the girl's heart, to be developed when the time should come: even the fierce relentlessness of Mary Stuart was to come out in this other Mary, who on her very deathbed refused forgiveness to those who had dared to lift a hand in rebellion against her race.

It is touching to read in the archduke's journal the simple and faithful record of his honeymoon, of his love and devotion, of his deep piety. He did his best to please his girl-bride by sharing her tastes; riding constantly with her over the wild mountains where there were no carriage roads. She was the most intrepid and untiring of horsewomen; never so happy as when in the saddle. Later, it was a very familiar sight in Modena to see her galloping her spirited little Sardinian courser all over the neighbouring country. Yet in spite of her husband's undoubted love and their friendly companionship, for five years after their marriage he was no more to her than her kind uncle.

With early autumn there came English ships to Cagliari with the welcome news of Wellington's victories in Spain and his entry into Madrid; then of the advance of Napoleon's eagles towards the Neva. The years 1812 and 1813 raged and thundered beyond the blue waters that encircled the rock-bound island. Moscow waved its banner of flame before the invader whose star declined over the Russian snows, and the once all-conquering hosts perished in the ice of the Beresina. The cannon of Lutzen and Leipsic shook the world. Blucher marched from Frankfoot, Wellington crossed the Bidassoa. But the peaceful home-life of Cagliari went on as if Sardinia were one of the Isles of the Blessed, far beyond the din of war and turmoil of politics: monotony broken only by the birth of King Victor's youngest child, Christina, and by an expedition of the archæological archduke to Pula to examine the famous antiquities there, described at length in his journal. English ships kept coming with news of all that went forward beyond the watery horizon; news of events hurrying stormily on, each big with fair augury for the cause of lawful sovereignty. On June 4, 1813, Admiral Sydney Smith entertained the Sardinian royalties on board his ship. Then letters came to Francis from his brothers in Vienna: his country was in danger and needed his presence and his services. He broke the news to his wife, the delicate girl who had never yet left her mother for very far or very long, and whose husband was not as yet by any means her world. But she was a daughter of Savoy and never hesitated a moment between happiness and duty. She saw at once that he must return to his troubled country, and bravely resolved to share with him the long dangerous journey through seas and countries distracted by a doubtful and desperate war. The king and queen, whom they consulted, were of the same mind, and praised the courage and resolution that outweighed affection and sorrow; because, to quote Galvani, the Houses of Este and Savoy know that all other affections must yield to the call of honour.

So on July 15, Mary Beatrice parted from her mother and embarked with her husband on board the English man-of-war *Tremendous*, a ship of seventy-four guns, commanded by a Campbell. An illustrious suite attended her. On the anniversary of that day in the following year, she and her husband made their state entry into Modena and ascended the throne of their ancestors.

But first there was much danger and difficulty to fight through. The archduke intended to touch at Malta by the way, but as the plague was raging there, they sailed instead to Zante, coasting Sicily. They were joined, while in sight of Malta, by more English ships on their way to unite with the fleet in the Adriatic. On the 23rd they landed at Zante. Among the dignitaries and officials who received them was the suite of Queen Caroline of Naples, who was returning from Sicily to Vienna, and who left nothing undone to prove her affection for her cousins while they were in the island. She had them with her constantly, entertaining them at her house or visiting them at their own. The way to Vienna continuing obstructed, Caroline decided to sail for Constantinople. She spent her last day in the island with Francis and Beatrice. They all went together to the Latin cathedral and her cousins saw the queen off when she set sail for the East.

The sojourn of Francis and Beatrice at Zante was forcibly prolonged, owing to Fiume and Trieste being still in French hands. But they had a very pleasant time in the beautiful little island, the "flower of the Levant," by its rocky bay and among its woods of myrtle and olive. They were most hospitably entertained by the English and Greek natives. They heard mass daily in the ancient cathedral that had inherited the name of St. Mark from Venetian rule. They rode a great deal over the level plain of the interior, sailed by moonlight on the warm purple sea, attended fêtes-champêtres, and saw all that was to be seen. The archduke found, examined, and described a magnificent collection of bas-reliefs and Greek sculptures that had originally formed the frieze of the Temple of Apollo on Mount Cotilius in Arcadia.

This prince, whom his enemies have accused of savage cruelty, had a very tender heart towards small weak things. It was related to Galvani by an eye-witness, one of the suite in attendance at Zante, how Francis and Mary Beatrice, passing by their kitchen on

1813. their way to enjoy a sail, came upon a basket of fish just bought by the cook for their table. Some of the fish were still living but writhing and gasping in the anguish of coming death. The pitiful prince and princess picked them carefully out from among those already dead and threw them back into the sea to give them another chance for life. When Francis returned to Modena, it was his daily custom to strew seed and crumbs before his closet window, taking keen pleasure in watching the confidence with which the sparrows came for their breakfast.

On September 10 the English ships brought good news of war auspiciously re-opened by the Allies, of the advance of Austria upon Italy, and the defeat of Soult and Souchet in Spain. These events inspired the archduke with a scheme which at first seemed impracticably Utopian—the recovery of Dalmatia by the House of Austria. He devoted himself to the direction of this enterprise, and never rested till by diligence and skilful statesmanship he had carried it through.

On September 25 the royal pair sailed from Zante to Lissa, a pretty little isle in the Adriatic. They left Lissa on October 15 for Fiume.

The Fiumese were enchanted at receiving the prince and princess and illuminated the town in their honour. Unfortunately the illuminations were spoilt by rain; as if, like the coincidental escort of English ships, English weather must naturally come to attend a princess who belonged dynastically to England. They went on by easy stages to Trieste, where again the people went wild with rapture, greeting them with acclamations, kissing their hands and clothes, and expressing in a thousand ways their ecstasy at finding themselves once more under the paternal rule of Austria; that very rule from which patriots assure us they are so anxious to be "redeemed." They rejoiced that an archduke and an archduchess should be amongst them, and again illuminations, banquets, and balls followed each other in brilliant succession; varied by exploration of the famous Grotto of Corniol and other places of interest. They stayed at Trieste till all the formalities connected with its restoration to Austria were completed, and presently arrived at Neustadt where they were met by the archduke's mother, and by his younger brother and sister. Then on to Vienna, where they remained until July 15 (1813), on which day they made their entry into Modena where they had a splendid reception as future duke and duchess.

But peace was not yet secured. Napoleon escaped from Elba, sent Pope and kings once more flying from their thrones, and occupied Modena. On March 20, 1815, the archduchess left Modena for Mantua. Her husband accompanied her part of the journey and returned to Modena to lead his army against the invader. Mary Beatrice herself worked and presented to the Guardia Nobile the banner under which they marched.

For twelve years, from his brother's abdication in 1802, Victor 1814. Emmanuel's kingdom had been restricted to the island of Sardinia, where he reigned in peace under English protection; a curious if not altogether unfitting state of things considering his dynastic position: which the English government did not consider. It was like the irony of fate. He ruled in the island wisely and well enough, until 1814 when the Allies sent Napoleon to Elba. Then he crossed the sea once more and established himself triumphantly in Turin. Piedmont was restored to him; Savoy later, and in 1815 the congress of Vienna added Genoa to his dominions. By the same treaty he ceded to the state of Geneva the circles of Carouge and Chesne, containing 12,700 inhabitants. France retained Savoy.

The Marquis d'Osmond was accredited to the restored Sardinian court as Louis XVIII.'s ambassador and his daughter, Madame de Boigne, who accompanied her parents, has much to say of its humours. The Genoese, she states, were at no pains to conceal their affliction at being re-united with Piedmont; they much preferred a great Napoleon to a merely good and kind Victor Emmanuel. If they might not be Genoese, they would much rather be French than Piedmontese. They became furious Bonapartists and correspondence passed continually between Genoa and Elba.

Unfortunately the reinstated Italian sovereigns could not set their proud footsteps to march with the times. Shutting their eyes to the changed conditions of the world, which if not improved was certainly past setting back, they immediately set to work, not only to undo the work of Napoleon but to repeal their own precedent reforms. Forgetting the lessons taught by adversity, Victor Emmanuel took up his position as an absolute sovereign of the extremest type. But he was a good soul, did no harm, and owing to his extreme *bonhomie* was very popular at first. He had brought from Cagliari one sole idea, says Madame de Boigne; to restore everything *en Novant-ott;* ('98 in Piedmontese patois) the date of his expulsion. Officers were compelled to take up their ranks as they left them, so that former pages, elderly men, took place beside boys just appointed to fill gaps made by death. Officers who had gained superior rank under the French could not remain in the army unless as cadets. It was the same in all civil offices. The sole exception to the law of *Novant-ott* was that on finding the taxes had been trebled by the French, the king accommodated himself kindly to *that* alteration and deigned to accept the Napoleonic increase of revenue. Napoleon had taken into his service the cream of the Piedmontese. This was judged to make them incapable of serving Victor Emmanuel, who filled their places with his Cagliari courtiers, not one of whom except his prime minister, de Valese, was fit to govern for a day. Scientific collections made by the French must all be destroyed. The king did not wish to be cleverer than his fathers. Then he made an exception of an

1814. ornithological collection which had charmed him. Would he have borne himself in corresponding fashion had he been called to reign in England; tried to set back the clock to 1688?

There remained nevertheless three legal codes in Piedmont, which caused great confusion; the old civil code, the military code, and the Code Napoleon. As one or other happened to be convenient, a royal note enjoined obedience. Society was for the most part of fabulous ignorance and foolishness, says Madame de Boigne.

The court went to Genoa to receive the queen who had lingered
1815. in Sardinia, and on February 27, the English commodore there held a small review to show the king the effect of some new fusees. Firing was interrupted for fear of hitting two little brigs, passing within shot. It seemed pretty certain afterwards that one of these brigs carried Napoleon and his fortunes from Elba to Cannes. He sailed on the evening of the 26th. One of those fusees might have saved much bloodshed, if by it the page of history had been the poorer by missing Waterloo.

Murat advanced from the south; the Sardinian cabinet meditated an arrangement with Napoleon; Victor Emmanuel went to Turin. Then Pius VII. came to Genoa, flying before Murat, and lived for a while under the protection of Savoy. The king and his daughter, Mary Beatrice, went to Genoa to welcome the Pope, the Archduke Francis joining them for a short time. The fugitive Pope was very cheery, reports Madame de Boigne, familiar and accessible with all, serene and dignified. He was followed by the Duchess of Lucca, queen of Etruria, and, after that saintly princess, by a very unsaintly and bizarre figure, Caroline, Princess of Wales, crazily in love with Murat, while Bergami, dressed to look like Murat, attended her in the circus-like chariot that was Murat's gift.

Mary Beatrice stayed with her father, her husband being obliged to return to Modena. Two ceremonies of unusual interest took place during the papal sojourn: First there was the exposition of the Holy Winding Sheet, which very sacred relic was enclosed in seven caskets, to the golden inmost of which the Pope kept the key, and his presence, therefore, made the opportunity. There was also the coronation by the Pope of a miraculous statue of the Blessed Virgin. This stood in a subterranean chapel through which ran a little stream of water on whose margin the Virgin appeared to a good old man, Antonio Botta, on March 18, 1536. The chapel was so tiny that the Pope was hardly visible amid the clergy and the heavy pillars.

On May 2, Mary Beatrice returned to Modena to find banners flying and a whole people rejoicing. Her husband was now firmly settled in his capital. Waterloo followed; the eagle was sent to beat his wings in vain in St. Helena, and Europe could settle down peacefully to setting her royal houses in order.

In the spring of 1817 came the welcome, almost despaired for intelligence that an heir might at last be expected to the ducal

house of Modena. The Queen of Sardinia went to Modena for the 1817.
event and to stand sponsor to the child. The heir disappointed his
friends and relations. The baby turned out to be a girl who arrived
on July 14, 1817. This princess, Maria Theresa Gaetana, born on
the anniversary of the storming of the Bastille and the eve of St.
Henry, so long the fête of French legitimism, lived to wear the shadow
of the French crown by marrying Henri V., Comte de Chambord.
In spite of her sex, the little girl was warmly welcomed by the
Modenese as the probable forerunner of many brothers, and she
was baptized with great splendour as befitted a princess of Este;
as might even have befitted a princess royal of England.

Two years later, in 1819, died Charles Emmanuel, ex-king of
Sardinia. He had abdicated the sovereignty of that country, but
as he had not abdicated his unclaimed position in the English
succession, Victor Emmanuel only now became head of the elder
line of England.

The Princess Maria Theresa Gaetana was duly followed on
July 1, 1820, by a brother, afterwards Francis V. After him was
born the Archduke Ferdinand, who through his only daughter was
to carry on the Stuart heirship to to-day. The fourth and last of
the family, Maria Beatrice, was mother of the present Don Carlos,
who, had Ferdinand's only child never been born or never married,
would have been heir-in-line of the House of Stuart.[1]

It was in the year following the birth of Francis, 1821, that 1821.
there broke out in Piedmont the military revolution which led to
the abdication of the king.

Though Victor Emmanuel had restored as far as possible the
old order of things, he confirmed the purchases of confiscated property made under French rule; restoring to the former owners
only the few estates which had not been sold, and allotting an
annual sum of £16,000 as some compensation to those whose
property had been plundered. He became a zealous member of
the Holy Alliance, brought back the Jesuits, established a very
severe censorship of the press, and introduced such restrictions on
the process of education in the universities, colleges, and seminaries
as he judged advisable to check the prevailing tendency to infidelity
and immorality. Unhappily, though monarchy had been restored
in Italy, faith and morals were as completely out of date as absolutism, and could not be restored either by military force or civil
pressure. These measures, combined with severe treatment of Jews
and Waldenses and with the alliance with ever-hated Austria, were
beheld with extreme disfavour by his turbulent subjects, infected
as they were by the modernist ideas in which all Europe had so
lately been submerged. Their affections became alienated: secret
societies, Carbonari and others, were revived and banded them-

[1] Thus claiming three thrones, England (? see page 330), France (with good right;
Bolingbroke said Philip V.'s renunciation was not worth the paper it was written on),
and Spain (according to himself and his party).

1821. selves together, their opposition smouldering for a time underground and in dark corners. On March 9, 1821, the flames of rebellion burst forth among the nobility and soldiers, headed by Santa Rosa and others, who imperiously demanded a constitution based on the same principles as those which the governments of Madrid, Naples, and Lisbon had just adopted. Prominent among the insurrectionists was Prince Charles Albert of Savoy-Carignano, distant cousin of Victor Emmanuel and heir-presumptive of the Sardinian crown after the king's youngest brother, Charles Felix. They took possession of the citadel of Alessandria, then of Turin, and addressed their ultimatum to the king.

Rather than yield to demands that were opposed to his conscience, and seeing no possibility of peaceful and efficient government in a kingdom permanently disaffected and demoralised, Victor Emmanuel abdicated in favour of his brother Charles Felix, March 13, 1821. He retired to Moncalieri. The proud soul of his daughter, Mary Beatrice, exulted at hearing how her father had laid aside his crown rather than govern against the ruling of his conscience, preferring a stainless name to sovereign power. She declared that she had never until then loved and appreciated him enough, and for years after, never alluded to that act of self-sacrifice without enthusiasm. Would she, too, have acted correspondingly, confronted by the rages and riots and fierce parliamentary struggles of the nineteenth century in England? The Sardinian king and queen settled themselves in Modena, to the great joy of their daughter. With them were the Princesses Marianna and Christina. Marie Thérèse had been married to the heir of the Duke of Lucca in the preceding year, 1820.

1824. On January 12, 1824, the good King Victor Emmanuel died at Moncalieri. He had been for five years the head of the elder royal line of Great Britain. At his death, that heirship devolved upon his eldest daughter, the English succession being heritable by females though the Sardinian was regulated according to Salic law and passed to his brother Charles Felix.

Charles Felix put down the insurrection in Piedmont, and, supported by Austria, restored the former system of monarchy. He occupied himself with the business of administration, made new roads and other improvements; yet he too had a stormy time of it, and during a temporary absence, the irrepressible heir-presumptive, Charles Albert, sought to hasten his own accession to sovereignty by assuming the regency, proclaiming the Spanish constitution of 1820, and establishing a provisional junta. Charles Felix, aided by Russia and Austria, was restored and undid his cousin's work, but at his death in 1831, leaving no son, the elder line of Savoy became extinct and Charles Albert, father of Victor Emmanuel II., great-grandfather of Victor Emmanuel III., succeeded to the throne.

It has sometimes been supposed that the present King of 1829. Italy might claim succession to the House of Stuart as heir of the Sardinian kings. He has no place whatever in the succession, being descended, not from Victor Amadeus II. and his wife Anne of Savoy, but from Francis Thomas, Prince of Carignan, third son of Charles Emmanuel I. who died 1630 and whose eldest son was grandfather of Victor Amadeus II.

The duchies of Massa and Carrara became united to Modena in 1829 on the death of Duchess Maria Beatrice Ricciarda. Her son, Francis, was then the richest prince in Europe, having besides the immense fortune of the Dukes of Modena, received a large dowry with his wife. Lord Normanby [1] testifies to the liberal way in which he spent his money, chiefly in the fostering of art and education.

He was a prince possessed both of legislative and executive power, and like the Stuarts of old, spared no pains to acquaint himself personally with the conditions and needs of his people. He travelled incessantly over his small dominions, inspecting fortifications, schools, public works, and everything else that was under way. Undoubtedly the most absolute of sovereigns, he had at heart earnestly and solely the real good of his people. Absolute sovereigns have in too many instances abused their power, but we who have heard so much of the Neros of ancient and modern days, have heard little of those "despots" who have quietly worked on for their subjects' good, fathers of their people, happy in the obscurity of peace and content which do so little towards the making of history. As one quietly and impartially searches the chronicles of their countries, it is amazing to find behind the mist of interested misrepresentation that these earnest, conscientious, beneficent sovereigns were the rule and not the exception. "The finances of a country," says Lord Normanby, "are considered a measure of its prosperity. When revenue increases without imposing new rates or making old ones more heavy, it is considered a proof that a state is not badly governed. Till the end of 1845 the revenues of Modena were six million francs" (the population was 600,000), "and in the last years of Duke Francis IV. they increased to seven millions. The bad harvests of 1846 and 1847, and the revolutionary disturbances of 1848, were injurious to the finances. After 1850 there was a large increase in the revenue, and it was mainly due to the progressive improvement in the circumstances of the country. The increase from 1850 to the overthrow of the duke's throne was an increase from seven to eleven millions, of which 2,722,000 francs can be referred to no cause except the advance of the population in wealth and comfort under the ducal government."

Lord John Russell testified in the same way to the prosperity, content, and good government of the neighbouring duchy of Tuscany

[1] " Vindication of the Duke of Modena from the charges of Mr. Gladstone," by the Marquis of Normanby.

1830. where he had resided for some time. He found it convenient for party necessities some years later, to forget those satisfactory experiences and the testimony he had borne to them. What of the finances of the " free and united Italy " we know to-day ?

These dukes devoted themselves also to the education of their people, founding numerous colleges, universities, and public schools. Francis IV. naturally aroused the suspicious dislike of revolutionised Italy by placing education in the hands of the Jesuits, as the wisest directors of youth, as they are certainly the kindest and most careful, but the Young Italy party, thoroughly and chronically unsettled, could endure no restraints whether of religion or government, and looked upon the Jesuits as bigots and torturers. In their eagerness to destroy the Duke's influence, these enthusiasts accused him of the basest ambition and tyranny, even of increasing his already enormous wealth by appropriation of public moneys. Strangest of all it is to find him accused of treachery against Italy, by wishing to unite the whole peninsula under his rule as representing through his wife the House of Savoy : a dream that was triumphantly realised forty years later amid the plaudits of the revolutionary party under the younger line of Savoy in the person of Victor Emmanuel. Authentic contemporary documents prove how grossly his actions and intentions were misrepresented.

In 1830 revolution broke out again in France, and Charles X. was banished. Francis IV. being requested by the French ambassador to recognise the régime of the Citizen King, refused. Modena, he declared, was a sovereignty so small as to have had the honour of being despised by France for its insignificance, so must naturally be dispensed from any necessity of such formal recognition.

His enemies now accused him of employing the services of the Carbonari and other secret societies, admitting to his friendship their leaders, Ciro Menotti and Enrico Mislei, for the furtherance of his ambition to become king of United Italy : of thus acquainting himself with their secrets to betray them remorselessly and give them up to the executioner. All of this is flatly and convincingly contradicted by Galvani, who from 1832 to 1839 had charge of the duke's private and most secret papers. The peace which Italy enjoyed since the tumultuous period of 1821 had not deceived the duke into relaxing vigilant watch over his doubtful subjects. He watched still more carefully the political immigrants from other states, to whose machinations the success of the revolution of July had given alarming impetus. Discovery was made of a conspiracy against the state of Modena under Ciro Menotti, whom Francis had honoured with his friendship and confidence and whose views he had done his best to study in hope of being able to meet them without compromising the peace and ultimate good of the State. Thirty of the chief conspirators were arrested and imprisoned, but only a few of them executed. Of these, one was, of course, the leader, Ciro Menotti, reverenced thenceforth as a martyr. Unfortu- nately the conspiracy had extended farther than the duke knew, and his *coup d'état* was the signal for revolution to burst from its hiding holes and corners.

The duke hastened to the head of his loyal troops; then bethinking himself that his wife and children might be alarmed at hearing of warlike preparations on such an extensive scale, and that their safety was certainly imperilled, he said to his staff, "Gentlemen, I am going to reassure Beatrice and the children. I shall be with you again in a moment." He dismounted and hurried to the palace where he found his wife with her little ones, the elder of whom were at lessons. She was brave, serene, and confident. She knew why he had come and did not flinch, but embracing him, she hung round his neck a relic of the true cross, saying, "Go in the name of the Almighty and be safe." The little girls cried, but the little boys begged for swords that they might fight at his side. Their mother comforted them, saying that the enemy might soon make their way into those very rooms, and then it would be their duty to defend her and their sisters. She said adieu once more to her husband, and when he had gone she gathered round her all the women of her household, from the ladies-in-waiting down to the last scullery-maid, and said the rosary with them for the safety of husband and state.

The duke, armed, returned to the hall, followed by two faithful servants carrying pistols. "I see him still," says Galvani, "his frank and noble countenance unflushed with anger, stop on the threshold, look round with satisfaction upon the ten of us; take off his hat, raise his right hand to his forehead and signing himself with the sign of redemption, say loudly, "Signori, in nomine Patris et Filii et Spiritui Sancti!" He blessed himself again twice in silence, and then cried, "Adesso, avanti, andiamo!"

Space does does not allow of a full description of a revolution that proved of little importance : its ultimate suppression and the rigorous but necessary punishment which followed. Francis would fain have been more lenient than his safety and the states demanded, but his wife insisted that her voice should be heard. She judged that her husband's leniency would give to his enemies the impression of a spirit weakened by troubles. She availed herself of the press to publish her sentiments, a more than inspired article appearing in the *Voce della Verità*, probably from the pen of the duchess herself. She declaimed against such mistaken indulgence. As one who on every opportunity, by word and countenance proved her horror of sects and subversive principles, she was not afraid to proclaim her hatred of the enemies of religion, monarchy, and social order. She, fierce daughter of Savoy, might not bear arms in her husband's cause, but other means would not fail her by which to avenge his wrongs and so combat his enemies with all her power. She had transfused these principles into her sons with her milk and

1831. had given them for a motto, " The honour of God and their father."
A very mediæval queen for modern England!

A subsequent plot against the persons of the ducal family was
baffled by a curious accident. It was their custom on St. Benedict's
Day to attend the Benedictine church of St. Peter, but the duchess
forgot the circumstance and promised to take her children to open
a spring festival. When reminded, she was sorry, being a very
devout lady and delighting in religious celebrations, but she would
not disappoint the children. Thus she perhaps saved her own life
and theirs, saved at least their liberty, the conspirators having planned
to seize the duke and duchess on their way to the Benedictine
church.

Even those historians who are most severe on Francis IV. for
his absolutism, admit that he wanted neither activity nor intelligence,
that he encouraged agriculture, and relieved in a great measure the
burdens of the poorer classes. He treated with great generosity the
emigrants who fled to his protection—Legitimists from France,
Carlists from Spain, Miguelists from Portugal. He encouraged by
large grants of money the scientific society of the Forty, resident at
Modena, presented 15,000 volumes to the public library, and formed
a museum of 30,000 coins and medals.

1840. In 1840 the duchess fell seriously ill : the wife, says Galvani,
with whom Francis had lived in such perfect union of heart and
mind for twenty-eight years ; " the pious, learned, large-hearted
woman whose tenderness was ever at the service of the unfortunate,
but who was immovable in what she held to be the principles of
right and truth." Early in the year her strength began to fail, and
she was much troubled by a cough that had begun two years before. For some time there was no alarm, no one knowing how very
weak she had grown. By August she was much worse, though in
writing to her absent children, she carefully avoided saying anything
of her health that might make them anxious. On September 5
she was so ill that it was necessary that she should receive the
last sacraments. Like Richard Cœur-de-lion, she had refused to
the last to forgive her political enemies, but some sort of submission to the condition of absolution must have been made. She
waited calmly for death, her family all at hand, her husband
watching by her every night. She passed away September 15,
1840.

Her son Francis has been accepted historically as heir to her
place in the line of succession, but a curious question arises to the
validity of his claim. His mother had married her uncle. Such a
marriage being illegal in England, would probably illegitimate
her children. Legists, however, have decided in favour of the
marriage, and her grand-daughter is universally recognised as heiress-
in-line of the House of Stuart. Were the marriage of Mary Beatrice
certainly null and void in England, the succession at her death must
have passed to one of her twin sisters, Mary Theresa of Savoy, then

Duchess of Lucca, later of Parma, or Marianna, Empress of Austria. 1842.
The empress died childless, but the Duchess of Lucca and Parma is
represented by her great-grandson Henry, Duke of Parma, and his
nineteen brothers and sisters. His father, Robert, was the son of
Ferdinand Charles III. and Louise of France, sister of the Comte de
Chambord.

On March 30, 1842, Francis married the still living Princess
Adelgonda of Bavaria, sister of the present Prince Regent Luitpold.
They had no children except a baby girl, born amidst the storms of
1848, who lived only a few months. No festivities hailed her birth :
no mourning marked her death. Italy was possessed again of the
frenzy of revolution and cared nothing for royal babes.

Francis IV., Duke of Modena, died January 21, 1846. His last 1846.
years were overshadowed by deep melancholy. It has been said
that like the guilty Richard III. he was continually haunted by the
ghosts of those whom he had been compelled to execute, his tender
conscience tormenting him with scruples, his naturally gentle soul
sick with unavailing remorse. Had it not been for the fierce counsels
of his stronger-minded wife, the blood of Ciro Menotti and his
accomplices would never have been shed. It was remarked that
after his wife's death he became milder, and his last years were
signalised only by beneficence. An ominous wasting, a mournful
lassitude warned him of approaching death. He fought bravely
against his physical weakness. He relaxed none of his many
cares, giving audiences and working with his ministers, until utterly
worn out, almost at his last gasp, he went to bed never to rise
again. One of his last acts was to accompany the Sacred Host,
torch in hand, to the bedside of an old servant of his daughter's.
All his biographers agree that he met death with the calm of a philosopher and the reverent humility of a Christian : confessing his
mistakes, excusing them on the ground of ever honest intention.
He was sincerely mourned by his people.

Francis V., Duke of Modena, King of England *de jure* in right
of his mother and her descent from Henrietta, Duchess of Orleans,
was a handsome youth, tall and graceful, with a fine colour, but
inheriting his father's short-sightedness which spoilt the openness of
his countenance in the same way. He had commanded a troop of
horse under his father, but had never been allowed to interfere in
state affairs. The anti-ducal Bosellini describes him as not given
to luxury, diffident of his own inexperience, ambitious of popularity,
but not ambitious to meddle in secrets of state. He was of a liberal
mind, hated the old detested institutions of the middle ages ; meditated forming a council of state ; was an Italian of the Italians and
averse from German influence. If he had had a friend to back him
in carrying out those early noble impulses of his, all might have
been different. But it seems to be the fate of princes who take to
liberalism in spite of family tradition, to become the family scape-
goats. He had near him only those who persuaded him that any

1846. reform would be a slight on his father's memory, and filial piety was strong in the Houses of Este and Savoy.

Shortly after his accession he gave his sisters in marriage, the elder to Henri, Comte de Chambord, by birth King of France; the younger to Don Juan de Bourbon, father of Don Carlos, Duke of Madrid, so long a claimant to the crown of Spain. The latter marriage was most unhappy. The Infante deserted his wife and her two sons and lived very privately in England until his death at Brighton in 1887.

In 1846 Pius IX. mounted the papal throne, and the watchword "Reform and Progress" rang from the Vatican itself. As we are supposed to be "all socialists now," so we were all reformers then! The national principle that was waking in Europe, arose high in Italy and in the soul of Francis V. On an English throne he would have led the van of progress, but his imperial relations bound him to the wheels of Austria, and he yielded, still diffident of his own inexperience, to their influence. The consequence was that Metternich contrived to make of Modena an Austrian province, and on December 20, 1847, the duchy was occupied by Austrian troops.

1848. When in 1848 the new constitutions were proclaimed throughout Italy, Francis, advised against his own wish and conviction by his uncle the Archduke Ferdinand, refused to treat with liberalism. A mild revolt consequently followed and the duke was compelled to depart from his dominions, but he returned triumphantly amidst public jubilation on August 10, 1848, to find everything exactly as he had left it, even to a watch which he had forgotten in his bedroom. The clement prince not only amnestied but retained in office the very men who had taken up arms against him, with the exception of twenty-five ringleaders whose only punishment was a prohibition against residing within the Modena frontiers (Normanby). Rizziati, who later attempted his sovereign's life, was sentenced to twenty years in the galleys. Montanari's sentence for life was by the duke commuted to ten, and after one or two years passed in the galleys, was further commuted to exile.

All rebellions against lawful authority must needs be more or less bolstered up with lies, but never was an honest, just, and conscientious man more foully and inexcusably slandered than Francis V. Not only Italian sympathisers, but a wise and honest English statesman like Lord Normanby, testify to the baselessness of the fabrications that were built up to justify his dethronement by the King of Sardinia. Lord Normanby testifies also to the duke's virginal and lofty mind. "His subjects are the best affected population in that part of Italy, conscious as they are that they live under a government which, however arbitrary in its nature, is equitably administered to all."[1]

"There is something very prepossessing in the simple, earnest

---

[1] "Vindication of the Duke of Modena against the charges of Mr. Gladstone."

manner of the duke," Lord Normanby writes to Lord Clarendon, 1849. August 23, 1856. "I hardly ever met in any rank of life with any one who more surely conveyed the impression of a thoroughly honest man who meant to do his duty, and although he has been found stern upon occasion, his love of justice has become proverbial amongst his subjects."

In the interval between the restoration of August 1848 and the battle of Novara April 1849, when his troops repossessed him of Massa and Carrara, he devoted himself to liberal reform. He disarmed the national guard, assigned to himself a modest civil list of 600,000 francs, and established four ministries of finance, home affairs (*buon governo*), justice, and religion. He also recalled the Jesuits, banished by the late turmoils. Francis V. governed as the father of a family and was accessible to all his people, as his predecessors had been; accustomed to give audience twice a week for three or four hours, at which the poorest of his subjects could present themselves, to whose grievances or demands he was ever ready to listen with that simple natural courtesy which characterised princes of his House. Travellers were amazed at the number of educational and charitable institutions with which Modena was filled. Francis V. had so much at heart the education of his people that he used to send abroad at his own expense youths of promise who had passed through the Modenese schools, to afford them every opportunity of wider study (Normanby.)

Lord Normanby reminds his readers of the peculiar interest due to the position of Francis V. in the royal succession of England, adding, "The only claim made by the Duke of Modena, the eldest of the lawful blood of our own exiled dynasty, is that we should not join his calumniators nor lightly credit every wild story invented by his enemies."

". . . Under the father of the present duke, in a reign of thirty-two years, there were but eight executions for political offences and capital crimes. In the first eleven years of the reign of the present duke (Francis V.) there was not one execution. In the two years which preceded the revolution, five executions for atrocious murders took place in Carrara, and they are the only cases in which the punishment of death has been inflicted by the duke."

The seven terrible charges brought against him by Mr. Gladstone in the English House of Commons in 1861 *confessedly on secondhand authority*, have all been annihilated by Lord Normanby. A more barefaced chain of guesses, falsehoods, and reckless conclusions was surely never produced even to serve a party! The second charge is a specimen of the utter groundlessness of all. A youth, seventeen years old, was convicted of a horrible murder under circumstances of peculiar atrocity. The law of Modena restricted capital punishment to criminals over twenty-one years of age except for sacrilege and high treason. Francis carefully made himself acquainted with the circumstances of the case, and then issued an edict ordaining that

1859. *in future* premeditated homicide should be excepted from a law so dangerously lenient. Mr. Gladstone, quoting not from official reports but from hostile hearsay, asserted that the duke had had the boy executed, altering the law for the purpose. Francis knew absolutely nothing of the charge until he read it in the English papers, and exclaimed that if he had done such a thing, he would have been morally guilty of murder.

Lord Normanby had some right of blood to act as champion of Francis V. He was not only descended from Sir Constantine Phipps, Queen Anne's Jacobite Chancellor of Ireland, advocate of Sacheverell, later of the Jacobite prisoners, but from James II. through the Duchess of Buckingham's daughter by her first marriage with Lord Annesley.

Destiny after all was too much for Francis V; the evil fortune that was his only Stuart inheritance and the destructive spirit of the age. The Italian princes were doomed: they must be sacrificed to the ideal of United Italy. Whether they were guilty or not of the sins attributed to them by the revolutionists is far too grave a question to be considered and answered in a few lines. They were painted so black by their adversaries that it is difficult to see what lights, even what form, was hidden by that thick coating. As the superabundant immoralities of Charles II. have coloured the reputation of all the Stuarts, so the iniquities of Neapolitan prisons have been used to darken the policies of all the sovereigns of the peninsula. Victor Emmanuel II. and Louis Napoleon marched upon Modena, and Francis had to fly. Italy believed that with insurrection and invasion an era of unity, liberty, prosperity, and above all of independence had begun. Unity Italy has secured and prosperity has, in the last few years, set in. But we have seen the new kingdom so starved by taxation that thousands of the free people have been reduced to beggary and driven to exile, weighted by a huge navy that serves no national need; serves only to ensure the safe aggrandisement of Prussia. And for the name of Independence, the once independent states have but exchanged independence under native rulers for dependence on the alien House of Savoy. Modena, like her neighbours, has exchanged the open-handed, kingly absolutism of the Este princes for ever-meddling municipal tyranny. Nor is the revolutionary spirit satisfied. Socialism is loud and strong, anarchism flings Italian bombs and brandishes Italian daggers before the mildest, most liberal of princes. Conspiracy has always been as glowing and enduring a force in Italy as the fires of her volcanoes.

Francis retired into Gratz in Styria where he died November 20, 1875. His widow, the devoted sister of the aged Prince Regent of Bavaria, is resident in Munich.

His younger brother, the Archduke Ferdinand, had predeceased him, leaving by his marriage with the Archduchess Elizabeth of Austria, one child, Mary Theresa Henrietta Dorothea, born July 2, 1849; married February 20, 1869 to Prince Louis of Bavaria, eldest son of the Prince Regent and heir-presumptive to the Bavarian throne. This is the lady known to Jacobitism as Mary IV., of Great 1908. Britain, France,[1] and Ireland, queen : heiress-in-line of the Royal Houses of Plantagenet and Stuart. Her mother, *en secondes noces*, married the Archduke Charles Ferdinand of Austria, by whom she became mother of Maria Christina, Queen Mother of Spain, and of the Archdukes Frederick, Eugéne, and Charles Stephen.

Of the twelve children of Princess Louis of Bavaria, the eldest, Prince Rupert, was born May 18, 1869. On July 10, 1900, he married his cousin, Marie Gabrielle, daughter of the oculist prince, Carl Theodor, Duke in Bavaria, by a daughter of the Portuguese pretender Dom Miguel. Their elder son, Luitpold Maximilian Ferdinand Charles, was born May 8, 1901 ; their younger son, Albert, on May 3, 1905. In these the elder line of the House of Stuart is continued to the present day.

[1] The French title having been abandoned only by George III., is retained by Jacobites among the *de jure* titles.

AUTHORITIES CONSULTED

Stuart Papers (Windsor Castle).
   „   ap. Browne's History of the Highland Clans, 1845.
   „   ap. Mahon's History of England.
   „   ap. Glover (J. H.), 1847.
Memorials of John Murray of Broughton: Scottish Historical Society : 1898.
Genuine Memoirs of John Murray of Broughton : 1747.
Carte MSS., Bodleian Library.
Archivi Segreti, Vatican.
Add. MSS., British Museum.
Stowe MSS., British Museum.
State Papers : Italian States. Record Office.
   „   Tuscany.   „
   „   George II. (Domestic) „
Les Derniers Stuarts : Campana de' Cavelli.
The Fallen Stuarts : F. W. Head.
Life of Prince Charles Stuart : A. C. Ewald.
Prince Charles Edward : Andrew Lang : second edition, 1903.
Pickle the Spy : Andrew Lang.
The Companions of Pickle : Andrew Lang.
Historical MSS. Commission Reports.
Lockhart Papers.
Æneas and His Two Sons. Pamphlet.
Walpole's George II. : 1846.
Letters of Sir Horace Mann.
Letters of Horace Walpole.
D'Argenson : Mémoires et Journal : 1857 and 1859.
De Luynes : Mémoires.
Saint Simon : Hommes Illustres.
Louis XV. et les Jacobites : J. L. A. Colin : 1901.
The Young Pretender : C. S. Terry, 1903.
Mann and Manners at the Court of Florence : Doran, 1876.
The Stuarts in Italy : *Quarterly Review*, December 1846.
The *Gentleman's Magazine*, 1788, 1807, &c.
Annual Register, 1788, 1807, &c.
Parliamentary Debates, 1744.
Coxe's Life of Walpole (Sir Robert).
Coxe's Life of Horatio, Lord Walpole, 1802.
L'Italie il y a cent ans : De Brosses, 1858.
Notes and Queries, 1st Series.
Northern Notes and Queries.
Dr. Charlton's Relics.

A Court in Exile : Marchesa Vitelleschi.
Maria Clementina in Italia ; MSS. University Library, Bologna.
Jacobite Lairds of Gask : Kingdon Oliphant.
Mémoires de la Comtesse de Boigne.
Storia dell' Immagine e Chiesa di Santa Maria in Portici di Campitelli, descritta da Carlo Antonio Erra : dedicato al Cardinale Duca di York : 1750.
Dennistoun's Life of Sir Robert Strange : 1855.
Reminiscences by L. M. Mure (privately printed).
The Four Last Popes, by Cardinal Wiseman.
Tales of the Century, by John Sobieski Stuart.
Diario del Cardinale Duca di York : Add. MSS. British Museum.
Diario del Cardinale Duca di York, by A. Ademollo ; Nuova Antologia, 1880.
Diario e Notizie di Bologna: Galeati : Vols. viii.–xiii.
Il Palazzo Vizani : A. Longhi.
MSS. Bologna Archives.
Insignie :   „   „
Memoirs of Alfieri.
The Countess of Albany, by Vernon Lee.
     „   „   by Von Reumont.
Hayward's Biographical and Critical Essays : The Countess of Albany.
Mémoires d'un voyageur : Louis Dutens.
A Visit to Abbotsford : Washington Irving.
Cornelia Knight : Autobiography.
On the Banks of the Seine : A. M. Falle.
Funeral Oration on the Cardinal of York ; Dom Marco Mastrofino.
Personal Recollections of Lord Cloncurry.
La Spedizione di Carlo Odoardo Stuarda : Cordara.
Storia di Casa Savoia : Dr. Felice Angeli.
Lives of Francis IV. and Francis V., Dukes of Modena, by Galvani and Bosellini.
Vindication of the Duke of Modena, by the Marquis of Normanby.
Coke of Norfolk, by A. M. S. Stirling.
Early Married Life of Maria Josepha Holroyd ; edited by J. H. Adeane, 1899.
Life of Lord Cloncurry : W. J. Fitzpatrick, 1855.
Mémoires du Cardinal H. Consalvi : second edition, 1866.
Züge aus dem Leben des Cardinals H. Consalvi : J. L. S. Bartholdy, 1824.
Diplomates et hommes d'état : le Cardinal Consalvi : Ernest Daudet.
Italy, by Sydney, Lady Morgan, 1821.
Historical Memoirs of His Own Time : Sir Nathaniel Wraxall, 1904.
Dictionary of National Biography
Almanach de Gotha.
Blason de España.

INDEX

A

Abdy, Sir Robert, 55
Acquaviva, Cardinal, 57, 58, 78
Adelaide of France, Madame, 72
Adelgonda of Bavaria, wife of Francis V. of Modena, 331, 334
Adrian IV., Pope, 22
" Æneas and his two sons," quoted, 33
Aiguillon, Duc d', 200
Ailesbury, Earl of, 203
Ailesbury, Countess of, presents the Countess of Albany at St. James's, 269
Aix-la-Chapelle, Peace of, 121, 125
Alamandini, Villa, 149
Albani, Cardinal Alexander, 21, 102, 130, 137, 164, 185
Albani, Cardinal John Francis, 163, 164, 165, 172, 184, 186
  Protector of Scotland, 181
Albano, 22, 23, 26, 29, 30, 33, 44, 58, 70, 136, 162, 164, 168, 174, 176, 192
Albany, Count of, 195, 229, 235, 256, 259 (see Charles Edward)
Albany, Countess of (see Louise)
Albany, Charlotte Stuart, Duchess of, 149, 172, 182, 189, 203, 204, 208, 240, 241, 242, 243, 244, 245, 246, 247, 248, 249, 250, 251, 252, 253, 253, 254, 256, 257, 258, 268, 269, 272, 274, 284, 287
  her birth, 158
  legitimatized and created Duchess, 234
  arrives in Florence, 235
  description by Mann, 239
  meeting with the Cardinal of York, 255
  her appearance in Rome, 259, 260
  her household, 267
  illness and death, 270
  her grave, 271
" Albany, Maria Matilda, Dowager Duchess of," 273
Albany, dukedom of, 236, 239
Albemarle, Earl of, British ambassador in Paris, 133, 152, 155, 157, 160, 166
Alberoni, Cardinal, 7, 19, 22, 32, 69, 147

Alberstroff, Countess (see Walkinshaw, Clementina)
Alfieri, Vittorio, poet, 201, 217, 218, 219, 220, 221, 224, 226, 227, 231, 233, 235, 242, 243, 244, 245, 246, 249, 250, 252, 260, 269, 292, 304, 305
  arrives in Florence, 216
  life with the Countess of Albany in Rome, 221
  turned out of Rome, 226
  visited by Lord Cloncurry, 284
  death and burial, 291
  at the court of Charles Emmanuel IV., 315
Alford, Earl of (see Græme, Sir John)
Amand, Abbey of St., 163, 167, 195
Amelot d', French War Minister, 53, 55, 61, 63, 65, 71
American colonies, Jacobites transported to, 103
American rebellion, 210
American overtures to Prince Charles, 211, 212, 214
Amiens, Peace of, 289
Anchin, Abbey of, 119, 144, 145, 195, 280
Anderson, a spy, 161
Angelelli, Chamberlain to the Cardinal of York, 148
Angelelli, Marquis, 148, 180
Anne, Queen of England, 199, 274, 301
Anne, Duchess of Savoy, Queen of Sardinia, 310, 311, 312, 327
Anne Henriette of France, Madame, 72, 86
Anson, Lord, 160
Antwerp, siege of, 97
Archinto, Cardinal, Vice-Chancellor and Secretary of State, 168
Argenson, Marquis d', French War Minister, 50, 68, 78, 80, 82, 87, 89, 90, 91, 92, 97, 100, 101, 104, 114, 115, 122, 123, 126, 134, 149, 154
  succeeds d'Amelot, 71
Argyll, John, second Duke of, 39, 40, 47, 48
Argyll, third Duke of (see Islay)
Arkaig, hidden treasure at Loch, 91
Arlingham Court, 152, 155, 157
Atholl, Duke of, 76, 77

Atholl, Duke of (*see* Tullibardine)

Atterbury, Francis, Bishop of Rochester, 11, 13, 15, 16, 17, 26, 27, 28, 78

Attry-Salviati, Duchess, 248, 254

Aubeterre, Marquis d', French ambassador at Rome, 183, 185, 186, 187

Avignon, James III. at, 16–19

Avignon, Charles at, 129, 130

Avignon, Henry at, 79

Azi, Marquis d', 199

B

Baden, Prince of, 134

Balhaldy (*see* Macgregor)

Balmerino, Arthur, Lord, 103, 139

Banville, Count de, visits Charles at Florence, 254

Barbieri, Abbé, 254, 258

Barbutane, Marquis de, 185

Barry, 64

Barrymore, Lord, 48, 55, 64, 78

Bath, Lord, 154

Bathurst, Lord, 63

Batoni, Pompeo, painter, 201, 206, 215, 302

Beaufort, third Duke of, 55

Beaufort, fourth Duke of, 78

Beauharnais, Eugène, viceroy of Italy, 316

Beaumont, Jacobite plotter, 36

Belloni, Casa, 149

Benedict XIII., Pope, 5, 12, 20

godfather of Henry, Duke of York, 4

Benedict XIV., Pope, 44, 48, 54, 70, 77, 90, 112, 118, 127, 128, 129, 130, 131, 132, 133, 134, 144, 145, 146, 149, 150, 151, 163, 164, 168, 169, 170

Berthier, General, marches into Rome, 281

Berwick, James Fitzjames, first Duke of, 7, 17, 41, 49, 328

Berwick, James Francis, second Duke of (Duke of Liria), 7, 9, 10, 13, 19, 20, 21, 29, 32, 33, 69

Berwick, James Francis Edward, third Duke of, 33

Berwick, Charles Ferdinand Stuart fourth Duke of (Marquis of Jamaica), 202, 222

Berwick, James Philip Charles, fifth Duke of, 270

Berwick, Charles Michael Stuart, sixth Duke of, 306

Berwick, J., Jacobite martyr, 139

Berry, Miss, correspondent of Horace Walpole, 269

Béthisy de Mézières, Bishop of Uzes, 280

Bianchini, Monsignor Francis, 136

Blacowe, Rev. ——, 153

Blyde, A., Jacobite martyr, 139

Boigne, Comtesse de, 277, 278, 323, 324

Bolingbroke, Henry St. John, Viscount, 2, 50, 65, 116

Bologna, 19, 20, 22, 132, 148, 149, 180, 182, 184, 188

Bolognetti, Madame de, 73

Bonaparte (*see* Napoleon)

Bonaparte, Pauline, 317

Borgia, Cardinal, 286

Boscawen, Admiral, 166

Bosellini, historian, quoted, 317

Boston (America), 210, 214

Botha, Marshal, Austrian Minister at Florence, 130

Bouillon, Duchess de, 36, 38

Bouillon, Duc de, 10

Bourbon, Duc de, 80, 90, 97

Bourke, Miss, 23

Bourke, Sir Toby, 23

Boyer d'Eguilles (*see* d'Eguilles)

Bradshaw, J. A., Jacobite martyr, 139

Brady, ——, Jacobite martyr, 139

Brampton (Cumberland), 83

Brand, ——, Jacobite martyr, 139

Braye, Lord, papers of, 199

Breteuil, Abbé de, Maltese envoy to Rome, 185

Brett, Colonel, 47

Bridgewater, Duke of, 154

Brionne, Madame de, 280

Broglie, Duc de, 200

Brosses, de, quoted, 41, 42, 43, 277

Broughton (*see* Murray, John)

Brunet, confidential adviser to the Cardinal of York in Paris, 182

Buchanan, Francis, of Arnprior, 76, 103, 139

Buckingham, Catherine, Duchess of, 13, 15, 23, 47, 52, 334

Bulkeley, Lady Sophia, 17

Buranello (*see* Galuppi, Baldassare)

Burdett, Sir Francis, 277

Burdett-Coutts, Baroness, 277

Burney, Dr. Charles, 142 *note*

Burney, Fanny, 38

Burns, Robert, 272, 284

Butler, Master of the Horse to Louis XV., 157

Byng, Admiral, 171

C

Calixtus, Pope St., 170

Cambrai, Archbishop of, 123, 160

Cameron, Allan, 8, 9, 15

Cameron, Dr. Archibald, 125, 153

Cameron, clan, 9, 77

Cameron (*see* Lochiel)

Cameron of Fassifern, 153

Cameron of Glen Nevis, 153
Cameron, H., Jacobite martyr, 139
Cameronians, 9
Campbell of Glenure (murder), 155
Campbell, clan, 9, 48
Campeggio, Cardinal, 171
Campo Formio, Peace of, 281
Cancellaria, Palace of the, 180, 218, &c., 268
Canillac, Monsignor, 57, 135
Canova, sculptor, 291, 303
Cantini, treasurer to the Cardinal of York, 218, 231
Cappock, Rev. T., "the Bishop," 103, 139
Carbonari, revived, 325, 328
Carignan, Princes of, 326, 327
Carignian (Prince ?), 199
Carlisle, surrender of, 83 ; atrocities at, 103
Caroline, Princess of Wales, 324
Caroline, Queen of Naples, 247, 248, 249, 321
Carlos, Don, Duke of Madrid, 325, 332
Carte, Thomas, 36, 38, 53, 64, 73, 152
Carteret, Lord, 64
Carthusians, Henry, Protector of, 144
Caryll, Lord, 66, 192, 197, 199, 201, 223, 230, 250, 260
Castille, Baron de, 234, 240
Catherine I., Czarina, 10, 12, 13
Catherine II., Czarina, 142
Cecil, Colonel William, 36, 52, 53, 55, 64, 65
Cesarini, Monsignor Angelo (Bishop of Milevi), 195, 221, 254, 256, 291, 295, 296, 301, 302, 304
Chadwick, T., Jacobite martyr, 139
Charles VI., Emperor, 6, 8, 10, 30, 45
Charles VII., Emperor, 47, 70, 71
Charles I., King of England, 293, 301, 310, 311
Charles II., 293
Charles III. (see Charles Edward)
Charles II., King of Spain, 311
Charles III., King of Naples, King of Spain, 247
Charles X., of France, 313
Charles Albert, King of Sardinia, 326
Charles Edward, Prince, 2, 3, 4, 5, 7, 12, 14, 19, 23, 24, 25, 26, 30, 31, 32, 33, 36, 43, 44, 45, 46, 51, 52, 55, 56, 60, 61, 63, 64, 65, 66, 69, 70, 71, 73, 74, 75, 78, 79, 80, 81, 87, 88, 89, 90, 91, 92, 93, 101, 102, 103, 104, 112, 113, 115, 116, 120, 122, 123, 124, 126, 128, 134, 135, 136, 139, 141, 142, 144, 145, 147, 150, 153, 154, 155, 156, 157, 158, 159, 160, 161, 164, 167, 168, 169, 171, 174, 176, 179, 182, 184, 187, 190, 191, 192, 194, 196, 203, 204,

Charles Edward, Prince, continued—
205, 206, 209, 210, 211, 213, 216, 218, 220, 221, 222, 223, 224, 227, 228, 231, 232, 233, 237, 238, 239, 240, 241, 242, 243, 244, 245, 246, 251, 254, 256, 257, 265, 266, 269, 270, 271, 272, 273, 276, 284, 285, 286, 287, 296, 298, 301, 303, 304, 307, 308, 312, 313
described by the Duke of Liria, 13
at the siege of Gaeta, 29
tour in Italy, 34, 35
described by Murray of Broughton, 37
to sail for England, 38, 40
described by de Brosses, 41, 42
plan to corrupt, 49, 50
as a sportsman, 52
invited to Paris, 54
leaves Rome, 57
journey to Paris, 58, 59
leaves Paris for Gravelines, 62
letter to Sempil, 67
returns to Paris, 68
wishes to marry Princess Anne Henriette of France, 72
sails for Scotland, 76
opens campaign, 77
marches south, 80–83
retreats, 83–85
meets Miss Walkinshaw, 86
wins the battle of Falkirk, 94
retreats northwards, 95
loses the battle of Culloden, 96
wanderings, 97
lands in France, 98, 99
attends French court, 100
his associates in Paris, 105, 106
quarrels with the Duke of York, 107
goes to Spain, 108
wild life in Paris, 109, 110, 111
rage at the Cardinalate, 114, 117, 118
refuses to leave France, 121, 123, 124, 125, 126
arrested at the Opera House, 127
at Avignon, 129
disappears, 130, 131
at Venice, 132, 133
plans of marriage, 132
turns Protestant, 137
proclaimed by Newcastle colliers, 138
joined by Miss Walkinshaw, 148
at Mereworth, 152
again in England, 166
left by Miss Walkinshaw, 172
at Coronation of George III. (?), 177, 178
invited to Rome by the Pope, 183
refused recognition as king by the Pope, 185, 186
arrives at Albano, 188
description of, 189

Charles Edward, Prince, *continued*—
audience of Pope, 193
leaves Rome, 195
new project of invasion and marriage, 197, 198
in Paris, 199, 200
meets the Duke of Gloucester at Genoa, 200, 201
to marry Louise of Stolberg-Gueldern, 202
marriage at Macerata, *ib*.
leaves Rome, 207
his supposed son, *ib*., 208
settles at Florence, 208
said to be in London, 211, 212
invited to America, 214
memorial from America, 215
left by his wife, 217
dangerous illness, 226
Louise's testimony to his character, 228
receives Gustavus III. of Sweden, 229
stroke of apoplexy, 230
legitimatises his daughter, 234
prepares to receive her at Florence, 235, 236
attends royal fêtes at Pisa, 247, 248, 249
applies for the jointure of Mary of Modena, 250
consents to leave Florence for Rome, 255
goes to Rome, 258
described by Sir J. T. Stanley, 259
death and funeral, 260, 261–263
memorial monument at Frascati, 264
will, 267, 268
removed to St. Peter's, 297
Charles Emmanuel III., King of Sardinia, 30, 57, 177, 198, 312
Charles Emmanuel IV., King of Sardinia, 293, 295, 301, 310, 313, 314, 315
Charlotte (*see* Albany, Duchess of)
Charlotte, Queen of George III., 269, 272, 293
Charlton, Dr. Edward, quoted, 138, 139
Charlton of Bowrie, 138
Charteris, Mr., brother of Lord Elcho, 153
Chatham, Earl of, 210
Chester, Prince Charles at, 83
Chesterfield, Lord, 39, 71, 79, 154
Choiseul, Duc de, 200
Cholmondely, Lord, 64
Christina of Savoy, Queen of Naples, 316, 320
Cisalpine Republic, 281, 316
Clancarty, Lord, 78
Clare, Lord, 89, 91

Clarendon, Earl of, 27
Clavering, Roland, Jacobite martyr, 139
Clement VI., Pope, 274
Clement XI., Pope, 2, 163
Clement XII., Pope, 39
Clement XIII., Pope, 146, 170, 173, 175, 183, 184, 185, 186, 193, 194
Clement XIV., Pope, 194, 197, 200, 201, 202, 203
suppresses the Jesuits, 206
Clementina, Queen of James III., 1, 3, 4, 5, 7, 12, 13, 14, 15, 18, 19, 20, 21, 22, 23, 24, 26, 29, 90, 118, 182, 222
marriage, 2, 149
death, 31
miracles, 26, 32, 129
monument, 48
Clermont, Count de, 97
Clifford, Lady, 74
Cloncurry, Valentine Lawless, Lord, 283
visits Louise and Alfieri at Florence, 284
visits the Cardinal of York, 290, 291
Cluny (Macpherson), 80
Cobham, Lord, 55
Coke, of Norfolk, 206, 207, 306
Colin, Charles, 160
Colman, British envoy at Florence, 23
Cologne, Elector of, 168
Colonna, Cardinal, 162
Concordat, 289, 294
Conflans, French Admiral, 177
Consalvi, Hercules, Monsignor: Cardinal Secretary of State to Pius VII., 163, 270, 278, 279, 286, 289, 293, 294, 304
Conti, Cardinal, 221, 222
Conti, Princesse de, 90
Conway, General, Secretary of State, 186, 206
Cope, Sir John, 77, 81, 82, 84
Cordara, S.J., quoted, 128, 302
Corsini, Cardinal, 135, 164
Corsini, Prince, 208, 221, 223
Cosmo III., Grand Duke of Tuscany, 6
Cotton, Sir John Hinde, 55, 64, 71, 78
Coutts, Mr., banker, visits the Cardinal of York, 377
Cowper, Rev. ——, 38
Craon, Prince and Princess de, 41
Crescenzi, Cardinal, 151
Crisp, Samuel, 38
Croix, La, spy, 135
Cruise, Father, 73
Cromarty, George, first Earl of, Clerk Registrar, 274
Cromarty, George, third Earl of, 103

Culloden, battle of, 96, 104, 130
Cumberland, Duke of, 82, 85, 94, 96, 102, 103, 104

D

Dalton, Simon, Jacobite correspondent, 212
Darcy, Mrs., 23
Dartmouth, Lord, Colonial Secretary, 209, 210, 211, 213
Dauphin (*see* Louis)
Dauphin (*see* Louis XVI.)
Dauphiness, 90
Dauphiness (second), 108
Davia, Cardinal, Protector of England, 20
Dawkins, James, 154, 155
Dawson, James, 85, 103, 139
Deacon, T., Jacobite martyr, 139
Deliard, M., Jacobite martyr, 139
Dennistoun, James, quoted, 165, 183, 267, 268
Derby, retreat from, 83, 84
Derwentwater, Charles, Earl of, 30, 55, 103, 139
Derwentwater, Countess of, 23, 103
Dicconson, treasurer to Mary of Modena, 277
Dodson, Rev. ——, 166
Dominicans, 28, 149, 191, 265
Doria, Cardinal, 148
Dormer, Mr., Jacobite agent, 156
Dorrett, Alexander, Jacobite agent, 211, 212, 213
Doutelle, ship, 76
Drummond (*see* Macgregor of Balhaldy)
Drummond, Lord John, 70, 82, 85, 95
Dunbar, Earl of (James Murray), 4, 5, 12, 13, 35, 41, 44, 58, 129, 147, 191, 198
Secretary of State, 20 ; resigns, 122
Dundas, ——, M.P., assists in procuring pension for the Cardinal of York, 287
Durham, Bishop of, 138
Durham, Dean of, 138 *note*, 154
Dutens, Rev. Louis, Rector of Elsdon, Northumberland, 214
Dymoke, Champion of England, 178

E

Eaton, Jacobite martyr, 139
Edgar, James, secretary to James III., 52, 123, 132, 133, 160, 165 ; his death, 179
Edward, Duke of York, 183, 279
Eguilles, Boyer d', 50, 78
Elcho, Lord, 56, 81, 125, 190

Elibank plot, 153
Elizabeth, Queen of Bohemia, 311
Elizabeth, daughter of Charles I., 311
Elizabeth (Farnese), Queen of Spain, 4, 6, 30
Elizabeth, Czarina, 132
Elizabeth, ship, 76, 193
Emmet, Robert, Irish rebel, 284, 290, 291
Errol, Earl of, at George III.'s coronation, 176
Eyre, equerry to Charles III., 188

F

Fabre, F. S., painter and sculptor, 201, 292, 301, 306
Fabroni, Abbé, Rector of the University of Pisa, 214, 215
Falconieri, Cardinal, 30
Falkirk, battle of, 94
Fane, British envoy at Florence, 35
Ferdinand IV., of Naples, 247
Ferdinand II., of the Two Sicilies (Bomba), 316
Ferdinand, Archduke of Austria, 316, 318
Ferdinand, Archduke of Austria, 332
Ferdinand, Archduke (Modena), 325, 334
Fitzgerald, Lord Edward, 282, 283
Fitzjames family, 203, 204
Fitzjames, Duc de, 80, 89, 198, 199
Fitzjames, Marquis de, 199, 200, 202
Fitzmorris, secretary to James III., 131, 147, 154
Fleetwood, in attendance on Prince Charles, 157
Fletcher, G., Jacobite martyr, 139
Fleury, Cardinal, French prime minister, 10, 39, 44, 52, 55
Florence, the Cardinal of York at, 180
Florence, residence of Charles Edward at, 208–257
Fontainebleau, Treaty of (1745), 82
Fontainebleau, Peace of (1763), 177
Fontainebleau, Pius VII., prisoner at, 318
Fontenoy, battle of, 82
Forester, Sir Mark, leaves legacy to James III., 30
Fortunata Maria, Princess of Modena, 132, 133
Foscolo, Ugo, writer, friend of the Countess of Albany, 292
Francis of Lorraine, Emperor, 41, 71, 131, 248
Francis IV., Duke of Modena, 316, 317, 318, 320, 321, 322, 324, 325, 329, 330
marries Mary Beatrice of Savoy, heiress of the House of Stuart, 319

Francis IV., *continued*—
his good government, 327
betrayed by Ciro Menotti and revolutionists, 328
death, 331
Francis V., Duke of Modena, 325
succeeds to heirship of House of
Stuart, 330
appearance and character, 331
revolt against, 332
Lord Normanby's testimony to, *ib.*,
333, 334
charges of Mr. Gladstone against
him, 333, 334
banishment and death, 334
Franciscans, 191, 260
Frascati, 174, 175, 176, 179, 193, 218,
219, 221, 225, 261, 263, 274, 275,
277, 281, 283, 289, 291, 296, 297,
298, 310
seminary at, 175, 279
Frazer, D., Jacobite martyr, 139
Frederick the Great, King of Prussia,
45, 61, 121, 154, 312

G

Gaetani, Duke, 57, 59
Galeati, quoted, 271
Galuppi, Baldassare, 142, 143, 147, 275
Galvani, historian of Francis IV. of
Modena, 317, 318
Ganganelli (*see* Clement XIV., Pope)
Garibaldi, 317
Garth, Mr., arrested with Carte, 65
Genoa, Prince Charles at, 200
Genoa, Lercari exiled to, 147, 151
George I., 14, 15, 18, 21
George II., 15, 16, 40, 42, 46, 48, 57,
61, 62, 63, 82, 84, 120, 127, 147,
155, 161, 173, 178
George III., 176, 182, 210, 213, 215,
224, 251, 269, 290, 293, 301, 318
coronation of, 177
grants pension to the Cardinal of
York, 286, 287, 288, 289
George IV., 214, 301, 302
raises the monument to the Stuart
princes, 303, 304
Gesvres, Duc de, 87, 88, 89
Gian Gastone de' Medici, Grand Duke
of Tuscany, 6
Gianuzzi, Felice, corporal of the police
at Frascati, 225
Gibraltar, 6, 7, 8, 14
Giraldin, Sir Nicholas, 13
Gladstone, W. E., charges against the
Duke of Modena, 327, 333
Glasgow, Prince Charles at, 85, 86
Gloucester, Henry, Duke of, son of
Charles I., 311

Gloucester, William, Duke of, son of
Queen Anne, 237, 251
Gloucester, William, Duke of, brother
of George III., 200, 201, 269
Gnesen, Archbishop of, 131
Godalming, 152
Gonzaga, Cardinal, 56
Gonzago, Valenti, tutor of Francis IV.
of Modena, 316
Gooderich, Sir John, 160
Gorani, economist, visits the Cardinal
of York, 277
Gori, Francesco, friend of Alfieri, 228
Goring, Henry, 127, 130
Gordon, Elizabeth, Duchess of, 28, 74
Gordon, Principal of the Scots College
at Paris, 158, 199
Gordon, Alexander, S.J., 82
Gordon, C., Jacobite martyr, 139
Gordon, Lord Lewis, 124
Gordon, General, 9
Gordon riots, 282
Gotti, Cardinal, 32
Gower, Lord, 71
Graeme, Sir John (Earl of Alford), 14,
17, 20, 79, 109, 126, 147, 172
created Earl and Secretary of State,
171
resigns, 181, 186
Grant, Abbé, 131, 191
Granville, Lord, 39
Grattan's Parliament, 282
Gray, Thomas, poet, 41
Greathead, Mr., visits Prince Charles
in Rome, 258
Gaulterio, Cardinal, 13, 20
Gustavus III., King of Sweden, 222,
229, 230, 248

H

Hamilton, fifth Duke of, 8, 22, 45
Hamilton, Rev. Ezekiel, 30
Hamilton, governor of Carlisle, 85, 139
Hamilton, in plot of 1775, 212
Hamilton, L., Jacobite martyr, 139
Hamilton, Emma, Lady, 192
Hamilton, Sir William, British envoy
at Naples, 192
gives news of the battle of the Nile
to the Cardinal of York, 285
Hanbury-Williams (*see* Williams)
Hansen, Captain John, 211
Hardwicke, Earl of, Lord Chancellor,
64, 161
Harrington, Sir James, 127
Harvie, Jacobite martyr, 139
Hawley, General, 94
Hay, John (*see* Inverness, Earl of)
Hay, Sir John, of Restalrig, created a
baron by Charles III., 188 ; leaves
Charles's service, 194

Hay, Theodore, 115
Henderson, Jacobite martyr, 139
Henri V., Count de Chambord, 325, 331, 332
Henrietta Anne, Duchess of Orleans, 264, 311, 331
Henrietta Maria, Queen of Charles I., betrothal ring of, 293
Henry Benedict Mary Clemens, Duke of York, 4, 14, 19, 22, 23, 24, 30, 31, 32, 34, 35, 36, 40, 41, 44, 49, 51, 52, 57, 61, 63, 72, 73, 74, 75, 84, 91, 94, 102, 105, 108, 110, 111, 114, 116, 117
  birth, 2, 3
  baptism, 4
  described by the Earl Marischal, 25
  his father's favourite, 29
  wants to ride to Gaeta, ib.
  intended for the Church, 33
  warlike spirit, 37
  his grace, 38
  described by de Brosses, 42
  described by Murray of Broughton, 43
  Tencin trying to obtain cardinal's hat for, 46
  cabal against him among Prince Charles's friends, 50
  divides Polish property with Charles, 52
  city of York wishes to present him with casket, 55
  not told of Prince Charles's flight from Rome, 56
  letter to his father, 59, 60
  letter to Prince Charles, 60, 61
  anxious to join Charles, 77
  leaves Rome for France, 78
  illness at Avignon, 79
  goes to Paris, 79
  reception of Sempil and adherents, 80
  audience of Louis XV., 87–89
  " Duchino di Yorck," 88 note
  acting with George Kelly, 89
  sends ships to Prince Charles, 90
  leaves Paris for Dunkirk, ib.
  complaints of his piety, 91
  story of his supposed cowardice, 92
  rumours of capture, ib., 93
  urges Sir Watkin Wynn to assist Charles, 93
  at the siege of Antwerp, 97
  Warren's approval of, ib.
  meeting with Charles, 99
  accompanies Charles to court, 100
  disliked by d'Argenson, 92, 100
  his economy, 101
  intercedes with British government for the Highlanders, 104
  expostulates with Charles, 106, 107

Henry, Duke of York, continued—
  quarrels with Charles, 107
  to go to Spain, but prevented by Charles, 108
  better able to take charge of affairs than Charles, 109
  unpopularity with Charles's friends, ib.
  leaves Paris for Rome, 111, 112
  to become a cardinal, 112–114
  consternation of Jacobites over, 115
  receives minor orders, 118
  receives the cardinal's hat, 118, 119
  promised the Abbey of Auchin, 119
  Cardinal of York, 120, 121, 122, 123, 124, 126, 127, 129, 130, 131, 133, 134, 135, 137, 147, 157, 164, 167, 171, 179, 184, 191, 192, 195, 196, 198, 201, 203, 205, 206, 208, 217, 219, 220, 221, 222, 223, 224, 227, 228, 230, 231, 232, 233, 235, 239, 240, 242, 244, 245, 246, 247, 248, 249, 250, 252, 253, 254, 256, 257, 258, 260
  decides on entering the priesthood, 128
  ordination, ib.
  acquaintance with Cordara, S.J., ib.
  story of kidnapping by pirates, 134, 135
  obtains an abbey in Naples, 136
  has smallpox, 138
  his parochial work, 141
  friendship with Galuppi (Buranello), 142
  quarrels with his father, 143, 144
  friendship with Lercari, 144
  his income, 144, 145
  Prefect of the Carthusians in Rome, 144
  Archpriest of the Vatican, 145
  presents chalice to St. Peter's, ib.
  severity with the chapter, 146
  quarrels again with his father, ib., 148
  dismisses Lercari, 147
  leaves Rome for Nocera, 148
  goes to Bologna, 149
  Walpole's criticism, 149, 150
  submits to his father, ib., 151
  receives commendam of the Sant' Apostoli, 152
  illness, 162
  promised Abbey of St. Amand, 163
  friendship with Cardinal John Francis Albani, ib.
  his hauteur and great expenditure, 165
  meets the Elector of Cologne, 168
  friendship with Stefanucci, S.J., 169
  appointed Camerlengo, ib.
  affronted by Austrian envoy in conclave, 170

Henry, Duke of York, *continued—*
consecrated bishop, *ib.*
acts for his father, 172
refuses to vote for beatification of
Palafox, 173
becomes Bishop of Frascati, 174
life and work at Frascati, 175
demolishes Temple of Jupiter Latiaris, 176
ill of typhus, 180
Vice-Chancellor of St. Peter's, 180
visits Pisa, *ib.*
holds synod at Frascati, 181
administers the King's charities, *ib.*,
182
re-opens communication with Prince
Charles, 182
urges Charles to come to Rome, 183
efforts to obtain recognition of
Charles, 185, 186, 187
medal struck, 187
negotiations with Miss Walkinshaw,
189, 190
accompanies Charles to the Pope,
193
finds benefice for young Routledge,
194
approves of Lumisden and the
equerries, *ib.*
receives Charles and Louise in state,
202
Louise takes refuge with him, 218
attempt on his life, 225
visits Charles at Florence, and is undeceived as to Louise and Alfieri,
226
protests against the legitimisation of
Charlotte, Duchess of Albany, 236,
237, 238
overtures from Charlotte, 241
begins correspondence with her, 243
his work in his diocese, 253
meets Charlotte at Montefreddo, 255
Henry IX., 262, 268, 269, 270, 271,
272, 274, 276, 280, 293, 294, 295,
304, 309, 310, 311, 313, 314, 315
accession to the royal dignity, 261,
264, 265
presides at Charles's funeral, 263
raises mural monument to Charles,
264
confirms the Countess of Norton,
267 *note*
appointed Protector of Capuchins
in Rome, 273
described by Cardinal Wiseman, &c.,
275
receives Mr. Coutts and daughters,
277
receives Gorani, *ib.*
receives Marquise d'Osmond, *ib.*
his domestic discomfort, 278

Henry, Duke of York, *continued—*
his affection for Hercules Consalvi,
ib.
receives Prince Augustus (Duke of
Sussex), 279
disposes of jewels to assist the Pope,
281
escapes to Naples, 281
perhaps approached with regard to
rebellion of '98, 283, 284
joy over the battle of the Nile, 285
meets Nelson, *ib.*
escapes from Naples to Venice, 286
receives pension from George III.,
286, 287, 288, 289
translated to Ostia and Velletri, 289
visited by Lord Cloncurry, 290, 291
visited by nuns, 292, 293
last illness and death, 296
his character, *ib.*, 297
burial, 297
oration at his funeral, 298, 299, 300
will and protest, 300
legacies, 301
portraits, 302
literary remains, *ib.*
his papers, *ib.*
commemorative tablet in the Muti
Palace, 303
tomb in St. Peter's, *ib.*
Hepburn of Keith, 124, 153
Herbert, Lady Mary, 40
Hervey, Augustus John, Lord, British
envoy at Florence, 258 *note*
Hervey, George William, Lord, 63
Hesse-Darmstadt, Princess of, 130
Heton, General, 288
Heys, Jacobite martyr, 139
Hint, Jacobite martyr, 139
Hippesley, Sir John Coxe, 286, 289, 301
represents destitution of the Cardinal
to George III., 287
Hoche, General, sails to invade Ireland,
283
Holdernesse, Lord, British Foreign
Minister, 155
Holt, Jacobite martyr, 139
Howard, Sister Rose, Jacobite agent,
28
Hume, David, historian, 177
Humphreys, Ozias, portrait painter,
214
Hunter, Jacobite martyr, 139
Hyndford, Lord, British ambassador
to Russia, 133

I

Ildefonso, Father, confessor to the
Cardinal of York, 144, 147, 148
Innes, G., Principal of Scots College at
Paris, 115

Innes, Lewis, 27, 274
Innies, I., Jacobite martyr, 139
Inverness, Earl of (John Hay), 2, 3, 4, 7, 12, 13, 15, 19, 20
conversion, 28
death, 44, 45
Inverness, Countess of, 3, 4, 20, 44, 122, 129
Irving, Washington, 215
Islay, Archibald, Earl of, 39, 48

J

J., C. W., agent, 212
Jacobites, 10, 22, 30, 36, 39, 48, 53, 55, 65, 78, 82, 85, 126, 132, 133, 135, 138, 139, 152, 154, 155, 159, 164, 165, 199, 200
Jane Frances de Chantal, St., canonisation of, 145
Jamaica, Marquis of (see Berwick, fourth Duke of)
Jamaica, Marquise de (Catherine Augusta of Stolberg-Gueldern), 201, 202, 251
James I., King of Scots, 1
James V., King of Scots, 1
James I., King of England, ix.
James II., King of England, 67, 117, 128, 148, 208, 238, 282, 301
James III. (Chevalier de St. George), 1, 3, 4, 6, 7, 8, 9, 10, 11, 12, 13, 14, 16, 17, 18, 20, 22, 23, 24, 25, 26, 27, 28, 29, 30, 31, 33, 34, 35, 37, 38, 39, 40, 41, 42, 43, 44, 45, 46, 49, 50, 51, 52, 53, 54, 55, 56, 58 n., 59, 60, 61, 62, 63, 65, 67, 68, 69, 70, 71, 72, 73, 74, 75, 77, 78, 79, 80, 81, 82, 88, 89, 91, 94, 96, 97, 98, 100, 101, 103, 105, 106, 107, 108, 109, 110, 115, 116, 117, 118, 119, 120, 121, 122, 123, 124, 125, 126, 128, 129, 130, 131, 132, 133, 134, 136, 137, 138, 141, 144, 145, 146, 150, 152, 153, 154, 158, 160, 162, 163, 165, 166, 167, 168, 169, 170, 171, 173, 176, 177, 178, 181, 182, 183, 186, 189, 190, 192, 194, 198, 199, 200, 201, 204, 205, 206, 237, 241, 251, 255, 264, 266, 273, 295, 296, 297, 298, 303, 304, 307, 308
marriage, 2
new attempt on England, 5
quarrel with Queen Clementina, 5
leaves Italy for France, 15
reconciled with Queen, 19
attempt to poison, 21
plan to marry Duchess of Parma, 32
issues circular letter (1741), 47, 48
appoints Prince Charles regent, 54

James III., continued—
takes farewell of Prince Charles, 57
sends for Henry from Paris, 111
letter on the cardinalate, 112–114
makes pilgrimage to Loreto, 127
attends Jubilee in state, 135
objects to Henry's friends, 142, 143
takes Lascaris as secretary, 147
new quarrels with Henry, 148
his residences in Bologna, 149
accepts Henry's submission, 151
asked to abdicate, 157
has a stroke of paralysis, 164
severe illness, 172
death, 184
burial, 187
Venture pretends to be his son, 223
Jesse, quoted, 21, 22
Jesuits, 173, 174, 175, 206, 311, 312, 325, 328
Jupiter Latiaris, temple of, 176

K

Keir, P., Jacobite martyr, 139
Keith, James, Field-Marshal, 40, 153
Keith, Roy, 159
Kelly, Friar, 105, 121, 160
Kelly, Rev. George, 69, 70, 76, 89, 105, 106, 124 note, 125
Kenmure, Lady, 124 note, 159
Kennedy, A., Jacobite martyr, 139
Kerrick, John, 179
Kilmarnock, Earl of, 103, 139, 176 note
King, Rev. Dr., 133, 155
King's evil, touching for, 36, 65
Kinnoull, Lord, 2, 3
Knight, Cornelia, lady-in-waiting on Princess Charlotte of Wales, quoted, 153, 223, 227, 228

L

Lafayette, Marquis de, 215
Lalande, visits the Cardinal of York, 192
Lally, Captain, 94, 166
Lamartine, quoted, 292
Lambertini Palace at Bologna, 149
Lambertini, Princess, 242, 265, 270
Lanze, Cardinal, represents Austria at conclave, 170
Lascaris, Monsignor, 133, 150, 151, 162, 167, 203, 218
secretary to James III., 147
Laurenti, physician to the Pope, 162
Law, John, of Lauriston, 6
Lee, Monsignor, Chamberlain to the Cardinal of York, 143

Legnani, Countess, 32
Legouz, Abbé, tutor to the princes, 5
Leith, captain, Jacobite martyr, 139
Leonora, Princess, of Tuscany, 118 *note*
Leopold, Grand Duke of Tuscany, 208, 247
Lercari, Abbé John, Chamberlain to the Cardinal of York, 143, 147, 148, 149, 150, 151, 164, 165
Lexington, battle of, 210
Lichfield, Lord, 78
Liechtenstein, Prince von, 180
Ligonier, Lady, loved by Alfieri, 216
Lindsey, P., Jacobite martyr, 139
Liria, Duke of (*see* Berwick, second Duke)
Lismore, first Earl of (Daniel O'Brien), 4, 17, 29, 31, 71, 80, 82, 89, 105, 111, 114, 115, 123, 153, 154, 160, 167, 171, 173
  Secretary of State to James III., 122
Lismore, second Earl of; Lord Tallow, 173, 182
Lismore, Countess of, 123, 159, 160, 167, 171, 182
Liverpool, Lord, writes to Canning on mourning for Charles Emmanuel IV., 315
Livingston, Chevalier, 279
Lockhart, George, of Carnwath, 9, 15
Lockhart, young, 124
Lochiel, Cameron of, 8, 52, 76, 122, 125
  takes Edinburgh by surprise, 81
  death, 125
Lochiel, young, 110, 125, 136, 153
Longhi, A., quoted, 271
Louis XIV., 5, 53, 311
Louis XV., 4, 18, 45, 47, 51, 53, 55, 56, 57, 59, 62, 68, 77, 78, 82, 87, 88, 91, 94, 97, 100, 101, 102, 104, 119, 120, 121, 123, 124, 125, 126, 144, 163, 172, 187, 204, 205
Louis XVI., 200, 234, 251, 267
Louis XVIII., 313
Louis Philippe, King of the French, 319
Louis, Dauphin of France, 88, 100, 108, 125
Louis, Dauphin of France (*see* Louis XVI.)
Louisa, Princess of England, 148, 208
Louise, Princess of France, 72
Louise of Stolberg, wife of Prince Charles Edward (Countess of Albany), 31, 201, 203, 207, 208, 209, 216, 218, 219, 220, 222, 223, 224, 226, 227, 228, 229, 230, 231, 232, 233, 235, 237, 238, 239, 242, 243, 244, 245, 246, 248, 249, 250, 251, 252, 253, 254, 260, 267, 268, 269, 270, 272, 278, 287, 291, 292, 296, 301
  marries Prince Charles, 202

Louise of Stolberg, *continued*—
  gives portrait to Coke of Norfolk, 206, 207
  escapes from Florence with Alfieri, 217
  divorced, 233
  presented at St. James's, 269
  summoned to Paris by Napoleon, 292
  residence at Florence with Alfieri, 284
  described by Lady Morgan, 304–306
  death, 304, 306
  monument in Santa Croce, 304, 306
Loudoun, Lord, 85, 95
Lovat, Lord, 77, 80, 85, 122, 139
Lumisden, Andrew, secretary to James III., 146, 147, 160, 165, 181, 182, 183, 185, 186, 187, 188, 191, 192, 194, 201
Luynes, Duc de, 53, 62, 87, 88, 102, 109, 149
Luynes, Duchesse de, 90
Lyon, Rev. R., Jacobite martyr, 139

M

Macallester, Oliver, spy, 174, 177
MacCormick (two), Franciscans, 260
MacDaniel, Dan., Jacobite martyr, 139
Macdonald, clan, 77, 96
Macdonald, Jacobite martyr, 139
Macdonald, Captain, Jacobite martyr, 139
Macdonald, Donald, Jacobite martyr, 139
Macdonald of Barisdale and son, 99
Macdonald of Boisdale, 76
Macdonald of Clanranald, 76
Macdonald of Glenaladale, 76
Macdonald of Glencoe, 9
Macdonald of Keppoch, 9
Macdonald of Kinlochmoidart, 76, 84, 103
Macdonald of Skye, 9
Macdonald, Æneas, 76
Macdonald, Sir John, 76
Macdonell of Glengarry, 9, 77
Macdonell of Glengarry, "Pickle the Spy," 51, 134, 136, 137, 152, 153, 155, 156
Macdonell, Angus, 77
Macdonell of Lochgarry, 77, 136, 153, 156
Macdonell of Scottas, 91
Macdonell, Rev. Myles, 105, 115
Macgregor of Balhaldy, 45, 47, 50, 51, 55, 56, 59, 69, 71, 74, 80, 89, 125, 157
Macgregor, James Mohr, 155–159
Macgregor, J., Jacobite martyr, 139

Macgregor, Rob Roy, 155
Macgregor, clan, 81
Mackenzie, clan, 9
Mackenzie, Jacobite martyr, 139
Mackintosh, clan, 9
Mackintosh, in attendance upon Prince Charles, 188
MacClain, J., Jacobite martyr, 139
Maclean, Sir Hector, 74, 134, 136
Macleod, clan, 77 ; chief of, 95
MacLewis, J., Jacobite martyr, 139
MacNaughten, J., Jacobite martyr, 139
Macpherson (*see* Cluny)
Mahon, Port, 6, 7, 14
Malzam, Mlle. de, 252
Mann, Sir Horace, British envoy at Florence, 48, 58, 62, 63, 74, 100, 109, 124, 127, 131, 134, 137, 150, 151, 167, 171, 172, 173, 174, 176, 179, 180, 183, 185, 187, 189, 192, 197, 198, 200, 204, 205, 210, 213, 223, 224, 226, 227, 229, 233, 234, 235, 239, 240, 241, 242, 255, 256
Mar, John, Earl and Duke of, 2, 3, 8, 28
Marefoschi, Cardinal, 201, 202
Marengo, battle of, 315
Maria Beatrice Ricciarda, Duchess of Modena, 316, 327
Maria Beatrice of Modena, married Don Juan of Spain, 325
Marianna of Savoy, Empress of Austria, 316, 331
Maria Theresa, Empress of Germany, 6, 45, 46, 47, 57, 61, 71, 169, 201, 248, 316
Maria Theresa, Infanta of Spain, 4, 7
Maria Theresa of Modena, Queen of Sardinia, 316
Maria Theresa Gaetana of Modena, Comtesse de Chambord, 325
Maria Theresa of Savoy, Duchess of Lucca, 316, 330
Mariano, favourite of Cardinal J. F. Albani, 163
Marie of Nemours, regent of Savoy, 311
Marie Antoinette, Queen of France, 223, 244, 247, 248, 249, 284, 292, 316
Marie Clotilde of France, Queen of Sardinia, 314, 315
Marie Leczcinska, Queen of France, 72, 90, 100
Marie Louise, Empress of the French, 317
Marischal, George, Earl, 10, 25, 48, 52, 55, 62, 66, 69, 77, 78, 121, 132, 154, 155, 157, 159, 160, 177
Mariscolli, Count, 73
Marlborough, John, first Duke of, 51
Mary, Queen of Scots, her veil, 301

Mary of Modena, Queen of England, 18, 148, 250, 260, 288, 316
Mary Beatrice of Savoy, Duchess of Modena (" Mary II. and III."), 316, 318
marries the Duke of Modena, 319, 320, 321, 329, 330
succeeds to the heirship of the Stuarts, 326
Mary Theresa of Modena, Princess Louis of Bavaria (" Mary III. and IV."), 334, 335
Mastrofino, Dom Marco, preaches funeral panegyric on the Cardinal of York, 298
Mathews, Jacobite martyr, 139
Maurepas, Marquis de, French War Minister, 78, 89
Mayson, B., Jacobite martyr, 139
Medard, Abbey of St., 167
Medici family, 6, 118
Menotti, Ciro, Italian revolutionist, 328, 329
" Mesdames," aunts of Louis XVI., 279 (*see* Adelaide and Victoire)
Mercier Dupaty, quoted, 259
Mereworth, 152
Merolli, Giacomo, attempts the life of the Cardinal of York, 225
Metternich, Austrian Minister, 317
Mézières, Eleanor, Marquise de, 36, 53, 64, 65, 73, 90, 114, 121, 152, 153, 159, 160
Mézières, Marquis de, 72
Mézières, agent, 160
Milford Haven, 212, 213
Mino da Fiesole, 171
Minorca lost, 171
Minto, Lord, British ambassador at Vienna, 287, 289
Mitchel-Nicholson, Jacobite martyr, 139
Modena, Rinaldo, Duke of, 6, 132
Modena, Ercole Rinaldo, Duke of, 316
Modena (*see* Francis IV., Francis V., &c.)
Monaco, Prince of, 66
Montauban, Prince de, 90
Montbazon, Duc de, 90
Montbazon, Princesse de, 36, 251
Montemorin, Count de, 267
Monterassino, visited by the Cardinal of York, 162
Montgomery, in attendance on Prince Charles, 192
Montlin, Château de, 159
More, Hannah, quoted, 270
Morgan, D., Jacobite martyr, 139
Morgan, Sydney, Lady, visits the Countess of Albany, 304, 305, 306
Moy, rout of, 95

Murat, Joachim, " King of Naples,"
324
Mure, Elizabeth, wife of Robert II.,
King of Scots, 238, 274
Mure, L. M., quoted, 146, 147
Murray, Alexander, of Elibank, 148,
153, 177
Murray of Abercairnie, 157
Murray, Lord George, 77, 81, 83, 84,
85, 94, 95, 96, 123, 125, 213
Murray, James (see Dunbar, Earl of)
Murray, John, of Broughton, 37, 43,
45, 50, 55, 56, 68, 69
Murray, J. T., Jacobite martyr, 139
Musgrave, Sir Christopher, 8

N

Nairne, Lord (Master of Nairne), 235,
260, 267
Napoleon, 280, 281, 283, 285, 290, 313,
314, 315, 316, 317, 318, 322, 323,
324
Napoleon III., 334
Negroni, Cardinal, 185
Nelson, Horatio, Lord, 192, 285
Newcastle, Duke of, 40, 58, 64, 152,
159, 160, 166
Newcastle-on-Tyne, colliers at, pro-
claim Charles III., 138
Nile, battle of the, 285
Nithsdale, Winifred, Countess of, gover-
ness to Henry, Duke of York,
14
her death, 131
Nithsdale, Earl of, 14
Nivernois, Duc de, French ambassador
at Rome, 130, 135
Noailles, Duc de, 53, 197, 212, 213
Normanby, Marquis of, 317, 327, 332,
333, 334
Norris, English admiral, 66
North, Lord, 210, 211, 282
Northumberland, 138, 139
Norton, Marie, Countess of, 235, 267,
270
Nottingham, Prince Charles at, 166
Novara, battle of, 333

O

Oakley, 287
O'Brien (see Lismore)
O'Dea, Denis, 265
Ogilvie, Lord, 81
Ogilvie, Jacobite martyr, 139
Oglethorpe, Anne, 36, 73, 152
Oglethorpe, Fanny, 36, 39
Oglethorpe, James, 85
Oliphant of Gask, 81, 188, 276, 279

Orleans, Duke of
Ormond, Duke of, 7, 10, 30, 39, 44, 45,
55, 66, 69, 75, 78, 79
Orrery, Lord, 16, 55, 78
Osmond, Marquis d', 323
Osmond, Marquise d', 277, 278
Ostia and Velletri, Henry translated
to see of, 289
Ossory, Lady, correspondent of Horace
Walpole, 203, 229, 235
O'Sullivan, 76, 106, 108
Oxburgh, 30
Oxford University, 153, 199

P

Padua, Prince Charles at, 132
Palafox, Bishop, 172, 173
Panmure, Lord, 9
Palidoro, Charles at, 191
Park, T., Jacobite martyr, 139
Parker, A., Jacobite martyr, 139
Parma, Duke of, 72
Parma, Dukes of (Appendix II.)
Parma, Duchess of, 32
Paterson, Sir Hugh, 86, 157
Patrizzi, Count, 41
Pelham, Henry, 63, 166
Pembroke, Lord, visited Charles at
Florence, 251
Perceval, Lord, 48
Perth, third Duke of, 55, 76, 81, 83, 109
Peter the Great, 9
Philip, Infante of Spain, 129
Philip V. of Spain, 4, 10, 311, 325 note
Pichot, Amédée, quoted, 13, 166
Piedmont, Prince of (see Charles
Emmanuel IV.)
Pirates of Barbary, 134
Pisa, 180, 195, 247, 248, 249
Pitt, niece of, visits the Cardinal of
York, 295
Pitt, William, 63, 179, 251, 282, 285
Pius II., Pope, letters of, 163
Pius VI., Pope, 221, 226, 227, 241,
281, 286, 294
Pius VII., Pope, 163, 278, 286, 293,
294, 303, 315, 318, 319, 324
Pius IX., Pope, 332
Poland, 198, 200
Pollnitz, Baron, quoted, 26
Polyxena, Queen of Sardinia, 312
Porten, Sir Stanier, Under Secretary,
211, 213
Pownall, ——, M.P., 211
Pragmatic Sanction, 6
Prestonpans, battle of, 79, 81, 82
Primrose, Sir Archibald, 103, 139
Primrose, Lady, 153, 155
Pringle, Sir John, 177
Proly, Count, 249

Pulteney, English Minister, 11, 154
Puysieux, French Minister, 121

Q

Quebec taken by Wolfe, 171
Queensberry, Duchess of, 212, 213
Quiberon Bay, French naval defeat,
   130, 171

R

Radcliffe (see Derwentwater)
Radcliffe, James Bartholomew, cap-
   tured in the Soleil, 92
Radziwill, Prince, 147
Radziwill, Princess, 131
Ramsay, Chevalier Andrew, 5
Read, L., Jacobite martyr, 139
Red or Rede, Mr., 65, 66
Riario, Cardinal, 180
Rezzonico, Cardinal, 187 (see Clement
   XIII.)
Rice, L. C. J., Ireland, 282
Richelieu, Duc de, 89, 90, 91, 92, 135
Richmond, Duke of, 125, 126
Ridley, Captain, carries news of in-
   vasion, 62
Ripperda, Duque de, Spanish Prime
   Minister, 7, 8, 9, 10
Riva, F., 148
Riviera, Cardinal, Protector of Scot-
   land, 112
Robert II., 1, 238, 274
Robert III., 238, 274
Robert, Duke of Parma, Appendix II.
Robertson, clan, 81
Rob Roy (see Macgregor), 153
Roche, La, spy, 109
Rochefoucauld, Duc de, French am-
   bassador at Rome, 112
Rochford, Lord, Secretary of State, 211
Rocquefeuil, French Admiral, 62, 66
Roebottom, J., Jacobite martyr, 139
Rohan, Prince de, Archbishop of
   Bordeaux, 234
Roper, Jacobite martyr, 139
Rosebery, Earl of, 103
Ross, Euphemia, Queen of Robert II.,
   239, 274
Routledge, of the Elizabeth ship, 193,
   194
Ruffo, Cardinal, Vice-Chancellor of
   St. Peter's, 168
Rupert, Prince of Bavaria, 335
Russell, G. W. E., quoted, 137
Russell, Lord John, quoted, 327
Ruth, Mr., 17
Ryan, Colonel, agent at Paris, 199, 200

S

Saint Aignan, Duc de, French ambas-
   sador at Rome, 44
Saint Aignan, Duchesse de, 29
   her sons, 33
Saints, English, commemoration pro-
   moted by the Cardinal of York,
   297 note
Saint Simon, Duc de, 204
San Clemente Palace, residence of
   Charles at Florence, 208, &c.
San Clemente, Duke of, 268
Sant' Andrea delle Valle, church of,
   297
Sant' Apostoli, church of, 152, 170,
   172
Santa Maria in Portici in Campitelli,
   church of, 128, 142, 151, 152, 167,
   168
Santa Maria in Trastevere, church of,
   170
Salviati, Duchess of, 35, 132, 146
Salm-Kryburg, Prince of, 249
Salm-Kryburg, Princess of, 199, 200,
   201
Sandwich, Lord, 154
Sardinia (see under kings of)
Savoy (see under Victor Amadeus II.,
   &c.)
Saxe, Count Maurice de, 43, 55, 62,
   65, 66, 74, 79
Saxony and Poland, Prince of, 38
Schaub, Sir Luke, British ambassador
   at Paris, 16
Scott, Sir Walter, 215
Sempil, Lord, 55, 56, 61, 65, 67, 69, 70,
   71, 73, 74, 80, 89, 121, 125
Sermoneta, Duke of, 169
Sheldon, Mrs., Prince Charles's nurse,
   3, 4, 5, 20
Sheridan, Sir Thomas, 5, 58, 69, 70,
   74, 76, 94, 105, 106
Sheridan, young, 106, 108, 121, 125
Siena, Charles at, 195, 198, 201
Silvagni, quoted, 128
Sixtus IV., Pope, 180
Smith, Mr., 157
Smith, Admiral Sir Sydney, 320
Sobieska, Clementina (see Clementina)
Sobieska, Caroline (see Bouillon, Duchess
   of)
Sobieski family, 14, 29, 37
Sobieski, John, King of Poland, 2, 37,
   43, 67, 101, 269
Sobieski, Prince James, 29, 35, 190
" Sobieski-Stuarts," 207, 208
Soissons (Fitzjames), Bishop of, 68, 71
Sophia, Electress, 310
Sophie, Madame, of France, 72
Southesk, Lady, 19

Spada, of Prince Charles's household, 220

Spinelli, Cardinal, 181

Staël, Madame de, 269

Stafford, equerry of Prince Charles, 188, 193

Stainville, de, French ambassador at Rome, 167

Stair, Lord, 62

Stanislas, King of Poland, 166

Stanley of Alderley, Lady, 306

Stanley, Maria Josepha, Lady, 259, 314

Stanley, Sir J. T., 259, 314

Stefanucci, S.J., 169, 206, 303

Stewart, Allan Breck, 155, 157

Stewart, Andrew, genealogist, 288

Statuvell, or Hatwell, 212

Stirling of Keir, 151

Stolberg-Gueldern, family, of, 203

Stolberg-Gueldern, Princess of, 222, 223

Stolberg-Gueldern, Catherine Augusta of (see Jamaica, Marquise of)

Stolberg - Gueldern, Louise of (see Louise)

Stoneleigh, Charles at, 166

Stonor, Monsignor, in attendance on the Duchess of Albany, 270

Stosch, Baron Philipp von (see Walton, John)

Strafford, Lord, 4

Strange, Lady, 146

Strange, Sir Robert, engraver, 182 note, 191, 279

Strathallan, Lord, 81, 85, 181

Strathallan family, 181, 182

Strathearn, Walter, Earl of, 238

Strickland, Francis, 49, 50, 72, 74, 76, 80, 81, 85, 105, 106, 122

Stuart of Ardshiel, 77

Stuart, Charlotte (see Albany, Duchess of)

Stuart, Sir John, 194, 230, 231, 232, 233, 234, 260, 267

Sturm, Baron, testifies to miracle by Clementina, 32

Suckling, Lieutenant, officer of Nelson's ship *Agamemnon*, 285

Sullivan (see O'Sullivan)

Sussex, Augustus, Duke of, 279, 290, 291, 302

Swan, Jacobite martyr, 139

Sweden, Princess of, 240

Swift, Dean, writes "Drapier's Letters," 282

Swinburne family, 139

Syddal, Jacobite martyr, 139

T

Taitt, upholsterer, 211

Taillandier, Réné, quoted, 197

Tallow, Lord (see Lismore, second Earl)

Talmond, Princesse de, 121, 129

Taylor, P., Jacobite martyr, 139

Tencin, Cardinal, 44, 46, 54, 55, 62, 71, 89, 105, 109, 111, 114, 148, 164, 190

French Prime Minister, 53

Tencin, Bailli de, 48, 57, 78, 112, 119, 148

Thompson, E., chargé-d'affaires at Paris, 62

Torrigiani, Cardinal, 187

Townley, Colonel Francis, 49, 83, 85, 103, 139

Townley, John, 49, 50, 72, 74, 80, 105, 122, 126

Trant, Mr., 157

Traquair, Lord, 51

Trotter, Alexander Pelham, 146

Tullibardine, Marquis of, 76, 81, 83

raises the standard at Glenfinnan, 77

Turenne, Prince de, 90

Tuscany, Grand Duke (see Leopold)

Tuscany, Grand Duchess of, 227, 247, 250

Tyrrel, Jacobite agent, 165

U

Urbino, 184

Urquhart, Colonel, correspondent for Scotland, 45

Urquhart, Mr., in attendance on Charles III.

V

Valenti, Cardinal, 112, 168

Valese, de, Minister of Victor Emmanuel I., 323

Vardil, Rev. John, 211

Vaudreuil, M. de, 258

Vaughan, Mr., 109

Venice, James III. at, 20

Venice, Charles Edward at, 34, 132, 133

Venice, Henry arrives at, 286; conclave at, 286

Venture, pretends to be son of James III., 223

Vergennes, de, French Foreign Minister, 242, 243, 244, 246, 249, 251, 252

Vernon, Admiral, 91

Vice-Chancellorship of St. Peter's granted to Henry, 180

Victoire, Madame, of France, 72

Victor Amadeus II., Duke of Savoy, King of Sardinia, 311, 327

Victor Amadeus III., 223, 233, 312, 313

Victor Emmanuel I., 315, 317, 318, 320, 323, 324, 325, 326

Messrs. Longmans and Co.'s New Books

AUTUMN 1908

THE MAID OF FRANCE. Being the Story of the Life and Death of JEANNE D'ARC. By ANDREW LANG. With Illustrations. 8vo.

HISTORICAL LETTERS AND MEMOIRS OF SCOTTISH CATHOLICS, 1625-1793. By the Rev. W. FORBES LEITH, S.J. With Illustrations. 2 vols., medium 8vo.

THE DAWN OF THE CATHOLIC REVIVAL IN ENGLAND, 1781-1803. By BERNARD WARD, F.R.Hist.S. President of St. Edmund's College, Ware. 2 vols. 8vo.

This book will treat of an important period which has not been fully covered by any modern writer. It will include a description of the state of English Catholics during the years which succeeded the death of Bishop Challoner in 1781, years which may fairly be considered the low-water mark of English Catholicity, when apathy and hopelessness reigned supreme; and the causes and influences which led to its unexpected and rapid revival, beginning with the Relief Act of 1791 which repealed the Penal Laws. The work has been written for the most part from original sources, the author having been allowed access to the archives of each of the four Vicariates into which England was formerly divided, as well as to those of the chief colleges and religious houses, and many documents hitherto unpublished will be given in full.

PERSONAL STUDIES. By WILFRID WARD. With 10 Portraits. 8vo.

CONTENTS :—A. J. BALFOUR, *Three Notable Editors* (J. T. DELANE. R. H. HUTTON, Sir JAMES KNOWLES), HENRY SIDGWICK, LORD LYTTON, FATHER IGNATIUS RYDER, GRANT DUFF, LEO XIII., THE GENIUS OF CARDINAL WISEMAN, CARDINAL NEWMAN, NEWMAN and MANNING.

THE KEY TO THE WORLD'S PROGRESS. Being some Account of the Historical Significance of the Catholic Church. By CHARLES STANTON DEVAS, M.A. Oxon., sometime Examiner in Political Economy at the Royal University of Ireland. New and Popular Edition. 8vo, paper covers, 6d.

A MYSTERY PLAY IN HONOUR OF THE NATIVITY OF OUR LORD. By ROBERT HUGH BENSON. With Illustrations, Appendices, and Stage Directions. Crown 8vo.

This Play was produced at Cambridge in December 1907 and January 1908. It was .ted by the girls of St. Mary's Convent School, whose ages were from six to eighteen.

THE INQUISITION. A Critical and Historical Study of the Coercive Power of the Church. By the ABBÉ E. VACANDARD. Translated from the French by BERTRAND L. CONWAY, C.S.P. Crown 8vo, 6s. net.

LONGMANS, GREEN AND CO.

LONDON, NEW YORK, BOMBAY, AND CALCUTTA

Messrs. Longmans and Co.'s New Books

AUTUMN 1908

THE JOURNAL OF ELIZABETH LADY HOLLAND
(1791–1811). Edited by the EARL OF ILCHESTER. With Portraits.
2 vols., 8vo, 21s. net.

THE LIFE OF HENRY IRVING. By AUSTIN BRERET
With 1 Photogravure, 22 Collotype Plates, and 23 other Illustratio
2 vols., 8vo, 25s. net.

HISTORICAL AND POLITICAL ESSAYS. By WILLI
EDWARD HARTPOLE LECKY. 8vo, 10s. 6d. net.

HENRY STUART, CARDINAL OF YORK, AND
TIMES. By ALICE SHIELD, Joint Author (with ANDREW LANG)
"The King over the Water." With Preface by ANDREW LANG, an
15 Illustrations. 8vo.

THOMAS GEORGE, EARL OF NORTHBROOK, G.C.S
A Memoir. By BERNARD MALLET. With Portraits and other Illu
trations. 8vo, 15s. net.

THE BERNSTORFF PAPERS: THE LIFE OF COUNT
ALBRECHT VON BERNSTORFF. By Dr. KARL RINGHOFFER.
Authorised Translation by Mrs. CHARLES EDWARD BARRETT-
LENNARD and M. W. HOPER. 2 vols., 8vo.

IN MOROCCO WITH GENERAL D'AMADE. B
REGINALD RANKIN, lately a war correspondent for the *Time*
Author of "A Subaltern's Letters to his Wife." With Pen-and-Ink
Portrait of Abdul-Aziz, a Map, and Illustrations from Photographs.
8vo, 9s. net.

THE RUSSIAN CONQUEST OF THE CAUCASUS. By
J. F. BADDELEY. With Maps and other Illustrations. 8vo. 21s. net.

A HISTORY OF ENGLISH JOURNALISM TO THE
FOUNDATION OF THE "GAZETTE." With Facsimiles. B
J. B. WILLIAMS. 8vo.

MEMORIALS OF TWO SISTERS: SUSANNA AN
CATHERINE WINKWORTH. Edited by their Niece, MARGARET
J. SHAEN. With 2 Photogravure Portraits. 8vo, 10s. 6d. net.

Catherine, the younger of these two sisters, is the better known of the two, as sh
translated the famous collection of hymns known as *Lyra Germanica*. Susanna Winkworth was the translator of several important works by Baron Bunsen, but her best known
work in that direction was that of the *Theologia Germanica*, issued in 1854, with a
preface by Charles Kingsley.

LONGMANS, GREEN AND CO.

LONDON, NEW YORK, BOMBAY, AND CALCUTTA

2

INDEX

Victor Emmanuel II., 311, 328, 334
Victor Emmanuel III., 326, 327
Vitelleschi, Marchesa, quoted, 293
Voltaire, quoted, 69, 143
Vulpian, solicitor to Charles III. in Paris, 246, 252

W

W., T., writer of intercepted letter, 212
Wade, Marshal, 82
Walton, John (Baron Philipp von Stosch), spy, 21, 22, 23, 30, 44, 49, 52, 58, 122, 127, 129, 131, 134, 147, 148, 154, 157, 162, 163, 168, 169
Wagstaffe, Rev. ——, Protestant chaplain to Prince Charles, 194
Waldegrave, Lord, British Ambassador at Paris, 62
Waldegrave, Lady, Duchess of Gloucester, 201
Walkinshaw, Clementina, Countess Alberstroff, 72, 86, 129, 148, 172, 173, 182, 189, 193, 203, 209, 235, 241, 267, 272
Walkinshaw of Scotstown, 161
Wallis, I., Jacobite martyr, 139
Walpole, Sir Robert, 11, 16, 38, 39, 40, 51, 73, 282
Walpole, Horace, 5, 50, 63, 79, 93, 149, 150, 152, 176, 177, 178, 185, 198, 200, 203, 205, 206, 226, 229, 235, 239, 242, 243, 255, 289
sees the Stuart Court in Rome, 42, 43
curious mistake as to the Cardinal of York, 224
Walpole, Horatio, British ambassador at Paris, 16, 17, 62
Walsh, Antoine Vincent, conveys Prince Charles to Scotland, 76, 78

Walsh-Serrant, Count de, 280
Warren, brings Prince Charles to France from Scotland, 94, 97, 122
Washington, George, 214
Waters, banker in Paris, 147, 182, 189, 269
Wedderburn, Sir L., Jacobite martyr, 139
Wellington, Duke of, victories, 320
Westmoreland, Earl of, 55, 137, 152, 155
Westmoreland, Countess of, 152
Whalley, Elizabeth, married by the Cardinal of York, 134
Wharton, Duke of, 7, 10, 14, 20
William II., Prince of Orange, Appendix II.
William III., Prince of Orange, 250, 251, 310, 311
Williams, Sir Charles Hanbury, English Ambassador to Dresden, offers to kidnap Prince Charles, 133
Wiseman, Cardinal, quoted, 101, 275
Wogan, Sir Charles, 1, 30, 36, 53, 64
Wolfe, General James, 171
Wood, Captain, Jacobite martyr, 139
Wraxall, Sir Nathaniel, quoted, 269
Wylam, meeting of Jacobites at, 138
Wynn, Sir Watkin Williams, 55, 78, 84, 93
Wynnstay, 137, 213

Y

Yate, owner of Arlingham Court, 153
York, city of, wishes to present casket to Henry, 55
"Yorke, Father Benedict," 93
Yorke, Sir Joseph, British Minister at the Hague

THE END

Printed by BALLANTYNE, HANSON & CO.
Edinburgh & London.

Z